Readings in Medieval Texts

Readings in Medieval Texts: Interpreting Old and Middle English Literature

Edited by David F. Johnson
and Elaine Treharne

L.C.C.DISCARDLIBRARY

OXFORD
UNIVERSITY PRESS

OXFORD
UNIVERSITY PRESS

Great Clarendon Street, Oxford OX2 6DP

Oxford University Press is a department of the University of Oxford.
It furthers the University's objective of excellence in research, scholarship,
and education by publishing worldwide in

Oxford New York

Auckland Cape Town Dar es Salaam Hong Kong Karachi
Kuala Lumpur Madrid Melbourne Mexico City Nairobi New Delhi
Shanghai Taipei Toronto

With offices in

Argentina Austria Brazil Chile Czech Republic France Greece
Guatemala Hungary Italy Japan South Korea Poland Portugal
Singapore Switzerland Thailand Turkey Ukraine Vietnam

Oxford is a registered trade mark of Oxford University Press
in the UK and in certain other countries

Published in the United States
by Oxford University Press Inc., New York

© Oxford University Press 2005

The moral rights of the authors have been asserted
Database right Oxford University Press (maker)

First published 2005

All rights reserved. No part of this publication may be reproduced,
stored in a retrieval system, or transmitted, in any form or by any means,
without the prior permission in writing of Oxford University Press,
or as expressly permitted by law, or under terms agreed with the appropriate
reprographics rights organizations. Enquiries concerning reproduction
outside the scope of the above should be sent to the Rights Department,
Oxford University Press, at the address above

You must not circulate this book in any other binding or cover,
and you must impose this same condition on any acquirer

British Library Cataloguing in Publication Data

Data available

Library of Congress Cataloging in Publication Data

Readings in medieval texts : interpreting old and Middle English literature /
edited by David F. Johnson and Elaine Treharne.
   p.   cm.
Includes index.
ISBN 0–19–926163–6 (alk. paper)
1. English literature—Old English, ca. 450–1100—History and criticism.
2. English literature—Middle English, 1100–1500—History and criticism.
I. Johnson, David F. (David Frame), 1956-   II. Treharne, Elaine M.
PR166.R43 2005
829'.09—dc22   2004030577

ISBN 0–19–926163–6 (pbk)

1 3 5 7 9 10 8 6 4 2

Typeset by RefineCatch Limited, Bungay, Suffolk
Printed in Great Britain by
Ashford Colour Press Ltd, Gosport

Acknowledgements

THE editors should like to express their gratitude to the contributors for their exemplary work and their prompt submission. We should like to thank Niall Brady and Michael Potterton of the Discovery Programme, Dublin, for their map. Our thanks also to Ruth Anderson at OUP for her helpful suggestions and support throughout the project.

Contents

List of Illustrations

List of Contributors

THOMAS BREDEHOFT University of Northern Colorado

ROLF H. BREMMER, JR. University of Leiden

PATRICK W. CONNER West Virginia University

ANNE MARIE D'ARCY University of Leicester

ALAN J. FLETCHER University College, Dublin

JILL FREDERICK Minnesota State University, Moorhead

ANDREW GALLOWAY Cornell University

NICOLE GUENTHER DISCENZA University of South Florida

THOMAS N. HALL University of Illinois

THOMAS D. HILL Cornell University

DAVID F. JOHNSON Florida State University

STACY S. KLEIN Rutgers University

SARAH LARRATT KEEFER Trent University

ROY M. LIUZZA University of Tennessee

PETER J. LUCAS Wolfson College, Cambridge

JAMES H. MOREY Emory University

AD PUTTER University of Bristol

WILLIAM A. QUINN University of Arkansas

DENIS RENEVEY University of Fribourg

NICOLA ROYAN University of Nottingham

MARY SWAN University of Leeds

ELAINE TREHARNE University of Leicester

MICHAEL W. TWOMEY Ithaca College

GREG WALKER University of Leicester

JONATHAN WILCOX University of Iowa

Introduction

David F. Johnson and Elaine Treharne

This volume is intended principally for literature students undertaking courses in Old and Middle English, and aims to assist them in reading a body of literature that can often appear alien at first glance. All of the contributors are experienced university teachers, who bring to bear on their chapters a knowledge of the difficulties encountered by students on their introduction to medieval literature. Each chapter addresses a text or set of texts that can be considered to represent a 'genre' (although, in many cases, the medieval authors themselves might not have thought in this way). Characteristics of the particular work under consideration are elucidated, scholarly criticism is evaluated, and reading strategies are proposed to highlight particular methods and approaches of understanding the nature, form, and function of the texts. These reading strategies can be applied to numerous other medieval texts, and can be thought of as a useful starting-point for students in their work on this substantial corpus of literature.

Most of the texts encountered in these chapters might be regarded as 'canonical'; that is, those literary works that often appear to be among the most highly valued and which are taught most often within a university syllabus. What is and what is not part of the canon is a matter for serious debate, and this volume does not intend to authorize particular texts as more worthy of study than others. Indeed, this volume aims to open up the issue of canonicity through its provision of valuable reading strategies, and it is hoped that students will use these interpretative approaches, acquire them as a set of skills, and adopt and adapt them in working with texts not included in the volume.

In addition to opening debates on canonicity, this volume attempts to examine a large body of literary material that is often divided up into two distinct periods: Old and Middle English. Students reading the whole volume will quickly recognize that there are many differences between the earlier texts from the Anglo-Saxon period and those which are written in the later Middle Ages. For example, the heroic literature of the Anglo-Saxons is, effectively, replaced by the romances of the thirteenth to fifteenth centuries. However, both 'genres' contain many similar features. As well as differences in the nature of the material there are also many types of literature that are in evidence throughout the period, from c.730 to c.1500. Among these would be sermons and saints' lives, penitential literature, and elegiac texts. In putting this volume together, we hope that comparisons that students can make between the works studied in each chapter will prove fruitful and interesting.

The volume begins with Treharne's brief overview of the context of medieval literature. She discusses the key issue of manuscript culture in a period in which all texts were produced by scribes, together with the concepts of date, authority, and authorship—areas of study that engage modern scholars in their work on the literature. Keefer's chapter begins with the most famous of Old English religious poems, *Cædmon's Hymn*, itself a text that exists in numerous versions, and uses this as a starting-point to examine through close reading and an investigation of the place of the liturgy the features of Old English religious poetry. Other religious texts from the Anglo-Saxon period, which are widely studied, are the so-called elegies. These are analysed by Conner in his chapter, which seeks to contextualize some of these poems specifically within the framework of the monastery and associated guilds in the tenth century. This provocative piece utilizes historical documents to demonstrate how an interdisciplinary and theoretical approach can be highly illuminating. Continuing the interpretation of works contained in the Exeter Book of poetry, Wilcox investigates the context, style, and function of the Old English riddles. He provides new readings highlighting the deliberate multivalency of the genre, and shows the delight of the riddlers in their exploitation of the linguistic and stylistic potential of the form. The third piece on Exeter Book texts is a discussion of Cynewulf's female saint, Juliana. In Frederick's chapter, the depiction of female saints is considered through a detailed reading of *Juliana*. The ways in which this virgin martyr saint responds to the challenges facing her are revealed through Frederick's investigation of 'flyting', and she is seen as a positive role model through this rhetoric.

We move from heroines to heroes. Bremmer's chapter offers an exemplary description and evaluation of the Germanic hero and heroic code. Bremmer focuses on those poems, including *Beowulf*, which treat the 'Germanic narrative heritage' and elucidate the heroic tradition of loyalty, praise, and glory. He then proceeds to compare the literary accounts with the historical 'reality' of texts such as *The Anglo-Saxon Chronicle*, before considering this *modus vivendi* in the propaganda of late Anglo-Saxon poetry. This chapter can be linked with the following one on *Beowulf*, widely regarded as one of the finest expressions of the heroic code in action. Liuzza examines the cultural significance of *Beowulf* both as a poem mediating between past and present, and as one that foregrounds issues of memory and, simultaneously, oblivion. As 'an act of the historical imagination', the poem nostalgically recreates days of former glory, but also recognizes the need to textualize a past already gone, but in danger of being lost completely. This is followed by Bredehoft's chapter on *The Anglo-Saxon Chronicle*. He offers a stimulating discussion on the important themes of memory and historical understanding, which are used by the compilers of the *Chronicle* to mark out key events in their own era.

Having introduced prose instigated in the reign of King Alfred in Bredehoft's chapter, Discenza's essay illustrates, through close analysis of Alfred's Preface to Gregory's *Pastoral Care*, the concerns that Alfred had for uniting his country and remedying the decline in learning. Attempting to remedy the sins of the Christian congregation, the homiletic tradition emerged in the tenth century to become one of the most prolific forms of literature during the medieval period. In Hall's essay, he examines a number of representative homilies, including some from the apocryphal corpus. He focuses principally on death and judgement in some interesting examples of the genre. Remaining with the Christian theme, Klein offers a feminist reading of Cynewulf's poem on the finding of the cross of Christ—*Elene*. She focuses on the depiction and interpretation of women, particularly queens, in the Anglo-Saxon church, and provides a stimulating and innovative discussion of the role of 'mother' within this cultural context.

The wisdom of the Christian women depicted in Anglo-Saxon poems like *Elene* and *Juliana* helps to illustrate the importance placed on being prudent and wise by Anglo-Saxon authors. In Hill's chapter, he tackles the nebulous body of literature that contains pithy apothegms, short universalist statements, and shared common knowledge, often deriving from the Bible: sapiential literature. His broad-ranging discussion encompasses texts such as *Maxims*, *Beowulf*, *Solomon and Saturn II*, and Old Norse and Welsh analogues.

With Morey's chapter on Middle English didactic literature, the volume's focus seemingly crosses the traditional separation of Old from Middle English literature, a divide generally located, on linguistic grounds, at *c*.1150. But, as Nicola Royan so trenchantly puts it in her chapter on Scottish literature later in the volume, '[L]ike all attempts to put clear dates on cultural phenomena, these boundaries stress discontinuity, whereas literary patterns and influence reach across political and temporal borders'. We hope that readers will recognize the continuities in such literary patterns and influences as they are reflected in the chapters in the second half of this volume.

Morey's chapter effectively complements Hill's, among others, in its consideration of the place and nature of didactic literature—understood to include 'sapiential' and moral literature—in the later Middle Ages. The passages he analyses are themselves concerned with a bridging of the inner and outer life in confession. Renevey's chapter considers the increased popularity of Early Middle English literature for women, and illuminates in particular the provocative and intriguing theme of community in the *Ancrene Wisse*, a theme that might at first seem counter-intuitive in a text aimed at solitary recluses.

Johnson's chapter on the Middle English verse *Brut* chronicles highlights the twin themes of violence and kingship in the first treatment of the Arthurian legend in English, and emphasizes the importance of consulting a medieval English author's sources and influences where known. Another romance from this earlier period is examined by Lucas in his discussion of the Breton lay *Sir Orfeo*, in which the private and public bonds of marital love and public loyalty are put to the test.

Fletcher's chapter illuminates an entirely different yet equally pan-European genre: debate literature. In so doing, he applies an extremely close reading to the genre's most superlative representative in English: *The Owl and the Nightingale*, examining 'socially productive binaries' and the role of debates in medieval English society as a means to understanding this fascinating poem.

Swan's chapter on religious writing by women provides a blueprint for reading such texts in Middle English even as it explicates passages from the *Book of Margery Kempe* and Julian of Norwich's *Revelation of Divine Love*. The methodology she outlines and demonstrates here shows how attention to such things as voice, vocabulary, syntax, imagery and patterning, rhythm, tone, attitude, and point of view all contribute to a stylistic analysis that can deepen our understanding of any medieval text.

Twomey's chapter continues the thread begun earlier of medieval English romance. He first considers the anonymous author of *Sir Gawain and the Green Knight* and his other works, then situates that most sophisticated of Middle English Arthurian romances in the contexts of medieval literature and contemporary scholarship on the poem.

In his work on medieval prologues, Galloway offers an intertextual reading of the importance of the openings of lengthy poetic works. Demonstrating how these seemingly stand-alone introductions are integral to the larger works, Galloway focuses on the interaction of the author with his audience through the prologue, of which he identifies four different forms in his broad-ranging discussion.

In her chapter, D'Arcy demonstrates how close reading and an interdisciplinary approach to the fascinating yet disparate corpus of Middle English lyrics can help us understand the form, purpose, and meaning of the secular and religious lyrics that have come down to us from this period.

Another very popular medieval literary genre, the dream vision, is defined and contextualized in Quinn's chapter, which culminates in an 'occasional' reading of Chaucer's *Book of the Duchess*. Quinn shows how dreaming itself is an act of healing and constitutes an 'interlude to mourning' for John of Gaunt following the loss of his wife Blanche, the Duchess. At the later chronological end of the period lies Malory's prose re-workings of earlier French and English romances, and Putter's discussion focuses on the *Tale of Balin*, one of the most intriguing episodes in this fifteenth-century author's massive Arthurian opus. Putter explores Malory's sense of adventure, even as he considers closely Malory's choice of prose as his medium.

Royan's chapter on Scottish literature underscores the continuities that transcend political, linguistic, and cultural differences between the medieval English and Scottish traditions. Here she surveys the literature in Older Scots between 1375 and 1513, analysing some of the best Scots literature in its cultural and historical context. Finally, Walker looks at two very different medieval English dramatic texts in his piece 'Medieval drama: the Corpus Christi in York and Croxton'. Of particular interest here is the way in which both of these plays focus on physical and theological implications of the suffering body of Christ within the fourteenth-century tradition of Affective Piety.

1

The context of medieval literature

Elaine Treharne

The origins of English literature

The history of literary production in English is a surprisingly long one, extending back to the seventh century during the lengthy period of the conversion to Christianity of the Anglo-Saxons. Christianity depends, by its very reliance on the Word of God, on some degree of literacy among its priests and bishops. With this specialist literacy came the production of the tools of religious instruction and clerical education: Latin manuscripts containing biblical texts, homilies or sermons, commentaries, and writings of the church fathers (those who formulated Christian doctrine based on interpretations of the Bible). Concurrent with this literary output in Latin lay a tradition of oral poetic composition in Old English as a means of entertainment and demonstration of the poet's skill. The products of this tradition may survive in a fragmentary and elusive manner through the mediation of scribes in later centuries. The story of Cædmon told by the monk Bede in his eighth-century *Ecclesiastical History of the English People* demonstrates how, through a miracle, this cowherd was able to recite religious poetry using the alliterative form traditionally used by the Anglo-Saxons and other Germanic tribes for their oral, heroic, secular poetry. Bede's inclusion of *Cædmon's Hymn* (written in Old English into the margins of the Latin *Ecclesiastical History*) is one of the earliest pieces of written English to survive (see, further, Chapter 2, by Keefer).

From this early propitious beginning, English literature has never ceased to be produced, and it represents the most sustained body of vernacular writing in Europe. The variety of textual production is naturally immense, and this is as true for the medieval period—encompassing the seventh to the early sixteenth centuries—as it is for later periods. What marks out the medieval period, perhaps, from those literary periods which follow is the nature and type of literary composition and production, together with our ability to discern the roles of, and relationships between, the author and audience of the texts.

Hand-made texts

All published books in contemporary society are published in print form, or, increasingly, electronic form. Mass reproduction of identical texts is a relatively straightforward process. From the emergence of printing in the fifteenth century to the present day, there has been a gradual move away from the centrality of the author's manuscript, his or her original composition, as far as the perspective of the recipient of the text is concerned.

Throughout most of the medieval period, the only means of 'publishing' a text was by hand: a book or series of parchment pages (paper begins to be used only from the fifteenth century) copied out by a scribe. Predominantly, this scribe was not the author, and in many cases the scribes acted as editors of the texts being copied, sometimes putting in their preferred spellings or changing the order of words, whether consciously and deliberately or unthinkingly. Not only, therefore, are surviving manuscripts of texts often one remove or more away from the author's original, but also each individual copy of a text is a unique witness to the way that the text was received and transmitted at its moment of writing.

Some texts survive in multiple copies, and it is possible to trace the evolution and relationship of these works through careful and detailed examination of all surviving copies. This is the case with some of the homilies written by Wulfstan, Archbishop of York, in the early eleventh century. It is also true of the Middle English debate poem, *The Owl and the Nightingale* (see Fletcher's essay, Chapter 17), which survives in two copies of the later thirteenth century. Perhaps the best-known example of a multi-copy work is Chaucer's *Canterbury Tales*, which survives in over eighty manuscripts and fragments from the fifteenth century onwards. While none of these manuscripts was written by Chaucer himself, meaning that no autograph copy is extant, the number of versions of the work testifies unequivocally to its popularity with contemporary audiences.

A significant proportion of texts, however, survives in only one manuscript. Among these are some of the most remarkable works from the medieval period. Fortunately, the unique manuscript of the Old English poems *Beowulf* and *Judith* survived a fire in Sir Robert Cotton's library at Ashburnham House in 1731. *The Battle of Maldon*, written after the Vikings defeated the English in 991, was not so fortunate, and does not survive in original form at all, but exists only in a seventeenth-century transcript made before its destruction in 1731. *Sir Gawain and the Green Knight*, a late fourteenth-century Arthurian romance, is extant in only one manuscript, with three other texts, probably by the same author; and the fifteenth-century *Book of Margery Kempe*, her autobiography dictated by her to a scribe, also exists in one manuscript, produced shortly after her death from an earlier text.

These texts, by virtue of their transmission in manuscript form, cause a number of problems for modern scholarly editors. Principally, where multiple copies of a text survive, it is often difficult to know which version is closest to that written by the author, and scholars must meticulously recreate an edition that they believe best reflects its original state. With unique manuscripts, particularly where the manuscript is damaged, or where scribes are clearly making errors in their copying, scholars have great difficulty in filling the gaps where text is missing, or supplying the necessary emendations. Unlike the modern printed book, with its relatively fixed textual identity, medieval texts are effectively arbitrated by the editor, using his or her preferred methods, and can thus be thought of as fluid, or mutable.

Authors and dates

A further aspect of the manuscript culture of the medieval period, which is exacerbated by the tendency of many authors not to put their name to their work, is the issue of date of textual composition. Scholars studying Dickens, or even the more shadowy Shakespeare, have useful information about the social and historical context in which these authors worked, together with a substantial body of knowledge about the authors themselves, their creative impetus, their intended audiences. In very many cases, nothing is known about the authors of medieval texts, or about the way in which the manuscripts of their works were compiled. In the case of the Old English Vercelli Homilies, for example, only the date of their inclusion in the Vercelli Book (c.970) is known. This is also true for the best-known poem in that book, *The Dream of the Rood*. When these texts were created, the date of their original composition, is not certain; who might have written the works, or who was responsible for their compilation into this manuscript, is also unknown. This lack of contextual informa-tion means that only the clues yielded by the texts themselves can be used to supply possible details of intended audience and method of composition. The same is true of later works, such as the lyrics con-tained in a fourteenth-century manuscript, London, British Library, Harley 2253, or indeed of the great religious poem *Piers Plowman*. In the latter case, the author is thought to be one William Langland, but the most detailed searches by scholars have yielded hardly any information about this inspired poet.

Even when authors are known, then, there are often many questions about them and their work that remain unanswered. Medievalists are still often unable to date poems even to a particular century, and cannot easily detect for what purpose or for whom a text was written. While such a vacuum of information can cause difficulties for critics, it also creates a wide range of interpretative possibilities. Partly for this reason, the medieval literary corpus is one of the most exciting and dynamic to study, with significant amounts of primary research yet to be done.

Authority and audience

Throughout this long period of English textual production, the church remained one of the most important producers and patrons of literature. The authority given to a work produced by one of the church's own could be very significant (see, for example, the work of the Old English homilist Ælfric, in Hall's essay, Chapter 10), and in the earlier period, up to about 1200, it is likely that a very large proportion of the Latin and English texts that were written down were done so by monks and other ecclesiastics. It is amusing to imagine the reaction of the monk who, in Glastonbury or Exeter, compiled the Exeter Book of Old English poems containing the Riddles, a few of which are inherently sexual in nature, if not in solution.

In the later medieval period, from the latter part of the eleventh century, professional, itinerant scribes become more important to a flourishing culture of literacy and the production of official documentation. By the thirteenth century, with the emergence of Oxford and Cambridge universities, workshops making manuscripts written in Latin, French, and English for scholarly or lay patrons became increasingly productive. The increase in literacy throughout society, with the probable exception of many of the peasantry, was an obvious catalyst in the development of professional writers and scribes, catering for tastes in secular, as well as the long-established religious, literary texts.

Tradition and innovation

Given the breadth and variety of texts produced in this, the longest of literary periods, it is near impossible to summarize all the forms and variations of literary fashion that occurred. There are, though, certain literary traditions that were maintained throughout the centuries, as well as notable shifts in the type of texts that were popular, particularly in the period after the Norman Conquest.

As society was very much dominated by the church, religious literature played a major role in the lives of the populace from the earliest period of production well into, and beyond, the Renaissance. Homilies or sermons, hagiography (the writing of saints' lives), religious poems and plays about biblical stories, and a diversity of works aimed at helping the Christian live a useful and pious life form the most prolific group of texts in both the Anglo-Saxon period and throughout the later Middle Ages. Key themes in these prose and poetic pieces were the emulation of the ideals of Christianity (as evinced in the lives of Christ and his saints), the need to beware of sin, to be alert to the imminence of Judgement Day and the transience of earthly life, to search persistently for salvation, and to meditate upon the great act of Christ's Passion to redeem mankind. From lengthy works like *Piers Plowman* or the *Ancrene Wisse* (the latter written *c*.1225 for a small group of women who lived in solitary contemplation of Christ) to densely compact lyrics and short poems, these themes emerge consistently in religious writings (in Latin and French, as well as English).

In the earlier period, the heroic ideal forms an important constituent of the extant body of English work. The Germanic code, necessitating acts of courage and loyalty by a band of warriors led by their lord, was an integral part of the literary re-creation of great deeds. The performance of these texts helped cement social cohesion and construct identity, reflected in the emphasis on kingship, leadership, warfare, and significant public events in historical works like *The Anglo-Saxon Chronicle*.

The public and performative nature of these texts—both religious and secular—is maintained throughout the medieval period, with texts usually being read aloud to a participative audience. The alliterative verse of Old English, to the rhyming octosyllabic couplets, or tail-end rhyme, or alliterative versification of Middle English benefit the modern reader's understanding greatly when spoken aloud. But alongside the continuity of the shared, performative text, there were numerous significant developments: the nature of the hero changed in the post-Conquest period, as much as did the compass of his deeds. One might arguably consider the evolution of romance in the twelfth century, derived from French literary forms, as best indicating the emergence of an individuated account of heroes. Arthur becomes the new Beowulf, but his knights—Gawain, Lancelot, Ywain, among them—have stories of their own too. The battle for a whole army of people (the Geats in *Beowulf*, the East Anglians in *The*

Battle of Maldon) becomes a battle for personal and spiritual development through the quest, real or metaphorical (in *Sir Gawain and the Green Knight, King Horn, Sir Orfeo*). These romances, like their heroic predecessors, idealize, mythologize, and reconceptualize the past of the audience, providing exemplars of human courage, wisdom, and self-awareness.

There is far more to medieval literature than simply religious, heroic, or romance literature, however. Medieval writers are as varied in their form and method, as sophisticated, profound, and creative as any subsequent authors. It is close and detailed reading that holds the key to unlocking the word-hoard of these writers—anonymous or known—and allows readers to gain an understanding of the proximity of these distant voices.

References and suggested reading

Bennett, J. A. W. *Middle English Literature*. Ed. Douglas Gray. Oxford: Clarendon Press, 1986. An excellent introduction to later medieval texts, offering detailed and clear readings of text by genre.

Burrow, John. *Medieval Writers and their Work: Middle English Literature and its Background, 1100–1500*. Oxford: Oxford University Press, 1982. One of the most interesting and lucid accounts of the ways in which medieval writers composed and created their literary works.

Clanchy, M. T. *From Memory to Written Record; England 1066–1307*, 2nd edn. Oxford: Basil Blackwell, 1993. An essential read for the post-Conquest period, this book analyses the growth in literacy and the types of documents produced from the eleventh century to the fourteenth within a trilingual society.

Godden, Malcolm, and Michael Lapidge, eds. *Cambridge Companion to Old English Literature*. Cambridge: Cambridge University Press, 1991. Essays by leading Anglo-Saxonists evaluate Old English literature from numerous different perspectives, and set these texts in their historical and literary contexts.

Le Goff, Jacques. *Medieval Civilization*. Trans. Julia Barrow. Oxford: Basil Blackwell, 1988. A standard volume on the most notable aspects of medieval culture.

Lester, G. A. *The Language of Old and Middle English Poetry*. Basingstoke: Macmillan, 1996. An immensely valuable volume, which demonstrates how Old and Middle English poetic texts can be read linguistically and stylistically.

Pulsiano, Phillip, and Elaine Treharne, eds. *Blackwell Companion to Anglo-Saxon Literature*. Oxford: Blackwell Publishers, 2001. An expansive collection of essays that trace the form and evolution of Old English and Anglo-Latin literature, and discuss the subsequent history of Anglo-Saxon scholarship into the twenty-first century.

Richards, M. P., ed. *Anglo-Saxon Manuscripts: Basic Readings*. New York: Garland Press, 1994. A collection of very useful essays discussing the implications of early medieval manuscript culture and of the practical ways in which manuscripts can be described and used by medieval students.

Treharne, Elaine, ed. *Old and Middle English c.800–1400: An Anthology*, 2nd edn. Oxford: Blackwell Publishers, 2003. Contains texts and *en-face* translations of numerous medieval English texts.

Wallace, David, ed. *Cambridge History of Medieval Literature*. Cambridge: Cambridge University Press, 1999. This extensive tome contains very significant essays on the later medieval period, covering most crucial aspects of literary culture from the twelfth century to the early sixteenth.

2

Old English religious poetry

Sarah Larratt Keefer

Introducing Old English religious poetry

' "What should I sing about?" Cædmon replied. "Sing about the Creation of all things," the other answered.'

> Nu sculon herian   heofonrices Weard,
> Metodes meahta   and his modgeþanc,
> weorc Wuldor-Fæder,   swa he wundra gehwæs,
> ece Dryhten,   or astealde.
> He ærest scop   ielda bearnum
> heofon to hrofe,   halig Scieppend.
> þa middangeard   manncynnes Weard,
> ece Dryhten,   æfter teode
> firum foldan,   Frea ælmihtig. (ASPR VI, p. 106)

Let us praise the maker of the kingdom of heaven, the power and purpose of our Creator, and the acts of the Father of glory. Let us sing how the eternal God, the author of all marvels, first created the heavens for the sons of men as a roof to cover them, and how their almighty Protector gave them the earth for their dwelling-place. (Bede's *Ecclesiastical History*, IV.24, p. 246)

This hymn, ascribed to the peasant cowherd Cædmon by Bede in his *Ecclesiastical History of the English Church and People* (hereafter *EH*), is considered to be the earliest example of religious poetry in Old English. The story goes that, as a simple man, Cædmon had no talent for verse composition and indeed feared social gatherings when people were called upon for impromptu song. Yet when approached in a dream by an angel and commanded to sing, he is suddenly gifted with an ability to compose vernacular poetry spontaneously in honour of God and his creation. Within Bede's account, this kind of spiritual creativity links lowborn and highborn, secular and professed: Hild, born into Northumbrian nobility (*EH* IV.23, p. 241), and Abbess of the double monastery at Whitby, recognizes Cædmon's gift and encourages him to enter the monastic order, making provision for him to learn Holy Scripture orally (since he is illiterate) and turn it spontaneously into alliterative vernacular narrative verse. Hild's historical tenure as Abbess at Whitby began after its foundation in AD 655 and ended with her death in 680, so these years mark Bede's imagined boundaries within which this first Old English poem to God could have been created; Bede himself lived between 672/3 and 735, so the first version of *Cædmon's Hymn*, set down in the Northumbrian dialect, is certainly no later than the third decade of the eighth century.

Bede tells us that the learned teachers at Whitby taught Cædmon the accounts of sacred history, which he then turned into Old English verse, and that his poems included 'the whole story of Genesis . . . Israel's departure from Egypt [and] their entry into the land of promise' as well as 'the Lord's Incarnation, Passion, Resurrection and Ascension into heaven, the coming of the Holy Spirit and the teaching of the apostles' (*EH* IV.24, p. 247). It is therefore no surprise that when early scholars, relearning Old English after the sixteenth century, discovered verse accounts of Old Testament events, they ascribed them without hesitation to Cædmon. Franciscus Junius the younger, a Continental Huguenot theologian and contemporary of John Milton's, was one of these new antiquarian scholars; he owned and edited a manuscript (known by his name and bearing the modern shelf-mark Oxford, Bodleian Library, Junius 11), which contains four poems of considerable length that are based on scriptural narrative. Junius gave these poems the editorial titles of *Genesis* (with two discernible versions known as *Genesis A* and *Genesis B*, a poem translated from Old Saxon into Old English, evident within it), *Exodus, Daniel* (again with one version of the poem interpolated into the other), and *Christ and Satan*, optimistically assuming that they were the work of Cædmon and therefore belonged to the very earliest Anglo-Saxon period. The first three poems are the work of one scribe who wrote in the late tenth or early eleventh century and they probably form a single book, while the fourth piece is written in three different hands of the first half of the eleventh century and may represent a second book bound with the first not long after it was written. These poems are not true translations of their Old Testament 'sources', but interpretations made of those sources from a Christian viewpoint, assuming the New Testament as an absolute point of departure. Modern scholarship does not believe that Cædmon wrote the poems of the Junius Manuscript, but instead that they were most probably each composed by a different author.

There are four main manuscripts that preserve most of the canon of Old English poetry, with the balance of minor poems found as inclusions in books containing other material: these four are the Junius Manuscript, preserved in Oxford's Bodleian Library, as we have seen, and dating from the first part of the eleventh century; the Vercelli Book (Vercelli, Biblioteca Capitolare CXVII), which dates from the last decades of the tenth century; the *Beowulf* or Nowell Codex (London, British Library, Cotton Vitellius A. xv), which was compiled around the year AD 1000; and the Exeter Book (Exeter Cathedral Library 3501), put together around the third quarter of the tenth century. The Junius Manuscript is unusual in that its entire content is religious verse. However, we find other poetry concentrating on religious topics in the remaining three major collections as well as among other minor poems, and their individual approaches can be roughly divided into three kinds of focus. First, there are those poems, like the verse in the Junius Manuscript, which take as their theme a scriptural narrative or event; secondly, there are poems that were inspired by the words or practice of church ritual, or by the lives of saints, and these may be termed 'liturgical poetry' and 'hagiographical poetry' respectively; finally, there are pieces about the Christian life that present interpretation or allegorization of religious subjects for the purpose of teaching, as well as individual meditations and creative outbursts of praise to God: *Cædmon's Hymn* actually fits best into this third category. But these three approaches are in no way mutually exclusive; some of the finest religious verse from Anglo-Saxon England incorporates elements of all three categories, and such a blend renders it truly remarkable.

Within the Nowell Codex that contains *Beowulf* stands another substantial poem that bears the editorial title *Judith* since it is based on the apocryphal book of Judith appended to the Old Testament. *Judith* is incomplete, in that it has lost its opening section, so that there is no way of knowing how long it originally was. Like the poems of the Junius Manuscript, it does not seek to present any kind of translation of its scriptural source, but again incorporates Christian overtones into a work based on an inherently Hebraic original.

The Vercelli Book contains a series of twenty-three prose sermons and a group of poems, some of which are fragmentary. Four of these poems deal with scripture or saints' lives, although such a restriction does them an injustice, as we shall presently see: *Andreas* is hagiographical in that it concerns the life of St Andrew, brother of St Peter, while *Fates of the Apostles* seems inspired by the New Testament book of the Acts of the Apostles. *Elene* is again hagiographical since it describes the finding by St Helena of the True Cross on which Christ was crucified; and *The Dream of the Rood* is the fourth, in which the True Cross recounts to the visionary poet the events of Good Friday. One of the two remaining fragmentary pieces is a lament by a human soul to its decaying body in the grave for all the sins into which it was led while it was in the flesh, while the other fragment deals with the issue of deceit: these pieces can still be termed 'religious' although they belong to the more amorphous, 'interpretative' group described above.

We should pause here to deal with a question of authorship. Within the centuries of European writing that preceded print, it was generally unusual to know the names of any poets composing verse; only after monarchs and courts extended patronage to poets in the later Middle Ages can we match compositions with authors, and even then this work is sketchy and is frequently the result of much painstaking academic historical research. Anglo-Saxon England is no exception to this rule. We have already seen that the name and a brief biography of Cædmon, but no readily ascertainable works, are all we know of this earliest of English poets; a second name, and the poems in which this name appears like a signature, represent the rest of our knowledge of the other named authors of Old English verse, sacred or secular. The poems in the Vercelli Book that have been given the editorial titles *Elene* and *The Fates of the Apostles* bear within them a series of runes, each one representing an individual word but when taken together spelling out the name 'Cynewulf'. Two other poems, *Christ II* or *The Ascension* and *Juliana*, this time in the so-called

Exeter Book, also contain Cynewulf's runic signature. The purpose of such a signature has been taken, from its explicit articulation in two of the poems, as a request for the prayers on the part of the audience for the soul of the poet so named.

The rest of the Exeter Book's contents are also poetry, all copied by the same scribe but, unlike the verse in the Junius Manuscript, these vary greatly in length, theme, focus, and quality. Two other poems, probably not by Cynewulf but copied on either side of his *Ascension*, have been traditionally grouped under the heading *Christ* as they were once assumed to be Cynewulf's work as well; these are known variously as *The Advent Lyrics*, *Christ A* or *Christ I*, and *Doomsday*, *Christ C* or *Christ III*. *Guthlac*, another fine example of 'hagiographical verse', retells the life of the Anglo-Saxon saint Guthlac of Crowland in two unfortunately incomplete versions that follow one after the other, and it is to be found after *Christ III*. After *Guthlac* comes *Azarias*, a poem based on the Old Testament Prayer of Azarias and Song of the Three Children in the book of Daniel; it may also once have been part of another now-lost 'Daniel' poem, since it contains elements of the Junius Manuscript's interpolated *Daniel 'B'* as well. Other religious pieces, primarily of the interpretative kind, make up the balance of the non-secular verse of the Exeter Book: these include allegories like *The Phoenix* and *Physiologus*, a second version of the same *Soul and Body* poem found in the Vercelli Book, and a much-damaged text, (Christ's) *Descent into Hell*.

We know that there was once a complete Old English metrical version of the book of Psalms, of which only the last hundred psalms (51–150) remain in one manuscript called the Paris Psalter (Paris, Bibliothèque Nationale, Latin 8824, copied around the early eleventh century), and a few verse-fragments from the first fifty are to be found in other manuscripts. This attempt at presenting the entire book of Psalms in Old English verse appears to have been made in the later tenth century, and the resulting poetry is uneven and more than a little technically unsatisfying. From approximately the same period in Anglo-Saxon culture comes an intriguing poem, written primarily in Kentish (though some West Saxon forms appear), in which the majority of each Latin verse of Psalm 50 is followed by a meditation upon it in Old English. In the same manuscript as this so-called *Kentish Psalm 50* is to be found another, shorter piece of religious verse, written once again in the Kentish dialect. Initially this poem, known editorially as *Kentish Hymn*, seems interpretative and not unlike *Cædmon's Hymn* but on closer inspection we see that it makes close reference in Old English to parts of better-known Latin liturgical pieces, and is therefore 'liturgical' in its inspiration. This bent for vernacular reinterpretation of the Latin liturgy is echoed in a poem from the tenth-century Exeter Book on the Lord's Prayer, and is carried through into compositions from the eleventh century, where two more Lord's Prayer poems, a verse version of the Apostles' Creed, and a metrical meditation on the *Gloria Patri* each contain the Latin texts of their liturgical original intercalated between the verses of Old English.

It therefore appears that, from its earliest records until its final decades, the culture of Anglo-Saxon England had poets for whom the turning of Christian scripture and saints' lives or the Latin liturgy of the church into Old English verse was a deep and rewarding impulse. However, it also seems evident that many of their longer religious 'poems', left to us in the canon of Anglo-Saxon writing, are in fact composite works made up of more than one version of a piece on a specific source; these were apparently collected as a second stage to their writing, reconstructed into single verse units, and compiled with other similar compositions for inclusion in their manuscripts with some distinctive purpose in mind.

Scholarship on Old English religious poetry

Very early scholarly work done on the longer poems focused, as we have seen, on an attempt to establish authorship and some kind of historical rationale for the composition of religious verse. This is the period of scholarship in which Cædmon was believed to have written the verse of the Junius Manuscript, and when the attempts were made to identify Cynewulf within extant records in order to date and perhaps explain the 'signed' poems in which his name-runes appear. The pieces in the Exeter Book were regarded primarily out of context as individual peculiarities, and the less well-known metrical Psalter and minor poems were studied, when they were studied at all, as examples of linguistic and dialect evidence in the language of Old English.

Later nineteenth-century scholarship was principally an exercise in 'cultural archaeology', in that it searched through the Old English verse canon for traces of a lost Germanic pagan reality: this interest led early scholars to focus on poems like *Beowulf* or *Widsith* more closely than on religious works, which they considered to have been 'contaminated' by the Christianization of Anglo-Saxon culture. But by the mid-twentieth century, such concerns with issues of 'Germania' had been rejected in favour of an equally over-focused study of 'Latina', the culture of the Christian West, in which both Anglo-Saxon poets and audiences were thought to have been steeped. This view presumed that any Germanic heroism present in Old English verse served as an allegory rather than as a narrative, and was intended to cast light upon 'higher truths', as they pertained to Christian learning and beliefs. Naturally, most of the major religious poems, not having been considered seriously hitherto, came under considerable scrutiny within this period, and were examined for their place within a context of patristic thought and Christian education (see Hill in Liuzza, p. 107). But because many religious poems of the canon of Anglo-Saxon verse contain elements of Germanic epic heroism (by way of example, *Andreas* in the Vercelli Codex seems to draw on a common original with *Beowulf* for its opening line, and describes its main figure by using heroic themes and diction), this interpretation of 'Latina' was often stretched to breaking point.

It is only more recently that scholarship has turned to a meticulous consideration of the entire manuscript context in which these poems are to be found. This more recent exploration of context for the poems seeks to examine all the evidence that might account for their inclusion with the other texts in their codex, such as the sequence of these pieces, the marginalia and art that accompany the sections of each book, the scribal corrections made to the material within the manuscripts, and the like. A study of what we can learn about the construction of each verse codex, undertaken over the last quarter-century, has therefore deepened our understanding of any given poem, through investigating the other texts with which it exists in its material context.

The Junius and Vercelli manuscript poems represent a classic case of having been ignored by Germania-orientated scholarship, only to be taken over in the later twentieth century as allegorical constructions by critics of the Latina approach. Current investigations, 'examining what is actually there for us to examine' (Hill in Liuzza, p. 12), have allowed scholars to appreciate Anglo-Saxon scribes as 'compilers and organizers as well as copyists. Each major Old English literary manuscript gives evidence of editorial planning' (Hall in Liuzza, p. 20). Here we can begin to appreciate the composite nature of poems such as *Genesis, Daniel,* or *Guthlac* as deliberate compilations, intended for inclusion within a major codex as part of a comprehensive collection of verse composition on specific subjects. New studies of each remaining codex of Old English poetry are now considering the overall structure of the book and the significance of context as well as content. The religious verse of the Exeter Book has fared in similar fashion: a new edition of this manuscript by Bernard Muir is accompanied by a CD-ROM presenting all pages of the manuscript in digitized facsimile images, with commentary on the layout of the book that is as thorough as the critical commentaries which once accompanied the more traditional print editions of the past.

Work on the canon of Old English liturgical poetry has been sparse. These short pieces were originally discussed in academic notes, identifying their linguistic peculiarities if they were not written in West Saxon (as, for instance, in the case of *Kentish Psalm 50* or *Kentish Hymn*), or their liturgical sources if those were not readily evident, but very little else was done with them. Current scholarship has sought to examine them as a sub-genre, looking at the impulse that caused them to be written in the first place, and examining the relationship, as the Anglo-Saxons saw it, between the Latin of the original liturgical text that is included in the poem, and the Old English that forms the response to it. In some instances, the Latin sentences of a given liturgical source are lacking either part of the grammatical whole (creating an incomplete sentence) or the second half of a complex statement. Investigation of this phenomenon shows that the syntactically incomplete Latin sentences of *Kentish Psalm 50* are the result of the scribe running out of vellum and therefore abbreviating material, which he assumed was familiar to his audience, in order to save space, while the Old English metrical *Creed* poem from Oxford, Bodleian Library, Junius 121 omits the second half of each Latin tenet of faith for another reason. Only the first half of each tenet of faith is intercalated in Latin: the missing half 'answers' each Latin 'prompt' as a short meditation in Old English verse. So, for example, the Latin *Credo in deum patrem omnipotentem*, 'I believe in God the Father almighty', finds its second half in lines 1–8:

> Ælmihtig fæder   up on rodore
> þe ða sciran gesceaft   sceope and worhtest
> and eorðan wang   ealne gesettest,
> ic þe ecne god   ænne gecenne,
> lustum gelyfe.   þu eart lifes frea,
> engla ordfruma,   eorðan wealdend,
> and ðu garsecges   grundas geworhtest,
> and þu ða menegu canst   mærra tungla

whose import is *creatorem caeli et terrae*, 'creator of heaven and earth' (Keefer, pp. 138–9). ['Almighty father up in the heavens, thou who hast shaped and wrought majestic creation, etc.']

This kind of investigation allows us to understand the ways in which Anglo-Saxon poets and their audiences apprehended the inter-action of two languages, the means by which the familiar Latin liturgy could find expression in the vernacular, and the approaches that were used in moving between the two to create something in verse that was at the same time personal and universal.

Reading Old English poetry

It is a given among current scholars of Old English poetry that one of its crown jewels is that poem in the Vercelli Book called *The Dream of the Rood*. This majestic piece is considered the earliest dream-vision poem in the English language, a genre which enjoyed great popularity in later medieval verse writing, and it represents a fascinating inter-section of the various approaches used by Anglo-Saxon poets when writing of God and the divine. Its premise has a narrator-Visionary describe 'the best of dreams' which he is given while 'other speech-bearers [people] are sleeping', thus, while he alone remains awake. He sees a splendidly adorned cross, covered with gemstones and shrouded with light and garments; nevertheless, it begins to change its appearance so that at times it remains a *crux gemmata* ('jewelled cross'), while at others it takes on the aspect of a rough wooden structure, stained with blood and pierced with gashes. This cross or Rood (Old English *rod*, the cross on which Christ died) begins to speak to him, and recounts the story of the Crucifixion from its own perspective in an astonishingly original, imaginative, and moving piece of writing. The poem ends with the Rood adjuring the Visionary to take up its tale of Christ's redemption of humanity on Good Friday and tell it to others, as indeed the poet is doing through composing the poem in the first place.

Two other verse texts exist in parallel with *The Dream of the Rood*, although they are much shorter and echo only central fragments of the poem: one is carved into the stone of the monumental Ruthwell Cross using runic characters, with the date of its inscription a matter of debate ranging from that of the monument itself (late seventh or early eighth century) to the tenth century. The other, equally brief, is carved on the Brussels Cross, evidently a reliquary from around the year 1000. The presence of these two variants suggests to some critics that a very early version of this poem, now lost, may have existed as exemplar for all three pieces. *The Dream of the Rood* grounds its narrative in the Gospel accounts of the Passion and Death of Jesus Christ, so it is inherently scriptural, but its poet makes substantial and significant changes to that source. The liturgy of Good Friday and Holy Saturday night appears in its lines, so that the poem is also liturgical by nature. But above all, it is a unique piece of composition, not at all a translation or even an attempt at retelling the Gospel story in Old English. For these reasons its fine complexities serve us well as an example of details to look for and ways in which to read Old English religious poetry. The section quoted and translated below occurs at the very beginning of the Rood's narrative concerning its history and the role it played on Golgotha when it served as the means by which Jesus Christ died (lines 27–48).

Ongan þa word sprecan   wudu selesta:
   'þæt wæs geara iu,   ic þæt gyta geman,
þæt ic wæs aheawen   holtes on ende,
astyred of stefne minum . . .
. . . Geseah ic þa frean mancynnes
efstan elne mycle   þæt he me wolde on gestigan.
Þær ic þa ne dorste   ofer dryhtnes word
bugan oððe berstan,   þa ic bifian geseah
eorðan sceatas.   Ealle ic mihte
feondas gefyllan,   hwæðre ic fæste stod.
Ongyrede hine þa geong hæleð   (þæt wæs god ælmihtig),

strang ond stiðmod;   gestah he on gealgan heanne,
modig on manigra gesyhðe,   þa he wolde mancyn lysan.
Bifode ic þa me se beorn ymbclypte;   ne dorste ic hwæðre bugan to
    eorðan,
feallan to foldan sceatum,   ac ic sceolde fæste standan.
Rod wæs ic aræred.   Ahof ic ricne cyning,
heofona hlaford;   hyldan me ne dorste.
Þurhdrifan hi me mid deorcan næglum;   on me syndon þa dolg gesiene,
opene inwidhlemmas.   Ne dorste ic hira nænigum sceððan.
Bysmeredon hie unc butu ætgædere.

The best of woods then began to speak with words:
   'That was long ago (I yet remember it)
that I was hewn down from the forest-edge
cut off from my trunk . . .
. . . Then I saw the lord of mankind
hasten with great zeal such that he desired to ascend on me.
In that place I then dared not, against the Lord's command
neither bow nor break, even when I saw
the earth's surface shudder. I might have felled
all my foes, but none the less I stood fast.
The young warrior then prepared himself (he who was God almighty),
strong and determined. He ascended upon the high gallows,
brave in the sight of many, when he wished to redeem mankind.
I trembled then when the warrior embraced me. Nevertheless I dared not
    bow to the earth,
fall to the ground's surface, but I was obliged to stand fast.
I was raised as the Rood. I lifted up the powerful king,
The lord of the heavens, and dared not bow myself down.
They drove me through with dark nails; on me the torment remains visible,
the open woundings. I did not dare injure any of them.
They mocked us both together.

This narrative account of the Crucifixion is startlingly original. Instead of a Jesus who is unresisting, obedient to God's will, this poem portrays a pro-active warrior who takes responsibility for his death on the Cross as part of his own determinism. Rather than being placed on the Rood by others, he prepares himself and ascends of his own volition. Here we find the sensibilities of a heroic culture in overlay with the Gospel narrative, since Jesus Christ is introduced as the *geong hæleð*, the young hero found in so many Germanic verse epics. This kind of construction, putting

Christian and Germanic cultural aesthetics into an innovative tension, appears in other Old English religious verse, such as the Junius Manuscript's *Exodus*, where Moses is depicted as the *heretoga* or 'war leader', or *Kentish Psalm 50*, where King David is described anachronistically as *soð sigecempa ... Criste liofest* ('a true battle-champion, dearest to Christ', lines 10a and 3b). Where once it would have been taken as a 'relic of Germanic heroic paganism' or as an 'allegorical representation of the Son of God as a warrior establishing his church', such a connection of disparate elements, verging on the 'metaphysical' as we understand the term when used of Donne or Vaughan, is now seen in a different way. It appears to present to its reader the intellectual challenge to weigh such a disparity in the mind as the piece unfolds, and to ponder the nature of the mystery thus represented.

Within this specific example, we find the Rood's repeated insistence that, while it might have destroyed those intent upon Christ's death, it nevertheless was obedient to the injunction of God (*dryhtnes word*) and stood fast, accepting its role as the instrument of the death of 'the powerful king, the lord of the heavens', just as Christ in the Gospels was obedient to the divine will. This kind of obedience would have been highly evocative of the obedience expected in epic tales of a warrior by his leader, and so the audience of *The Dream of the Rood* would have been encouraged to associate the relationship between the Rood and Christ with something that they knew from their own cultural stories, that being the *comitatus*, or warband, whose fighters owe their allegiance and obedience to their own earthly lord. This kind of close, intensely loyal bond is reinforced in the poem with the image of the dark nails, driven through Christ's body into the wood of the Rood and thus linking the two with the same scars (*On me syndon þa dolg gesiene, opene inwidhlemmas*, 'on me the torment remains visible; | The open woundings'), and by the half-line *Bysmeredon hie unc butu ætgædere*, 'they reviled us both together'. The dual pronoun *unc* literally means 'the two of us', and use of the dual in Germanic languages is generally reserved for intimate binary relationships between man and woman, lord and warrior, or in this case as a means by which to challenge the Anglo-Saxon reader to think deeply about the configuration of Rood and crucified Christ.

Part of the phenomenon of presenting their themes in such

disparate terms shows us that the Anglo-Saxon poets of religious verse were able to take delight in reinterpreting the stories and characters of Christian scripture through a cultural lens all their own. But this particular configuration (the startling depiction of Christ as a Germanic hero, the insistence by the Rood on its *thegn*-like obedience to the Lord's command, the evocative image of the nails that join Christ and the Rood into a unit, and that unity affirmed by the dual pronoun *unc*) also introduces another, even more important element to the poem: it constructs something mysterious. This forces the reader to read in a new way something which superficially appears to be a familiar story (in this case, the account of the Passion in the Gospels), so that we move from the known into the unknown as we interpret, and that movement mirrors the movement of the human soul from the transitory to the eternal. Many of the Anglo-Saxon riddles have at their core a 'speaking creature' whose identity must be guessed from what it tells us about itself, and *The Dream of the Rood* has long been associated, however peripherally, with such a genre. There are 'cross' riddles within the canon of Old English *enigma* (riddle) writing, and while *The Dream of the Rood* is many other things as well, it certainly shares some of the *enigma* features. These challenging features of the mystery at the heart of its narrative create a puzzle that the reader must solve, since the riddlic question 'what am I?' is implicit in the changes that are imposed on the Bible's version of the Crucifixion. Indeed, one must ask those questions which the poem thus provokes: can we see Christ as a hero and not a victim? Why does the Rood repeat so frequently that it dared not fall? If we allow that Christ and the Rood are irrevocably joined into a single reality by the nails, can we see one as purely passive and obedient, the other purely active and authoritative? What then does this do to our understanding of the Crucifixion? Christ's death on the Rood must therefore also be understood as a mystery, of necessity challenging the Christian reader to reassess it from a new angle, and to consider the complexities of the meaning of redemption.

In addition to such innovation, appealing to the aesthetics of their culture, the Anglo-Saxon writers of this kind of verse made use of their own language to create patterns of semantics in thematic development, which would also have had resonance for their audience. The Rood tells us that it was *astyred of stefne minum*, 'cut off from my tree-trunk', but there are at least two meanings to the word *stefn*, depending on whether one takes it as a masculine or a feminine noun: *stefn*, masculine, means 'tree-trunk' or 'root', while *stefn*, feminine, means 'voice'. The single word, with its different meanings that are both being used here, thus serves to move the theme of the poem forward and develop it: that which was once a tree with a trunk has now, through God's intervention, become something different in that it is able to speak with a voice and recount a history in words. Other instances of these word-plays, used to create a sense of development through the power of God, appear not only in the rest of *The Dream of the Rood* but in many other Old English religious poems as well. As with the earlier riddlic dimension that is constructed in the poem, this polysemy (or more than one meaning for the same word at the same time) encourages a much more creative and inquiring mindset in considering the mysteries of the Crucifixion and Resurrection, and the ways in which one reality (a tree-trunk, a woman, a Visionary) can be changed into another (the speaking Rood, the mother of God, the poet who writes his vision as a witness of the Christian faith) through the power of God.

From the foregoing, we can see that this kind of verse has many layers upon which a listener or reader can build their understanding. While *The Dream of the Rood* is a stylistic and aesthetic masterpiece, it is not atypical of other poems on religious subjects within Anglo-Saxon writing; as a group and across the three types of focus described earlier, these poems readily serve as meditations upon the spiritual dimensions of life that the Anglo-Saxons found so compelling. The voice of the Anglo-Saxon religious poet is a singular one, drawing from the rich tradition of Germanic epic, elegiac composition, and metrical design, and embedding that richness within a new and evocative revisiting of the Christian world-view.

References and suggested reading

Bede. *A History of the English Church and People.* Harmondsworth: Penguin, 1968. Trans. Leo Sherley-Price. revised R. E. Latham. The standard translation of Bede's monumental work.

Farrell, Robert, ed. *Daniel and Azarias.* London: Methuen, 1974. An important and useful edition of two of the central Old English religious texts.

Irving, Edward B., Jr., ed. *The Old English Exodus.* New Haven: Yale University Press, 1953. A full and invaluable edition of the poetic account of the Israelites' journey out of Egypt.

Keefer, Sarah Larratt. '*Ic* and *We* in Eleventh-Century Old English Liturgical Verse'. In Katherine O'Brien O'Keeffe and Mark Amodio, eds., *In Unlocking the Wordhord: Anglo-Saxon Studies in Memory of Edward B. Irving, Jr.* Toronto: University of Toronto Press, 2003, pp. 123–46. Discusses forms of address in Anglo-Saxon verse.

Krapp, George Philip, and Elliot van K. Dobbie, eds. *The Anglo-Saxon Poetic Records.* New York: Columbia University Press, 1931–42. 6 vols. Still the fullest and most cited edition of all Old English verse.

Liuzza, Roy Michael, ed. *The Poems of MS Junius 11.* New York and London: Routledge, 2002. An important collection of some of the most significant critical works on the Junius poems. See especially Joyce M. Hill, 'Confronting Germania–Latina: Changing Responses to Old English Biblical Verse', pp. 1–19; and James R. Hall, ' "The Old English Epic of Redemption": Twenty-Five Year Retrospective', pp. 20–52.

Lucas, Peter, ed. *Exodus.* London: Methuen, 1977. A full edition, with glossary, of the Old English *Exodus* that elucidates the liturgical significance of the poem, and seeks to place it within its manuscript context.

Muir, Bernard J., ed. *The Exeter Anthology of Old English Poetry,* 2nd edn. Exeter: Exeter University Press, 2001. 2 vols. + CD-ROM. A full edition of all the poems contained in the Exeter Book, with notes, glossary, and useful introduction.

Remley, Paul G. *Old English Biblical Verse.* Cambridge Studies in Anglo-Saxon England 16. Cambridge: Cambridge University Press, 1996. An essential study of the verse of the Junius Manuscript, and other texts deriving ultimately from biblical sources.

3

The Old English elegy: a historicization

Patrick W. Conner

Poems in the Old English elegiac tradition

Since the sixteenth century, the term 'elegy' has been used to describe a funeral song or lament. Therefore, when John J. Coneybeare began to publish the sad Old English poems he found in his researches in the early nineteenth century, it is no surprise that he chose to call them 'elegies'. A curious fact about the Old English elegy, however, is that every free-standing poem we have that anyone has ever been willing to call an elegy is to be found in manuscript 3501 of the Dean and Chapter Library of Exeter Cathedral, better known as 'The Exeter Book'. There are elegiac passages in longer poems, such as the so-called 'Lay of the Last Survivor' and the 'Father's Lament' in *Beowulf*, but only in the Exeter Book does the genre sustain a composition. Those poems deemed by critics and scholars to be Old English elegies include *The Wanderer, The Seafarer, The Riming Poem, Deor, Wulf and Eadwacer, The Wife's Lament, Resignation A* and *B, The Husband's Message,* and *The Ruin*.

That this genre is claimed by a single manuscript may be an accident of survival or it may be indicative of a localized interest in the form. Early medieval topography was, as the historian Jacques Le Goff reminds us, 'made up of economic, social, and cultural cells'.[1] Indeed no institution better symbolizes this concept of economic and social insularity than the monastery, where most surviving Old English poetry was copied. It is too often imagined that monasteries shared the same culture throughout western Europe, but in every detailed way which remains in the textual and archaeological record, this is not true. The varied contents of numerous mass-books and other service books make clear how local interests and opportunities could determine even the universal liturgy of the church. That we have never been able to write, as Joseph Harris has noted, a satisfactory literary history of the Old English elegy may have to do with the assumption that the form was ubiquitous in Anglo-Saxon culture when its presence in a single manuscript suggests that knowledge of the form was circumscribed.

The Exeter Book has resided at Exeter since at least *c*.1050 and I think the manuscript was in fact written there. Although there are several ways to read these intriguing poems, many of which will be found in the list of further reading for this chapter, I want to read them against culturally important documents written in the same period and to relate them to the determining issues of the day. I shall therefore take what is known as a 'New Historicist' approach to the Old English elegies. Such a New Historicist project may rescue them from the romantic but unfortunate notion that they are timeless.

The prayer-guild: an elegiac milieu and context

The Exeter burial guild offers the proper milieu for the composition, presentation, and reception of several of the elegies we find in the Exeter Book. Its charter, or 'Guild-statutes', is preserved on the surviving leaf, folio 75, of an eighth-century gospel-book in London, British Library, Cotton Tiberius B. v, vol. 1. The text is datable to the middle of the tenth century. Because the Exeter Book was copied *c*.950 × *c*.970, the Guild-statutes are contemporary textual witnesses to Exonian culture at the time the elegies were copied. Five sets of Guild-statutes are known for the period,[2] but Exeter's document is the most concerned with the valuation of membership duties and the commodification of monastic work:

+Ðeos gesamnung is gesamnod on Exanceastre for Godes lufun 7 for usse saule þearfe, ægþer 'ge' be usses lifes gesundfulnesse ge eac be þæm æfteran dægun þe we to Godes dome for us sylfe beon willaþ. Þonne habbaþ we gecweden þæt ure mytting sie þiwa on .xii. monðum: ane to Sancte Michaeles mæssan; oðre siðe to Sancte Marian mæssan ofer midne winter; þriddan siþe on eallhælegna mæssedæg ofer Eastron. 7 hæbbe ælc gegilda .ii. sesteras mealtes 7 ælc cniht anne 7 sceat huniges. 7 se messepreost asinge two mæssan—oþre for þa lyfigendan frynd, oþere for þa forðgefarenan—æt ælcere mittinge; 7 ælc gemænes hades broður twegen salteras sealma— oðerne for ða lifgendan frynd, oþerne for þa forðgefarenan. 7 æt forðsiþe ælc monn .vi. mæssan oððe .vi. salteras sealma; 7 æt suþfore ælc mon .v. peninge; 7 æt husbryne ælc mon ænne peninge. 7 gif hwylc mon þone andagan forgemeleasige æt forman cyrre .iii. messan, æt oþerum cyrre .v., æt þriddan cyrre ne scire his nan man butun hit sie for mettrumnesse oððe for hlafordes neode. 7 gif hwylc man þone andagan oferhebbe æt his gescote bete be twifealdum; 7 gief hwylc monn of þis geferscipe oþerne misgrete, gebete mid .xxx. peninge. Þonne biddaþ we for Godes lufun þæt ælc man þæs gemittinge mid rihte healde swa we hit mid rihte gerædod habbaþ. God us to þæm gefultumige.

+This council is convened at Exeter for the love of God and for our souls' need, both for our welfare in life and in the afterlife, too, which we hope may be granted us as God's judgement on our lives. To that end, we have agreed that we shall have three meetings in twelve months: one at St Michael's Mass; a second time at St Mary's Mass after mid-winter; a third time at All-Saints' Massday after Easter. And each guildsman shall have two sesters of malt and each retainer one, and a sceat's worth of honey. And the priest shall sing two masses—one for friends who are living, the other for those passed away—at each meeting; and each brother of common degree, two psalters of psalms—one for friends who are living, the other for those passed away. And for a death, each man [is assessed] six masses or six psalters of psalms; and for a pilgrimage south, each man [is assessed] five-pence; and for a house fire, each man [is assessed] one penny. And if anyone misses the stipulated day, he [is assessed] three masses for the first instance, five masses for the second instance, and for the third instance he may not exculpate himself except it be on account of sickness or his lord's needs. And if any man omits his payment for that day, let him pay double in compensation; and if any man from this fraternity insult another, let him pay in compensation thirty pence. So we ask for the love of God that each man duly observe this assembly as we have duly ordered it. May God support us in this.

The Exeter Guild-statutes suggest a familiarity with a central idea which is also played out in the elegies: what is the soul's need in this life that will properly prepare it to be judged worthy of eternal joy in the next? The answer to that is styled in the mode of barter or exchange. Gold hoarded in life may not purchase the desired afterlife, as *The Seafarer* will make clear but, as the Guild-statutes assume, it can purchase the saying of masses and singing of the psalter to the benefit of the soul, and so figure the coin of salvation.

Members of the guild contracted with the monastic community for liturgies (forms of worship) during three regular meetings per year. We must assume that they paid the community for a priest to sing two masses for the living and the dead and for each monk's chanting the psalter once for the living and once for the dead. The *opus Dei*, the work of God, was clearly commodified. For the monastic community, the death of a guildsman amounted to their greatest realization of capital: if the guild had but ten surviving members, which seems a small number for such an elaborate set of statutes, then the monastery would receive funds for sixty masses and psalters, which is five times the number of such services that would be required by the guild in a year when there were no deaths. The larger the guild membership, the more dramatic are the economic benefits to the monastery at a guildsman's death, not only because each death results in more masses being ordered, but also because the larger the membership, the more likely that at least one member will die during any given period. Such conspicuous largesse to the monastery led the individual guildsman to expect that his own death would occasion an equivalent production and this encouraged the continuation of the arrangement.

This system was probably a consequence of the social development of lay piety that arose in the attempt to graft monastic virtue onto noble families, and we can be reasonably certain that the members of the guild were wealthy people of high status. Models of piety for such families abounded at Exeter in men like Kings Æthelstan, Edward, and Edgar, and Abbot Sidemann, all of whom shared the deeper ideologies of monasticism. Æthelstan favoured Exeter in many ways, most piously in establishing a treasury of holy relics there, and Abbot Sidemann tutored King Edgar's son, Edward the Martyr, at Exeter. Relics from Edward's body were kept with the large collection of martyrs' relics there.[3] What greater glory could his life have purchased than to be included among the saints whose relics King

Æthelstan gave to Exeter 'for God's praise, for the deliverance of his own soul and for the eternal salvation of all those who seek out and worship the holy place' and were thus identified as 'the most precious treasures which might ever be purchased on this earth'? ('The Old English Relic-List' §§1 and 4, in Conner, *Anglo-Saxon Exeter*, pp. 176–7).

By agreeing to pay for masses or psalters upon the death of a colleague, each member assured himself that a similar number of liturgies would be said at his own death. Thus he could not be accused of hoarding his wealth, and he could guarantee his own purchase of salvation. It is, in short, my contention that several of the elegies in the Exeter Book once functioned to perpetuate, to guarantee, and to strengthen the social relationships necessary to the production of a monastic economic hegemony. These same bonds were further strengthened in the feasts that were given at each of the three annual guild meetings, wherein the malt and honey required for brewing was allotted by the monks per the Guild-statutes. Such gatherings would have required programmes of some sort, and the reading of appropriate vernacular poems, such as the elegies, would have been in order. In what follows, then, my reference to the 'reader' of these poems is primarily to the Anglo-Saxon listener, who—I want to suggest—can be identified with the members of the guild.

The Seafarer

The Old English elegy appropriates the voice of an imperilled aristocrat grappling not merely with the transient nature of glory in the world (Fell, p. 176), but with the intransigent nature of human fate: *wyrd bið ful araed*, 'providence may not be changed'. The elegies assert the value of monastic capital in such a world by employing a rhetoric which both identifies the subject of each poem with the reader, and defers that identification, forcing the reader to admit that he or she could yet become such a subject, and thus ensuring further participation in the monastic/guild enterprise. Deferral of that identification permits the reader to believe that he or she will not be caught on the frozen sea but can perceive him or herself superior to the subject, which ensures further participation in the monastic project:

Mæg ic be me sylfum   soðgied wrecan,
siþas secgan,   hu ic geswincdagum
earfoðhwile   oft þrowade,
bitre breostceare   gebiden hæbbe,
gecunnad in ceole   cearselda fela,
atol yþa gewealc,   þær mec oft bigeat
nearo nihtwaco   æt nacan stefnan,
þonne he be clifum cnossað.   Calde geþrungen
wæron mine fet,   forste gebunden,
caldum clommum,   þær þa ceare seofedun
hat ymb heortan;   hungor innan slat
merewerges mod.

(lines 1–12a)

I can recite a true-tale about myself—tell my experiences—how, during my working days, I often suffered times of turmoil, abided the bitter cares of the heart, encountered many meeting places of sorrow in my vessel, where the hard night-watch at the ship's prow often fell to me when the grim heaving of the waves dashed against the cliffs. My feet were tormented with cold, bound with frost, shackled with iciness, where cares, hot within my heart, moaned; a hunger from within pierced the spirit of the sea-cursed man.

The narrative of misery extending beyond mere physical discomfort occupies the largest part of *The Seafarer*. It is at once the means to establish the subject's (and, perhaps, the author's) authority for suggesting that, without spiritual comfort, the impermanence of physical comfort leaves one empty indeed, but this narrative of misery is also the means to establish an identification with the reader. Cold feet and *angst* are universal problems, but the reader will also comprehend within him- or herself the context in which mere physical discomfort represents a spiritual lack; the Anglo-Saxon reader shared an ideology which read physical pain in spiritual terms.

The context of misery is not perceived in *The Seafarer* as the business of seafaring, but rather as the recollection of seafaring. When the subject recalls, *hu ic geswincdagum | earfoðhwile oft þrowade*, or 'how, during my working days, I often suffered times of turmoil' as the context of the *soðgied* or biographical précis he recites, the reader is concurrently made aware of a subject who has constructed a text for (and, perhaps, from) his past. We can generalize this to all the elegies: the past is always the subject's means of determining the present. But there is a crux in these poems where the past and present are unexpectedly juxtaposed or linked. In bringing up his hardships as a thing of his past whose significance the reader will comprehend, the subject signals that he has resolved those problems, but he defers telling the reader how this resolution was accomplished. It is in this situation that we find the ideological nexus of the poem: 'I was lost, but now am found; was blind, but now I see', as the sometime seaman of John Newton's hymn, 'Amazing Grace', has it. At the heart of such an ideology is the notion that transformation is desirable, and from it will spring the more desirable future:

> Forþon cnyssað nu
> heortan geþohtas,   þæt ic hean streamas,
> sealtyþa gelac   sylf cunnige;
> monað modes lust   mæla gehwylce
> ferð to feran,   þæt ic feor heonan
> elþeodigra   eard gesece.   (lines 33b–38)

So now the thoughts of my heart stir that I myself may try the deep waters, the play of the salt waves; all the time my mind's desire urges my spirit to go forth, so that I may seek a home among pilgrims, far from here.

The poet relates *cnyssað* in line 33b and *cnossað* in line 8a, both having to do with unrelenting motion. Where the waves beat against the cliff at the beginning of the poem, the subject's thoughts beat within his breast in this second segment; where the rolling of the waves was *atoll* or 'grim' at the outset, it is *gelac*, in motion but not grim, in the second segment; where he was given a hard night-watch in his ship in the beginning of the poem, he seeks a desirable dwelling away from here in the second segment. The subject's desire is set up in almost exact opposition to his experience. Perhaps the most important phrase in the passage is *elþeodigra eard*, 'a home among pilgrims'. The rhetorical opposition of these two passages just discussed requires an ideological interpretation which the reading of *elþeodigra eard* merely as 'foreign land' will not support, because the past must be inflected with the subject's present desire: once I was forced to be wretched and now I want to be blessed. The creation of such desire in the reader reproduces the conditions of production that define the relationship between the guild and monastery:

> Simle þreora   sum þinga gehwylce,
> ær his tid aga,   to tweon weorþeð;
> adl oþþe yldo   oþþe ecghete

fægum fromweardum   feorh oðþringeð.
Forþon þæt [bið]eorla gehwam   æftercweþendra
lof lifgendra   lastworda betst,
þæt he gewyrce,   ær he on weg scyle,
fremum on foldan   wið feonda niþ,
deorum dædum   deofle togeanes,
þæt hine ælda bearn   æfter hergen,
ond his lof siþþan   lifge mid englum
awa to ealdre,   ecan lifes blæd,
dream mid dugeþum.

(lines 68–80a)

Each of three things is always uncertain before its time arrives; illness or age or violence will take life from a doomed and dying man. And so for every man, the praise of the living—those who speak after he is gone—is the best testimonial, which he may bring about before he must be away, with accomplishments on earth against the fiends' devising, with worthy deeds against the devil, so that the sons of men may afterwards praise him, and his praise—the joy of eternal life and delight among the hosts—may then live with the angels always and forever.

The subject desires salvation in the face of a world which he deems condemned, but he is no longer interested in recalling the sea, whether as a reminder of mortal tribulation or as a metaphor for the pilgrim's final journey. Instead, this desire is manifested in terms of the value of a living person's praise of the dead. The subject's focus is not on the dying man's soul finding a place in heaven, but rather on the way in which eternal life is supported by those living on earth. This sentiment is an exact counterpart to the Guild-statutes' requirements that members sponsor masses or psalters to be said at the death of a fellow member, constituting one of the monastery's most lucrative functions. *The Seafarer* defines both the subject's and the reader's desire in terms of monastic capital.

The lawcode known as V Æthelstan, promulgated at Exeter by King Æthelstan and his council in *c.*927 × 937, required every minster to sing fifty psalms each Friday 'for the king and for all who desire what he desires and for the others, as they may deserve'.[4] If we read the decree as a means of making the monasteries integral to English culture and society, then it is a short step to the commodification of monastic ritual, and an equally short step to the idea that holy praise effects a heavenly response:

> Þeah þe græf wille   golde stregan
> broþor his geborenum,   byrgan be deadum,
> maþmum mislicum   þæt hine mid wille,
> ne mæg þære sawle   þe biþ synna ful
> gold to geoce   for godes egsan,
> þonne he hit ær hydeð   þenden he her leofað.   (lines 97–102)

Although the brother will strew with gold the grave of his kinsman, bury him among the dead with a variety of treasures which he wants to go with him, gold cannot serve as a help before the awesomeness of God for the soul which is full of sin when he had hoarded it while he lived here.

The Seafarer follows a peroration on the transient nature of the world and the physical degradation of the body with this passage on how gold, once hoarded, has no value when strewn on the grave of the departed. These lines directly embrace the stated purpose of the Exeter Guild-statutes. The subject is no longer a seafarer in any sense; the subject is a homilist, and the message being preached is that the reader must properly share his or her capital while living. Extending the homiletic mode, the poem reaches its final exhortation:

> Uton we hycgan   hwær we ham agen,
> ond þonne geþencan   hu we þider cumen,
> ond we þonne eac tilien,   þæt we to moten
> in þa ecan   eadignesse,
> þær is lif gelong   in lufan dryhtnes,
> hyht in heofonum.   Þæs sy þam halgan þonc,
> þæt he usic geweorþade,   wuldres ealdor,
> ece dryhten,   in ealle tid. Amen.
>   (lines 117–24)

Let us consider where we may have a home and then contemplate how we may come there, and then we may also labour that we may be able to come into the eternal blessedness, joy in heaven, where life is dependent upon the love of the Lord. Thanks be forever to the Holy One, the King of Glory, the Eternal Lord, who determined our worth.

That the verb, *tilian*—from which we derive the Modern English agrarian term 'to till'—signifies 'to labour' is telling in this reading of the poem, for it emphasizes the exchange of capital (of labour or the coin which represents labour) for monastic capital. That God should be thanked because humans have been *geweorþade* is also telling. *Geworþian* means 'to set a value upon', and the semantic range of the verb includes this mercantile dimension. The point appears to be a basic economic one: our value lies in our will to purchase salvation, with all of the ramifications of the market place that implies.

The Seafarer presents us, then, with a paradigm for reading the elegies. The subject presents a contrast between a dismal past and a present in which there has been a resolution of the earlier pain. This is the 'confession' component of the paradigm. The subject purchases the conditions of deliverance from mortal pain and generates in the reader a desire for a similar delivery. This component of the paradigm is the 'production of desire'. Next, the subject establishes the value of monastic capital as the means of satisfying this desire, the 'identification' between desire and the commodity which will satisfy it being the third component of the paradigm. The 'exhortation', the last component of the paradigm, asks the reader directly to reproduce the conditions of monastic capital.

Other elegies

All of the elegies do not match the paradigm in all four components, but they all draw from a single, coherent body of imagery, and they are all found in one codex, constituting sufficient reason to see how each formulates the described paradigm within the culture which produced the Guild-statutes.

The subject of *The Wanderer* focuses on the production of desire. The poem's subject speaks by observing the wanderer from a position of comfort which he identifies with age and wisdom. The subject's opening observations suggest the importance of desire in the poem and simultaneously identify what will satisfy that desire:

> Oft him anhaga   are gebideð
> metudes miltse,   þeah þe he modcearig
> geond lagulade   longe sceolde
> hreran mid hondum   hrimcealde sæ
> wadan wræclastas.   Wyrd biþ ful aræd!   (lines 1–5)

Often the wanderer prays for honour, the mercy of the Creator, though he, weary at heart, must needs stir the ice-cold sea with his hands through the water-routes and ramble the paths of exiles. Fate is fully determined.

It is *ar* or honour which the wanderer seeks, and which would negate the narrative of misery which most of the poem articulates. But, in the second line of the poem, *ar* is identified with God's mercy; *ar* may be translated as respect or even divine grace, but it also is used for real capital, including property, estates, and ecclesiastical benefices. Thus, the *ubi sunt* catalogues of things which are gone are dramatic demonstrations of the inability of items in this world to satisfy, in themselves, the desire which the poem sets up:

> Wel bið þam þe him are seceð,
> frofre to fæder on heofonum,   þær us eal seo fæstnung stondeð.
>
> (lines 114b–115)

It will be well for him who seeks honour, comfort with the father in heaven, where the agreement stands for us all.

Here, it would seem as if *ar* is being used both in its abstract and concrete meanings; if we read this exhortation against the reading of *The Seafarer*, then *The Wanderer* is a poem in which the hoarding of private capital is also vain.

The subject of *The Riming Poem* states the condition of physical death, to dramatize the importance of understanding the Christian alternative. The confession is interesting because, while it recalls a pleasant and happy past at first, it shows the turn of fortune that inevitably comes with death. The subject's present, which the reader understands to be *beyond* the grave, creates the production of desire. The reader does not desire the idyllic past which was first described in the poem, because death is shown to make that a cruel comfort; instead, the reader desires to know what the subject has already realized and can proclaim. This is described not in the first person (in which he described his own death), but in the third-person subjunctive, the style appropriate to the exhortation:

>   Ne biþ se hlisa adroren.
> Ær þæt eadig geþenceð,   he hine þe oftor swenceð,
> gemon morþa lisse.   Her sindon miltsa blisse,
> hyhtlice in heofona rice.   Uton nu, halgum gelice,
> scyldum biscyrede,   scyndan, generede
> wommum biwerede,   wuldre generede,
> þær moncyn mot,   for Meotude rot,
> soðne God geseon   ond aa in sibbe gefean.
>
> (lines 78–87; Macrae-Gibson)[5]

Fame may not have gone under. The blessed man considers that early, exerts himself more often as defence against harsh sin, thinks of the better joys, the sweet reward where delight is in mercy and hope confirmed in heaven. Then let us hasten with the saints to where, cut off from sins, saved and protected from all evils, gloriously saved, mankind, glad before the Lord shall see true God, and rejoice among the kindred of peace for ever.

The identification of desire with its satisfaction depends upon the word *halgum*, 'saints'. *Halgum gelice* means 'like unto the saints', and it brings the whole cultural significance of the saints to bear in this reading. To be urged to exert oneself to be like the saints in a poem is, of course, a piety which the reader would no doubt have taken seriously, but it may have been also an invitation to participate in the monastic economy that depended often on the income from relics of the same saints.

The two *Resignation* poems are quite different. *Resignation A* is a prayer of confession, and it has been analysed as a psalm, so that we might say that it references the psalter in its own form. But like the other elegies, the subject of *Resignation A* speaks of her own soul. The poem is no vernacular textualization of monastic capital; it is rather a poem made in the context of the same ideological apparatus which gave rise to the Guild itself. It associates the content of the statutes with the emotion such practices require. Opening like one of John Donne's 'Holy Sonnets', *Resignation A* identifies the desire for union with God as the means of satisfying the shortcomings of the past:

> Age mec se Ælmihta god,
> helpe min se halga dryhten!   Þu gesceope heofon ond eorþan
> ond wundor eall,   min wundorcyning,
> þe þær on sindon,   ece dryhten,
> micel ond manigfeald.   Ic þe mære god,
> mine sawle bebeode   ond mines sylfes lic,
> ond min word ond min weorc,   witig dryhten
> ond eal min leoþo,   leohtes hyrde,
> ond þa manigfealdan   mine geþohtas.
>
> (lines 1–9)

Possess me, Almighty God, help me Holy Lord! You made heaven and earth, and all the great and manifold wonders, my King of Glory, which are thereon, Eternal Lord. I offer you, glorious God, my soul and my own body, and my words and my labour, wise Lord, and all my hymns and my various thoughts.

The poem's subject speaks a general confession, without the sort of detail evident in the confessions of *The Seafarer* and *The Wanderer*, but it amplifies the production of desire by continually focusing on heaven. The subject repeatedly requests God to act for the good of his soul, and to sustain and defend him. The poem breaks off before it explores the possibility that monastic practice may satisfy spiritual hunger. However, the last two and a half lines of the poem suggest that the poem's lost lines would have engaged the exchange of temporalities for spiritualities:

> Đe sie ealles þonc
> meorda ond miltsa, þara þu me sealdest.
> No ðæs earninga ænige wæron mid ...   (lines 67b–69)

May thanks be to you for the rewards and mercies which you have given me. No such rewards were with ...

That the beginning of *Resignation B* is missing is unfortunate. We nevertheless have part of the poem's confession preserved, and it is intriguing in its implications. The subject suspects that he has angered God, and thus fears dying. Although his labours (*wyrhto*) were once focused on worldly things, *fyrhto in folce*, 'fear among the people', replaces *wyrhto* or worldly labours. Fortune renders him an exile, too destitute to buy the boat that would take him away from his painful existence:

> ... hwy ic gebycge bat on sæwe,
> fleot on faroðe; nah ic fela goldes
> ne huru þæs freondes, þe me gefylste
> to þam siðfate, nu ic me sylf ne mæg
> fore minum wonæhtum willan adreogan.   (lines 100–4)

... with which I may purchase a boat on the sea, a ship in the current; I have not so much gold nor so many friends who may aid me on the journey, now that I cannot carry out my own desire on account of my poverty.

The passage clearly identifies capital with salvation. The subject should have taken the trip when he had the wherewithal to purchase a boat, but then, in a passage parallel with the last line of the poem, he found 'martirdom' too intense to carry out.[6] The confession, then, is not complete, but it represents a painful past which is not ameliorated in the present; even so, the subject focuses so clearly on the relationship between the fiscal and the physical worlds that the object of desire is clear, and so is the means of its satisfaction. The exhortation is a gnomic passage with no particular homiletic overtones: *Giet biþ þæt selast, þonne mon him sylf ne mæg wyrd onwendan, þæt he þonne wel þolige*, 'It is best, when a man cannot change fate himself, that he then suffer well'. But the poem implies that *wyrd* could have been changed if the subject had been able to purchase that which is figured by the boat. In the context of the guild at Exeter and of King Æthelstan's decrees, the means to change *wyrd* is psalters and masses, which this poor exile did not buy.

Of the poems usually listed amongst the elegies, *Deor*, *Wulf and Eadwacer*, *The Wife's Lament*, *The Husband's Message*, and *The Ruin* have not been discussed here, because they do not obviously share the paradigm of a desire for monastic capital with those poems that have been discussed. They are laments, and as such they probably had a place in the same programme where the elegies were read before the guild members, but unlike the elegy, they do not exhort one to participate in purchasing the production of the monastery. The laments do not sell salvation, the elegies do.

Notes

1. Jacques Le Goff, *Medieval Civilization*, 2nd edn., trans. Julia Barrow (Oxford: Basil Blackwell, 1988), p. 131.
2. Dorothy Whitelock *et al.*, eds., *Councils & Synods with Other Documents Relating to the English Church*, i. AD 871–1204 (Oxford: Oxford University Press, 1981), pt. 1, no. 16, pp. 57–60; no. 67, pp. 516–20. Also see Gervase Rosser, 'The Anglo-Saxon gilds', in J. Blair, ed., *Minsters and Parish Churches: The Local Church in Transition, 950–1200*, Oxford University Commission for Archaeology Monograph 17 (Oxford, 1988), pp. 31–4.
3. David Rollason, *Saints and Relics in Anglo-Saxon England* (Oxford: Basil Blackwell, 1989), pp. 142–3; on his relics at Exeter, see Conner, *Anglo-Saxon Exeter*, p. 173.
4. Whitelock *et al.*, pp. 53–4.
5. O.D. Macrae-Gibson, ed., *The Old English Riming Poem* (Cambridge: D.S. Brewer, 1983).
6. See Phillip Pulsiano, 'Spiritual Despair in *Resignation B*', *Neophilologus*, 79 (1995), 155–62.

References and suggested reading

Conner, Patrick W. *Anglo-Saxon Exeter: A Tenth-Century Cultural History.* Studies in Anglo-Saxon History 4. Woodbridge: Boydell Press, 1993. A study of Exeter texts and institutions supporting the conclusion that the Exeter Book was probably compiled and copied at Exeter in three separate parts, and including new editions of the Guild-statutes, the relic-lists, and other locally identified documents. See Richard Gameson, 'The Origin of the Exeter Book of Old English Poetry', *Anglo-Saxon England*, 25 (1996), 135–85 for a contrary opinion; also see Robert M. Butler, 'Glastonbury and the Early History of the Exeter Book'. In Joyce Tally Lionarons, ed., *Old English Literature in its Manuscript Context.* Medieval European Studies V. Morgantown, WV: West Virginia University Press, 2004.

Conner, Patrick W. 'Religious Poetry'. In Phillip Pulsiano and Elaine Treharne, eds., *A Companion to Anglo-Saxon Literature and Culture.* Oxford: Blackwell Publishers, 2001, pp. 250–67. Using an anthropological approach to religion espoused by Clifford Geertz, Conner catalogues surviving Old English poetry according to four modes describing degrees of religious content. The elegies are considered under the 'social mode'.

Fell, Christine. 'Perceptions of Transience'. In Malcolm Godden and Michael Lapidge, eds., *The Cambridge Companion to Old English Literature.* Cambridge: Cambridge University Press, 1991, pp. 172–89. A careful essay that explores the voice of the imperilled aristocrat or noble individual grappling with the transient nature of glory in the world.

Greenfield, Stanley. *The Interpretation of Old English Poems.* London: Routledge and Kegan Paul, 1972. A classic introduction in which Greenfield's New Critical approach leads to solid readings of the elegies as well as of other Old English poems.

Green, Martin, ed. *The Old English Elegies: New Essays in Criticism and Research.* Rutherford, NJ: Fairleigh Dickinson University Press, 1983. Contains thirteen essays undertaking a variety of readings and scholarship on the corpus of Old English elegies. In particular, see Joseph Harris, 'Elegy in Old English and Old Norse: A Problem in Literary History', pp. 46–56.

Klinck, Anne L., ed. *The Old English Elegies.* Montreal: McGill-Queen's University Press, 1992. Described as 'a critical edition and genre study', this book provides facsimiles of all the elegies in the Exeter Book with editions and a full critical apparatus, an essay on the genre, analogues from numerous traditions, an extensive bibliography, and a glossary.

Mora, Maria José. 'Modulation and Hybridization in the Old English Elegies'. In Teresa Fanego Lema, ed., *Papers from the IVth International Conference of the Spanish Society for Medieval English Language and Literature.* Santiago de Compostela: Universidad de Santiago de Compostela, Servicir de Publicacións e Intercambio Cientifico, 1993, pp. 203–11. Mora traces the history of identifying the poems in question with the term 'elegy' from its first application by John J. Conybeare and examines generic issues relevant to the corpus of Old English elegies.

O'Keeffe, Katherine O'Brien, ed. *Old English Shorter Poems: Basic Readings.* Basic Readings in Anglo-Saxon England 3, Garland Reference Library of the Humanities 1432. New York: Garland Publishing, 1994. The Old English elegies are among the poems considered in this collection, including *The Wanderer, The Seafarer, The Wife's Lament,* and *Wulf and Eadwacer.* General essays grouped under the title 'Critical Perspectives' also offer valuable insights into reading the elegies.

Vickery, John F. ' "The Seafarer" 12–17, 23–30, 55–57: "Dives" and the Fictive Speaker', *Studia Neophilologica,* 61 (1989), 145–56; 'The Seafarer 97–102: "Dives" and the Burial of Treasure', *Journal of English and Germanic Philology,* 94 (1995), 19–30; 'The Seafarer 111–15: "Dives" and the Ultimate Futility', *Papers on Language and Literature,* 28 (1992), 227–41. These three essays offer a close reading of *The Seafarer* informed by Psalm 48 (49) and the Christian *topos* of wealth.

4

'Tell me what I am': the Old English riddles

Jonathan Wilcox

'What goes on four feet in the morning, two feet at noon, and three feet in the evening?' asks the Sphinx in the most famous early example of a genre that extends ubiquitously across cultures and times. Riddles themselves stalk through Anglo-Saxon literature in a variety of forms. Free-standing riddles survive in both Latin and in Old English collections. A set of one hundred by the late Latin poet Symphosius provided a model for subsequent Anglo-Latin collections. Aldhelm, abbot of Malmesbury, bishop of Sherbourne, and a major Anglo-Latin scholar (died 709 or 710), wrote a sequence of one hundred *enigmata*, mostly short works which encapsulate expressions of wonder at the natural world; Boniface, the missionary to Germany (*c.*675–754), wrote twenty *enigmata* on virtues and vices; while Tatwine, archbishop of Canterbury (died 734), wrote a sequence of forty, which was rounded out with a further sixty by the otherwise unknown poet Eusebius. Latin riddles, then, had some popularity in educated Anglo-Saxon circles, and these provide a context for the vernacular examples, of which a single collection of about a hundred survives.

These Old English riddles are preserved in three sequences in the Exeter Book, the great poetic codex (see also Chapters 3, 5, and 12 by Conner, Frederick, and Hill). Vernacular riddles presumably circulated more widely than this since one example from the Exeter Book is also preserved in an earlier Northumbrian version, known after the present location of the manuscript as the Leiden Riddle, but the forces that controlled the recording of Old English texts—primarily the monastery, secondarily the court—were not kind to the preservation of such secular non-didactic verse. What does survive is a group of almost a hundred riddles, mostly quite short, on varying subjects. It is hard to give a precise number since the Exeter Book text is damaged in some places during the riddles, while the precise boundary of individual riddles is contested—the standard edition of Krapp and Dobbie gives ninety-five, while the more recent edition of Williamson gives ninety-one. It is this body that will be investigated in the present chapter.

A most ingenious paradox

Riddles work by describing something recognizable from an unusual perspective and thereby make the familiar strange. The object described, often termed in Old English by the unrevealing catch-all noun *wiht*, 'creature', is sometimes characterized in the third person and sometimes presents itself in the first person, often making use of a particular form of personification known as prosopopoeia, whereby an inanimate object is made to speak. Such a device also underlies the famous devotional poem *The Dream of the Rood* (discussed in Chapter 2), which, like many Old English poems, is certainly riddling in its form and conceit, and yet is longer and more profound than is typical of the riddles themselves. Rather than building up to the edification dramatized in *The Dream of the Rood*, Old English riddles are quite short and instead reflect upon objects of little consequence. Whereas the Anglo-Latin *enigmata* generally circulate with titles that name the object described, the Old English riddles highlight their playful challenge by lacking any stated solution. While the solution is often not difficult to arrive at, many riddles enact a form of reversal by the very act of making some humble object central to the poetic imagination. Reversals and frustrations of expectations are central to the riddles, which revel in paradoxes of all kinds and delight in presenting a world turned upside down, sometimes analogous to the world of inversion seen in the grotesque marginalia of medieval manuscripts.

An example will help establish the form and illustrate the standard expectations. In this case, the *wiht* is presented in the third person and the riddler's challenge is implicit, if unmissable (Riddle 34 in Krapp and Dobbie; Riddle 32 in Williamson. The translation is my own):

> Ic wiht geseah   in wera burgum,
> seo þæt feoh fedeð.   Hafað fela toþa;
> nebb biþ hyre æt nytte,   niþerweard gongeð,
> hiþeð holdlice   ond to ham tyhð,
> wæþeð geond weallas,   wyrte seceð
> aa heo þa findeð,   þa þe fæst ne biþ;
> læteð hio þa wlitigan,   wyrtum fæste,
> stille stondan   on staþolwonge,
> beorhte blican,   blowan and growan.

> I saw a creature in the dwellings of men,
> it feeds cattle (*or* fuels prosperity). It has many teeth;
> its snout is useful, it proceeds downward,
> plunders loyally and draws to home,
> it hunts around walls, seeks out roots;
> it always finds those which are not firm;
> it lets those beautiful ones, firm in their roots,
> still stand in their established place,
> shine brightly, grow and flourish.

This riddle works through many characteristic conventions. The *wiht* seems to be a living animal in view of its array of body parts: *fela toþa*, 'many teeth', *nebb*, 'a nose'. The verbs play up the personification: the creature has the ability to travel (*gongeð*, 'it goes') and to enjoy volition (*seceð*, *findeð*, 'it seeks, finds'), and even judgement (*læteð*, 'it lets'). Other verbs set up a tension as to whether the object is benign or not: it feeds (*fedeð*), yet it also plunders, draws to home, and hunts. The verbs make the personification unmissable, yet the creature is grotesque because the body parts fail to add up to a recognizable body: why teeth and nose but not other parts of a head? The setting provides further clues. The object is domestic (*in wera burgum, geond weallas*, 'in dwellings of men', 'around walls') and visible to the presumably human persona of the opening. It is twice collocated with *wyrtum*, which carries both the sense of 'plants' in line 5 and the specific anchor of those plants, 'roots', in line 7, and which provides a further localizing clue.

As often, the riddle rests on a central paradox. The utility of the creature is suggested a few times, in the useful nose, the feeding, and the suggestive prosperity of the plants blossoming at the end, yet there is a tension encapsulated in the oxymoron *hiþeð holdlice*, 'it plunders (or lays waste or ravages) loyally (or graciously or kindly)'. The verb *hyðan*, 'to plunder', is collocated elsewhere in Old English with *herian*, 'to ravage', and is the activity of fire, for example, or that which the devil promises to undertake in the kingdom of heaven, could he but win his contest against God. *Holdlice*, by contrast, derives from the adjective *hold*, 'loyal, gracious, kind', a quality highly prized throughout the Old English corpus. The creature of the riddle is a wonder of body parts and actions encapsulated by this tighter paradox of potential destruction and yet loyal utility. Such tension, however, lacks the gravity of a poem like *The Dream of the Rood* since the whole paradox is played out in the vegetable world of *wyrte*, 'garden-plants'. What has many teeth, a particularly useful nose, operates in the domestic sphere, and both seeks out and secures roots by finding out those which are not secure? By the end the solution is not particularly difficult; the creature that embodies this miracle of vegetal probing is, of course, a rake.

The mixture of the serious and the lighthearted here and the unstable border between the two is entirely characteristic of the riddles. Indeed, this whole short description hints at various other possibilities in a manner that is typical for riddles. Line 3 presents hints of the abject or at least the humble: the *wiht* travels *niþerweard*, 'downward' or in some way cast down, and such humility is picked up by the usefulness of the nose, which hints that the creature is less cerebrally august than doggedly practical. And yet the function of this humble being hints at judgement and moral uprightness since it discovers *þa þe fæst ne biþ*, 'those who are not secure', hinting at, for example, a pastor's ability to distinguish the morally upright from those in his flock with loose foundations who are not *on staþolwonge*, 'in their established place'. Loyalty is stressed in the central paradox, *Hiþeð holdlice*, 'it plunders loyally', and the activity of this humble *wiht* apparently contributes to the reward of the steadfast, who get to the bliss implied in the aurally emphatic triple infinitives of the last line—that is, the joy of shining brightly and the positively rhyming, almost tautological, *blowan and growan*. The *wiht*, then, has something of the value of the morally militant. Yet all this implied metaphysical valence is subsumed within an earthy practicality—the *wiht* is just a rake, after all. The riddle moves the hearer's universe by making such a humble and downturned utilitarian object briefly glorious, upright, and morally upstanding, but such a shift in world outlook is only a temporary part of the playfulness of the riddle.

A different playfulness perhaps also lurks beneath the surface. The embodied nature of riddles often hints at the bawdy, which in other riddles is exploited to the full. Here the bawdy subtext is the merest hint for the salaciously-inclined listener. Most importantly, the embodied *wiht* is proceeding *niþerweard*, 'in a downward manner', an inversion of normal bodily hierarchies that hints at exposure of the taboo nether regions. While this is by no means worked into a full *double entendre* here, the wholesome fecundity with which the riddle ends encourages thoughts of propagation engendered by that useful snout.

Much of the pleasure of the riddles is that their enigmatic quality requires an interpreter to consider multiple possibilities, even as, paradoxically, the implied riddling challenge goads the listener to settle on just one. That one reading here is clearly the garden imple-ment, yet the blind alleys of humble reprover or of strutting mascu-linity give added value to the obvious answer: what a wonderful thing a humble rake proves to be! Riddles reward close reading. The pleasure of interpretation comes from attending to language that is both paradoxical and multivalent.

Most of the Old English riddles similarly build up their subject through a series of paradoxes, often with one central paradox domin-ating. The riddler wonders, for example, at a *wiht* that is masculine, youthful, and drinking from four fountains: 'that creature, if it survives, will break the hills; if it perishes, it will bind the living', building up a paradox of the living form that injures the inanimate, while its inanimate form injures the living, in the presentation of a young calf that in life will pull the plough and in death become leather (Riddle 38). Part of the point presumably lies in the extreme power of the living ox, which is paradoxically nullified yet also amplified in its posthumous use. The same paradox is brought out in a fuller account of the potential uses of ox-leather that plays up its sexual potency as well as its power to bind (Riddle 12). A similar paradox of the transfiguration of the powerful lies at the centre of the description of an iceberg, whose mother is also its daughter, reflecting on the movement from water to ice to water (Riddle 33). The paradox of manufacture is a frequent focus for the riddles. A sword enters into human vengeance structures and emblematizes human masculinity yet laments that it will not have heirs and that no one will take vengeance for the violence of its production (Riddle 20). A mail-coat is poignant in lamenting the pain of its production for all the blows it withstands in its later life (Riddle 35), while gold's account of the trauma of its production motivates in part its power to bind humans in slavery (Riddle 83). Riddles are slanted to reveal the paradoxes that prove to lie almost everywhere.

The sexual dilemma

Stitching together body parts, as a riddle's hearer is often asked to do, runs the risk of laying bare taboo areas, as was suggested in the reading of the rake above. Sometimes such salacious hints are built up with consistency so as to suggest an apparent sexual solution. In these cases, the riddles also build up to a possible innocent solution. Such *double entendre* presents a paradox of sexual licence and prudery. On the one hand, these riddles encourage the extensive pursuit of a sexual reading; on the other hand, such a reading is taboo enough to need to be discarded and replaced with a more innocent one. Sexual *double entendre* provides another version of the paradox of the multiple possibilities of language. In this context, it also presents a puzzle as to what such sexual play is doing in a monastic manuscript. Delight lies in playing with a taboo as well as in the ingenuity of the double vision.

Some eight or so riddles maintain such *double entendre* throughout. One short example is Riddle 45 (in Krapp and Dobbie; 43 in Williamson):

> Ic on wincle gefrægn   weaxan nathwæt,
> þindan ond þunian,   þecene hebban;
> on þæt banlease   bryd grapode,
> hygewlonc hondum,   hrægle þeahte
> þrindende þing   þeodnes dohtor.

> I learned of I know not what growing in a corner,
> swelling and sticking up, lifting a covering;
> a wife grasped that boneless object,
> a haughty one, a lord's daughter, with her hands,
> covered with a garment the rising thing.

Some of the vocabulary and the tricks here are characteristic of the sexual riddles. For a start, there is much emphasis on the gender and sexual status of the named human: she is *bryd*, a sexually-loaded term, cognate with Modern English 'bride', although somewhat broader in application; she is *hygewlonc*, literally 'proud of mind', perhaps hinting at the next descriptor, but also suggesting lasciviousness since the second element, *wlonc*, is remarkably consistent for its use in slightly steamy contexts; and she is of strikingly high status, the daughter of a *þeoden*, 'lord, chief, master'. The activity of this slightly sexualized, slightly stuck-up, woman is clear: she grasps something with her hands (an emphatic tautology?) and covers it with a *hrægle*, 'a garment, dress, or cloth'. The place of the action is also clear, *on wincle*, 'in the corner', where, presumably, things can be concealed somewhat.

Most ambiguity resides in the description of the object so handled. First of all, this object is explicitly called *nathwæt*, 'I know not what', a mini-riddle in itself that occurs with striking frequency in the sexual riddles. The object is *banlease*, 'boneless', which of course establishes the expectation that its lack of bone is somehow significant—that it should normally have a bone or is in the same set as objects which are supported by bones but itself happens to lack one. The greatest verbal ingenuity lies in what this suggestive object is doing. First the enquirer's discoveries lead to a sequence of parallel verbs in the infinitive: the object is heard to *weaxan, þindan, þunian, hebban*. The first of these is a standard term for 'to grow', the next two are more anatomical in register, 'to swell up' and 'to stand up' or 'stick out'; all of the first three are intransitive verbs while the fourth is a transitive verb, 'to raise'. So much is this the defining characteristic of the I-know-not-what that the attributive present participle in the final line defines it through the verb *þrintan*, 'to swell', establishing three near-synonyms that have close identity of sound: *þindan, þunian, þrintan*. In a miniature version of poetic justice, this thing that raises a garment (*þecene hebban*) is in turn covered with a garment (*hrægle þeahte*). Apparently it is not to be seen exposed.

The slightly sexualized, slightly high-status woman, then, is grasping and covering in a corner a boneless object that is rising, swelling, distending, and sticking up. The resolution of these conundrums at a sexual level is obvious. At another level, she is engaged in some fecund process of production that involves grasping and covering this rising object—presumably the kneading of bread dough. Within the sexualized solution, the status of the woman adds an additional paradox through the implication that even those with the dignity of an elevated status resort to the same basic bodily functions when it comes to satisfying sexual desires (*Amor vincit omnia*, as Chaucer says in a different context). The paradox of such a temporary upending of status is frequently explored in the riddles. In Old English, the implications of status and of sexuality carry special resonances for the respectable solution in view of the most common term for a high-status woman: *hlæfdige* 'lady' is a dead metaphor for the kneader of the loaf, perhaps here brought to life alongside the overtones of a bun in the oven.

Other sexual riddles revel in an impressive array of different paradoxes, usually with some interesting resonance between the sexual and the innocent solution. They display, for example, the paradox of the biter bit in the useful object that wets the eye of the woman who grasps at it (the onion of Riddle 25), the fecund bulging object that serves its servant (the bellows of Riddle 37), the long and firm object beneath a man's garment that fills a familiar equally long hole (the key of Riddle 44), the young man who jiggles like crazy but tires before he can satisfy the desire of the one he embraces (the butter churn of Riddle 54), the object, locked up by a lady, that is filled with a masculine hairiness (the helmet or shirt of Riddle 61), the warm object thrust forward by its lord (the borer of Riddle 62), or the one that is kissed and embraced (the drinking glass of Riddle 63). Sexual riddles broaden the range of paradoxes since all this otherwise undescribed activity proves to be mappable onto such a wide range of inanimate objects.

The significance of form

While part of the pleasure of riddles comes from mastering their clues and appreciating their paradoxes, sometimes in a context of sexual licence, these short works also abound in the pleasure of poetic effects. The listener's attentiveness to the multiplicity of clues, indeed, encourages attentiveness to the sound of the verse, which sometimes provides onomatopoeic clues to the object described. The very uncertainty of the listener probably helps open the ears to a riddle's aural effects. Again, a single example will help illustrate the point, this time related in the first person (Krapp and Dobbie Riddle 7, Williamson 5):

> Hrægl min swigað,   þonne ic hrusan trede,
> oþþe þa wic buge,   oþþe wado drefe.
> Hwilum mec ahebbað   ofer hæleþa byht
> hyrste mine,   ond þeos hea lyft,
> ond mec þonne wide   wolcna strengu
> ofer folc byreð.   Frætwe mine
> swogað hlude   ond swinsiað,
> torhte singað,   þonne ic getenge ne beom
> flode ond foldan,   ferende gæst.

> My garment is silent when I tread on the earth
> or dwell in the camp or stir the seas.
> Sometimes my ornaments and this high air
> raise me up over the dwellings of men
> and then the strength of the clouds carry me
> far and wide over the people. My trappings
> whistle loudly and sound out,
> sing brightly, when I am not resting upon
> the sea and the land, a travelling spirit.

Here the paradoxes pile up revolving around location (the subject moves on land and on water and in the air), the implied relation to humans (the subject has its own habitation and yet passes with apparent confidence close to those of humans), the nature of its covering and its sound. A series of words for garment or clothing or covering or adornment echo each other as they vary through the poem: *hrægl min, hyrste mine, frætwe mine*. The parallelism between the first and third instance extends to parallel-sounding following verbs: *swigað, swogað, swinsiað, singað*. The heavy parallelism here is played up through sound: these verbs not only grammatically rhyme and alliterate, they also chime with echoing vowels and echoing consonant clusters (*-īg-, -ōg-, -in-, -ing-*). Such parallelism might lull the inattentive listener from attending to the central paradox: that *swigian* means precisely the opposite of *swogan, swinsian, singan*, 'to be silent' as opposed to 'to sound out'.

The nature of that sounding is conveyed in the sound of line 7, which matches the swooshing sound of the creature's feathers carrying it through the air, a Mute Swan in flight. In addition, such emphasis on sound also plays thematically into the poem's suggestive climax. The subject passing overhead is a *ferende gæst*, either 'a travelling guest' (a variant on *giest*) or 'a passing spirit' (a variant on *gāst*). The idea of a passing guest picks up on the independence and yet proximity to humans. The passing spirit, on the other hand, in this sound-heavy context, carries with it probable echoes of a swan-song, the idea, common in classical tradition, that swans sing only at the point of death. The suggestive creature here is poised poignantly between worlds, with the satisfying paradoxes not only adding up to a particular wild animal that masters three incompatible environments but also hinting at the metaphysics of the moment of death.

Such aural clues reverberate in many of the riddles. The iceberg riddle, for example, includes the sound of the powerful creature, which:

> cleopode to londe,
> hlinsade hlude— hleahtor wæs gryrelic.
> (Riddle 33, lines 2b–3)

called out to the land
resounded loudly, the laughter was terrible.

where the *hl-* alliteration supplemented by the echoing dental (*d* and *t*) sounds suggests the eerie screeching of the mass of ice, here imagined as a warrior. Like other poems, riddles create worlds through sound, which the riddle interpreter is wise to listen to.

Enigmatic enigmata

Old English riddles require sensitivity to poetic effects and a consideration of paradoxes to arrive at the object described. In a few special cases, the answer is named explicitly in the text, albeit in code. In one instance, Riddle 23, the name of the *wiht* is given in reverse as the opening word of the riddle at line 1: *Agof* [for *Agob*] *is min noma eft onhwyrfed* ('Wob is my name turned around again'). In other instances, the solution is embedded within the text through runic clues. The copulating chickens of Riddle 42, for example, are literally spelled out *þurh runstafas*, 'by means of runic letters', as the appropriate rune names are included in the description. In a few other cases, embedded runic letters spell out the name or additional clues (as in Riddle 19, perhaps ship; Riddle 24, jay or magpie; Riddles 75 and 76, brilliantly solved by Williamson as piss). Riddle 36 preserves within the text a line of code that spells out 'man', 'woman', 'horse', for all of which generous clue the solution remains not obvious (Williamson argues for ship). Apart from these special cases, though, the texts do not provide any explicit solution. As a result, a few riddles remain unsolved.

One such is the brief Riddle 57 (55 in Williamson):

> Ðeos lyft byreð   lytle wihte
> ofer beorghleoþa.   þa sind blace swiþe,
> swearte salopade.   Sanges rope
> heapum ferað,   hlude cirmað,
> tredað bearonæssas,   hwilum burgsalo
> niþþa bearna.   Nemnað hy sylfe.

> This air carries little creatures
> over the hillsides. Those are very dark,
> black, dark-coated ones. Bountiful of song
> they travel in groups, call out loudly,
> tread the wooded cliffs, sometimes the town buildings
> of the children of men. They name themselves (*or* name them yourselves).

In the paradox given most stress here, these creatures are carried by air *ofer beorghleoþa*, 'over hillsides', tread *bearonæssas*, 'wooded cliffs', but sometimes also the built domestic structures of humans (*burgsalo*). They are both of the air and of the ground, both in wild places and in the domestic structures of humans. There are plenty more clues. They are bountiful of song and call out loudly. They are little, black, dark, dark-coated. They travel in groups. And, in what may or may not be a clincher, they possibly name themselves. The trouble for homing in on an answer is that this abundance of clues seems to allow too many possibilities, so that it is hard to guess which clues are to be taken as they appear and which are obfuscatory metaphors.

Many more or less convincing solutions have been proposed for this riddle. The movement through different mediums—air/land, wild/domestic, remote/human—and the movement in flocks and the singing encourages the possibility that these are birds. As such the riddle would be parallel to the swan riddle considered above. Solutions posited include swallows, starlings, swifts, jackdaws, crows, and house martins. The same clues could also suggest insects, which would also pick up on the smallness, and gnats, bees, or midges have all been suggested. Other solutions posit greater ingenuity and see the more obvious elements as masking metaphors. Suggestions include damned souls and demons; stormclouds, hailstones, raindrops; and musical notes. If the final half-line is a clincher, the satisfying paradox may be that the creature names itself in an onomatopoeic cry. Suggestions include a projected *ca as the name for a jackdaw, or *beon*, the name for bees. Along similar lines but with a different form of self-naming, flies might be an attractive insect solution, OE *fleoge*, where the self-naming is conceptual rather than onomatopoeic, related as the name surely is to the verb *fleogan*.

This riddle, then, joins some ten or so others that do not (yet) have any certain or convincing solution. It is striking that this does not prohibit the enjoyment of the riddle. Indeed, in this case the clues can be teased out, some of the satisfying paradoxes can be appreciated, and the sound-effects of the poem can be heard, even without settling on an overwhelmingly convincing solution. The pleasure of the riddles lies more in attending to their multiplicity than in their resolution.

All the world is a riddle

A few of the Old English riddles are translations of surviving Anglo-Latin examples, and a few more probably derive from scholarly tradition. The opening riddle or riddle sequence is a 104-line description of a storm that provides an account of the power of God to control nature (Riddles 1–3). Another lengthy example translates a riddle by Aldhelm to describe creation (Riddle 40: 108 lines survive, but the text is fragmentary at the end due to the loss of a manuscript leaf). Most of the Old English riddles are significantly shorter and more playful. More presumably derive from literary tradition: icebergs would not have been a common sight in Anglo-Saxon England (Riddle 33), while Lot and his two daughters is a solution that is clearly drawn from texts (Riddle 46). Most, though, appear to derive from observation of the world around. The weather-cock of Riddle 81, for example, represents such recent technology that there is no known Latin term for the object before the thirteenth century (according to Williamson). Myriad aspects of the Anglo-Saxon world that are not usually worthy of literary attention here take centre-stage, from the humble rake to the ludicrous bagpipes (Riddle 31), from book and quill (Riddles 26 and 51) to horn and sword (Riddles 14 and 20); from wild creatures such as the nightingale (Riddle 8) and the barnacle goose (Riddle 10) to the earth-shine visible on a new or waning moon (Riddle 29).

Saga hwæt ic hatte, 'Say what I am called', is the recurring refrain of the riddle object, and this forces the listener into a set of judgements that require attentiveness to poetic language in its full richness of semantic denotation and connotation and an ear for poetic effects. Riddles with their multiple possibilities become ideal microcosms for the interpretative act of reading all Old English poetry. As a result, riddles richly reward close reading. They provide a window on Anglo-Saxon imaginative engagements that are different from those more characteristic survivals, namely the high-culture preoccupations of heroic literature or of didactic and pious religious literature. In the love of paradox, in the delight in comic inversions, in the temporary disruptions of social order, riddles hint at a literature of licence and of play that has otherwise been mostly lost in the transmission of a culture from a thousand years ago.

References and suggested reading

Barley, Nigel F. 'Structural Aspects of the Anglo-Saxon Riddle', *Semiotica*, 10 (1974), 143–75. This essay provides an interesting structural analysis of the Old English riddles.

Crossley-Holland, Kevin. *The Exeter Book Riddles*. Harmondsworth: Penguin; rev. edn. 1978.

Irving, Edward B., Jr. 'Heroic Experience in the Old English Riddles'. In Katherine O'Brien O'Keeffe, ed., *Old English Shorter Poems: Basic Readings*. New York: Garland Publishing, 1994, pp. 199–212. Irving offers a close reading of riddles that shed light on the heroic world.

Kitson, Peter. 'Swans and Geese in Old English Riddles', *Anglo-Saxon Studies in Archaeology and History*, 7 (1994), 79–84. Kitson provides an ornithologically informed reading of some of the bird riddles, including riddle 7.

Krapp, George Philip, and Elliott Van Kirk Dobbie, eds. *The Exeter Book*. New York: Columbia University Press, 1936. The fundamental edition of the poems of the Exeter Book.

Niles, John D. 'Exeter Book Riddle 74 and the Play of the Text', *Anglo-Saxon England*, 27 (1998), 169–207. Niles provides an exemplary reading of one contested riddle and suggests a process for reading Old English poetry.

Pepicello, W. J., and Thomas A. Green. *The Language of Riddles: New Perspectives*. Columbus: Ohio State University Press, 1984. This book provides a structural study of riddles across cultures.

Smith, D. K. 'Humor in Hiding: Laughter between the Sheets in the Exeter Book Riddles'. In Jonathan Wilcox, ed., *Humour in Anglo-Saxon Literature*. Cambridge: D. S. Brewer, 2000, pp. 79–98. This essay provides an excellent reading of the mechanism of the sexual riddles, showing how they play with and yet also exemplify underlying taboos.

Stewart, Ann Harleman. 'Kenning and Riddle in Old English', *Papers on Language and Literature*, 15 (1979), 115–36. Stewart presents an ingenious structural reading that relates the Old English riddles to a characteristic technique of Old English poetry.

Wilcox, Jonathan. 'Mock-Riddles in Old English: Exeter Riddles 86 and 19', *Studies in Philology*, 93 (1996), 180–7. This essay suggests the self-consciousness of the riddle form evident in two playful riddles that appear to present particularly difficult solutions.

Williamson, Craig, ed. *The Old English Riddles of the Exeter Book*. Chapel Hill: University of North Carolina Press, 1977. A full edition of the Riddles.

Williamson, Craig. *A Feast of Creatures: Anglo-Saxon Riddle-Songs*. Philadelphia: University of Pennsylvania Press, 1982. Translations of the Riddles.

http://www2.kenyon.edu/AngloSaxonRiddles/
This website gathers together material on the Old English riddles. In particular, it has a text and translation for each riddle (from Williamson 1977 and Williamson 1982 respectively) and an ongoing bibliography of riddle scholarship.

5

Warring with words: Cynewulf's Juliana

Jill Frederick

Genre and context

The Old English narrative poem *Juliana* can be categorized within
the popular medieval genre of the *passio*, which narrates the story of a
saint's martyrdom. Conventionally, a *passio* follows a structure where
a male or female saint, having professed Christianity within a pagan
community, is brought before pagans and ordered to disavow his or
her faith, either by sacrificing to the local gods, or in some other way
offering worldly allegiance to the pagan overlords. Because the saint
categorically refuses to obey these instructions, he or she is tortured
at great length and finally killed. Numerous other examples from Old
English literature survive, including the prose *Life of Saint Agnes* and
The Life of Saint Edmund in Ælfric's *Lives of Saints*. With a saint's life,
whether a *passio* or a *vita* (which recounts a saint's entire life from
birth to natural death), literary originality is never the author's main
creative impetus. Authors regularly follow a similar compositional
template, because it is the pattern that teaches 'the truth of faith
through the principle of individual example', as Thomas Heffernan
puts it (*Sacred Biography*, p. 19). Whether or not the story or characters
ring true to life is not important. Their relevance derives from the
example set by the saint, who provides a model to which Christians
are meant to aspire. A saint by definition leads a paradigmatic life;

consequently the life of any person claimed to be among the community of saints must follow the accepted literary paradigm of sanctity.

Most early medieval texts are anonymous, but *Juliana* is one of a number of Old English poems that can be attributed to a named author, in this instance someone who 'signed' the poem by incorporating into its closing verses runes spelling out his name, Cynewulf. (The others also containing the signature runes are *The Fates of the Apostles, Christ II,* and *Elene.*) While there has been a great deal of scholarly exploration into the identity of this author, research on Cynewulf remains speculative (scholars have suggested, for example, that he might have been an abbot, a bishop, or a priest). Though *Juliana* itself was written into its manuscript in the later tenth century, its actual date of composition is another question that vexes scholars. It is now extant in a varied collection of Old English poems known as the Exeter Book (Exeter Cathedral Library 3501, folios 65b–76a). In its present incomplete state, it comprises approximately 731 lines; the text has two gaps, and seems to be missing two manuscript pages incorporating material that would have fallen between lines 287 and 288 and between lines 558 and 559.

The poem is unique in the canon of Old English literature. While other Old English poems do have female protagonists, *Judith* and *Elene* among them, *Juliana* is the only Old English text that renders into poetry the *passio* of a female saint. *Judith*, contained in the *Beowulf* manuscript (London, British Library, Cotton Vitellius A. xv), relates the story of the Old Testament heroine's encounter with Holofernes, while the Vercelli Book's *Elene* focuses not on the life of the saint but on her search for the True Cross. As with most Old English saints' lives, whether in prose or poetry, Juliana's story derives from earlier Latin prose texts, the most accessible version of which is found in the *Acta Sanctorum*, on her feast day of 16 February. In addition to this representative text, other Latin prose versions of Juliana's life also exist, most notably in a collection thought to have been compiled by the Venerable Bede—his *Martyrology*. None of these texts has survived in Old English. Cynewulf seems to have known a Latin version similar to that which appears in the *Acta Sanctorum*, but the evidence of his Old English poem itself suggests that he probably also made use of other sources that no longer exist.

Cynewulf, then, presents the legend of Juliana, a pious Christian girl living in the city of Nicomedia, who refuses to marry the pagan Eleusius, chosen by her cruel father Africanus, a theme conventional within the genre. Juliana reiterates repeatedly her wish to remain a virgin, dedicating herself to Jesus Christ, and pays the ultimate penalty for her disobedience, torture and death. While Juliana is imprisoned, a demon arrives to torment her but she turns the tables on him, forcing him instead to confess his crimes at painful length. Once Juliana defeats the demon, she is subjected to further trials that fail to harm her, then beheaded. In divine retribution, Eleusius and his thanes drown in a storm at sea and are consigned to hell.

Given the interest in the place of women in medieval society and culture during the past two decades, *Juliana*, with its unyielding and courageous heroine, would seem an ideal focus for contemporary critics. Unlike those of her literary sisters Elene and Judith, however, Juliana's story remains comparatively under-examined and generally undervalued. The central question about the poem's literary quality revolves around the character of Juliana herself: has Cynewulf created a figural type who moves disinterestedly through a stilted and conventional allegory, as has been the general critical consensus? Or is she a strong, complex, and autonomous woman, functioning within a unified and artful narrative, as more recent criticism has suggested? Part of the difficulty stems from the poem's genre: even the most appealing saint's life requires a different set of aesthetic criteria from those usually valued by a modern audience.

Themes and motifs

In telling the story of St Juliana, Cynewulf has fused the highly conventional structure of the Latin source with Old English poetic tradition in the manner that has come to define Old English religious poetry. Most obviously, the poem's actions occur within the metaphorical framework of the primary Anglo-Saxon social construct, what Old English calls a *dryht* (also referred to by the Latin term *comitatus*), the relationship between a lord (the *dryhten*) and his retainers (*þegns*). The Anglo-Saxon heroic ethos requires that a good king provide his men with protection, food, and shelter, and reward them with a share of whatever they have earned in battle. In return, his retainers pledge themselves completely, vowing to follow the king's orders unswervingly and to die on the field rather than to desert him in battle. Cynewulf depends on this theme throughout *Juliana*, making use of the traditional diction and motifs that Anglo-Saxon poets employ to talk about battle. Consequently, neither plot nor diction can be termed unique to the author or his text.

However, in this poem Cynewulf has moved beyond merely imitating Old English heroic tradition or simply recreating the original Latin version. Here he has shaped the legend to his own purposes using several strategies. His broadest means to his ends are to omit details that an Anglo-Saxon audience would not have found pertinent and to elaborate sections that would have enhanced the poem's relevance and appeal. Most obviously, he exaggerates the qualities of the main characters, Juliana and Eleusius. Heightening the contrast between them strengthens the poem's underlying Christian motif, the cosmic struggle between good and evil. And in placing greater emphasis on the dialogues between Juliana and the demon sent to torment her, he gives greater weight and definition to the larger spiritual battle that underlies the personal sparring. As he draws on his audience's common understanding of Anglo-Saxon *dryht* imagery to give dramatic tension and irony to his story, Cynewulf holds *Juliana* together by other, less exclusively Anglo-Saxon, patterns as well. The poem is infused with light and dark imagery, the relationship between fathers and children, the idea of conversion, and the use of scriptural and apocryphal symbolism, such as the Harrowing of Hell. Ultimately, however, woven throughout Cynewulf's language in *Juliana* is the juxtaposition of perspective corrupted and truth discerned that characterizes the battle between pagan and Christian, which moves the struggle between individuals—however one-dimensional they might be perceived to be—onto the cosmic level.

The battlefield

Very often in a text the important themes and motifs are evident from its earliest lines, whether explicitly or implicitly, and in *Juliana* Cynewulf presents the poem's thematic boundaries in lines 1–17:

> Hwæt! We ðæt hyrdon   hæleð eahtian,
> deman dædhwate,   þætte in dagum gelamp
> Maximianes,   se geond middangeard,
> arleas cyning,   eahtnysse ahof,
> cwealde cristne men,   circan fylde,
> geat on græswong   godhergendra,
> hæþen hildfruma,   haligra blod,
> ryhtfremmendra.   Wæs his rice brad,
> wid ond weorðlic   ofer werþeode,
> lytesna ofer ealne   yrmenne grund.
> Foron æfter burgum,   swa he biboden hæfde,
> þegnas þryðfulle.   Oft hi þræce rærdon,
> dædum gedwolene,   þa þe dryhtnes æ
> feodon þurh firencræft.   Feondscype rærdon,
> hofon hæþengield,   halge cwelmdon,
> breotun boccræftge,   bærndon gecorene,
> gæston godes cempan   gare ond lige.

Listen! We have heard that warriors bold in deeds praise and proclaim that which occurred in the days of Maximian, the heathen battle-prince, a king without honour, who glorified persecution throughout the earth, killed Christian men, destroyed churches, shed the blood of saints, righteous warriors, God's worshippers, on the grassy plain. His kingdom was broad, wide, and splendid over his people, over almost all the wide world's ground. His prideful thanes journeyed throughout cities as he had commanded. Often they raised violence, evil deeds, those men who in their wickedness hated the Lord's law. They did evil, raised idols, murdered the holy, killed the book-learned, burned the chosen people, frightened God's champions with spear and flame.

Compared with the Latin source, these lines in the Old English are much expanded. As set down in the *Acta Sanctorum*, the legend notes only *Denique temporibus Maximiani Imperatoris persecutoris Christianae religionis, erat quidam Senator in civitate Nicomedia, nomine Eleusius, amicus Imperatoris* ('Briefly told, in the times of the emperor Maximian, the persecutor of the Christian religion, there was a certain senator in the city of Nicomedia, Eleusius by name, a friend of the Emperor'). While no one can be certain that a Latin life did not exist with the sort of itemized list that the Old English presents, it seems very likely that Cynewulf has deliberately altered the Latin life in order to plunge the audience into a world of fire and sword, a world that would have been familiar, and at least theoretically appealing to an Anglo-Saxon audience accustomed to war, imaginative and actual. Even though the poem describes the legions of a pagan emperor laying waste to the land, the activities and the language that Cynewulf uses evoke the familiar military action found in poems like *The Battle of Maldon* or *The Battle of Brunanburh*. Here, however, the language used to describe the pillage elevates the stakes to a much higher level and the external battle mirrors the battle of will and wit between the demon and Juliana to come later on.

The opening interjection 'Hwæt!' also occurs in the opening proclamation of *Beowulf* as well as in other significant Christian narratives in Old English such as *Andreas*, *Exodus*, and *The Dream of the Rood*. More particularly, however, the syntax of the poem's first sentence at lines 1–3a above also contains the same epic sweep as the first sentence of *Beowulf*: 'We have heard about the glory of the Spear-Danes, the tribal kings, how the noble men performed courageous deeds in days gone by.' The earthly courage and nobility elucidated in *Beowulf*, however, contrasts with the context of wilful destruction and waste set up in *Juliana*'s opening lines. Moreover, the description of the emperor Maximian's brutal assaults and judgements against Christians creates an implicit contrast with God's love and protection.

Cynewulf emphasizes the earth-bound nature of Maximian's authority and desires, situating his influence *geond middangeard* ('throughout the earth', line 3), and observing that Maximian's retainers cause the blood of Christian men to be shed *on græswong* ('on the grassy plain', line 6). The king himself is portrayed as *arleas* (line 4), a term with several levels of meaning: he is both without honour and mercy-less. *Ar* can also denote 'property', however, and ironically, Maximian does lack the real property of heaven. (By contrast, in the final lines of the poem Cynewulf confesses that he himself is in need of mercy, *arna biþearf* (line 715), requesting that his audience, whoever it may be, pray for him, and thus lead him to heavenly possession.) Maximian's thanes cut a cruel swath through cities, and their violence enumerated in lines 14b–17b—raising idols, murdering the holy, killing those knowledgeable about books, burning God's chosen people, frightening the champions of God with weapons and fire—broadly foreshadows the actions against Juliana herself, particularly in lines 227–33a and 573–93. The emperor's previous conquests, however, which resulted in a domain covering almost the entire world, will count for very little in the face of the saint's uncompromising devotion to Christ. The saint in her prison cell is a small piece of unconquerable territory. God's champions might have been frightened by spear and flame, but Juliana is not. Ultimately, she will hold firm even in the face of death.

The vicious deeds of Maximian's men pervert the idea of the courageous fidelity an Anglo-Saxon retainer owes his lord, the allegiance demonstrated by the brave warriors of *Beowulf*, *The Battle of Maldon*, or *The Battle of Brunanburh*. In line 13 the deeds of Maximian's men are described as *gedwolene*, a term which also carries multiple layers of meaning. Translating *gedwolene* simply as 'evil' ignores its connotations of activity twisted by delusion and misperception. This idea is so important to the focus of the poem, as Robert Bjork points out, that Cynewulf uses it at least four more times during his narrative, at lines 138b, 202b, 301a, and 363b ('Saintly Discourse', p. 45). The word captures how those representing the forces of evil in the poem wilfully distort what is real and truthful; the stakes of the battle are not what they appear to be, so that part of Juliana's task as she confronts the demon is to force him—and by extension, the audience—to examine the truth and dimensions of his existence.

Fighting and *flyting*

While its first lines may suggest the poem will have an epic sweep, the poem's narrative arc is remarkably small: not much really happens. The battles in *Juliana* are wars of words, psychological intimidation, and here again a contrast with *Beowulf* is instructive. When Beowulf and his men land on the shores of Denmark, the Danish shoreguard first challenges them, then acknowledges their worthiness, observing, at lines 287b–289: 'A clever shield-warrior, a man who thinks well, must know the difference between each of these two things, words and works.' In other words, there is a time for speech and a time for action, and actions must perforce follow a warrior's assertions. Juliana's words always engender her actions, so while Cynewulf never describes the saint with words denoting a warrior, her speech enacts the conduct of a warrior: she does battle, resists conquest, with her words. One can argue, in fact, that she engages in a behaviour called *flyting*, a kind of rhetorical battle found in other Old English poems. Her eloquence is apparent from the very first scenes with her father and would-be suitor, and it moves to centre-stage once her father tosses her into prison to contemplate her filial disobedience. She continually answers her persecutors boldly—one might say tactlessly—and without fear, never backing down.

The importance of her rhetorical facility is apparent from the amount of space devoted to it. The heart of the poem, taking up well over 300 lines of the extant 731, deals with the series of verbal engagements between Juliana and the demon sent to test her piety, a motif common among both *vitae* and *passiones*, seen, for instance, in the Old English lives of St Guthlac and St Margaret. In each exchange, the demon is at a distinct disadvantage. Although this demon is disguised as an angel—another instance of the perversion and delusion suggested by the word *gedwolene*—Juliana sees through his disguise and turns the tables, interrogating him without mercy until he explains his evil mission and offers a thorough confession. He details at great length his crimes, but no matter how much information he gives, he falls short of Juliana's demands. Juliana, on the other hand, says little but speaks forcefully enough each time to coerce further disclosure. This pattern emerges in lines 289–311b, the demon's first confession (which is fragmentary, as it falls in one of the missing folios). Following his explanation of how he instigated the deaths of Christ, and the apostles Peter, Paul, and Andrew, he seems too overcome to continue further. The unbending Juliana, however, will not accept any of his words at face value, and requires him to confess still further:

> '. . . þus ic wraþra fela
> mid minum broþrum   bealwa gefremede,
> sweartra synna,   þe ic asecgan ne mæg,
> rume areccan,   ne gerim witan,

heardra heteþonca.'   Him seo halge oncwæð
þurh gæstes giefe,   Iuliana:
'Þu scealt furþor gen,   feond moncynnes,
siþfæt secgan,   hwa þec sende to me.'   (lines 311b–318)

'Thus I performed many evil deeds in malice with my brothers, dark sins, which I cannot talk about, account for in detail, nor even know the number of the hard and hateful acts.' The holy woman, Juliana, answered him through the grace of the spirit: 'You will tell about your journey still further, who sent you to me, enemy of humankind.'

Despite the brevity of her demand, the demon obeys *forht afongen, friþes orwena* ('held in fear, despairing of peace', line 320). All told, this pattern of the demon's lengthy confession framed by the saint's brief but forceful encouragement occurs five times between lines 289 and 530. These encounters demonstrate how easily the demon betrays Satan's charge, thereby transferring his thaneship to Juliana, however temporarily.

Dryhten and *þegn*

Two more of the demon's subsequent confessions provide further instances of how Cynewulf uses the language and motifs of the *dryht* to configure his story and its central theme of unswerving allegiance to God, even in the face of death. The first, at lines 321–41, emphasizes and inverts the relationship between lord and thane. In this second of five speeches which elucidate his wretched existence, the demon's description of his journey creates a picture antithetical to the manner in which a benevolent lord of a *dryht* would behave to his men. He tells Juliana:

'Hwæt, mec min fæder   on þas fore to þe,
hellwarena cyning,   hider onsende
of þam engan ham,   se is yfla gehwæs
in þam grornhofe   geornfulra þonne ic.
þonne he usic sendeð   þæt we soðfæstra
þurh misgedwield   mod oncyrren,
ahwyrfen from halor,   we beoð hygegeomre,
forhte on ferðþe.   Ne biþ us frea milde,
egesful ealdor,   gif we yfles noht

gedon habbaþ;   ne durran we siþþan
for his onsyne   ower geferan.
Þonne he onsendeð   geond sidne grund
þegnas of þystrum,   hateð þræce ræran,
gif we gemette sin   on moldwege,
oþþe feor oþþe neah   fundne weorþen,
þæt hi usic binden   ond in bælwylme
suslum swingen.   Gif soðfæstra
þurh myrrelsan   mod ne oðcyrreð,
haligra hyge,   we þa heardestan
ond þa wyrrestan   witu geþoliað
þurh sarslege. . . .'   (lines 321–41a)

'Listen: my father, king of the hell-dwellers, who is in that house of woe more eager for evil than I, sent me on this journey to you, hither from the narrow home. When he sends us so that we may change the minds of the steadfast, through error turn them away from salvation, we are sad in spirit, frightened in our heart. A terrifying prince, he is not a merciful lord to us if we have accomplished no evils; nor dare we afterward ever travel before his countenance. Then he sends his retainers from the shadows through the wide earth, has them raise violence if they encounter sight of us on the earth-way, if we are found either far or near, so that they should bind us and have us toil in the miseries of funeral-flames. If the minds of the righteous, the spirits of the holy, are not perverted through offence, we endure the hardest and the worst punishments through painful blows.'

Satan is described in all of the ways that an Anglo-Saxon audience might expect a deviant lord to be described, a lord who would undermine their social contract: Satan is a stay-at-home king. Rather than accompanying his warriors into the fray, he sends them out on their own. One could argue that a king's place is not at the front but, leaving this question aside, the passage makes clear that the hearts of these warriors are not in their work; rather than revering their king, they fear him. They do not move into their metaphoric battles with righteous men willingly, as true thanes move willingly into battle. They do not receive treasure for their efforts; instead they receive violent punishment. Satan sends his men out from *þam engan ham* ('the narrow home'), an image in opposition with the epitome of the Anglo-Saxon hall found in *Beowulf*, Heorot, described, for example, as *heah ond horngeap* ('high and horn-gabled', *Beowulf*, line 82a). It is certainly at odds with the vast roof of heaven described in *Cædmon's Hymn*. Rather than a place of light and hope, the home of the hell-dwellers is a *grornhof* ('a house of woe'), and they carry that misery with them as they move *hygegeomre | forhte on ferþðe* ('sad in spirit, frightened at heart'), about the earth seeking souls to corrupt. They have no enthusiasm for their mission, since their bond is based on punishment rather than reward with treasure: they are fettered, forced to work in the fire, beaten if they fail at their tasks. The demon makes explicit the passage's implicit sense of coercion as he concludes his first confession, telling Juliana in lines 343–4a that he was threatened continually to seek her out. By contrast, Juliana's own allegiance to God, even in the face of her own punishment, remains joyfully steadfast throughout the poem.

The soul under siege

The demon's third confession, at lines 382–405, in which he explains to Juliana how he gathers up souls for Satan, consistently uses the conventional diction of the battlefield:

'Gif ic ænigne   ellenrofne
gemete modigne   metodes cempan
wið flanþræce,   nele feor þonan
bugan fram beaduwe,   ac he bord ongean
hefeð hygesnottor,   haligne scyld,
gæstlic guðreaf,   nele gode swican,
ac he, beald in gebede,   bidsteal gifeð
fæste on feðan,   ic sceal feor þonan,
heanmod hweorfan,   hroþra bidæled,
in gleda gripe,   gehðu mænan,
þæt ic ne meahte   mægnes cræfte
guðe wiðgongan,   ac ic geomor sceal
secan oþerne   ellenleasran,
under cumbolhagan,   cempan sænran,
þe ic onbryrdan mæge   beorman mine,
agælan æt guþe.   Þeah he godes hwæt
onginne gæstlice,   ic beo gearo sona,
þæt ic ingehygd   eal geondwlite,
hu gefæstned sy   ferð innanweard,
wiþsteall geworht.   Ic þæs wealles geat
ontyne þurh teonan;   bið se torr þyrel,

ingong geopenad,   þonne ic ærest him
þurh eargfare   in onsende
in breostsefan   bitre geþoncas . . .'   (lines 382–405)

'If I meet any brave warrior of God, bold in courage, with an arrow-storm, who will not flee far from there, away from the fight, but who wise in mind raises his weapon in opposition, the holy shield, the spiritual armour, nor will not abandon God, but he, bold in his prayers, makes a stand fast in his tracks, I must turn heavy-hearted far from there, deprived of joy, into the fire's grip, lament the misery that I cannot overcome in battle with the power of force; but I must mournfully seek another, less courageous under the wall of weapons, a duller warrior whom I can ferment with my yeast, hinder at the battle. Although he might begin somewhat good in spirit, I am soon ready so that I see all through his inward thought, how secured his inner strength might be, his defences constructed; I open this wall's gate through my iniquity; the tower is pierced, its entrance opened, when in a flight of arrows I first send bitter thoughts into his mind . . .'

At the centre of this passage is the image of a soul as a fortress under siege, a motif common in Latin Christian texts but which does not occur in the legend printed in the *Acta Sanctorum*. Cynewulf seems to have added it to his version of the story, suggesting that he wanted his audience to think of this very Latin saint in more familiar, Anglo-Saxon, terms. Though the image of the beleaguered citadel is common in Christian allegory, the catalogue of weaponry here— *flanþræce* ('flight of arrows'), *bord* and *scyld* (both meaning 'spear'), *guðreaf* ('armour'), and the especially evocative metaphor *cumbolhagan* (literally, 'a hedge of battle-standards')—gives this spiritual battle a palpable earthly existence, and clearly characterizes its participants as Anglo-Saxon warriors, *cempan* ('champions'). The layout of the fortress is unmistakable, with its defensive walls, tower, and gate. Although the demon recounts his own individual assaults on humankind, his speech reinforces the larger narrative theme that Christians are always engaged in the eternal battle against sin. As the demon explains his strategies to Juliana, he seems resigned that his tricks have failed to penetrate her soul. None the less, while she can resist his spiritual subterfuges, she cannot forever defend her physical self against her execution.

Cynewulf's runes

Although the conventions of the *passio* require that Juliana survive and transcend the various tortures—hung by her hair, beaten, imprisoned, boiled in a cauldron of molten lead—to which she is subjected, she cannot survive her decapitation. The inevitable generic conclusion of her death, however, does not end the poem: her persecutors find their way to hell as the saint's body is carried inside the city's walls for veneration and, presumably, for the resulting saintly intercessions. Leaving his audience with this closing image allows Cynewulf to conclude his poem in lines 695–731 with a traditional request for both their prayers and those of the saint. This concluding passage fuses time and space: past, present and future merge, as do Nicomedia and Anglo-Saxon England, linking the original participants of the saint's passion with Cynewulf's contemporary audience, and then enlisting the participation of any future audience for the poem.

Consequently, the larger passage has a three-part structure that acknowledges its thematic concerns for time, space, and salvation. Lines 695–708 establish the poet's present condition while lines 709–17 look back in a confessional mode on his sinful life. Lines 718–31 point to the promise of future reward, given the saint's intercession and the prayers of anyone who encounters the poem. (This sort of conclusion also appears in Cynewulf's poem *Fates of the Apostles*, and is common within medieval literature, perhaps most notably in Chaucer's use of it in his *Retraction*.) Embedded in the first section, however, the seven lines containing Cynewulf's runic signature (703b–709a) arguably have elicited more popular attention than the poem itself. While Cynewulf has arranged the runes differently in his other poems, in *Juliana* he sets them out as groups of three, three, and two. Scholars have disagreed about how these eight runes should be read: as individual letters spelling out Cynewulf's name, eight individual words meaningful within the passage, or as three words spelled out in runes. This ambiguity has made understanding the passage difficult, though if we take each set of runes as spelling out a word, as R. W. Elliott has suggested ('Cynewulf's Runes in *Juliana*', p. 202), these lines may mean something like: 'Humankind [CYN] passes away, sorrowing.

The King, the Giver of victories, is stern when his sheep [EWU], stained with sin, terrified, awaits what will be judged to him after the deeds of his loaned life. The weak man [L F] trembles, lies sorrowful.' No matter how these lines are translated, however, Cynewulf has used them to insert himself into the action of the poem, the middle of the battle, exhorting his audience to pray with and for him, reminding it—and us—that the struggle against sin presented in *Juliana* is both personal and universal.

References and suggested reading

Bjork, R. E. *The Old English Verse Saints' Lives.* Toronto: University of Toronto Press, 1985. Ch. 2, 'Saintly Discourse and the Distancing of Evil in Cynewulf's *Juliana*', pp. 45–61. As part of a larger stylistic analysis of Old English poetic hagiography, Bjork's chapter argues that Juliana's rhetoric fuses with and enacts her deeds, revealing the saint's immutable and refined spiritual condition.

Calder, D. G. *Cynewulf.* Twayne's English Authors Series 327. Boston: G. K. Hall, 1981. Calder provides a comprehensive overview of the poet and each of the works attributed to the poet, with narrative summaries and critical analyses.

Doubleday, J. F. 'The Allegory of the Soul as Fortress in Old English Poetry', *Anglia*, 88 (1970), 503–8. This article provides the context for an important motif in *Juliana* as well as some discussion of the motif's function in the poem.

Elliott, R. W. V. 'Cynewulf's Runes in *Juliana* and *Fates of the Apostles*', *English Studies*, 34 (1953), 193–204. Elliott's article does not offer the last word on the subject, but it is a good place to begin.

Garnett, J. W. 'The Latin and the Anglo-Saxon Juliana', *Publications of the Modern Language Association*, 14 (1899), 279–98. Although dated, the article makes useful comparisons between the Old English poem and its Latin sources.

Heffernan, T. H. *Sacred Biography: Saints and Their Biographers in the Middle Ages.* Oxford: Oxford University Press, 1988. This study provides a solid outline of the genre of hagiography and its accompanying issues.

Olsen, A. H. 'Cynewulf's Autonomous Women: A Reconsideration of Elene and Juliana'. In H. Damico and A. H. Olsen, eds., *New Readings on Women in Old English Literature*. Bloomington: Indiana University Press,

1990, pp. 222–32. Olsen argues against the view of Juliana as a flat, allegorical figure, claiming for the saint a complex psychology that renders her autonomous, active, and heroic.

Wittig, J. S. 'Figural Narrative in Cynewulf's *Juliana*', *Anglo-Saxon England*, 4 (1975), 37–55. Rprt. in R. E. Bjork, ed., *Cynewulf; Basic Readings*. New York: Garland, 1996, pp. 147–69. Wittig explicates *Juliana* from a typological perspective, which provides a critical *apologia* for the poem's presumed literary shortcomings.

Woolf, R., ed. *Juliana*. London: Methuen, 1955; rev. edn. Exeter: University of Exeter Press, 1993. Woolf's is the standard edition of the poem, and includes an introduction to the poem, its text, notes and commentary, and a glossary. The bibliography is comprehensive up to 1992.

6

Old English heroic literature

Rolf H. Bremmer, Jr.

What makes a hero?

Heroes are quite a common phenomenon these days, it seems. When the American President welcomes back home the troops, he calls them 'our heroes'. But from the thousands of ranks and files that the camera shows us, we fail to isolate the 'illustrious warrior', as the *Concise Oxford Dictionary* defines the word 'hero'; or the 'person, esp. a man, admired for noble achievements and qualities (e.g. courage)'. In these days of high-tech warfare it is hardly possible for soldiers, be they man or woman, to distinguish themselves in such a way as to comply with the dictionary definition. Clearly, either the dictionary is insufficient in its definition or the President's notion of what makes a hero has been subject to inflation. In reality, heroes are rare and hard to find. In fiction, however, they are alive and kicking, especially on the silver screen. One of the best-known heroes of modern times is Ian Fleming's creation of James Bond, the British secret agent with a licence to kill. Initially 'the principal main character in a literary work' (*COD*), Bond particularly owes his unprecedented popularity to the deft formula with which Fleming's novels have been turned into films.

Old English does not have a separate word for 'hero'. However, according to the *Thesaurus of Old English*, for 'warrior' there are no fewer than seventy or so words, expressing a vast spectrum of nuances. One of these is *eorl*; and while translators have used the abstract noun *eorlscipe* to refer to what we would call a deed of heroism, the word literally means 'having the qualities of a warrior'. Indeed, the French loanword *hero* is not recorded in English until the late fourteenth century, and then it is an isolated case. Only with the Renaissance rediscovery of the ancient authors did the word gain wide acceptance, first with reference to heroes of the classical Greek and Latin world, and then soon after to other men of extreme valour. The Romantic fascination with the individual character whose virtues are 'larger than life', the Gothic movement, a growing national sentiment, and the publication of *Beowulf* (1815) and its subsequent reception have greatly influenced our idea of the Germanic hero. We are so accustomed now to the Old English literary genre called 'heroic' that it seems worthy of definition. Basically, the genre comprises poems that deal with warriors endowed with often superhuman courage whose actions are motivated by a special set of values, the 'heroic ethos'. Successful in their early career, such warriors are eventually confronted with impossible choices or set such choices for themselves (such as choosing between conflicting loyalties or engaging in an unequal fight). They accept their decision knowingly and willingly, which leads either to victory and honour or to defeat and death, yet with the satisfaction of posthumous fame. Tragedy, therefore, is often an essential component of heroic literature. In this respect, the genre differs markedly from modern Bond stories and the like which predictably end with the hero's triumphant success.

The heroic ethos

The heroic ethos or code is typical for an unstable, tribal society that depends on fighting for its survival. For England, the two centuries following the Anglo-Saxon invasions and subsequent conquest by individual groups proved formative, but the principal ingredients of the ethos reach back to Continental Germany. The invading warrior-lords managed to carve a piece of British territory for themselves and their kindred and to maintain or even to extend their power base. Though the individual martial feats of these leaders have been lost in the mists of time, their names still survive in place-names such as Hastings (OE *Hæstingas*, 'Hæsta's people') and Barking

(OE *Bericingas,* 'Berica's people'). To achieve success in battle, a lord (*hlaford, frea,* or *dryhten*—to mention some of the ten words used for a leader in *Beowulf*) depended on the unswerving loyalty of his retainers (*gesiþas* or *þegnas*), which he secured by bonding his retainers to himself through a variety of means. He treated them in his hall to ceremonial banquets with food and mead, ale and wine. Publicly and generously, he shared out precious gifts such as weapons, rings, torques, and brooches. 'A king must in his hall distribute rings' (*Maxims II,* 28–9): the act was even proverbial. In this capacity a lord is referred to, for example, as *sinces brytta* 'distributer of treasure' or *goldwine* 'gold-friend'. The reciprocal obligations had a spiralling effect: attracting retainers enabled a lord to extend his power and by gaining more power he became an even more attractive lord for new retainers. According to Tacitus, in his ethnographic description of the Germans around AD 100, 'both [a lord's] prestige and power depend on being continuously attended by a large train of picked young warriors, which is a distinction in peace and a protection in war' (*Germania,* 13). Protection too was mutual, as a place in a band guaranteed a young man guidance in battle-skills, social esteem, support in feuding, and a career with a prospect to become a lord himself one day. Retainers vied with each other for their lord's attention by vowing (or 'boasting') in public to perform deeds of valour in battle.

The band of warrior-retainers (variously called *dryht* or *folgað,* or *comitatus* with the lord included) usually consisted of two groups. The core was made up by the *duguð,* reliable veterans who had long proved their mettle in the mêlée and who had advanced in years and in position. They owned land and a hall of their own and were married. Then there were the junior warriors, the *geoguð,* adolescent, unmarried, little tried in battle but impetuous and eager to make a name for themselves. In addition to bravery, the concept of honour and shame figured prominently in this warrior culture. A man's place in this aristocratic society was greatly constituted by the public esteem he enjoyed. Honour, or the lack of it, made or broke a man's standing and thereby his role in the social fabric. This aspect of the heroic code applied to both the lord and his followers. Again, according to Tacitus, 'on the field of battle it is a disgrace to a chief to be surpassed in courage by his followers, and to the followers not to equal their chief's courage. And to leave a battle alive after their chief has fallen means lifelong infamy and shame' (*Germania*, 14). The ultimate aim of heroism was acquiring an honourable reputation (*dom*) and praise (*lof*) which guaranteed a prominent place in the community not only during life but even more so with posterity, through stories and songs.

It is precisely the literary, fictional legacy of the Anglo-Saxons which informs us about the heroes of the past. Remarkably, in 'factual', historical sources we find few traces of the heroic ideal. This paucity of information must alert us to a possible discrepancy between the ideal as expressed in works of literature and its practical application or modification as we find it in, for example, annalistic narratives such as the *Anglo-Saxon Chronicle*.

More specifically, Old English heroic poetry relates or alludes to the exploits of heroes of the Germanic past that took place in the Migration period, roughly between 400 (the fall of the Roman Empire) and 600 (the consolidation of the new situation). The manuscripts in which these poems are found, however, all date from the late tenth and early eleventh centuries. A dramatic gap exists, therefore, between the time to which the heroes can be dated on historical evidence and that from which our written documents stem. This time interval between pre-conversion origin and post-conversion documentation has been the cause of intense scholarly debate in recent decades. The transition to Christianity took place between 600 and 700 and brought with it cultural and ethical changes whose impact cannot be gauged precisely. This poses the problem of the transmission of narrative material through the centuries. Did the heroic ethos as described by Tacitus—himself a biased reporter of 'noble savages' with a hidden agenda for his decadent Roman home front—survive so many centuries and cultural changes undiluted?

Old English traditional heroic poetry

Some five poems survive which together make up the corpus of the Old English heroic literature whose subjects share in the common Germanic narrative heritage. They are *Widsith*, *Deor*, *Waldere*, *The Finnsburg Fragment*, and *Beowulf*. These five poems differ remarkably in both length and format: *Deor* is stanzaic and numbers 42 lines. *Widsith*, 143 lines long, is more a catalogue of heroic figures than a narrative proper. Both poems are included in the late tenth-century Exeter Book of poetry. Both *Waldere* and *The Finnsburg Fragment* survive as fragments, the former as two single leaves of 63 lines in all, the latter as a late seventeenth-century copy of a stray leaf, now lost. How large these two fragmentary poems once were is hard to establish, but estimates run to 1,000 lines for *Waldere* and 250 to 300 lines for *The Finnsburg Fragment*. *Beowulf* is by far the longest poem—in fact, it is *the* longest Old English poem—with 3,182 lines.

Not only do these five poems differ in length, they also vary greatly in content and purpose. *Widsith* is generally held to be a composition of the seventh century. It is not so much a narrative poem as an autobiographical account of a poet who reveals himself in the opening lines (1–4a) as follows:

> Widsið maðolade,   wordhord onleac,
> se þe [monna] mæst   mægþa ofer eorþan,
> folca geondferde;   oft he [on] flette geþah
> mynelicne maþþum.

Widsith spoke, unlocked his treasure of words, he who of all men had travelled through tribes and peoples; often he had received on the floor of the hall some memorable treasure.

In the lines immediately following, Widsith reveals his family background and proudly informs his audience that he had begun his career as the personal poet of Ealhhilde when she departed from Angeln to become the queen of Eormanric, king of the Goths. As a persona, Widsith is a successful poetic creation. His name means 'far traveller', and that is precisely how he appears in the remainder of his poem, which consists of three sets of 'catalogues' of still famous, but even more of long forgotten, figures from the Germanic heroic past. The first set (lines 10–49) consists of names of famous rulers of whom he has heard; the second (lines 50–108) lists the tribes and rulers with whom he has sojourned; the third (lines 109–34) sums up the tribes and rulers whom he has visited. All in all some 180 names of tribes and rulers parade through the poem, which no longer make for entertainment or reflection (unless, for us today, it shows that fame does not always last). However, occasionally, Widsith interrupts his monotonous listings by giving a few details, for example:

> Hroþwulf and Hroðgar   heoldon lengest
> sibbe ætsomne,   suhtorgefædran,
> siþþan hy forwræcon   wicinga cynn
> ond Ingeldes   ord forbigdan,
> forheawan æt Heorote   Heaðo-beardna þrym.   (lines 45–9)

Hrothwulf and Hrothgar, father's brother and brother's son, kept peace together for a very long time, after they had driven off the tribe of pirates and humiliated the vanguard of Ingeld, cut down the host of the Heothobards at Heorot.

Suddenly it appears that Widsith shows familiarity with at least some of the episodes of *Beowulf*, and that the latter poem—or at least some of its narrative substance—was more widely known in England than we may assume on the grounds of its unique survival. Further, the mention of Eormanric occasions Widsith to dwell on that king's remarkable generosity when he presented him with a collar in which there was 'six hundred coins'-worth of refined gold, counted by shillings' (lines 91–2). Back home, Widsith, in turn, passed it on to his own lord, Eadgils, who now could pride himself on possessing this precious ornament and reciprocally increase his honour by entrusting to his retainer, Widsith, the authority of the latter's ancestral lands. Also Queen Ealhhild, according to Widsith, added to her record of international praise (*lof*) by giving the poet a similar collar. The poem thus turns from a catalogue of past heroes into a billboard for Widsith's own supreme qualities as a court singer (*scop*) and concludes with a general statement that entertainers (*gleomen*) wander through many lands extolling in song the generosity of some leader 'who wishes to have reputation (*dom*) heightened in front of the company of his veteran warriors and his valour shown [. . .]. Such a man attains praise (*lof*), he has a lasting reputation under heavens' (lines 140–3). The poet's purpose, then, is to emphasize the notion that reputation cannot exist without singers who attractively give shape and permanence to the glorious deeds of past warrior-lords. Recounting the exploits of past heroes as role models at feasts of aspiring heroes is one effective—and peaceful—means for lords to establish their fame. To this end, catalogues as applied in *Widsith* were circulating among the professional singers.

Another such (fictive) singer is Deor, persona of the eponymous poem, likewise preserved in the Exeter Book. Deor begins by recounting four episodes from the heroic past. First he devotes two stanzas to the legendary Germanic smith Weland's tragic adventures and subsequent cruel revenge. Were it not for the detailed information we have from Scandinavian sources, notably the *Saga of Weland*, the allusions to Weland, to his capturer King Nithhard, and to the killing of the king's two sons and seduction of his daughter Beathuhild (he makes her pregnant) would have been lost on us. Such is indeed the case with the second episode in the poem, dealing with an otherwise unknown pair of lovers, Geat and Mæthhild. It has remained uncertain until now to which Theoderic the third stanza alludes, whether to the legendary Theoderic the Great, king of the Visigoths, or to a lesser-known Frankish king. With Eormanric, king of the Goths, we are on safer ground again, for many sources confirm Deor's opinion that Eormanric was 'a fierce king' (line 23). What makes these four stanzas so intriguing is that each ends with the same refrain: *þæs ofereode; þisses swa mæg*, 'As for that it passed; so can this'. Apparently, mutability is of great concern to Deor, and after stanza four, he comforts himself (and his audience) that God is in control of changes in this world. On a more personal note, the poem ends with Deor confiding a dramatic change in his own life: his position as his lord's favourite singer has been awarded to a *leoðcræftig* ('skilled in song') competitor, Heorrenda, *scop* of the Heodenings ('the group or tribe of Heoden').

Such cursory allusions to famous heroes in *Deor* and *Widsith* suggest that their adventures were quite well known by professional singers in Anglo-Saxon England and also, in some form, by their intended audience. Further familiarity with the heroes of old is supported by the fragmentary poem *Waldere*. Again, the story of Walter of Aquitaine is known to us from non-English sources as diverse as the continental tenth-century Latin epic *Waltharius*, the thirteenth-century Old Norse *Þiðrikssaga*, and the eleventh-century North Italian *Chronicon Novaliciense*. Son of King Alphere (OE Ælfhere), Walter is sent to the court of the Hunnish King Attila, almost simultaneously with Hiltgunt, daughter of King Hereric of the Burgundians. The two are meant to be married by their fathers, but Attila's queen wishes to tie the popular Walter to her court by marrying him off to a Hunnish princess. Walter and Hiltgunt escape, taking two chests of gold with them. On their way home they have to cross the land of Gunther, king of the Franks (mentioned as Guðhere in *Waldere* and in *Widsith*), who refuses them passage. A fight ensues in which Walter, strategically positioned at the entrance of a gorge, kills eleven of Gunther's men. The next day, when facing the king himself, he ventures out of his position and cuts off the king's leg. At this point, one of Gunther's faithful retainers, Hagano (mentioned as Hagene in *Widsith*), intervenes and strikes off Walter's hand. After Walter has pierced Hagano's eye and also cut out six of his teeth—making him appear ghastly and permanently shameful—the two men reconcile and Walter and Hiltgunt marry to rule their land for thirty happy years: all this according to the *Waltharius*.

It is hard to decide which of the two leaves on which *Waldere* survives takes precedence in the narrative sequence, but it is quite clear that both of them deal with Waldere's fight in the gorge. On one leaf, Waldere is encouraged by a woman, presumably *Hildegyð (as her name would have been in OE). Her long speech is full of heroic sentiments. For example, she formulates the fate Walter is facing: 'Now the day has come that you, son of Ælfhere, must do one of two':

> lif forleosan oððe l[an]gne dom
> agan mid eldum . . .   (I, 8–11)

lose your life or possess lasting reputation among men . . .

She praises him for never having shunned battle or fled to a place of safety. She repeats the heroic choice a little later to Waldere, but negatively this time. Now it is Guðhere who 'must either leave this fight and return without rings [i.e. empty-handed and shamefully] or die first [i.e. heroically]'. The other leaf contains two speeches, the former by an unidentified speaker, the latter by Waldere himself. They belong to the traditional exchange of taunts—'come and get me if you dare'—typical of battle descriptions in heroic poetry.

Speech also fills a good deal of the *Finnsburg Fragment*. Were it not for the fact that the event and many of the characters related in these 39 lines are also familiar to us from *Beowulf*, we might not have guessed their relevance. In *Beowulf*, the story is told as after-dinner entertainment at a banquet in King Hrothgar's hall. Hnæf, a Danish prince, accompanied by sixty warriors, is visiting his sister Hildeburh, wife of Finn, king of the Frisians. Hildeburh, like many other women of her rank, had been married to Finn as a *freoðu-webbe* ('peace-weaver') in order to forge a stable alliance between potentially competing tribes. For some reason or other (revenge?), the Frisians suddenly attack Hnæf and his men. Eventually not only Hnæf, but also Hildeburh's unnamed son, fall in battle. Owing to the Danes' brave resistance, the outcome of the battle is a draw and in a truce it is decided that the Danes should share Finn's hall and participate in the ceremonial activities. All winter, relations seem peaceful, until in the spring bitter feelings revive and Hengest, Hnæf's successor, decides to avenge his lord's death and reopens hostilities. This time, Finn is killed, his hall plundered, and Hildeburh taken home in triumph. In *Beowulf*, the emphasis is not so much on violent action as on the moral implications of revenge, the taking and breaking of oaths, and the cruel outcome, especially for Hildeburh, of predominantly male preoccupations with honour and shame. The *Fragment* deals with the beginning of the enmities. For five days the Danes have managed to withstand the Frisian onslaught and encouraged themselves with speeches. The 'beasts of battle'—often looming in poetic battle scenes—are paraded to announce the impending carnage: 'The birds [of carrion] will be singing, the grey-coated wolf baying' and 'the raven was hovering, black and with dusky gleam'. Admiringly, the poet exclaims that 'never have I heard of young warriors [the word used is "bach-elors"] better and more honourably repaying the shiny mead than these youngsters paid Hnæf', their lord. Cunningly, the poet here links the warriors' motivation for risking their lives with the festivities in their lord's meadhall and the reciprocal bond of the heroic ethos.

Beowulf is particularly rich in celebrating heroic ideals. In the preliminaries to the actual story in and around the hall of Hrothgar, king of the Danes, one of his ancestors is being praised. This praise leads the poet to the first of many sententious remarks with which he comments on the actions in the poem:

> Swa sceal geong guma   gode gewyrcean,
> fromun feohgiftum   on fæder [bear]me,
> þæt hine on ylde   eft gewunigen
> wilgesiþas,   þone wig cume,
> leode gelæsten;   lofdædum sceal
> in mægþa gehwære   man geþeon.   (lines 20–5)

Thus a young man must achieve goodwill with excellent precious gifts while in his father's protection, so that dear retainers remain with him as an adult, when battle comes, (and so that) men may stand by him; through praiseworthy deeds a man is sure to thrive in every tribe.

With some modifications, Beowulf is such a man. In barely five lines (194–98a) he is introduced to us as *þegn* of Hygelac, his mother's brother and king of the Geats, a tribe in South Sweden. Beowulf enjoys a good reputation amongst his people—the poet simply says that he was 'good'. Moreover, we are told that he was the strongest man in his time, of noble birth, and had that extra quality (*eacen*) it takes to be exceptional. In his youth he ventures with a band of fourteen picked warriors (*cempan gecorene*, line 206) to Denmark to help King Hrothgar get rid of the monster Grendel. Having completed that mission, Hrothgar bestows on Beowulf twelve precious gifts, a number of which Beowulf, upon his return home, magnanimously passes on to his lord, Hygelac. Beowulf's adventure in Denmark appears to have been his last 'rite of passage' towards adulthood, for Hygelac honours him with his father's (and Beowulf's grandfather's) gold-ornamented sword, seven thousand hides of land, a hall, and a princely throne. Nowhere is there mention of Beowulf's fourteen companions receiving valuable gifts. Would their having joined such a brave man have been enough reward for them?

When fifty years after his Danish adventure Beowulf again takes up a challenge—to kill a fire-breathing dragon—he advances to his opponent with eleven retainers. The dragon appears to be so frightening that ten of them rush shamefully to the woods. Only one, Wiglaf, remains resolute and reminds his coward companions of the mead drinking, the receiving of rings, and the making of promises to their lord to repay him for the many war-equipments he had given to them. As for himself, he would rather be burnt to cinders than forsake his lord. Wiglaf then rushes to his lord's aid and together they kill the dragon, even though it costs Beowulf his life.

Beowulf ends with the hero's complex ceremonial funeral. Twelve warriors ride around his memorial tomb and acclaim his *eorlscipe*. The poet approvingly comments that it is fitting to praise a *winedryhten* ('friend and leader') after his death, and he summarizes the song of Beowulf's 'hearth-companions': [Beowulf was] wyruldcyninga

manna mildust	ond monðwærust,
leodum liðost	ond lof geornost. (lines 3180b–3182)

of (all) the world's kings the most generous of men and the most loyal to his men, gentlest to his people and most eager for praise.

Generosity, loyalty, fairness in conduct, and ambition for fame— these qualities sum up a hero's profile. At the same time, they offer material for critical comparison. Let us take loyalty as an example.

We have seen that, according to Tacitus, it was a disgrace for a retainer to survive his lord on the battlefield or at least to leave his death unavenged. Wiglaf appeals to this code when he scolds his companions and joins Beowulf in his combat with the dragon, and in doing so gains the poet's (and our) approval. But how are we to consider Hengest's decision to conclude a truce with King Finn after his lord Hnæf had been killed in fighting the Frisians? Or again, what about Hengest's breaking his solemn oaths to Finn when he resumed hostilities in spring and killed Finn after all? The poet does not give us an answer, leaving it to his audience to solve these moral questions. The heroic code cannot apparently be adhered to under all circum- stances. Previous generations of scholars have often judged the ideals of the warrior ethics too absolutely and have closed their eyes to its finer workings. Particularly in *Beowulf*, not only the ideals but also the shortcomings of the heroic ethic are critically sounded.

The heroic code in historical 'reality'

The heroic code seems to have been more a concern within poetry than outside it. In any case, examples of heroism are not easy to find in historical, 'factual' prose. Outside the traditional heroic poetry, evidence for its reality in Anglo-Saxon England is hard to find. More than once we read of treachery, exile, and the killing of kings in the frequently terse prose of the *Anglo-Saxon Chronicle*. King Æthelbald of Mercia was murdered by his own bodyguard (annal 757) and one year later the same fate befell King Oswulf of Northumbria. Osred, king of the Northumbrians, was betrayed and driven from his kingdom (annal 790). When two years later he ventured to return, he was captured and killed. His successor Ethelred was killed four years later 'by his own people'. Examples of Tacitean loyalty are also present: Theobald, brother of the Northumbrian King Æthelfrith, fell in the Battle of *Degastan* against the Scots 'with all his troop' (annal 603).

Best known in this respect is the remarkably long annal for 755, which begins with the disposal of King Sigebriht of Wessex by Cynewulf with the support of important counsellors. The reason for this unusual action is that after having reigned for only one year, Sigebriht had committed (too many) 'unjust deeds' instead of showing himself, like Beowulf, *leodum liðost*. Equally unusual is that Sigebriht is not driven from the country but is allowed to keep Hampshire. Some of his retainers remained loyal to him in his degraded position, but instead of rewarding gratitude he even killed the Ealdorman Cumbra who stood by him longest. For this most unloyal deed (the opposite of Beowulf's *monðwærost*), Sigebriht was exiled to the vast forest of the Weald. Eventually, a swineherd stabbed him there to avenge Cumbra. The years pass on until in 788 Sigebriht's brother Cyneheard, in an attempt to regain the throne for his line of the family, plots against King Cynewulf when the latter with a small following—the greater part of his company camps outside the enclosure—is visiting a woman in Merton. Under cover of night, Cyneheard and his men sneak into the enclosure and surround the chamber (a detached small building outside the hall) in which the king spends the night with the (unnamed) woman. Aroused by the noise outside, Cynewulf goes to the door and nobly defends himself until he notices Cyneheard, rushes towards him, and wounds him severely. However, Cyneheard's followers attack Cynewulf and he is killed. Meanwhile, Cynewulf's *þegnas* have come from the hall to his assistance. Despite Cyneheard's offer to them of *feoh ond feorh* 'money and life', they fight until all of them are dead but for one member of their party, a Welsh hostage. The next day, Cynewulf's other men find the gates closed to them and a triumphant Cyneheard who offers them money and land if they would support him as the new king. This they refuse. Thereupon Cyneheard, obviously intent on avoiding a new fight, informs Cynewulf's men outside that some of their kinsmen are inside. The men outside then retort determinedly that 'no kinsman was dearer to them than their own lord, and they would never follow his slayer'. Further negotiations, in which

Cyneheard even offers his opponents the right of 'self-judgement', founder. In the ensuing fight, Cyneheard and his rebellious men are killed, again with one survivor. The delicate balance of this report with its two to-the-last-man fights, motivated by the heroic qualities of loyalty and revenge, carries the air of structured composition, complete with its two 'sole survivors'. Whether it is the residue of oral tradition or an embellished imaginative recreation of an actual event continues to be a moot point amongst the critics. So much is clear that long after the conversion the time-honoured ethos was still alive in literature. Earlier critics considered this ethos irreconcilable with Christ's teachings of non-violence with such precepts as 'love thine enemy' and 'turn the other cheek'. Rather, the new religion had accommodated the ancient warrior code. Both *Hildegyð and Waldere invoke God, as does Hildebrand in the Old High German heroic *Hildebrandslied*. *Beowulf* in its own peculiar way is the work of a Christian, even though Christ is never mentioned.

From ethos to propaganda

Two poems remain to be discussed that employ the heroic ethos but celebrate contemporary events of the late tenth century rather than the deeds of ancient Germanic heroes. *The Battle of Brunanburh*, preserved as the annal for 937 in the *Anglo-Saxon Chronicle*, glorifies in 73 lines the victory of King Athelstan over the joint forces of five Viking and Scottish kings at Brunanburh. Vivid battle scenes with many phrases and kennings reminiscent of the traditional heroic poetry fill most of the account, but the poet never focuses on the prowess of individual warriors nor highlights moments of heroic dilemmas. The poem praises in stock heroic terms the king of the Anglo-Saxons and thus of the nation as a whole. By this method the poet creates a link with the heroic genre of old and expressly refers back to the days of the Anglo-Saxon invasions:

> Ne wearð wæl mare
> on þis eiglande   æfre gieta
> folces gefylled   beforan þissum
> sweordes ecgum,   þæs þe us secgað bec,
> ealde uðwitan,   siþþan eastan hider

> Engle and Seaxe　　　up becoman,
> ofer brad brimu　　　Brytene sohtan,
> wlance wigsmiþas,　　　Wealas ofercoman,
> eorlas arhwate　　eard begeatan.　　　(lines 65–73)

Nor has there been more slaughter of folk by swords' edges in this island ever before this, as books, ancient scholars, tell us, since Angles and Saxons came hither from the east, invaded Britain from over the wide sea. Proud battle-smiths, they overcame the Welsh. Warriors eager for glory, they gained the land.

Significantly, the poet appeals to 'bookish' authority: the heroic past is no longer the domain of a shared oral discourse of the warrior-aristocracy, but has been appropriated by a literate élite for purposes of glorifying a united England.

The Battle of Maldon is quite different in form from *The Battle of Brunanburh*, even though their (modern) titles suggest similarities. The poem commemorates the killing and defeat of Earl Byrhtnoth and his band by the Vikings in 991. Composed not many years after the event, the poet recreates the battle—on which the *Anglo-Saxon Chronicle* expends only a few words—into hundreds of lines (325, but the poem survives as a fragment and we do not know how many lines are missing). The poem is at once realistic, fictional, chauvinistic, and traditional. Realistic in that it outlines the natural site of the battlefield and records the death of Byrhtnoth and his men at the hands of the Vikings, its fictionality appears from the long speeches attributed to Byrhtnoth and his retainers. Chauvinism is apparent in the contrast between 'us'—*þysne eðel*, 'this native land', *urne eard*, 'our country', mention of Essex and Northumbria, Christians—and 'them'—*wicinga werod*, 'band of pirates', *wælwulfas*, 'carrion-wolves', *hæðene*, 'pagans'. Finally, by using the stock heroic phraseology the poet has successfully attempted to place his work in the epic tradition, yet applied to contemporaneous, historical characters. Many elements of the *comitatus* spirit are present: vows spoken over mead in the hall, reference to the presenting of gifts, the wish to gain *dom* in dying rather than to live on in shame afterwards and the formulation of the dilemma: *lif forlætan oððe leofne gewrecan* ('abandon life or avenge the dear one', line 208). The almost monotonous expression of successive retainers of their suicidal resolve to avenge Byrhtnoth has often been adduced as evidence for the continuity of the heroic code until late Anglo-Saxon times.

More likely, though, in retrospect of the historical reality of Byrhtnoth's fight and defeat, the poet has used the poetic ingredients of traditional epic to transform and elevate just another defeat against the Vikings into a memorable celebration of the English fighting spirit.

There are signs in *The Battle of Maldon* of 'bookish' knowledge. When Byrhtnoth, dying, commends his soul to God, his words are an almost literal translation of a part of the (Latin) Office for the Dead as prescribed in the Roman Missal. Apparently, the poet was a clergyman. In a different way, bookishness introduced a new, more romantic kind of hero, as exemplified by the first English 'novel', *Apollonius of Tyre*. Translated from Latin at the same time as *The Battle of Maldon* was composed, the story narrates a series of adventures that Prince Apollonius has to experience in exile before he is finally reunited with the princess he loves. It is hardly fortuitous that Byrhtnoth's death coincided with the birth of a new type of hero. The time was ripe for a change.

References and suggested reading

Bazelmans, Jos. *'By Weapons Made Worthy': Lords, Retainers and their Relationship in Beowulf*. Amsterdam: Amsterdam University Press, 1999. The first in-depth anthropological study of the sociocosmic universe as described in *Beowulf*, paying special attention to the exchange of gifts.

Bremmer, Jr., Rolf H. 'The Germanic Context of "Cynewulf and Cyneheard" Revisited'. *Neophilologus*, 81 (1997), 445–65. A reading of the *Chronicle* annal against a broader Germanic background.

Caie, Graham D. 'The Shorter Heroic Verse'. In Henk Aertsen and Rolf H. Bremmer, Jr., eds., *Companion to Old English Poetry*. Amsterdam: VU University Press, 1994, pp. 79–94. A critical appreciation of Old English heroic poetry, except *Beowulf*.

Hill, Joyce, ed. *Old English Minor Heroic Poems*, 2nd edn. Durham Medieval Texts 4. Durham: Department of English, 1994. A useful student edition of *Widsith*, *Deor*, *Waldere*, and *The Finnsburh Fragment*.

O'Brien O'Keeffe, Katherine. 'Heroic Values and Christian Ethics'. In Malcolm Godden and Michael Lapidge, eds., *The Cambridge Companion to Old English Literature*. Cambridge: Cambridge University Press, 1991, pp. 107–26. A critical appreciation of the heroic ethos and its place in relation to Christian doctrine.

Roberts, Jane, *et al. A Thesaurus of Old English*, 2 vols., 2nd edn. Amsterdam and Atlanta, GA: Rodopi, 2000. A very useful tool to explore the various semantic fields of the Old English language relevant to the heroic ethos, particularly chapter 13: 'Peace and War'.

Tacitus. *The Agricola* and *The Germania*. Trans. H. Mattingly, rev. S. A. Handford. Harmondsworth: Penguin, 1970. An introduction to and translation of one of the earliest descriptions of the Germanic warrior society.

7

Beowulf: monuments, memory, history

Roy M. Liuzza

The Old English poem *Beowulf* has all the hallmarks of an ancient text, and is usually placed at the beginning of anthologies and surveys of English literature, but its literary history is really only two centuries old. We know nothing about its status in Anglo-Saxon times, and very little about its history before the nineteenth century. The single surviving copy of the poem (now London, British Library, Cotton Vitellius A. xv) was made shortly after 1000; it lay unknown for centuries after the Norman Conquest and was preserved by sheer chance, narrowly escaping incineration in a devastating fire in 1731 and who knows what perils before that. The poem was not published in full until 1815, and not well understood on even the most literal level until a generation later. It might be said that if *Beowulf* is a monument of English literature, the monument was erected in the nineteenth century.

Beginnings

Beowulf is in any case an unlikely candidate for its role as inaugural work of the English literary tradition. The story takes place entirely in Denmark and Sweden, and none of its characters is English; its subject is not great battles or struggles for empire, like the epics of Homer or Virgil, but rather a series of solitary adventures set in a fairy-tale world of caves, curses, dragons, and monsters, punctuated by generally cryptic allusions to feuds and treacheries; over the whole tale hangs a melancholy cloud of doom and defeat. Opening and closing with the depiction of a funeral, it seems more like a poem about endings than beginnings. Moreover, *Beowulf* is a profoundly retrospective poem: when we look back towards it, we find it too looking back to a vanished age, for all we know seeking the same things we are hoping it will provide. The first lines of the poem offer not the promise of novelty or the confidence of new beginnings but an assertion of its own belatedness, its repetition of matters already known:

> Hwæt, we gar-Dena in geardagum
> þeodcyninga þrym gefrunon,
> hu ða æþelingas ellen fremedon. (lines 1–3)

Listen! We have heard of the glory in bygone days of the folk-kings of the spear-Danes, how those noble lords did lofty deeds.[1]

Whatever else *Beowulf* intends to be, it is evident from the outset that it does not intend to be a surprise. Equally notable is the fact that the narrator begins in the first person plural, assuming a common identity with his audience—'we' have heard this story already. This initial conjunction of repetition, retrospection, and community is a good place to begin to understand the poem's larger purpose and structure; by its recurrence it becomes one of *Beowulf*'s fundamental themes.

After insisting on familiarity and repetition, *Beowulf* does tell a story of origins, but it is a strange and uncanny one: a foundling named Scyld arrives out of nowhere, rises through conquest to become king of the Danes, and at his death is given back to the same sea from which he came, where we are told that 'men cannot say . . . who received that cargo' (lines 52–4). Then follows a story of origins which go horribly wrong: Scyld's grandson Hrothgar prospers in war, and to secure his renown builds the magnificent hall Heorot; no sooner is the hall established than it is invaded by a monstrous creature named Grendel. Grendel's bloody reign of terror makes a mockery of Hrothgar's aspirations; after twelve humiliating years a young warrior of the Geats named Beowulf comes to the king's aid. First the hero undergoes a series of verbal challenges, the last and most aggressive of which involves a sharp-tongued character named Unferth and conflicting interpretations of a story about a swimming contest from Beowulf's youth—the hero's own origins are questionable and his history in dispute.

Beowulf then faces and defeats Grendel in a wild wrestling match, but the ensuing celebration is premature; the next night Grendel's mother attacks the hall in revenge for the death of her son, carrying off the body of one of Hrothgar's most trusted companions. The king sinks into what must by now be his accustomed state of despair but Beowulf, nothing daunted, tracks Grendel's mother to an underwater lair and kills her with the help of an oversized sword he finds hanging in her cave (the sword, mysterious heirloom of the race of giants who were destroyed in the biblical Flood, is yet another instance of an uncanny originary tale, an explanation that explains nothing). After much feasting, storytelling, and gift-giving, and a sententious warning by Hrothgar against the danger of pride, Beowulf returns to his homeland leaving behind the heartbroken old king and a royal hall still in peril, facing imminent treachery by the king's nephew Hrothulf and ultimate destruction by his son-in-law Ingeld.

After presenting a long and somewhat embellished account of his adventures to his uncle Hygelac, king of the Geats, Beowulf generously gives away most of the gifts he has earned, gaining glory and considerable wealth in return. The young hero has gone forth, proven his courage, earned his reward, and returned safely home: this would be a lovely place to end the story, but *Beowulf* has other things on its mind. Fifty years fly past in a few hectic lines, and suddenly the hero is himself an aged king facing a monstrous attack. This time it is a dragon, who has for 300 years guarded a hoard of ancient treasure in an underground barrow; the treasure's origin, as one might expect, is mysterious—buried by the anonymous 'Last Survivor' of an unnamed race whose fate is not explained, and protected by a lethal curse whose precise nature is not clear. The aged Beowulf sets out to fight the dragon armed with a fireproof shield and accompanied by a troop of men; in his hour of need all his companions desert him, except for a young warrior named Wiglaf. Together they slay the dragon, but Beowulf is mortally wounded; he dies gazing upon the treasure, hopeful that somehow it will ensure the future safety of his people. We are told, however, that the bloody past of the Geats will shortly catch up with them and they will be violently scattered into exile. Amid grim predictions of their ghastly destruction, Beowulf's people bury him in a magnificent barrow on a cliff by the sea. A dozen thegns ride around Beowulf's tomb, lamenting his death and recounting his deeds: the poem ends looking back upon itself, with a song about a fallen hero.

Memory

This final image of repetition, retrospection, and community shows that Beowulf has achieved what he had hoped to accomplish: he will be remembered after his death. For all the ring-giving and treasure-taking in the poem, and the delight in the glitter of rich objects, heroic action is not driven by greed or economic necessity but by the desire for *lof* or *dom*, words usually translated 'fame'. After his fight with Grendel, Hrothgar assures Beowulf that his *dom* will live *awa to aldre* 'forever and ever' (line 955); after the unexpected attack of Grendel's mother, Beowulf consoles the grieving Hrothgar with the statement that:

> Ure æghwylc sceal   ende gebidan
> worolde lifes.   Wyrce se þe mote
> domes ær deaþe;   þæt bið drihtguman
> unlifgendum   æfter selest.   (lines 1386–9)

Each of us must await the end of worldly life; let him who can achieve fame before death—that will be best later on for a lifeless nobleman.

And the very last word on Beowulf is that he was *lofgeornost*, 'most eager for fame' (line 3182). His motive, then, is not wealth or power, though these certainly come his way, but reputation and renown; he seeks not to be rich but to be remembered. *Beowulf* is about life after death, for the hero and for his story.

The Old English word *dom* still survives in the word 'doomsday'; its literal meaning is 'judgement'. Heroic *dom* may be earned by exceptional deeds, but it can only be granted by the judgement of the community that witnesses, remembers, and recounts those deeds. The desire for *dom* is the engine of heroic self-fashioning; once achieved, *dom* is both the judgement of society upon an individual's actions and the source of the criteria by which such judgements are made. By insisting that acts of individual self-assertion will always be subject to communal evaluation, the circulation of *dom* is a way of both eliciting and containing the pride and violence that sustain the military band in the meadhall. More than this, however, *dom* and the stories that bestow, preserve, and transmit it are depicted as the threads that stitch together the fabric of society. Social groups, whether families, clubs, gangs, schools, ethnic subcultures, or nations, define their identity in various ways: kinship, rituals and religious practices, a shared language, common customs and traditions. One of the most important tools for shaping cultural identity is the com-memoration of famous figures who embody the group's ideals and promote a set of common values. In the world of *Beowulf*, the exemplary figures are those who have achieved long-lasting *dom*; their stories are the pattern to which others aspire and against which they will be measured.

This process is by no means limited to 'primitive' or ancient societies; film and television play a tremendously powerful role in contemporary society in spreading models of 'manly' behaviour, normative patterns of social interaction, or ideals of 'elegant' living. The Christian cult of the saints provided (and still provides) role models for all nations, trades, and stations of life; saints are heroes of the faith whose courage we must admire and whose piety we should imitate, just as they imitated the model of Christ's life. Like the life of a saint, the story of Beowulf offers a pattern of exemplary behaviour; tales of famous figures from the past express and validate a group's present identity and inspire individual emulation, which in turn ensures future remembrance and the continued existence of the group. *Dom*, then, is another name for the relationship between culture and time: those who have achieved lasting *dom* (in this world or the next) are both memory and model, mediating Janus-like between the past and future.

Such stories of exemplary individuals are subject to powerful pressures of conformity and tend to be assimilated to an existing archetype—truly eccentric figures are rarely remembered, being either cast into a more familiar form or forgotten for want of the language to preserve them. One medieval saint is pretty much like another, just as most cowboys or detectives or gangsters bear a strong family resemblance; one becomes exemplary by losing one's individuality. But even if cultural role models are traditional and homogeneous, they are not necessarily static. Because societies are dynamic and complex, exemplary figures can be as well, changing or challenging the expectations of their audience by blending, blurring, or otherwise inflecting an inventory of traditional stories and patterns. The creative work involved in composing new exemplary narratives out of traditional forms and themes can be seen in such works as the *Dream of the Rood*, in which Christ's passion is re-imagined as a heroic battle, or Ælfric's *Life of St Edmund*, in which the traditional expectations of kingship are reversed when the hero chooses martyrdom over the defence of his people. Cultural memory is fluid, and stories of the past bend to the changing contours of the present. Yet such changes are often invisible: the narratives through which new ideals of behaviour or new patterns of social order are disseminated generally retain their air of ancient authority and their insistence upon the antiquity of their tradition.

Memory and emulation are among the most powerful forces at work both within and upon *Beowulf*. At every point in the story the past presses upon the present and makes claims against the future; tradition and memory form the core of both Beowulf's world and the poet's. The poem begins with the invocation of what we have already heard, and is concerned throughout with what is memorable or remembered; the poem itself is a memory and a memorial of the life of its hero, and a reminder to us that such memories are good and useful things.[2] Characters are defined by their lineage; Beowulf is repeatedly called 'son of Ecgtheow'. The Danes and Geats make sense of events by fitting them into a framework of poetic histories: the death of Grendel is celebrated by retelling the story of Sigemund; when the Danes return to their hall they celebrate by retelling the story of Finn and Hengist; Beowulf turns his own deeds into a story when he returns to the court of his uncle Hygelac. Such moments are models of the poem's own mediation between the past and present. The generalizing maxims scattered throughout the poem moor the present to the past, and even though the gulf that divides the pagan characters from the Christian audience is acknowledged and even at times insisted upon, the events of *Beowulf* still occur in what the poet calls 'that day of this life'.

Oblivion

And yet for all its insistence upon the power of memory and narrative to make the past and present cohere, *Beowulf* is haunted by images of destruction and forgetting, of the difficulty of preserving and comprehending the past, and of the disruptive and violent potential of memory. Beowulf dies childless, having secured his *dom* but not his kingdom. The lingering memory of unavenged deaths stirs characters like Hengist into violent action (lines 1066–1159) despite good intentions and oaths to the contrary; the remembrance of past deeds is as likely to destroy a hall as to bring it together. The rusted hoard, the poem's starkest image of the ravaging power of time, brings destruction on Beowulf and his people when it is unearthed—in this case, connecting the past and the present has terrible consequences. Lasting memory can seldom be willed; Hrothgar builds the great hall of Heorot so that he will be remembered forever (67–70), but no sooner is it completed than we glimpse its future destruction:

> Sele hlifade
> heah ond horngeap,   heaðowylma bad
> laðan liges;   ne wæs hit lenge þa gen
> þæt se ecghete   aþumsweoran
> æfter wælniðe   wæcnan scolde.   (lines 81b–85)

The hall towered high and horn-gabled—it awaited hostile fires, the surges of war; the time was not yet near when the sword-hate of sworn in-laws should awaken after deadly violence.

This monument to Hrothgar's *heresped* 'success in battle' (line 64) will be burned to the ground in an attack by his son-in-law Ingeld, destroyed by the human inability to tame the very passions it celebrates. The king's desire for a lasting memorial will be defeated by the power of memory itself—the 'awakening' of old grievances between the Danes and the Heathobards that refuse to be forgotten, old wounds that cannot be healed by love or diplomacy.

Memories are preserved in stories, but also attached to objects; just as today a souvenir or heirloom can serve as a touchstone of personal history or cultural tradition, so the cups, rings, necklaces, and swords of *Beowulf* are powerfully charged conduits between past and present, reminders of past events and incitements to future action. But again the course of memory cannot always be controlled: Queen Wealhtheow gives Beowulf a beautiful necklace to commemorate his success, but it will become a far less pleasant souvenir when it is looted from the corpse of Beowulf's dead uncle on a battlefield in Frisia (lines 1202–14). Swords are particularly unruly engines of memory, each the embodiment of a series of violent narratives—the fame of the great deeds they have performed, the names of the dead warriors from whose hands they were pried, the guilt of the blood that has stained them, the weight of the revenge they impose. At one of the most dramatic moments in the entire poem, when Wiglaf draws his sword to rush to Beowulf's aid, the narrative pauses to give fourteen lines of background on the weapon's lineage; its history implicates Wiglaf's father (and thus his son, heir to his father's guilt along with his sword) in three generations of bloody and unresolved hostility between the Geats and the Swedes. The traces of the past in the present are not always happy ones, and memory's power can be centrifugal as well as centripetal, as likely to tear apart the hall as to preserve it.

By the end of the poem all the paraphernalia of heroic *dom*, the cups and rings and helmets and harps and coats of mail so gloriously deployed in celebration of Beowulf's triumph, is shown rusting and decayed, abandoned by the nameless remnant of a forgotten race from the poem's own *geardagum* 'days of yore' (line 2233), who consigns his world—the poem's world—to oblivion. His haunting eulogy over the treasure's grave (lines 2247–70) clings to the poem like a pall of smoke until it settles upon Beowulf's own tomb, the *beadurofes becn* 'beacon of the battle-brave [man]' (line 3160) built over his funeral pyre. Like Scyld, Beowulf choreographs his own funeral; like Hrothgar, he plans a monument to his memory, and with practically his last breath tells Wiglaf:

> 'Hatað heaðomære   hlæw gewyrcean
> beorhtne æfter bæle   æt brimes nosan;
> se scel to gemyndum   minum leodum
> heah hlifian   on Hronesnæsse,
> þaet hit sæliðend   syððan hatan
> Biowulfes biorh,   ða ðe brentingas
> ofer floda genipu   feorran drifað.'   (lines 2802–8)

'The brave in battle will order a tomb built bright over my pyre, on the cliffs by the sea; it will tower high over Whale's Head as a reminder to my people, so that seafarers afterwards shall call it "Beowulf's Barrow", those who drive from afar their broad ships over the dark flood.'

Beowulf's soul then flies off to seek a more personal and perhaps less certain *dom*, the 'judgement of the righteous' before God (line 2820). The monument surrounding his pyre is built to his specifications, *heah ond brad, wegliðendum wide gesyne* 'high and broad, visible from afar to seafarers' (lines 3157–8), but his hopes for the dragon's treasure are not fulfilled: taking no *maððum to gemyndum* 'treasures as a remembrance' (3016), his people return the entire hoard to the grave, where the narrator tells us that it *nu gen lifað, eldum swa unnyt swa hit æror wæs*, 'still lies there, as useless to men as it was before' (lines 3167–8). Conflated in this way with the Last Survivor's lost world and the suspended animation of the dragon's anti-hall, Beowulf's heroic tomb becomes a beacon of both *dom* and despair, a monument of memory and loss mocking its own aspirations to immortality.

The poem does not end on this suggestion of the insufficiency of human monuments before the abyss of oblivion, however, but rather with the image of twelve Geats riding around Beowulf's tomb. They wish to

> ceare cwiðan   ond kyning mænan
> wordgyd wrecan   ond ymb wer sprecan;
> eahtodan eorlscipe   ond his ellenweorc
> duguðum demdon.   (lines 3171–4)

voice their cares and mourn their king, tell stories and speak of the man; they praised his lordship and judged his brave deeds.

In his last generalizing maxim, the narrator pronounces this act *gedefe* 'proper' (line 3174) even today. Beowulf's ambivalent memorial filled with useless treasure is surrounded, literally, by a scene of *dom* in the making: an act of communal storytelling which reinforces social identity and offers an exemplary model for future behaviour. For all its anxiety about unruly memory and untimely oblivion, the conclusion of the poem seems to imply that the poetic commemoration of a heroic life can be more stable and reliable than physical monuments subject to rust, collapse, theft, or loss; his *dom* secured, the story of Beowulf begins to become the poem we are hearing, and the circle of memory seems complete. In the world of Beowulf, *dom* is a process, not a product; monuments may fall, but memory stands.

History

It is sometimes useful to think of a work of literature as being the answer to a question, the pearl formed around some irritating speck of cultural or philosophical grit; we might well wonder what sorts of question would provoke a response like *Beowulf*. There is no scholarly consensus on where, when, why, how, or by whom the story was first created, but whatever its origins, the text that has survived is not a living portrait of heroic society but an act of the historical imagination. The poem's Christian author, looking deep into the pagan prehistory of his own culture, sees both admirable virtues like strength, courage, sacrifice, generosity, and loyalty, and tragic ignorance of the true meaning of the world—we know, for example, that Grendel is a descendant of Cain, but Hrothgar has no idea where he comes from; he does not know his history. Characters are presented in a carefully flattering light (they are extraordinarily pious, for example, but never make explicit reference to any pagan god, using instead generic epithets like 'the Almighty' or 'the Ruler'), but the story is framed by long depictions of distinctively pagan customs forbidden by the church, a ship burial for Scyld and a cremation pyre for Beowulf. The author of *Beowulf* is mindful of the differences as well as the connections between the past and the present, and is concerned with difficult questions of the continuing relevance of those *geardagum* to the present; in this fundamental sense, *Beowulf* is a work of history. It is also, and not unlike many other heroic poems, a profoundly nostalgic work, recreating a world that no longer exists, mourning a way of life that is no longer possible. Migration, conversion, and the twists and turns of several centuries of political development rendered the world of the meadhall practically as distant to the eleventh-century audience of the *Beowulf* manuscript as they are to us.

In her *Inventiones: Fiction and Referentiality in Twelfth-Century English Historical Writing*, Monika Otter notes how frequently twelfth-century historical writing contains the story of a subterranean journey or excavation which unearths a cup or other treasure; she suggests that the excavator is 'a stand-in for the author and the episode a reflection on the complexities of the historian's work' (p. 129). So too in *Beowulf*, like the hapless, nameless thief who plunders the dragon's cave, the poet rifles the hoard of the past to unearth both gleaming treasure and useless trappings. Otter accounts for this sophisticated historical self-consciousness by noting that twelfth-century historians were 'at a threshold between largely oral and largely written modes of historical tradition and therefore more acutely aware than [their] colleagues at most other times of the precariousness of historical transmission' (p. 51). The same may be said of *Beowulf* a century (or more) earlier: it is a poem derived from (or imitating) old stories and songs which had circulated in oral and memorial form, but composed by a Christian author and copied in a manuscript alongside lives of saints and works of pseudo-learned classical geography like the *Letter of Alexander to Aristotle* and the *Wonders of the East*. The story is set firmly in the old heroic world of the meadhall, filled with vibrant song and boasting speech, but the poem is set just as firmly in a manuscript among texts derived from Latin sources, and shelved in the cloistered silence of a monastic library. Like many works of Old English literature, the poem bears the imprint of the effort required to negotiate this passage from older to newer ways of remembering, recording, and retrieving the past. The poem's fascination with *dom*, commemoration, and memorials may reflect its author's awareness that this heroic world was slipping into oblivion, disconnected from the world of written texts and Christian learning, its very memory in danger of being lost.

The Continental tribes who migrated to Britain in the fifth century brought no written histories, only collections of stories and songs; their cultural identity was in part contained in, and their social order legitimized by, this remembered and recited body of praise-poems and heroic tales. Conversion to Christianity offered not only political advantages (such as alliance with the Continental Franks and the Roman/papal *imperium*) but also new motives and structures for centralizing authority, new narratives of universal and sacred history, and new technologies of writing and reading for exploiting these resources. Yet whatever spiritual or practical benefits it might have conferred, the transition to Christianity presented profound challenges as well, and had the potential to disrupt nearly every aspect of daily life from baptism to burial, from the rituals of the agricultural cycle to the ethics of the royal court. In practice, Christianity seems to have accommodated rural customs—seasonal festivals, offerings of propitiation, the wearing of protective amulets, the recitation of charms over medicinal herbs—fairly easily, simply by replacing older sources of symbolic power with new Christian ones like the Cross, the Paternoster, or the saints. But the spread of Christianity in the royal courts and the creation of powerful abbeys and episcopal sees—the story told in Bede's *Ecclesiastical History*—created new centres of cultural gravity; abbots and bishops, some of noble ancestry themselves, had good reason to question the role played by the old stories of heroic ancestors in sustaining the ideological infrastructure of English nobility.

For some, full conversion required not just turning towards Christ and Rome but turning away from the pagan past. Around AD 800 Alcuin, trained at York but schoolmaster in the court of Charlemagne, admonished the head of an English religious house:

Let the Word of God be read at the clergy's meals. There it is proper to hear the reader, not the harpist; the sermons of the Fathers, not the songs of the heathens. What has Ingeld to do with Christ? The house is narrow, it cannot hold them both. The King of heaven will have no fellowship with so-called kings who are pagan and damned, for the Eternal King reigns in Heaven, while the pagan is damned and laments in Hell. The voices of readers should be heard in your houses, not the crowd of revellers in the streets.[3]

Ingeld the Heathobard prince plays a supporting role in *Beowulf* and is mentioned in a jumbled concatenation of heroic lore known as *Widsith*; Alcuin's casual allusion suggests that his story was well known. Alcuin's literary style no less than his spiritual identity was firmly anchored in the Latin textual tradition; he saw no place in the monastery—which effectively held a monopoly on learning, literacy, and manuscript production—for the secular histories of the mead-hall. Their heroes, and by implication those who honoured or imitated them, were consigned to hell. To reject such stories, however (and thus, in the absence of written record, to forget them), was to undo the knots which knit together the secular world. Not all were ready to make such sharp distinctions and countenance such loss: less than a century after Alcuin urged the banishment of secular heroic tales from the monastery, the West Saxon kings were promoting a royal genealogy which traced their ancestry back through legendary figures like Scyld and Sceaf, and pagan gods like Woden, to biblical figures like Noah and Adam.[4] Ancient heroes were still used to authorize royal power, but now they were interpolated into the framework of Christian history. For many, less dogmatic than Alcuin, Ingeld and Christ may have seemed like equally solid pillars of secular aristocratic identity.

The promotion of new narratives of cultural identity for a Christian England occurred in consort, however, with the spread of writing; this necessarily involved the incorporation of stories and traditions, which had existed only orally, into the new archive of textual records. The problem of what to include, what to omit, and where to locate historical and textual authority is faced by nearly all Anglo-Saxon writers who turned memory into written record, from Bede in the early eighth century to hagiographers promoting the cults of local English saints, to the compilers of the *Anglo-Saxon Chronicle* in the ninth-century court of King Alfred. When these writers constructed coherent narratives out of annals, documents, testimonies, and local traditions of varying degrees of completeness and reliability, they had both pragmatic and ideological reasons for including some stories and omitting others; crafting new genealogies for the English was a process of omission and elision as well as construction and preservation. The corpus of songs, stories, sayings, proverbs, rituals, and traditions, which formed the common field of cultural memory, was winnowed, the wheat transcribed into the textual record and the chaff lost to the wind.

Oral performance and textual records are by no means mutually exclusive categories, and their complex interaction in medieval culture has been noted by many scholars. But the difference between 'text' and 'song', however oversimplified, is a useful shorthand to characterize two distinct ways of preserving and transmitting literary or historical information. Songs, which are depicted in *Beowulf* as the primary vehicle for historical remembrance, are performed before an audience and re-created anew at each telling; they are communal acts of 're-membering', which survive only in their circulation. Texts, like the manuscript in which *Beowulf* is preserved, are individual, highly technical products, expensive to produce, copied by learned specialists, and stored in libraries; their contents, relatively fixed in form, are preserved from oblivion but limited in access and subject to individual control. A vivid image of this shift in the locus of historical authority is found in Gaimar's twelfth-century Anglo-Norman *Estoire des Engles*. In the days of Alfred the Great, he asserts,

The clerks kept record. Chronicles it is called, a big book. The English went about collecting it. Now it is thus authenticated; so that at Winchester, in the cathedral, there is the true history of the kings, and their lives and their memorials. King Alfred had it in his possession. And had it bound with a chain. Who wished to read it might well see it, but not remove it from its place.[5]

The accuracy of Gaimar's account is itself questionable, but it offers a striking reminder of the collusion of interests between church and state, each of which had a stake in the construction of historical narratives and the control of cultural memory, and a vivid image of the institutionalized triumph of the textual record. Instead of a shifting collection of stories circulating among and weaving together a community of people, the 'true history' of the English was kept in a book chained in a church, visible but not portable, authorized, sanctified, and privatized. The past had become property.

The song is the dream of the text

In the course of such a great cultural shift, it must have struck more than one copyist or composer of a vernacular text that 'the medium is the message': the transcription of living memory into a textual artefact altered the nature and content of that work as well as the context in which it was produced and received. The development of vernacular textuality made possible not only new ways of recording the past, but also new perspectives on it—songs transmitted by memory keep the past firmly in service to the present, always ancient but always new; texts create a fixed record, separable from both its author and its audience. Their very materiality makes vividly clear that whatever its usefulness or value to the present, the past is firmly Other—old stories either adjust themselves invisibly to changing cultural needs or they disappear from memory, but old books, their texts stubbornly unchanging, simply grow old, ageing into an incoherence which requires translation or commentary, losing leaves or accruing annotations and continuations, stored in the scriptorium or shredded into scraps for more immediate use. The past becomes truly visible only at the fissure of its separation and the moment of its disappearance; a 'sense of history' is inevitably a sense of loss. The energy and anxiety of *Beowulf*'s sense of history arise, I believe, from the poem's situation precisely in the contested cultural area where questions of aristocratic self-formation and national identity met new technologies of memory and a growing recognition of the profound consequences of the shift from oral to textual sources of cultural authority. *Beowulf* is not only about a particular history of certain Danes and Geats, but about History itself: the meaning of the past, the means by which it is recorded, and its remaining value to the present.

We can imagine the world of 'oral culture' only through its traces in a text like *Beowulf*; these traces outline an imaginary cultural space of their own in which the text containing them is somehow invisible or unnecessary, the dream of a poetics without the corporeal restrictions of textual practice, a pastoral of pre-textuality. *Beowulf* strives to set the living world of song and the sustaining power of poetic fame above the insufficiency of material objects to secure lasting memory; the instability and ambivalence of monuments—from Hrothgar's hall to Beowulf's barrow—is unfavourably contrasted with the enduring power of narrative commemoration ('remembering-together'). But the heroic world of oral poetry, gleaming with treasure and gloomy with treachery and the terror of defeat, is in a state of imminent collapse at the end of the poem: the exemplary bravery of Beowulf does not preserve his life, provide for his succession, or even persuade his men to come to his aid; *dom* fails to hold the hall together; and memory is either useless, like the rusted treasures of the dragon's hoard, or destructive, like the simmering feuds which will presumably wipe out Beowulf's people after his death. The past is passing, and where it is not passing, its lingering presence is dangerous and troublesome.

Even those moments in the poem in which a storyteller dramatizes the process of cultural memory itself by making a poetic link between the past and the present—the so-called 'digressions' on Sigemund or Hengist, for example—are more fractured by complexity and ambivalence than they first appear. Sigemund's highly irregular origins, well-known from other traditions, are elided, but obliquely present in cryptic allusions; his exemplary success as a dragon-slayer and treasure-hunter only mocks Beowulf's later failure to achieve the same ends.[6] The story of Hengist is told from the perspective of Hildeburh, helpless witness to the orgy of heroic violence that destroys her family; she places her sons and her brother on the same funeral pyre, endures the murder of her husband at the hands of her kinsmen, and is last seen being carried like a piece of plunder back to her father's hall. Putting her pathos in the foreground prevents us from sharing whatever feeling of triumph the story might have been meant to arouse in the Danes. Neither tale, in effect, unambiguously celebrates the *dom* of a heroic role model or offers a reassuring guide to the present order; as each story falls short of its role as an exemplar, the reader of *Beowulf* is drawn into a more critical position towards the life of Beowulf himself, more attuned to its own ambiguities and insufficiencies. In this way *Beowulf* offers with one hand what it takes away with another; its fantasy of the world of heroic *dom* cannot survive its awareness that such a world is irretrievably gone and cannot, and should not, be recovered.

To some extent, every Old English poem makes a leap of imagination into the cultural gap between the past and the present, the oral and the textual, secular Germanic and Christian Latin values; every vernacular poem is an act of imagined solidarity with the very past it supplants and erases by the poem's existence in a textual community. Situated on the border between two worlds, every line of it is fictive, appropriated, and to that extent contested, discourse. The tension between monuments and memory in *Beowulf* arises from the ambivalence of its cultural circumstances: a textual simulacrum of an oral poetics, a history of heroic society in a post-conversion, post-migration world. The fact that we are able to make such claims at all, of course, is a tribute not to the lasting power of poetic fame but to the tensile strength of parchment and the random play of chance across the inventories of old libraries; our fascination with *Beowulf* is equally a tribute to our enduring need to seek authorization and value in some point of origin in the past. The poem's complex sense of history is a reminder that we should not expect the Anglo-Saxons—assiduous inventors of their own past, obsessed with their own belatedness, negotiating their own competing historical narratives, suffering their own nostalgia for imaginary points of origin—to supply that place of pure, simple, stable presence from which we can derive an 'English literary tradition'. *Beowulf* offers instead a deeply conflicted reflection on the uses of history, the inaccessibility of the past, and the deceptive and ambivalent roles played by memory and literature in the creation of culture. We might hope it will open a window onto the past; we find instead a mirror.

Notes

1. Quotations from *Beowulf* are taken from the edition of Friedrich Klaeber, *Beowulf and the Fight at Finnsburg*, 3rd edn. (Boston: Heath, 1950); translations are my own and are generally adapted from those in R. M. Liuzza, *Beowulf: A New Verse Translation* (Peterborough, ON: Broadview Press, 2000).

2. My thinking on this matter has been profoundly influenced by Eileen Joy, '*Beowulf* and the Floating Wreck of History' (Diss., University of Tennessee at Knoxville, 2001); I am grateful to Professor Joy for sharing this work and her insights with me.

3. For this text and its context, see Donald A. Bullough, 'What Has Ingeld to do with Lindisfarne?' *Anglo-Saxon England*, 22 (1993), 93–125.

4. See David N. Dumville, 'The West Saxon Genealogical Regnal List: Manuscripts and Texts', *Anglia*, 104 (1986), 1–32, and the earlier study of Kenneth Sisam, 'Anglo-Saxon Royal Genealogies', *Proceedings of the British Academy*, 39 (1953), 287–348.

5. Cited in James Campbell, 'What is not Known about the Reign of Edward the Elder', in N. J. Higham and D. H. Hill, eds., *Edward the Elder, 899–924* (London and New York: Routledge, 2001), pp. 12–24, at p. 15.

6. See M. S. Griffith, 'Some Difficulties in *Beowulf*, lines 874–902: Sigemund Reconsidered', *Anglo-Saxon England*, 24 (1995), 11–41.

References and suggested reading

Bjork, Robert E., and John D. Niles, eds. *A Beowulf Handbook*. Lincoln: University of Nebraska Press, 1997. A collection of essays by distinguished scholars on many aspects of the poem and its context; not only a fine guide to the history of *Beowulf* criticism but a reminder of how many of the poem's mysteries remain unsolved.

Earl, James W. *Thinking about 'Beowulf'*. Stanford: Stanford University Press, 1994. A provocative meditation on the poem's meaning to its original audience and to modern scholars.

Frank, Roberta. 'The *Beowulf* Poet's Sense of History'. In Larry D. Benson and Sigfried Wenzel, eds., *The Wisdom of Poetry: Essays in Early English Literature in Honor of Morton W. Bloomfield*. Kalamazoo, MI: Medieval Institute Publications, 1982, pp. 53–65. An elegant study of the depth of the poem's own historical focus.

Hutton, Patrick H. *History as an Art of Memory*. Hanover, NH: University Press of New England, 1993. The field of what might be called 'memory studies' has spread vigorously in the past generation; this book is a useful summary of its development and a guide to its major authors.

Ong, W. J. *Orality and Literacy: The Technologizing of the Word*. London: Methuen, 1982. Ong often overstates his case, but his work remains one of the fundamental starting-points for all later discussions of writing and culture.

Orchard, Andy. *A Critical Companion to 'Beowulf'*. Cambridge: D. S. Brewer, 2003. This excellent recent work explores the stylistic and thematic complexities of the poem.

Otter, Monika. *Inventiones: Fiction and Referentiality in Twelfth-Century English Historical Writing*. Chapel Hill: North Carolina University Press, 1996.

Robinson, Fred C. *'Beowulf' and the Appositive Style*. Knoxville: University of Tennessee Press, 1985. A brief, elegant, and compelling study of the poem's language and style, one of the most widely read modern interpretations of *Beowulf*.

Schaefer, Ursula. 'Ceteris Imparibus: Orality/Literacy and the Establishment of Anglo-Saxon Literate Culture'. In Paul E. Szarmach and Joel T. Rosenthal, eds., *The Preservation and Transmission of Anglo-Saxon Culture: Selected Papers from the 1991 Meeting of the International Society of Anglo-Saxonists*. Studies in Medieval Culture 40. Kalamazoo: Medieval Institute, Western Michigan University, 1997, pp. 287–311. An important introduction to current work on the complex relationship between written and oral works in Anglo-Saxon England.

8

History and memory in the *Anglo-Saxon Chronicle*

Thomas A. Bredehoft

Introduction

Surviving today in seven principal manuscripts, the *Anglo-Saxon Chronicle* is a year-by-year historical account of events (focused on happenings in Britain) from Caesar's invasion in 60 BC up to—and through—the Anglo-Saxon period. Although it was primarily written in Old English prose, the *Chronicle* also includes a handful of poems, including the well-known heroic poem *The Battle of Brunanburh*, which suggests just how closely the *Chronicle* was connected to the literary and political concerns of its time. Further, as it was written by various hands and in various centres from the 890s to the 1150s, the *Chronicle* seems comfortably to straddle the boundary modern readers often draw between Old and Middle English. Linguists consider the earliest section of the Parker Chronicle (Cambridge, Corpus Christi College, MS 173. See plate 2.) as an important example of 'early West Saxon', while portions of the *Peterborough Chronicle* (Oxford, Bodleian Library, Laud Misc. 636) frequently appear in anthologies of Middle English prose. Yet, as the very title '*The Anglo-Saxon Chronicle*' suggests, there is an important sense of continuity and consistency in this work, despite the range and diversity of its origins in space and time, that makes it equally important for us to read the *Chronicle* as a coherent whole. The very continuation of the *Chronicle* across the cultural dislocations prompted by the Norman Conquest stands as a powerful sign of a continuing Anglo-Saxon perspective on English history and a reminder that not all historical accounts are written by the winners.

The *Chronicle*'s vernacularity

The *Chronicle* is unique in relation to contemporary medieval historical literature in its extensive use of the vernacular (Old English) rather than Latin, which remained the European standard for historical composition long after the *Chronicle* was first begun. Almost certainly, the *Chronicle*'s use of Old English stemmed from King Alfred's famous programme of translation and English literary instruction; the *Chronicle* was first composed during Alfred's reign and may well have begun as an extension (and translation) of the 'Chronological Epitome' appended to Bede's *Ecclesiastical History*. Regardless of its specific origins, however, the *Chronicle*'s use of Old English had striking consequences: Old English made the *Chronicle* especially accessible to Anglo-Saxons, and a translation of the *Chronicle* into Latin by the late tenth-century nobleman Æthelweard clearly shows that it was at least sometimes read and appreciated by secular figures, even though the surviving manuscripts seem to have been housed in ecclesiastical centres. As an Old English document, with a palpable cultural presence, the *Anglo-Saxon Chronicle*'s very existence coloured their view of their own history in ways no Latin chronicle could have. Indeed, in this chapter, I will explore some of the most specific ways in which the existence of an Old English *Chronicle* interacted with the Anglo-Saxons' own idea of their history: those places where the chroniclers explicitly identify some event as being unparalleled in the history (or historical memory) of Britain.

The form of the *Anglo-Saxon Chronicle*

Before examining the portions of the *Chronicle* that refer to historical superlatives, it is useful to make a brief survey of the nature of the *Chronicle* and its surviving manuscripts. The first compilation of the *Chronicle*, undertaken during Alfred's reign (and probably under his direction), is now called the Common Stock; after a preface recounting Caesar's invasion, it includes annalistic information from the year one right up until the 890s, when the Common Stock was completed. Not every year has information recorded, but as the Common Stock approaches its present, annals get both more frequent and more extensive, until the Common Stock's record approaches a full-fledged historical narrative. The extensive record of Alfred's reign, of course, supports the notion that the *Chronicle* was first written under Alfred's influence.

The Common Stock gets its name because it is the root from which all of the surviving *Chronicle* manuscripts grow. These manuscripts span the late ninth century to the twelfth century, and together they represent a remarkable record of more or less continuous annalistic activity, since the manuscripts generally brought the *Chronicle*'s record up to date at the moment of their copying, and they often appear to have continued that record for some years afterward. Besides the Parker manuscript (see Pl. 2; conventionally designated as manuscript A: Cambridge, Corpus Christi College, MS 173), originally copied around the turn of the tenth century and with sporadic annals extending to the Norman Conquest, full *Chronicle* manuscripts survive into modern times from the tenth century (B: London, British Library, Cotton Tiberius A. vi), the eleventh century (C: London, British Library, Cotton Tiberius B. i; D: London, British Library, Cotton Tiberius B. iv; and G: now mostly burnt, with fragments preserved in London, British Library, Cotton Otho B. xi); and the twelfth century (E: Oxford, Bodleian Library, Laud Misc. 636; F: London, British Library, Cotton Domitian viii). A single additional twelfth-century leaf (manuscript H: London, British Library, Cotton Domitian ix, folio 9) and the lost exemplars that lie behind some of the surviving manuscripts indicate that the *Chronicle* certainly existed in significantly more copies than now survive, and hence it must have been an important book for the Anglo-Saxons. The very latest entries, in the E manuscript, attest to the *Chronicle*'s continuing relevance nearly ninety years after the Norman Conquest. The *Chronicle*'s record thus undermines easy generalizations that suggest that the Norman Conquest meant the death of Old English as a literary language.

Further, the poems of the *Chronicle* provide crucial evidence of a major literary shift involving formal versification techniques in the tenth and eleventh centuries: the earlier poems (such as annal 937 in manuscripts A, B, C, and D, *The Battle of Brunanburh*) employ the classical alliterative metrical style, while later poems (such as annal 1036 in C and D, *The Death of Alfred*) follow different poetic rules. The use of rhyme in *The Death of Alfred* (annal 1036CD) and in *William the Conqueror* (annal 1086E), in fact, seems to anticipate that aspect of Laȝamon's verse. The possibility that the *Chronicle* poems provide evidence for poetic continuity connecting *Brunanburh* to Laȝamon makes them especially valuable to students of literary history.

The *Anglo-Saxon Chronicle*, then, includes a complex web of interrelated manuscripts spanning two and a half centuries of composition and production. Across this span, it is a nearly continuous (and often nearly contemporary) record of Anglo-Saxon history, sometimes from different, even conflicting, perspectives. Including simple prose narrative, genealogies, poetry, and even some brief passages of Latin, it is both a historical document and a literary monument, one that served as a crucial source for many of the Latin historians of the twelfth and later centuries, including William of Malmesbury, John of Worcester, and Henry of Huntingdon. The *Chronicle*'s use and re-use during the Anglo-Saxon period and well into the twelfth century mark it as one of the most enduring cultural documents of its time, and it is these very features that make the *Chronicle* important for our understanding of the Anglo-Saxon period.

The *Chronicle* and vernacular historiography

Since no tradition of vernacular historiography preceded its composition, there is a sense in which the *Chronicle* needed to make up its own rules as it went along. Although it seems clear that some features of the *Chronicle*, such as the year-by-year format, probably owe their origin to the example of Bede, the late ninth-century chronicler (or chroniclers) nevertheless faced the daunting task of developing a historiographic idiom in Old English. The effort was remarkably successful, and even a cursory reading of the *Chronicle* reveals how powerfully the mode of expression found in the Common Stock set the pattern for later entries. To take just one prominent example, the frequent victories of the Danes are often recorded in the Common Stock with the formulaic phrase, *þa Denescan ahton wælstowe gewald* ('The Danes held the place of slaughter'—annal 833A; cf. also annals 837, 840, and 871).[1] The same phrase is used a century later in annals 999CD (999E has *þa ahton þa Dæniscan wælstowe geweald*) and 1010CDE. Even annal 1066C records the result of the battle between the English under Morcar and Edwin and the Norwegians under Harald and Tostig with the phrase *ond Norman ahton wælstowe gewald* ('And Northmen held the place of slaughter'). It may be going too far to suggest that, in these later examples, the late tenth- and eleventh-century Danish and Norman invasions and victories were intentionally identified with the invasions of the middle ninth century, but it is clear that the patterns of vocabulary and expression that the Common Stock set out (the basic tools of Anglo-Saxon historiography) continued to have a living force for chroniclers generations and even centuries later. The passages which are my main concern in this chapter are the references to the greatest or worst events in memory or in historical time, and these show a similar continuity of expression across two hundred years of the *Chronicle*; as such they can provide useful insights into the world of Anglo-Saxon historiography itself.

The greatest events in memory

Although the references to the greatest events on record or in memory make up only a small portion of the *Chronicle* as a whole, they happen to be associated with many of the *Chronicle*'s most interesting features. Such references span from the Common Stock to the final stretch of the Peterborough manuscript, and they occur in passages of poetry as well as prose. In addition, such references fall rather neatly into two separate categories. On the one hand, the *Chronicle* includes numerous claims about some natural event or circumstance being the greatest in the memory of men, while on the other hand, a number of politically orientated events are identified as superlative with specific reference to preceding historical circumstances: invasions, reigns of kings, and so forth. To understand the *Chronicle*, we must approach an understanding of these references to history and memory; I turn first to the *Chronicle*'s invocations of human memory as the basis for superlative claims.

It is, perhaps, surprising to modern readers to find that most prominent among the claims of the greatest events in living memory are notices of massive cattle plagues. In annals 1041E, 1111E, 1115E, and 1131E, we read of such cases of *orfcwealm*. Typical is this notice from annal 1111E: *ond gewearð se mæsta orfcwealm þe ænig man mihte gemunan* ('And there was the greatest killing of cattle that any man might remember'). As the dates of these notices suggest, several of these cases of *orfcwealm* may indeed have occurred within the span of one chronicler's memory; but it is important to note that, for readers, the force of the superlative remains. The *Chronicle*'s record implies a succession of cattle plagues, each worse than the last; the chroniclers' decision to sequence the superlatives may not have been intended to suggest increasingly destructive plagues, but to readers of the *Chronicle* such was surely the resulting effect.

Most of the other events identified in the *Chronicle* as being remarkable within the memory of men involve similar sorts of natural occurrence. We see notices of the greatest wind in memory, for example, in annals 1009E, 1103E, and 1118E. A series of other events from the natural world are recorded in similar terms: harsh winters in annal 1046C (with both *mancwealm* and *orfcwealm*) and annal 1115E, famines in annals 1005E and 1043E, sea-floods or ebb-tides in annals 1099E and 1114E, a great wildfire in annal 1032E, and remarkable circles around the sun in annal 1104E. The frequency with which the memory of men is used to indicate the exceptional nature or degree of these natural events is notable: clearly the chroniclers felt that human memory was the proper time-frame in which to assess (or describe) the impact of such natural disasters and occurrences. Such events deserve a place in the historical record, the *Chronicle* implies, not because they necessarily stand out in the narrative of historical time, but rather because their prominence in the memory of men gives them a historical significance.

The greatest events in history

By contrast, the kinds of event referred to as the greatest ever or as the greatest in history tend to concern political or military events from the world of men; only one purely natural event is identified as the greatest ever: the sea-flood described in annal 1014E. Likewise, only one strictly political event is identified as the greatest in memory, when we read in annal 1107E, *ðera wæron swa fela swa nan man næs þe gemvnde þæt æfre ær swa fela to gædere gyfene wæron* ('Of these [bishoprics and abbacies] there were so many that there was no man who could recall that so many were ever before given away together'). But both of these clearly stand as counter-examples to the general trend, which associates human memory with exceptional natural events and historical time with political events. And it is the latter sort of events and records that give us the clearest insights into the *Chronicle*'s vision of history.

The earliest passage in the *Chronicle* which invokes such a historical comparison falls in annal 851 of the *Chronicle*'s Common Stock. The earliest surviving record of this annal is in the Parker (A) manuscript, where we read of the Danish invasions of that year, concluding with the claim that Æthelwulf and his army *þær þæt mæste wæl geslogon on hæþnum herige þe we secgan hierdon oþ þisne ondweardan dæg* ('[They] there accomplished the greatest slaughter of a heathen army that we have heard tell of to this present day'). This passage is remarkable for the phrase *secgan hierdon*, which is a familiar formula from the poetic tradition, where it serves to identify things or events known from common report. It is significant that, during the composition of the Common Stock, when there were (as yet) no English books of history, the chronicler's invocation of historical time falls back upon a formulaic phrase from the poetic tradition: before the *Chronicle*, the only recourse for making historical comparisons in the Old English tradition lay in the common report of men and in the memory of poets.

Fascinatingly, the next such historical comparison in the *Chronicle* falls within the *Chronicle*'s first poem, *The Battle of Brunanburh*. This poem's concluding lines read:

> Ne wearð wæl mare
> on ðis eiglande   æfre gieta,
> folces gefylled,   beforan þissum
> sweordes ecgum,   þæs þe us secgað bec,
> ealde uðwitan,   siþþan eastan hider
> Engle *ond* Seaxe   up becoman,
> ofer brad brimu   Brytene sohtan,
> wlance wigsmiðas,   Weealles ofercoman,
> eorlas arhwate   eard begeatan.
>
> (annal 937A, lines 65b–73)

There was never before on this island greater slaughter, peoples felled by the edges of swords, before this, as books tell us, old authorities, since Angles and Saxons came up here from the east over the broad seas, proud war-smiths sought Britain, bold earls overcame the Welsh, seized the homeland.

Here, the historical comparison explicitly invokes books of English history; although *The Battle of Brunanburh* itself is a poem, the superlative comparison derives its strength now from the authority of books, rather than the common report of annal 851.

In later annals, books are rarely invoked to identify historical superlatives as explicitly as in *Brunanburh*, although a passage concerning a great fleet of ships in annal 1009CDE uses the same *þes ðe us bec secgað* formula. Rather, later entries pick up on *Brunanburh*'s reference to some earlier historical event to support the superlative. In *Brunanburh*, Æthelstan's victory is identified as the greatest since the Saxon invasion of Britain. In a brief poetic passage in annal 979DE, the same comparison is made regarding the murder of Edward the Martyr:

> Ne wearð Angelcynne nan wyrsa dæd   gedon þonne þeos wæs
> syððon hi ærest   Brytonland gesohton
>
> (979E, lines 1–3; relineated)

There was no worse deed done amongst the English race since they first sought the land of Britain.

In the annal 1036CD poem, a similar claim is made about the murder of Alfred Ætheling, although the time-reference now points back to the Danish conquest of the island rather than the Saxon conquest:

> Ne wearð dreorlicre dæd   gedon on þison earde
> syþþan Dene comon   *and* her frið namon.
>
>   (annal 1036C, lines 6–7)

There was no more miserable deed done in this land since the Danes came here and made peace.

The shift in the specifics of the historical comparison (from the worst deed done since the English came to the worst since the Danes came) serves to identify the English treachery as worse than any perpetrated by the Danes (who, in this poem, are the peacemakers). But in both cases, the power of the superlative derives from the reference to a specific event in English history. The record of the *Chronicle* itself underlies the rhetorical effect of these superlative claims; such claims are possible only once the *Chronicle* itself has come into existence.

Other claims of historical superlatives generally do not make reference to specific historical events, instead identifying occurrences as the greatest ever, or the greatest ever seen. In annal 1045C, for example, there was a great ship-army gathered, *swa nan man ne geseh scyphere nænne maran on þysan lande* ('such that no man had seen any greater ship-army on this land'). This particular claim seems especially interesting because it falls within a short series of annals with repeated superlative claims (although not all of them fall within the main scope of this chapter). Thus we read of the following things in the following annals:

Famine; corn more dear than in memory	annal 1043E (1044C)
Greater ship-army than ever seen	annal 1045C
Stronger winter than in memory	annal 1046C
A very great plague	annal 1047C
A great earthquake	annal 1048C
An immeasurable army	annal 1049C

Some of these items are reflected in D as well, although often without the claims of great size or extent seen in the C manuscript. A pattern such as this one may well reflect the habits of a particular chronicler, since the C manuscript's annals for the late 1040s (starting with annal 1045C) seem to reflect contemporary chronicling activity. The possibility that the C-chronicler's apparent penchant for superlative expression also marks him as the primary author for at least annal 1044C (and thus annal 1043E) would seem to be worth further investigation. Just as the patterns of expression shared by the chroniclers in general attest to a shared historiographic idiom, evidence such as this seems to suggest that individual chroniclers may at least sometimes also have had identifiable habits or characteristic modes of expression.

Other examples of events being 'the greatest seen' or 'the greatest ever' abound. In annal 1066CD, there are great tokens in the heavens (including Halley's comet) *swylce nan mann ær ne geseh* ('such as no man had seen before'). Here the juxtaposition of natural events (the appearance of a comet) with the political and martial upheavals of 1066 suggests the comet itself (in the *Chronicle*'s use of this trope) takes the greater portion of its significance as a betokening of significant human, political events than from its status as a natural phenomenon. In annal 1129E, the election of competing popes led to the following comment: *Nu wearð swa mycel dwylde on Cristendom swa it næfre ær ne wæs* ('Now there was such great heresy in Christendom as there never before was'). In annal 1077E the burning of London was *swa swyðe swa heo ær næs syðþan heo gestabeled wæs* ('As great as it never was before since it was established'). Such widespread and varied examples attest to the continuing power and usefulness of this mode of historical comparison.

In annal 1066CD, we see a similar usage in reference to the great armies raised by Harold to oppose Tostig. In the C manuscript, we read, *þa \ge/gadorade he swa mycele scipfyrde ond eac landfyrde swa nan cingc ær her on lande ne gegaderade* ('Then he [Harold] gathered so great a ship-army and also a land-army as no king here in [this] land had previously gathered'). Remarkably, the D version of the same passage reads somewhat differently: *And Harold cyng, his broþor, gegædrade swa micelne sciphere ond eac landhere swa nan cyng her on lande ær ne dyde* ('And Harold the king, his brother, gathered such a great ship-army and also a land-army as no king here on [this] land had previously done'). The changes between these versions provide a good illustration of some of the difficulties of working with the *Chronicle*. Like the C version, the D manuscript here explicitly identifies Harold as *cyng*, but the specific words used in D (*sciphere* rather than *scipfyrde*) may provide significant clues about the annal. As is generally recognized, *scipfyrde* always refers to the English army, while *sciphere* was used to refer to either the English or the Danes. Considering that Tostig's army, rather than Harold's, is usually associated with the invading northerners, the lexical choice seen here in D seems interesting, at the least. It seems clear that the different accounts of the events of 1066 seen in the C and D versions of the *Chronicle* reflect different political or historical perspectives, but assessing the precise implications of those perspectives is often, as here, quite difficult.

The *Chronicle*'s final invocation of this historiographic strategy falls within the very passage from annal 1137E that is frequently anthologized in collections of Middle English literature: *Wes næure gæt mare wre\c/cehed on land. ne næure hethen men werse ne diden þan hi diden* ('There was never before such wretchedness in the land, nor did heathen men ever do worse than they did'). The forms of the language had certainly changed by the time this annal was composed (probably shortly after 1154), but it is fascinating to see that this twelfth-century chronicler employs much the same rhetorical strategy to describe the horror of Stephen's reign as had been used by previous chroniclers in tenth- and eleventh-century annals. Indeed, this passage explicitly refers to the invasions of pagan Danes in previous centuries: the force of the comparison makes powerful use of the *Chronicle*'s own record of those invasions.

Conclusion

The significance of the two modes for drawing superlative historical comparisons that I have described in the *Chronicle* should not be underestimated. As I have shown, exceptional natural events are generally identified in the *Chronicle* as the greatest or worst in memory, while political and military events are assessed against spans of historical time (the greatest ever, or the greatest since some specific historical event). Indeed, the historical record as preserved in history books is sometimes explicitly invoked. On the one hand, the dual nature of this historiographic strategy tells us something crucial about the Anglo-Saxon idea of history: natural events are interesting, even outstanding, in terms of human lifespans and human memory, while political events take their significance in terms of historical events and of historical time itself. For Anglo-Saxons, 'history' was certainly understood as political history.

Further, it is worth while to note the degree to which the linkages between natural events being superlative in memory and human events being superlative in comparison to historical time remained remarkably consistent in the *Chronicle*, occurring across nearly the full two and a half centuries that spanned the *Chronicle*'s composition. Such a consistency certainly reflects the cultural pervasiveness of the *Chronicle*'s perspective. Once the pattern had been set, generations of chroniclers seem both to have understood that pattern and to have followed it. The existence of the *Chronicle* itself, it seems, powerfully reflected and, arguably, coloured the Anglo-Saxon view of history, in ways both subtle and significant.

It is especially important to realize the implications of the continuation of the *Chronicle*—and its habits and perspectives—for nearly ninety years after the Norman Conquest. In the mid-twelfth century, a time that a modern perspective often identifies as solidly Norman in its outlook, Anglo-Saxon chroniclers continued to write the *Anglo-Saxon Chronicle*, and in their continued invocations of historical time and the memory of men, they sustained a fascinatingly (and characteristically) Anglo-Saxon viewpoint on events. Even in, and perhaps especially in, the post-Conquest records of cattle plagues and great winds, we see the *Chronicle*'s continuation as both a cultural document and a cultural force, far into the Norman period.

Note

1. Throughout, I identify quotations from the *Chronicle* through the simple expedient of identifying the relevant annal number followed by the letter of the manuscript. Doing so, however, risks obscuring the actual sources of my quotations, and so it is necessary to spell out those sources here. All quotations are taken from the respective multi-volume edition of *The Anglo-Saxon Chronicle: A Collaborative Edition*. Quotations from the A (or Parker) Chronicle are taken from 'MS A', ed. Janet Bately, *The Anglo-Saxon Chronicle*, iii (Cambridge: D. S. Brewer, 1986); manuscript C is cited from 'MS C', ed. Katherine O'Brien O'Keeffe, *The Anglo-Saxon Chronicle*, v (Cambridge: D. S. Brewer, 2001), while those from manuscript D are cited from 'MS D', ed. G. P. Cubbin, *The Anglo-Saxon Chronicle*, vi

(Cambridge: D. S. Brewer, 1996). Charles Plummer, ed., *Two of the Saxon Chronicle Parallels* (Oxford: Clarendon Press, 1892–9) remains the standard edition of manuscript E. If a passage is present in more than one manuscript, I usually cite it from the earliest. Throughout, conventional manuscript abbreviations are expanded, with the expansions generally indicated by italics.

References and suggested reading

Bately, Janet. '*The Anglo-Saxon Chronicle*': Texts and Textual Relationships. Reading: University of Reading, 1991. This book examines textual evidence for the interrelationships of the various *Chronicle* manuscripts and related works such as Asser's *Life of Alfred* and Æthelweard's *Chronicle*. Dense, but packed with information.

Bredehoft, Thomas A. *Textual Histories: Readings in the 'Anglo-Saxon Chronicle'*. Toronto: University of Toronto Press, 2001. This book examines the prose, verse, genealogies, and Latin passages of the *Chronicle* in their manuscript context and traces the cultural significance of the *Chronicle* across time.

Clark, Cecily. 'The Narrative Mode of *The Anglo-Saxon Chronicle* before the Conquest'. In Peter Clemoes and Kathleen Hughes, eds., *England Before the Conquest*. Cambridge: Cambridge University Press, 1971, pp. 215–36. This essay discusses continuities and shifts in the *Chronicle*'s strategies of narration.

Dumville, David. 'Some Aspects of Annalistic Writing at Canterbury in the Eleventh and Early Twelfth Centuries', *Peritia*, 2 (1983), 23–57. This essay looks at the manuscripts of the *Chronicle* located at Canterbury near the end of the Anglo-Saxon period and identifies this time and place as being especially important for our understanding of the *Chronicle* and its manuscripts.

Swanton, Michael, ed. and trans. *The Anglo-Saxon Chronicle*. London: J. M. Dent, 1996. This book is the most recent translation of the *Chronicle*, a page-by-page rendering of Charles Plummer's multi-text edition of 1892–99. It contains numerous and useful notes and genealogical tables.

Thormann, Janet. 'The *Anglo-Saxon Chronicle* Poems and the Making of the English Nation'. In Allen Frantzen and John D. Niles, eds., *Anglo-Saxonism and the Construction of Social Identity*. Gainesville: University of Florida Press, 1997, pp. 60–85. This essay discusses many of the *Chronicle*'s poems and suggests their importance for understanding Anglo-Saxon conceptions of an English national identity.

9

The persuasive power of Alfredian prose

Nicole Guenther Discenza

In the ninth century 'England' did not yet exist. Over the decades, Viking wars helped whittle the several separate Anglo-Saxon kingdoms down to two, Wessex and Mercia, while the rest became the Danelaw, an area under Viking control. Alfred the Great was born around the middle of this tumultuous century, the youngest son of the king of Wessex. After his four older brothers died, in 871 Alfred became king of a land beleaguered by Vikings—and promptly retreated into a swamp. He fought his way back out and drove the Vikings out of Wessex and the kingdom of Mercia, which he brought under Wessex influence. By his death in 899, he had secured an Anglo-Saxon kingdom that formed the core of what his son and grandson would make England.

Yet Alfred did not spend all his time on military matters. He initiated a programme of translation and education, and he translated four Latin texts himself. Latin was the language of learning and the élite, an international language of churchmen and churchwomen. Almost all books, from schoolbooks to the Bible to the writings of the church fathers, were available only in Latin; Greek had been lost, and evidence shows very little translation or original writing in Old English before Alfred.

Alfred began his programme with a letter known as the Preface to the *Pastoral Care*, his translation of Gregory the Great's *Regula pastoralis* (*Rule for Pastors*). The Old English text (see Pl. 3) is often reprinted and translated, making this short piece of writing now Alfred's best-known work—and with good reason. The Preface is both a landmark historical document and a complex literary text. It explains Alfred's goals and methods in establishing his programme of translation and education, alerting both historians and literary scholars to its significance. The Preface also exemplifies many qualities of the programme itself. Its syntheses of varied sources with Alfred's own words, and moral with practical elements, embody the programme's methodology. The Preface looks to the biblical and classical past but seeks to bring important texts into the Anglo-Saxon present and establish an Anglo-Saxon future through a new kind of education and new treasures. Alfred's rhetorical and literary strategies contribute power and artistry to a developing English prose style. Thus the Preface gives us a brief but memorable introduction to the era's prose.

Alfred's programme

Alfred's Preface seems so rich and complete that it is often anthologized alone, or occasionally with small excerpts from other Alfredian-era texts. Yet the Preface was never meant to stand alone. It introduces one of Alfred's own translations, the *Pastoral Care*, serves as an invitation to all the translations, and exemplifies the methods and goals of the Alfredian translation programme as a whole.

To write his Preface, Alfred weaves together the familiar format and wording of contemporary writs (official letters) with sources ranging from Jerome, one of the church fathers, to Sirach (also known as Ecclesiasticus, one of the lesser-known scriptures of the secondary canon). The mix of recognizable and difficult sources parallels his work in his own translations, where he often weaves together his main source text with a range of other sources to clarify and develop the meaning of the text. At the same time, much of the Preface has no direct source; Alfred follows models and takes quotations from a number of sources but supplies very much his own emphasis and argument.

All the translations synthesize practical and moral elements;

earthly and spiritual success go hand in hand in the translations of Alfred's programme. Both religious and lay audiences incapable of reading Latin texts can find in the programme a Christian way of life that is also a successful Anglo-Saxon way of life. As Alfred adapted different sources for use in his Preface, so the translations adapt, to a greater or lesser extent in different texts and in the hands of different translators, a Christian lifestyle to the Anglo-Saxon leader.

The body of Alfred's *Pastoral Care*, his translation of Gregory the Great's work for pastors, tells both religious and lay leaders how to live a Christian life and how to direct and care for those under them. His translation of the first fifty Psalms remains fairly close to the scriptural text, but adds introductions drawn from other sources to help readers understand the figurative and moral meanings of the Psalms and apply them to their own lives. His *Boethius*, a translation of Boethius's *Consolation of Philosophy*, exhorts readers to pursue what is truly worth while: God. They should abandon worldly concerns as much as possible, though (in a departure from Boethius's own text) they must fulfil the earthly responsibilities God has given them. Finally, Alfred's *Soliloquies* (from Augustine of Hippo's text) argues that the soul lives eternally, giving men and women a responsibility to live well here so as to deserve a good afterlife. Alfred finishes Augustine's incomplete two books with a third compiled from other sources.

Other translators follow much the same lines. Wærferth's *Dialogues* translate another text by Gregory the Great, this one illustrating the power of leading a holy life with many stories of saints and miracles. The *Orosius*, an anonymous translation of Paulus Orosius's *History against the Pagans*, sometimes draws on other sources as well. It demonstrates the futility of empire and the superiority of Christian nations. The *Bede*, an anonymous translation of Bede's *Ecclesiastical History of the English People*, was probably part of Alfred's programme and perhaps even a coda to it. This work demonstrates God's work in English history and the English people turning from their old religions to Roman Christianity. Finally, *The Anglo-Saxon Chronicle* creates an original account of the English people, which culminates in the successful reign of Alfred himself (until later continuators added later events). Thus Alfred's Preface, and his own translations, set the tone for a whole programme of translation.

Past, present, and future

In Alfred's age, Latin was the clerics' language, and kings were warriors, not scholars. Very few people could speak or read Latin at all, and not many Anglo-Saxons could read their mother tongue, Old English. The king had to persuade readers to value royal teachers and written English texts. The Preface draws its authority first from history. Alfred describes a Golden Age of Anglo-Saxon learning and prosperity in the distant past:

me com swiðe oft on gemynd, hwelce wiotan iu wæron giond Angelcynn, ægðer ge godcundra hada ge woruldcundra; ond hu gesæliglica tida ða wæron giond Angelcynn; ond hu ða kyningas ðe ðone onwald hæfdon ðæs folces on ðam dagum Gode ond his ærendwrecum hersumedon; ond hie ægðer ge hiora sibbe ge hiora siodo ge hiora onweald innanbordes gehioldon, ond eac ut hiora eðel gerymdon; ond hu him ða speow ægðer ge mid wige ge mid wisdom; ond eac ða godcundan hadas hu giorne hie wæron ægðer ge ymb lare ge ymb liornunga, ge ymb ealle ða ðiowotdomas ðe hie Gode don scoldon; ond hu man utanbordes wisdom ond lare hieder on lond sohte . . . (3.2–12)[1]

it comes very often to my mind, how many wise men there were formerly around England, both in religious offices and secular; and how happy times were around England then; and how the kings who had the rule of the people in those days obeyed God and his messengers; and they held peace and proper conduct and authority within, and also expanded their rule outward; and how they succeeded both in war and in wisdom; and also how eager the religious orders were both concerning lore and learning, and concerning all the services which they owed to God; and how men from abroad sought wisdom and learning here in this land . . .

The Anglo-Saxons' own past sets a precedent for Alfred's revival of learning and for wisdom among both religious and lay people. Yet after this Golden Age, learning declined badly in England: knowledge of Latin was lost, few could even read English, and Anglo-Saxons went abroad to learn. Instead of trying to re-establish Latin learning as in the past, when Anglo-Saxons could not imagine Latin being lost, Alfred will revive learning by rendering important books into English: *we eac sumæ bec, ða ðe niedbeðearfosta sien eallum monnum to wiotonne, ðæt we ða on ðæt geðiode wenden ðe we ealle gecnawan mægen* ('we also render some books, those which are most necessary for all men to know, into that language which we can all know', 7.6–8).

Because these were not just any books, but authoritative religious texts, Alfred drew precedent also from Judaeo-Christian heritage traced through Greco-Roman tradition:

Ða gemunde ic hu sio æ wæs ærest on Ebreisc geðiode funden, ond eft, ða hie Creacas geliornodon, ða wendon hie hie on hiora agen geðiode ealle, ond eac ealle oðre bec. Ond eft Lædenware swæ same, siððan hie hie geliornodon, hie hie wendon ealla ðurh wise wealhstodas on hiora agen geðiode. Ond eac ealla oðræ Cristnæ ðioda sumne dæl hiora on hiora agen geðiode wendon. (5.25–7.5)

Then I recalled how the law was first established in the Hebrew language, and again, when the Greeks learned it, then they turned it all into their own language, and also all other books. And again the Romans did the same: as soon as they learned it, they translated it all through wise translators into their own language. And also all other Christian peoples translated some portion into their own language.

Alfred knew that the Hebrew Old Testament had been translated into Greek, and then the Bible was translated into Latin. What 'other Christian peoples' Alfred might have meant is uncertain; the Anglo-Saxonist Francis P. Magoun speculates (in 'Some Notes', p. 100) that Alfred might have known of translations into Syriac, Coptic, or Slavic, and probably Wulfila's Gothic Bible or some Old High German renderings. In any case, Alfred presents his programme as part of a long and prestigious tradition.

Alfred's Preface not only draws upon past precedents, but situates itself very much in the Anglo-Saxon present. Recently, he says, few on this side of the river Humber could read any Latin, and not many on the far side; Alfred thanks God that they have any teachers at all now. Much has been lost. The churches have been sacked, their books and other treasures destroyed. Still, a circle of learned men at court can read Latin and aid Alfred: he names Archbishop Plegmund, Bishop Asser, and the priests Grimbold and John. Alfred and his helpers will renew English by providing the churches with books that readers can understand, as they learn to read their own native language, and with more tangible treasures.

Alfred reveals his vision for a future England. As Kathleen Davis points out ('National Writing in the Ninth Century', pp. 620–1), Alfred's history includes no mention of past wars between kingdoms, nor any acknowledgement that there *were* separate kingdoms; he unites the people with one term, *Angelcynn*, meaning both the English people and this land they inhabit. Moreover, Alfred projects a future of wealth and wisdom for the Anglo-Saxon people.

Wealth and wisdom

The 'wisdom' Alfred mentions repeatedly in his Preface emerges in his translations as a knowledge of God, a participation in divine wisdom. Yet this virtue is not merely an intellectual one; while books can form and inform wisdom, the learner must practise it or forget it like any other skill. Modern readers might separate practical know-ledge from 'book learning', but Alfred's term 'wisdom' slips easily and unselfconsciously between the two: *Ure ieldran, ða ðe ðas stowa ær hioldon, hie lufodon wisdom ond ðurh ðone hie begeaton welan ond us læfdon* ('Our ancestors, who held these places before, loved wisdom, and through it they acquired wealth and left it to us', 5.13–15); the Anglo-Saxons have now lost *ge ðone welan ge ðone wisdom* ('both the wealth and the wisdom', 5.17).

Wisdom is a treasure in itself, an intangible but great good. Yet perhaps more importantly for some readers, wisdom brings more tangible treasures such as those that used to fill the Anglo-Saxon churches, and losing wisdom caused the loss of physical treasures. The linkage of wealth and wisdom, concepts not always allied in the Anglo-Saxon mind, provides a central theme of the Preface— and an incentive for readers to follow Alfred's programme. The investment of labour in learning to read and, for some, in writing and copying books, will pay off. Books are both possessors of sym-bolic value, in the knowledge in their pages, and valuable objects in themselves, the products of significant labour and expense. Books are among the treasures that belonged to the churches before the pillaging, which also included gold and silver objects such as chalices and crosses.

Alfred's programme will restore both kinds of treasure. The king and his helpers will produce books to further wisdom among the Anglo-Saxons. This particular book, the *Pastoral Care*, will bear a more tangible treasure: *on ælcre bið an æstel, se bið on fiftegum*

*mancessa. Ond ic bebiode on Godes naman ðæt nan mon ðone æstel
from ðære bec ne do, ne ða boc from ðæm mynstre* ('on each [book]
shall be an *æstel*, which shall be worth fifty mancuses. And I command in God's name that no one shall remove the *æstel* from the
book, nor the book from the minster', 9.1–3). The meaning of *æstel*
has long been the subject of dispute, with suggestions ranging from a
bookmark or pointer to a book cover. Whatever it was, it must have
been ornamented with gold and gems: based on Magoun's estimates
(in 'Some Notes', p. 105), it would seem that each *æstel* consisted of
130 ounces of gold or its equivalent. The books would enrich the
churches intellectually and physically, and they were to be sent to
every bishop in the land, and copied later. With Alfred's programme,
wealth and wisdom will once again abound in Anglo-Saxon England,
the Preface declares.

Rhetorical and literary strategies

Of course, when Alfred embarked on his radical programme of
education and translation, he had to convince his readers to commit
time, effort, and resources to reading and perhaps writing—skills the
laity did not usually plan to learn. His invocation of the past and
vision for the future could only go so far in persuading church leaders
who might see no need for an educated laity, and warrior nobles who
would want to re-establish wealth, but probably without investing
their own intellectual energies. Alfred therefore uses several further
strategies to win over readers.

First, he appeals directly to his addressees, church leaders whose
support he would need. The Preface begins as a letter: *Ælfred kyning
hateð gretan Wærferð biscep his wordum luflice ond freondlice* ('King
Alfred bids Bishop Wærferth to be greeted with loving and friendly
words', 3.1–2), one copy of the Preface starts; each copy would have
the name of a different bishop, making a personal appeal to the
bishops of Canterbury, Dorchester, Exeter, Hereford, Lichfield,
London, Rochester, Sherborne, and Worcester. Alfred's later explicit
thanks to his four helpers not only gives Plegmund, Asser, Grimbold,
and John a pat on the back, it demonstrates that the king remembers
those who assist him in his efforts and thanks them publicly. Both

religious and lay leaders could see that their efforts would not be forgotten.

Alfred next co-opts his audience by appealing to their best intentions: phrases such as *forðon ic ðe bebiode ðæt ðu do swæ ic geliefe ðæt ðu wille* ('therefore I ask that you do as I believe that you want to do', 5.1–2), and *Forðy me ðyncð betre, gif iow swæ ðyncð* ('Therefore it seems better to me, if so it seems to you', 7.6) both draw readers into agreement with Alfred while seeming to defer respectfully to their judgements, which he *knows* are for the best. Telling the bishops not to allow the *Pastoral Care* to be taken from the minster except to lend it or have it copied suggests to the bishops that they should circulate the book when they can and keep it carefully the rest of the time. Alfred refrains from outright commands, instead simultaneously urging and praising his readers.

Even more subtly, the Preface takes as a given the king's crucial role in Christian education and seeks to inculcate a similar sense of responsibility in all the readers, as do all the programme's translations. Anglo-Saxon and Continental kings sponsored scholars and writers, who dedicated texts to their patrons, but for a king to undertake translation himself was unprecedented. Alfred spends no time defending his work but presents it as the obvious choice, forcing his audience to adjust their assumptions about kings.

The king devotes more attention to his prospective students. He carefully explains that his programme of education will not draw men away from important matters:

eall sio gioguð ðe nu is on Angelcynne friora monna, ðara ðe ða speda hæbben ðæt hie ðæm befeolan mægen, sien to liornunga oðfæste, ða hwile ðe hie to nanre oðerre note ne mægen, oð ðone first ðe hie wel cunnen Englisc gewrit aædan: lære mon siððan furður on Lædengeðiode ða ðe mon furðor læran wille ond to hieran hade don wille. (7.10–15)

all the youth of free men which are now in England, who have the means that they might devote themselves to it, be set to learning, as long as they are not capable of other employment, until they can read English writing well; afterwards teach a man further in the Latin language as much as you want to teach him and to promote him to higher office.

The king begins by reassuring families that they will not lose sons when they need them. He also appeals to their pride. Only those with the *sped*—the means, opportunity, and ability—will be educated.

These would be the children of the élite, not boys who would work the land but those who would become fighters and leaders. Some few will continue their studies, but only if they are to attain higher positions in the church or government. Alfred offers his readers a win-win situation: noble boys will become further distinguished from their social inferiors. Some will then assume family responsibilities, while some few (perhaps younger sons?) will take other positions of authority after further schooling.

The passage assumes that just as the king has a responsibility for his people's learning his officials have a responsibility to learn. *Gewrit* means 'writing', but also 'official letter': the future leaders of England must know how to read a letter from their king or bishop. Less obviously, Alfred's sponsorship of the programme, and his own work of translation, puts leaders, both lay and religious, in the king's debt: they owe their wealth and wisdom to him. The programme envisions a land in which the most powerful share the same education, binding them to each other, to the king, and to the particular set of ideals and values he has selected for their training.

Alfred weaves potentially controversial statements together with points of consensus. Who would not like to recall a golden past of wealth and learning? Who could deny the recent troubles? When Alfred suggests this programme as a solution to the problems, his advice seems as natural as his reading of history. When Alfred writes, *Geðenc hwelc witu us ða becomon for ðisse worulde, ða ða we hit nohwæðer ne selfe ne lufodon ne eac oðrum monnum ne lefdon: ðone naman anne we lufodon ðætte we Cristne wæren, ond swiðe feawe ða ðeawas* ('Think what punishments then will await us for this world, when we neither loved [wisdom] ourselves nor allowed other men to do so; the name alone we loved that we were Christian, and very few of the practices', 5.5–8), he makes a very serious accusation, but without quite blaming the reader. He levels the charge conditionally: great punishments await, *unless* we act as Christians. Earlier he appealed to readers' dreams of wealth and power; now he speaks to fears of loss well-founded in these years of Viking attacks. Including himself in the first-person plural pronoun also lessens the potential sting of the warning. He then outlines what it means to live as a Christian.

Moreover, Alfred constructs much of the Preface as an internal debate. He speaks several times of what he thinks or remembers: *me com swiðe oft on gemynd* ('it has very often come into my mind', 3.2), *gemunde* ('I remembered', twice in 5.8; once each in 5.18, 5.25, and 7.15). He also questions himself and then answers: *ða wundrade ic swiðe swiðe . . . Ac ic ða sona eft me selfum andwyrde ond cwæð* ('then I wondered very greatly . . . But then I answered myself soon again and said', 5.18–19, 21–2). Therefore he need not argue directly against anyone but can rebut possible objections. Alfred's confiding tone seems to let us in on his own thoughts, binding writer and readers together.

Thus the Preface offers implied arguments: that this particular programme of translation and education is necessary for the future; that the Anglo-Saxons *have* a future, in a unified England (not a foregone conclusion during the Viking wars); that the bishops should commit themselves to this programme; and that all those who can participate should learn as much as time and ability permit. While these claims are radically new, Alfred's argumentation is subtle and consequently potent: he makes it very difficult to identify his arguments as arguments and hence to object to them. His use of history to authorize the programme gives him a solid foundation on which to build his other appeals.

The Preface also outlines a specific method of translation to reassure readers that, even if they never learn Latin, they will benefit from these originally Latin texts. The passage quoted above about translations of scripture does not just give historical justification; as Kathleen Davis writes, 'This carefully detailed sequence corresponds closely to Alfred's sequential description of his own translation process: *when* the Greeks and Romans had learned the law and the books, *then* they translated them through wise interpreters; *when* Alfred had learned *Pastoral Care* from his bishops and priests, *then* he interpreted it and turned it into English' (in 'The Performance of Translation Theory', pp. 154–5). Alfred's programme relies on a core group of learned men with Alfred at its heart and on a process of learning before writing. Alfred's method of translation seems simple and straightforward: *ða boc wendan on Englisc ðe is genemned on Læden Pastoralis, ond on English Hierdeboc, hwilum word be worde, hwilum andgit of andgiete* ('to translate into English the book which is named in Latin *Pastoralis* and in English *Shepherdbook*, sometimes word for word, sometimes sense for sense', 7.18–20) as his helpers taught him the book: *Siððan ic hie ða geliornod hæfde, swæ swæ ic hie forstod, ond swæ ic hie andgitfullicost areccean meahte, ic hie on English awende* ('After I had learned it, just as I understood it,

and as I could most meaningfully render it, I turned it into English',
7.23–5). Alfred's 'sometimes word for word, sometimes sense for
sense' derives from Jerome's explanation of how he rendered the
Hebrew and Greek Bible into the Latin Vulgate, avoiding the loss of
meaning an excessively literal translation causes. Alfred's most
learned readers would recognize his use of a formulation by one of
the church fathers. Yet Alfred's practice is not as clear as it may
seem from these simple phrases: *when* is it word for word, and *when*
sense for sense? How much input did Alfred's helpers have in the
final translation? Alfred's explanation of his translational practice at
times sounds as though it explains more than it truly does, but its
simplicity and apparent clarity seem calculated to inspire confidence. Even if they do not recognize his quotation of Jerome, the
audience can rest assured that Alfred knows exactly what he is
doing.

Through argumentative skill and literary art, Alfred crafts a Preface
to win over a variety of readers to his views on wisdom and responsibility. For Alfred silently asserts the ability of the English language to
convey arguments with beauty as well as authority. At one point,
Alfred visualizes the loss of learning:

Swelce hie cwæden: Ure ieldran, ða ðe ðas stowa ær hioldon, hie lufodon
wisdom ond ðurh ðone hie begeaton welan ond us læfdon. Her mon mæg
giet gesion hiora swæð, ac we him ne cunnon æfterspyrigean, ond forðæm
we habbað nu ægðer forlæten ge ðone welan ge ðone wisdom, forðæmðe we
noldon to ðæm spore mid ure mode onlutan. (5.13–18)

As if they said: 'Our ancestors, those who held these places before us, they
loved wisdom, and through it they produced wealth and left it to us. Here one
may yet see their track, but we do not know how to follow after them'—and
therefore we have now lost both the wealth and the wisdom, because we did
not want to bend our minds to that track.

This vivid imagery calls to mind what must have been a favourite
occupation of many readers, hunting, and aligns it with a new
occupation, learning.

Alfred also illustrates his Preface with a series of contrasts between
the former splendour of England and its near ruin. The long opening
passage quoted above populates readers' minds with wise men, servants of both God and king, who valued peace but were successful in
war, knew their books and performed their duties, both lay and

ecclesiastical, and attracted students from other lands. This contrasts with the recent past:

Swæ clæne hio wæs oðfeallenu on Angelcynne ðæt swiðe feawa wæron behionan Humbre ðe hiora ðeninga cuðen understondan on Englisc, oððe furðum an ærendgewrit of Lædene on Englisc areccean; ond ic wene ðætte noht monige begiondan Humbre næren. Swæ feawa hiora wæron ðæt ic furðum anne anlepne ne mæg geðencean besuðan Temese ða ða ic to rice feng. (3.13–18)

So completely had [learning] declined in England that there were very few on this side of the Humber who could understand the services in English, or further render a letter from Latin into English; and I think that there were not many beyond the Humber. So few of them were there, moreover, that I cannot think of a single one south of the Thames when I succeeded to the kingdom.

Specific geographical details in the two passages paint first a lively portrait crowded with successful officials before the downfall of learning and then a more recent picture populated by few men of learning. The order of past and present is reversed a little later when Alfred recalls *ærðæmðe hit eall forhergod wære ond forbærned, hu ða ciricean giond eall Angelcynn stodon maðma ond boca gefyldæ* ('before it was all ravaged and completely burnt, how the churches around all England stood filled with treasures and books', 5.9–10). The rich churches contrast with the total destruction, the intensifier *for-* added to the verbs of pillaging and burning.

With these briefly sketched but striking images, the Preface persuades readers to see the past, present, and future through Alfred's eyes and to value what he values. His construction of the English language and people, with the repeated word *Angelcynn*, meaning both the English people and the land they occupy, simultaneously instils and plays upon Anglo-Saxon pride. The argumentation and literary craft together demonstrate that English, the language of the people, can convey complex and subtle content—whether the reader is a sophisticated churchman, who may recognize Alfred's scriptural references and subtle argumentation, or a layman or poor cleric just learning to read, who can marvel at the vividness of the king's short letter.

Conclusion: the Preface's afterlife

To what extent Alfred's programme succeeded in crafting a new Christian, Anglo-Saxon reader is a subject for another essay. The effects of the programme apparently did not match the dream the Preface offers, for we find no evidence for a sudden explosion in lay literacy and spirituality. Yet an increasingly educated and centralized government followed Alfred as England became the unified land that his term *Angelcynn* envisions. Continuators *did* add to the *Anglo-Saxon Chronicle*, and scribes copied the works of Alfred and his circle for later readers. The Benedictine Reform in the century after Alfred may have realized more of his vision, as monks grew in learning and spirituality while maintaining a hand in governance.

Alfred's Preface to the *Pastoral Care* is a very powerful piece of writing and provides an excellent point of entry to one of the most important authors in Old English, and indeed one of the most fruitful periods of Old English prose. The Preface, with its combination of learned sources and originality, argument and ornament, persuasion and co-option, offers more than a short chapter can hope to reveal. Well over a millennium after its writing, in a world vastly changed from what the king knew, Alfred's Preface still rewards careful readers.

Note

1. All primary text citations refer to *King Alfred's West-Saxon Version of Gregory's Pastoral Care*, ed. Henry Sweet, EETS 45, 50 (London: N. Trübner and Co., 1871); translations are my own.

References and suggested reading

Keynes, Simon, and Michael Lapidge. *Alfred the Great: Asser's Life of King Alfred and Other Contemporary Sources*. New York: Penguin, 1983. Keynes and Lapidge offer good introductions, translations, and notes to Asser's life of Alfred and several selections from Alfred's own works, including the Preface to the *Pastoral Care*, which they translate on pp. 124–6.

King Alfred's West-Saxon Version of Gregory's Pastoral Care. Ed. Henry Sweet. Early English Text Society 45, 50. London: N. Trübner and Co., 1871. This is the standard edition of Alfred's Old English translation, including the Preface. Sweet provides an introduction and a modern English translation of the entire text.

Davis, Kathleen. 'National Writing in the Ninth Century: A Reminder for Postcolonial Thinking about the Nation', *Journal of Medieval and Early Modern Studies*, 28 (1998), 611–37. Davis analyses Alfred's work, especially the Preface, as it helps to create an early English nation.

Davis, Kathleen. 'The Performance of Translation Theory in King Alfred's National Literary Program'. In Robert Boenig and Kathleen Davis, eds., *Manuscript, Narrative, Lexicon: Essays on Literary and Cultural Transmission in Honor of Whitney F. Bolton*. Lewisburg, PA: Bucknell University Press, 2000, pp. 149–70. This essay examines Alfred's approach to translation as explained in the Preface and how Alfred's programme helps create a sense of an English nation.

Discenza, Nicole Guenther. 'Wealth and Wisdom: Symbolic Capital and the Ruler in the Translational Program of Alfred the Great', *Exemplaria*, 13 (2001), 433–67. This essay explores in detail the cultural, social, and political work of Alfred the Great's programme, using the Preface to the *Pastoral Care* as one of the base texts for understanding Alfred's goals and methods.

Discenza, Nicole Guenther. ' "Wise wealhstodas": The Prologue to Sirach as a Model for Alfred's Preface to the *Pastoral Care*', *Journal of English and Germanic Philology*, 97 (1998), 488–99. This item identifies and analyses Alfred's use in his Preface of the Prologue to Sirach, a book from the Bible's secondary canon (which Catholics call deuterocanonical and Protestants call apocryphal).

Magoun, Francis P., Jr. 'Some Notes on King Alfred's Circular Letter on Educational Policy Addressed to his Bishops', *Mediaeval Studies*, 10 (1948), 93–107. This seminal article illuminates many different aspects of the Preface and forms a foundation for later work.

Shippey, T. A. 'Wealth and Wisdom in King Alfred's *Preface* to the Old English *Pastoral Care*', *English Historical Review*, 94 (1979), 346–55. Shippey examines Alfred's conception of wisdom and his representation of history in the Preface.

Szarmach, Paul. 'The Meaning of Alfred's *Preface* to the *Pastoral Care*', *Mediaevalia*, 7 (1980), 57–86. This essay examines Alfred's sources, use of rhetoric, and conception of wisdom.

10

Old English religious prose: rhetorics of salvation and damnation

Thomas N. Hall

Even though they were all nominally Christian by the time King Alfred came to power in the late ninth century, most of the inhabitants of early medieval Britain could claim only a rudimentary grasp of Christian theology as gleaned from the Lord's Prayer and Creed and what little instruction they received from the clergy, who were themselves poorly educated. The weighty questions that had occupied the church fathers on the meaning of grace, the nature of the Trinity, and the relationship between Christ's divinity and his humanity were largely unknown to the average person. But an area of inquiry that gripped their imagination and that kept them in touch with a long tradition of Christian speculation was the fate of the soul after death. What happens to the righteous and the wicked when they die? Where do they go? What are their rewards and punishments? What does the physical landscape of the world beyond the grave look like? Where are paradise and hell located? What role do the angels and demons play there? And what should the living do now to prepare ourselves for Doomsday? To judge from the abundant supply of literary texts from pre-Conquest England that address these questions, the Anglo-Saxons were deeply curious about such matters, which all fall within the category of religious thought known as eschatology (from the Greek *eschatoi*, meaning 'the last things'). Numerous works of Old English religious prose, including dozens of sermons, homilies, and saints' lives from the tenth and eleventh centuries, provide excruciatingly detailed (and from a modern perspective highly entertaining) answers to these questions, and their depictions of death, Judgement, and the afterlife are among the most memorable in all of early medieval literature.

Biblical and apocryphal models

When seeking answers to questions on any aspect of religious belief, the Anglo-Saxons naturally started with the Bible as the foundational document of Christianity, but the Bible turns out to be disappointingly reticent on the central problems of eschatology. True, the biblical book of Revelation (or Apocalypse, as it was known in the Middle Ages) speaks at length about the signs presaging Judgement Day and the advent of Antichrist, but in highly abstract and symbolic language that did not suit the concrete imagination of the early Middle Ages. Besides, Christ's own pronouncement concerning the timing of the Last Judgement that 'of that day and hour no one knows, no not the angels of heaven, but the Father alone' (Matthew 24: 36) made it clear that answers to questions about the last things constituted hidden knowledge, unavailable from the Bible, that would have to be sought elsewhere.

So elsewhere the Anglo-Saxons turned, finding a ready store of information about the last things in the sprawling body of ancient and medieval writings known as apocrypha, some loosely imitative of canonical books of the Bible, some embodying literary traditions inherited from ancient Jewish apocalypticism. Chief among these is a popular Latin narrative known as the *Vision of St Paul*, a late-antique apocryphon that fuelled much medieval visionary literature and that even survives in a partial Old English translation from eleventh-century Canterbury. In the *Vision of St Paul*, the apostle Paul is transported bodily to the third heaven, where he is given a tour of the abode of the righteous by an angelic guide, then is conveyed to the abyss, where he is shown the dwelling-place of the damned. In the process he discovers that the rewards of the blessed in paradise and the torments of the damned in hell are all calculated to reflect the crimes or merits of the individual soul, a notion of corresponding justice—of punishment fitting the crime—that exerted a lasting influence on medieval representations of divine otherworld judgement (as worked out, for instance, in Dante's *Divine Comedy*). In the hell depicted in the *Vision of St Paul*, sinners who in life mocked the church must gnaw their tongues for eternity, while those who broke their fast prematurely are chained just out of reach of mouth-watering foods. Other features of the *Vision of St Paul*, such as an ascent through multiple heavens, a weekly respite for the damned, a daily accounting to God of each soul's deeds by a guardian angel, a torment whereby sinners hang from their hair or eyebrows above a river of billowing flame, and a treacherous bridge over which damned souls must cross into hell, all became standard features of medieval visionary literature from the Old English period onwards.

A second apocryphon that informed Anglo-Saxon eschatology is the *Apocalypse of Thomas*, a fifth-century Latin text that purports to be a letter from Christ to his apostle Thomas containing a prophecy of the tumultuous events that will take place on the last seven days leading up to Doomsday. On day one, a mighty voice will cry out in heaven and blood will rain upon the earth. On day two, the earth will tremble, the gates of heaven will open, and smoke and fire will cover the sky. On day three, the air will be filled with the stench of brimstone, and so on. The work survives in four separate Old English prose translations as well as an Irish verse translation from the seventh century, and the catalogue of signs marking the last days spun off several independent lists of the portents of Doomsday, which grew to include bleeding trees, groaning sea monsters, and the loss of human language. Like the *Vision of St Paul*, the *Apocalypse of Thomas* was freely adapted for Old English sermons in the tenth and eleventh centuries, presumably for purposes that included preaching to lay communities, and while virtually nothing is known about the authors and translators of these texts or about the audiences to whom they were directed, their survival in the vernacular may be taken as a sign of the appeal which apocryphal literature held for a broad segment of the population, not just the educated élite.

Visions of death

A critical focus of much eschatological literature is the moment of death, an event defined in the early Middle Ages as the parting of body and soul. For those who had lived a good life, this was of course a thoroughly positive experience, a welcomed entry into eternal bliss. The deaths of saints are accordingly joyful occasions often foretold in visions and accompanied by miracles. According to a story told by Bede in his *Ecclesiastical History*, the death of St Ethelburga, a seventh-century abbess of Barking Abbey, was foreseen in a waking vision by one of her nuns, Tortgyth. One morning just before dawn, Tortgyth witnessed a human body wrapped in a shroud and shining brighter than the sun levitate out of the house where the sisters slept. As Tortgyth watched, the body was raised into the open heavens, lifted by cords that were brighter than gold. The vision came true when the devout abbess died just a few days later. As Bede tells it, 'her soul was drawn up to heaven by her good deeds as though by golden cords'. In the entry for 15 June in the ninth-century *Old English Martyrology*, the simultaneous deaths of the child martyr St Vitus and his companion, St Modestus, are marked by a public vision of their joint ascension. After a series of adventures in southern Italy, Vitus and Modestus meet their end when, in the words of the Martyrologist:

Godes engel hine [St Vitus] þa gelædde ond his festerfæder mid hine, Sanctum Modestum, on þæs flodes neaweste se is cweden Siler. Þær gesegon Cristne men heora sawle fleogan to heofonum swa swa culfran, ond hi wæron seofon siðum hwittran þonne snaw.

An angel of God then led him [St Vitus] and his fosterfather St Modestus with him into the vicinity of a river called Siler. Christians there watched their souls fly to heaven just like doves, and they were seven times whiter than snow.

Other saints foretell their own deaths. St Cuthbert, in Book 4 of Bede's *Ecclesiastical History*, informs his good friend the hermit Herebert that the day of his own death is fast approaching, and Herebert is understandably dismayed. So tightly knit are Cuthbert and Herebert in the bonds of spiritual friendship, in fact, that they both expire on the same day, and their souls are together borne aloft by angels. In the version of the *Life of St Benedict* which Ælfric includes in his second series of *Catholic Homilies*, compiled in the 990s, Benedict announces his own impending death, arranges for his grave to be dug a week in advance, and expires only after the church has made suitable preparations. The eighth-century Mercian saint Guthlac of Croyland, whose life is memorialized by several prose and poetic texts in Latin and Old English, is warned by an angel of his coming death, which he reluctantly reports to his attending servant and understudy, Beccel. On the day of Guthlac's death, Beccel knows the hour is at hand when he sees Guthlac's hermitage lit up with a fiery brightness from midnight till dawn, and an ambrosial odour like the nectar of sweet-smelling flowers emanates from Guthlac's mouth. As Guthlac sends forth his spirit, a tower of light fills the house stretching from earth to heaven and guides his soul to its eternal home.

The deaths of sinners are depicted less often in Old English, but not because the Anglo-Saxons knew no stories about the grisly demise of wicked men. Exemplary tales of exactly this kind abound in medieval sermon literature, including a Latin sermon by Gregory the Great (died 604) that was adapted by Ælfric for two of his *Catholic Homilies*. The story concerns a pompous Italian nobleman named Chryserius who was afflicted with inordinate pride and avarice. At the very moment he was about to leave his body, he was visited by a swarm of black spirits who threatened to snatch him away to the dungeons of the lower world. Chryserius trembled and cried out for help, turned this way and that to escape the gaze of the demons, and begged for a reprieve from death until at least the next day, but to no avail. As his family looked on, his soul was wrested from his body and was carried off to hell. Ælfric concludes the story by adding the cold moralizing comment that *seo gesihð him wearð æteowed for oþra manna beterunge na for his agenre* ('this vision was presented to him for the improvement of other men, not for his own'). A comparable demonic encounter concludes Gregory's nineteenth Gospel homily, which was twice translated into Old English, first by Ælfric and then in an anonymous eleventh-century Lenten sermon known as Bazire-Cross Homily VI. All three texts relate the anecdote of a young monk who had never seriously embraced his profession and lived a dissolute life even in the monastery. When stricken with the plague one summer, he found himself on his deathbed facing a vision of a dragon that had risen from hell to devour him. His fellow monks implore him to sign himself, but he exclaims: 'I want to sign myself, but I cannot! The dragon is holding me down! The foam from its mouth is spread over my face! It has me by the throat! I cannot sign myself! It is squeezing my arms together, and it has already swallowed my head!' The insistent prayers of the monks at his side fortunately succeed in chasing the dragon away, and the young man hastily converts, but never fully recovers. As in other death-scene narratives, the moment of death opens a window to the soul that reveals the individual's true spiritual state, implicitly aligning the soul with either the blessed or the damned even before judgement has taken place.

Visions of judgement

Meditations on death led inevitably to speculation about the fate of the soul after death and on when exactly the soul should receive its final reward, whether as soon as the soul vacates the body (an immediate individual judgement) or at a far distant time on Doomsday (an ultimate universal judgement). Both doctrines have their proponents, backed by an arsenal of biblical and patristic argument, and an Old English poem from the tenth century known as *Soul and Body* even allows for a compromise position, claiming that the departed soul of a wicked sinner must return to the grave where its body is housed once a week for up to three hundred years before it is sent to hell for eternity. Each week when it returns to its body, the soul condemns its flesh for the multitude of carnal sins it committed during life, enacting a recurrent sabbatical judgement from which the body has no escape. In other Anglo-Saxon texts, such as a sermon by Ælfric for the octave of Pentecost, a suspended state of the soul in an interim paradise between death and final judgement anticipates the later medieval doctrine of purgatory, which was not clearly defined until the twelfth century.

The most colourful judgement scene in all of Old English prose occurs in a sermon from the tenth-century Vercelli Book known as Vercelli Homily IV. In Vercelli IV, first the soul and body of a good man, then the soul and body of a wicked man, in each case having been separated since death, are brought back together on Doomsday to confess their sins and face judgement before God. As God directs his angels to receive the soul and body of the blessed man into heaven, the soul addresses its body, praising it for its good works and virtues, including constancy and moderation. The narrator then pauses to describe the metamorphosis that the body goes through as it transforms from dead flesh to a resplendent vessel of light fit to house the blessed soul in heaven:

Men þa leofestan, utan geðencan hu glædlice ⁊ hu wynsumlice ⁊ hu fægre ⁊ hu mildlice heo sprycð, sio sawl, to hire lichaman, ðonne hio ærest ðas word sprycð þe ic ær nemde. Þonne bryt se lichoma on manigfealdum bleon; ærest he bið on medmicles mannes hiwe, þonne æt nehstan on þam fægerestan manes hiwe; swa æt nehstan þæt he þara wyrta fægernesse, lilian ⁊ rosan, ⁊ þonne swa forð þæt he hæfð gelic hiw golde ⁊ seolfre ⁊ swa þam deorwyrðe-stan gymcynne ⁊ eorcnanstanum; ⁊ æt nehstan þæt he glitenað swa steorra, ⁊ lyht swa mone, ⁊ beorhtað swa sunna þonne hio biorhtust bið scinende.

Most dearly beloved, let us consider how gladly and how joyfully and how beautifully and how mercifully she speaks, that soul, to her body when she first speaks those words that I have just related. Then the body turns into various forms: first it has the appearance of a small man, then secondly the appearance of a most beautiful man. Then after that it possesses the beauty of those plants the lilies and roses, and then so forth, until it has a colour like that of gold and silver and like the most valuable gems and precious stones. And afterward it twinkles like a star and gleams like the moon and shines like the sun when it is shining most brightly.

The body and soul are then reunited and are ushered into eternal rest singing praises to God. Then follows the judgement of the wicked man. In a fearful voice, the wicked soul rebukes its body for neglect-ing to think about the fate of its soul, and for wallowing in the sins of gluttony, slander, theft, and immoderate laughter. The soul's lament continues until the castigated body can take no more, and the corpse undergoes a morbid transformation from sin-stained flesh to coal-black imp, a transformation that is paralleled by a corresponding shift in the colour of the soul:

Men þa leofestan, þonne stent ðæt deade flæsc aswornod, ⁊ ne mæg andwyrde syllan þam his gaste, ⁊ swæt swiðe laðlicum swate, ⁊ him feallað of unfægere dropan, ⁊ bryt on manig hiw. Hwilum he bið swiðe laðlicum men gelic, þonne wannað he ⁊ doxaþ; oðre hwile he bið blæc ⁊ æhiwe; hwilum he bið collsweart. 7 gelice sio sawl hiwað on yfel bleoh swa same swa se lichoma, 7 bið gyt wyrsan hiwes. 7 standaþ butu swiðe forhte 7 bifigende onbidað domes.

Most dearly beloved, the dead flesh then stands confounded, and he can give no answer to his soul and sweats with a very foul sweat, and unpleasant drops fall from him, and he changes into many colours. At first he is like a very loathsome man, when he grows black and darkens; another time he is pale and colourless; at another moment he is coal-black. And likewise the soul transforms into an evil colour in the same manner as the body, and yet it is of a worse colour. And they both stand very afraid and await judgement with trembling.

The devil then steps forward to claim the wicked soul and body as his own, and together they enter the house of perdition. In this judgement scene, interestingly, God plays only a minor role, leaving the job of enumerating the virtues and vices to the soul itself. According to the understanding of sin, salvation, and judgement pre-supposed here, the capacity for good or evil resides within the body, not the soul, and the ultimate fate of the soul is determined not by God but by the soul through its public confession before an assembly of witnesses, a concept that makes sense only within the early Insular tradition of penitential confession. As a proverbial statement found in several Old English sermons declares, it is better to suffer shame for one's sins before a single man (the confessor) in this life than it will be to have one's sins openly paraded before God and all angels and demons and men at the Last Judgement.

From a separate tradition entirely comes the dramatization of the last days in Pseudo-Wulfstan Homily XLII, an account of the advent and career of Antichrist based on Adso of Montier-en-Der's tenth-century Latin tract *On Antichrist*. As a summation of early Christian teachings on this mysterious figure, who is only dimly represented in the Bible, Adso's tract constructed the first fully-fledged biography of Antichrist from his birth in Babylon following the reign of a last world emperor to his ultimate battle with the risen Christ on Doomsday. With the devil's assistance, Antichrist will gather followers about him by preaching in Jerusalem and raising men from the dead, and he will perform a series of unnatural miracles to demonstrate his awesome and unholy powers:

He deð ðæt fyr cymð færlice ufan swylce hit of heofonum cume and egeslice forswælð fela þinga on eorðan. And treowa he deð færlice blowan and eft raðe asearian. And sæ he deð on lytelre hwile beon ungemetlice and ungecyndelice swyðe astyrode and þærrihte eft sona smylte. And mistlice gesceafta he awent of heora gecyndum: wæter he deð þæt yrnð ongean stream; þas lyfta and windas he astyrað to ðan swiðe þæt mannum þincð heora dead leofra þonne egesan to gehyranne.

He will cause fire to descend swiftly from above as if it were coming from heaven and would terrifyingly engulf many things on earth. And he will cause trees to bloom suddenly and then quickly wither. And he will cause the sea within a short time to be extremely and unnaturally churned up and immediately after that to be calmed. And he will turn various creatures away from their natural state: he will make water flow upstream; he will stir up the skies and winds to such an extent that it will seem to men that they would rather die than hear such terrifying things.

But at length Antichrist's identity will be revealed by the prophets Enoch and Elias, whose preaching will also convert the Jews to Christianity. The timing of these events is not far off, the homilist warns, and we should begin preparing now lest we be caught unawares by Antichrist's deceptions. Together with the Doomsday scenarios inspired by the *Vision of St Paul* and *Apocalypse of Thomas*, accounts of Antichrist such as this one borrowed from Adso provided ample material for literary representations of the final days.

Visions of heaven and hell

From the Bible and the apocrypha as well as from ancient Germanic and classical mythology, the Anglo-Saxons inherited a nuanced range of ideas about the nature and physical make-up of the otherworld. In sermons detailing the joys of heaven and pains of hell these ideas typically become compressed into a small number of highly mannered rhetorical formulas. Accounts of heaven routinely rely on the contrastive formula 'x without y' to portray heaven as a place defined just as much by the absence of bad things as the presence of good things. In Vercelli Homily XXI, for instance, the joys of heaven include life without death, youth without age, beauty without alteration, honour and bliss without end, joy without unhappiness, light without darkness, and tranquillity without clouds. By comparison hell is a place typified by sorrow without joy, toil without respite, darkness without light, pain without end, fire without extinction, and discord without peace.

Vercelli Homily IX provides an especially elaborate and rhetorically sophisticated account of hell that hinges on the idea that the torments of hell are so unspeakably awful that no living human can possibly express them. As the homilist puts it:

Þeah .vii. men sien, ⁊ þara hæbbe æghwylc twa ⁊ hundsiofontig gereorda, swa feala swa ealles þysses middangeardes gereorda syndon, ond þonne sy þara seofon manna æghwylc to alife gesceapen, ⁊ hyra hæbbe æghwylc siofon heafdu, ⁊ þara heafdu ælc hæbbe siofon tungan, ⁊ þara tungena ælc hæbbe isene stemne, ⁊ þonne hwæðre ne magon þa ealle ariman helle witu.

Even if there were seven men, and if each one had seventy-two languages (as many languages as there are in this world), and then if each of those seven men were granted eternal life, and if each one had seven heads, and if each head had seven tongues, and if each tongue had an iron voice, still they would not be able to enumerate all the pains of hell.

Rhetorically this passage makes use of two conventions that are frequently employed in early medieval religious writings with clear antecedents in classical literature. One is the *topos* of inexpressibility (hell is so terrifying that it cannot be put into words). The other is a rhetorical device known as numerical *gradatio* which functions as a mathematical formula: each man has seven heads, each head has seven tongues, and so on exponentially, giving the impression that the sum total is practically infinite but governed none the less by a strict ordering principle. The capacity of these seven hypothetical men to give voice to the pains of hell is paradoxically both unimaginably great and precisely measurable, yet in the end it is still inadequate to reduce the pains of hell to language. Both rhetorical devices are brought together as early as Book 6 of Virgil's *Aeneid*, where in the midst of their tour of the nether regions, Virgil's Sybil attempts to convey to Aeneas the inexpressible severity of the torments suffered by the denizens of Hades when she declares that 'If I had a hundred tongues, a hundred mouths, and a voice of iron, I could not sum up all the forms of crime or rehearse all the tale of torments.' The *gradatio* device in Vercelli IX can thus be traced back to Virgil, but it is structured around an incremental multiplication of the number seven, a number of common biblical import, and it is supplemented by a reference to the seventy-two languages in the world, an apocryphal motif based on the number of disciples in the New Testament. (In the early Middle Ages it was commonly believed that there were seventy-two nations in the world, seventy-two languages, seventy-two disciples, and seventy-two books in the Bible, a witness to the numerical consistency of the divine plan.) The passage thereby neatly folds together elements of classical, biblical, and apocryphal learning into a tightly knit numerically ordered package.

Similar feats of rhetorical dexterity carry through the rest of the homily. Later in Vercelli IX another numerical *gradatio* is employed to describe a beastly hound of hell that appears to be a distant cousin of the classical Cerberus:

On helle sy an hund . . . He hafað hundteontig heafda, 7 he hafað on ælcum heafde hund eagena, 7 ælc þara egena is fyre hat, 7 he hafað .c. handa, 7 on ælcre handa hundteontig fingra, 7 on ælcum fingre .c. nægla, 7 hyra is ælc on nædran wisan ascyrped.

In hell there is a hound . . . He has a hundred heads, and in each head he has a hundred eyes, and each of his eyes is as hot as fire, and he has a hundred hands, and on each hand a hundred fingers, and on each finger a hundred nails, and each nail is sharpened in serpent fashion.

And another of the homilist's efforts to characterize the horrors of hell results in an inexpressibility formula the gist of which is that if a damned soul in hell were ever permitted to escape, he would be so relieved that he would sink into a peaceful slumber so deep that nothing could ever wake him up:

Þeah mon þone garsecg mid isernum weallum utan betyne, 7 hine þonne fyres afylle up oþ heofnes hrof, 7 hine þonne utan besette mid smiþnylium 7 heora æghwylc oðrum ætrine, 7 sy to ælcum þara man togeset and ælc þara manna hæbbe Samsones strenge . . . 7 man þonne sette iserne þele ofer þæs fyres hrof 7 þæt sy eall mid mannum afylled 7 heora æghwylc hæbbe hamor on honda, 7 hit þonne aginne eal samod brastlian 7 þa bylias blawan 7 þæt fyr dynian 7 þa hamoras beatan, hweþere for eallum þyssum gedyne ne mæg seo sawl awacian seo þe wæs ær ane niht on helle.

Even if the ocean were closed up from the outside with iron walls and then filled with fire up to the roof of heaven and then surrounded by smiths' bellows so that each one touched the other, and if a man were placed at each bellows, and if each of those men had the strength of Samson . . . and if an iron plate were then placed over the roof of the fire, and if it were all filled with men and each had a hammer in his hand, and if they all then began to bang on it together and blow the bellows and cause the fire to roar and beat the hammers, none the less in spite of all this commotion the soul that earlier resided in hell for a single night could not wake up.

In another Old English homily, from the tenth-century Blickling collection, an attempt to provide a more realistic description of hell relies on a portion of St Paul's account of hell from the *Vision of St Paul* blended with several lurid details familiar from Old English heroic poetry:

Swa sanctus Paulus wæs geseonde on norðanweardne þisne middangeard þær ealle wætero niðergewitað 7 he þær geseah ofer ðæm wætere sumne harne stan 7 wæron norð of ðæm stane awexene swiðe hrimige bearwas 7 ðær wæron þystrogenipo 7 under þæm stane wæs niccra eardung 7 wearga 7 he geseah þæt on ðæm clife hangodan on ðæm isgean bearwum manige swearte saula be heora handum gebundne 7 þa fynd þara on nicra onlicnesse heora gripende wæron swa swa grædig wulf 7 þæt wæter wæs sweart under þæm clife neoðan.

St Paul was looking at this northern part of the world, where all waters go down, and there he saw over the water a grey rock, and to the north, grown all the way out of the rock, were frosty groves, and in that place were mists and darkness, and under the rock was the dwelling-place of water-monsters and wolves. And he saw that on the cliff many black souls were hanging on the icy groves, bound by their hands; and the hellish enemies of those black souls, in the likeness of water-monsters, were taking hold of them even as a greedy wolf would do; and the water was black under the cliff from beneath.

Hell is located in the north, as it often is in Old English poetry, and the hellish terrain centred on the river of torment and hanging punishments from the *Vision of St Paul* has been populated by water-monsters and greedy wolves, both fixtures of Old English secular verse. As in the ornate descriptions of hell in Vercelli Homily IX, one can see multiple literary traditions falling together here.

Not only is Old English religious prose the largest, the earliest, and the most diverse body of religious prose among early medieval European vernaculars, but its intellectual heritage is far richer than that of neighbouring literatures. As the passages touched on above suggest, Anglo-Saxon authors had a hearty appetite for biblical, apocryphal, classical, and patristic writings, especially if such writings ventured into eschatological territory. The Old English sermon corpus is unparalleled for its synthesis and embellishment of competing eschatological traditions drawn from numerous quarters. While many of these Old English sermons are direct translations from Latin, a reflex of the centuries-old method of Latin-based textual study in Anglo-Saxon schools, the merging of Latin themes and rhetorical devices with home-grown literary conventions cultivated specifically for the English idiom shows how fully Anglo-Saxon authors had seized control of this literary form for their own tastes and purposes.

References and suggested reading

Caie, Graham D. *The Judgment Day Theme in Old English Literature.* Copenhagen: Publications of the Department of English, University of Copenhagen, 1976. A useful introduction to Old English literature concerned with death, Doomsday, and the afterlife.

Gatch, Milton McC. *Preaching and Theology in Anglo-Saxon England: Ælfric and Wulfstan.* Toronto: University of Toronto Press, 1977. Analyses writings on Doomsday, with a full discussion of the two most prominent Anglo-Saxon homilists.

Healey, Antonette diPaolo, ed. *The Old English Vision of St. Paul.* Cambridge, MA: Harvard University Press, 1978. The eleventh-century Old English version of the *Vision of St Paul* edited (but not translated).

James, M. R. *The Apocryphal New Testament.* Oxford: Oxford University Press, 1924; repr. with corrections, 1953. Modern English translations of both the Latin *Vision of St Paul* and the *Apocalypse of Thomas.*

Kabir, Ananya Jahanara. *Paradise, Death and Doomsday in Anglo-Saxon Literature.* Cambridge Studies in Anglo-Saxon England 32. Cambridge: Cambridge University Press, 2001. A full and fascinating account of what Anglo-Saxons believed to happen in the years intervening between death and Judgement Day in Old English texts.

Scragg, Donald G. ed. *Vercelli Homilies and Related Texts.* Early English Text Society o.s. 300. Oxford: Oxford University Press, 1992. Contains editions and sources of all the Vercelli Homilies, together with a full introduction and a glossary.

Wright, Charles D. *The Irish Tradition in Old English Literature.* Cambridge Studies in Anglo-Saxon England 6. Cambridge: Cambridge University Press, 1993. Discusses in detail many intriguing correspondences between Old English and early Irish eschatological literature.

11

Centralizing feminism in Anglo-Saxon literary studies: *Elene*, motherhood, and history

Stacy S. Klein

Introduction

One of feminist theory's most profound commitments is to the study of gender, or the myriad of social, psychological, and political values assigned to masculinity and femininity that have prevented women (and to a lesser extent men) from living full and meaningful lives. When feminists speak of apprehending certain aspects of the world as intolerable and of creating a more just one, what many have in mind is a world in which gender roles are taken up as a variety of playful possibilities rather than as a set of cultural norms enforced in strict accordance with biological sex. Feminist literary criticism is driven by the belief that representational systems such as literature may help to create such a world—by contributing to enhanced understandings of gender norms and their construction, and by enabling readers to envision new ways of living as gendered beings. As Drucilla Cornell reminds us, 'There is a necessary aesthetic dimension to a feminist practice of freedom.'[1] In other words, freedom from gender stereotypes begins with the ability to imagine alternatives. This essay seeks to show how reading Old English poetry through the lens of feminist criticism sheds new light on the myriad of gender stereotypes that have accrued to motherhood, a cultural phenomenon which remains one of the most difficult and debated issues in feminism.

Motherhood stands at a crucial nexus between biology and social practice and has provoked profoundly divided responses among feminists. Many have rejected motherhood on the grounds that its strong associations with female physicality and infant care-giving both epitomize and contribute to women's exclusion from realms of intellectual, political, and social privilege, and to the entrenchment of cultural myths centred on women's 'natural' propensities for self-sacrifice and domesticity. Others have embraced motherhood as a specifically female form of experience which promises to erode imagined boundaries between self and other that historically have underwritten acts of domination and colonization, and as a form of social interaction that heralds the possibility of remaking the world in the image of maternal love. The radical possibilities of motherhood are memorably encapsulated in Helen Cixous's contention that 'She [a woman] writes in white ink', which envisions a powerful link between women's capacities to produce the 'good mother's milk' that sustains infant life and an emancipatory poetics of political resistance that might sustain us all.[2]

Yet the continued tendency in Western culture to either devalue or to romanticize motherhood, as well as the practical conflicts between motherhood and economic success, makes clear that neither a wholesale rejection or embracing of motherhood will prove an effective political position for changing the material realities and cultural conceptions of motherhood. What has emerged among feminists instead is a shared sense of the need to change the social conditions of mothering (e.g. by increasing access to child-care facilities), as well as to re-envision cultural understandings of motherhood in ways that neither minimize the distinctly female character of birthgiving nor that overemphasize it and thus limit women's potential for self-determination by consigning them to motherhood as biological destiny. But how?

This question is posed in a complex and thoughtful way by one of the founding mothers of medieval Christianity: St Helena, the fourth-century Roman empress and mother of Constantine, whose voyage to Jerusalem was believed to have resulted in the recovery of both the lost Cross and the historical context of the crucifixion. The only surviving Old English poetic rendition of the Invention of the Holy Cross is Cynewulf's *Elene*, a text that may have been composed in late eighth- or early ninth-century Mercia and that survives in a single manuscript, the Vercelli Book, which dates to the later tenth century. Although *Elene* relies heavily on the Latin *Inventio Sanctae Crucis* as its main source, Cynewulf significantly rewrites various portions of the Latin text. As he transports Helena out of an imagined Roman past into an Anglo-Saxon present, Cynewulf creates an image of motherhood that challenges cultural myths of maternity as synonymous with self-sacrifice, domesticity, and loss of personal identity. By depicting Elene as at once the biological mother of Constantine, the spiritual mother of the Jews, and the mother-muse who inspires his own poetry, Cynewulf envisions an important role for biological mothers in the founding and perpetuation of Christianity, and, at the same time, expands social definitions of motherhood to encompass roles that move far beyond the conception and bearing of children. Cynewulf's account of motherhood both draws on and recasts the meanings typically assigned to mothering in Anglo-Saxon heroic poetry and in so doing urges readers to remember 'Woman' differently within the historical record.

Of sons and mothers

As the mother of Constantine—the first emperor to bring Christianity under the official recognition of the state—Helena was strongly associated with motherhood. Not surprisingly, when Cynewulf introduces Elene, he refers to her simply as Constantine's mother (*his modor*, 'his mother', line 214b).[3] Similarly, Elene's most memorable act, her sea-voyage to Jerusalem, is explicitly described as having been undertaken in the name of maternal duty: it is because *Elene ne wolde ... ðæs wilgifan word gehyrwan*, | *hiere sylfre suna* ('Elene did not wish ... to scorn the word of the ruler, her own son', lines 219–22a) that she immediately prepares to obey his orders that she recover the lost Cross. The semantic range of the term *willgifa* ('ruler' or 'gracious giver'), which connotes both the earthly and the heavenly ruler, constructs the fulfilment of maternal duty as synonymous with Christian obedience. For Elene to scorn the word of her earthly ruler Constantine would be to scorn the word of her heavenly ruler Christ, an act that is presented throughout the poem as a defining feature of Judaism and that would be unthinkable for a model Christian queen. Moreover, in constructing Elene as a single mother carrying out her son's will in the world, Cynewulf allies her with the only other named woman in the poem: the Virgin Mary, who appears frequently in Elene's speeches to the Jews as the vessel for carrying the son of God. The association between Elene and Mary would have been familiar to many Anglo-Saxons, as patristic and early medieval writers drew frequent comparisons between the two women; for them, Helena was the mother who would continue the Virgin's work of redeeming humanity. As Ambrose states in his *De obitu Theodosii oratio*: 'Mary was visited to liberate Eve; Helena was visited that emperors might be redeemed.'[4]

By presenting Elene as a kind of secular version of Mary, Cynewulf reminds readers of the importance of biological mothers within Christian culture. Indeed Anglo-Saxon mothers, especially royal mothers, served as powerful patrons of the church, and it was of course Mary's motherhood that made it possible for Christ to be known in the world. Yet in spite of mothers' practical and theoretical importance in the establishment of Christianity, patristic and early medieval theologians tended to devalue biological mothers on account of their strong associations with secular life and sexuality. Most of the female figures who are celebrated in Anglo-Saxon religious writings are women who actively reject biological motherhood: virgin martyrs such as Juliana and Agatha, who choose to die rather than to relinquish their chastity; childless widows such as Judith and Oswyn (Edmund's caretaker), who devote their lives to prayer and the Lord's work; or chaste wives such as Cecilia and Basilissa, who engage in 'spiritual marriages' marked by an absence of sexual relations. By depicting Elene as Mary's secular counterpart, Cynewulf revalues biological motherhood and in so doing creates a more accessible exemplar for Anglo-Saxon mothers—women who, unlike the Virgin, had indeed 'known men' and who were thus, according to medieval theology, entitled to a lesser reward in heaven.

Moreover, by placing Elene's travels to Jerusalem under the rubric of maternal duty, Cynewulf revises the Marian model of motherhood, in which mothers are seen as fairly passive figures whose primary role is to serve as vessels for male children. The idea of the mother as a woman who simply feeds her child and is powerless to influence its future is not confined to homiletic or hagiographic writings that deal explicitly with Mary nor to voices that are intended to represent the fruits of Christian wisdom. Witness, for example, the Chaldean prince Saturn's remarks on motherhood in the Old English poem *Solomon and Saturn*:

> Modor ne rædeð,   ðonne heo magan cenneð,
> hu him weorðe geond worold   widsið sceapen.
> Oft heo to bealwe   bearn afedeð,
> seolfre to sorge. . . .
> Forðan nah seo modor geweald,   ðonne heo magan cenneð,
> bearnes blædes,   ac sceall on gebyrd faran
> an æfter anum;   ðæt is eald gesceaft.[5]

When a mother bears a child, she cannot predict how his long journey through the world will be shaped. Often she feeds the child, who then comes to nothing but grief, to her own sorrow. . . . When a mother bears a child, she has no control over his fate but must simply follow along with his destiny, the one after the other. That is the old tradition.

Much like this anonymous poet, Cynewulf depicts motherhood as powerfully shaped by the destiny of one's son. It is Constantine's new-found Christian belief and his desire to make that belief known beyond Rome that motivates him to send Elene to Jerusalem. Yet unlike the anonymous poet, who envisions mothers as powerless figures, lost in their own sorrow and following in the tracks of their sons' wide journeys, Cynewulf envisions motherhood as a role that necessitates a woman's own wide journeys. Cynewulf's depiction of motherhood thus presents a sharp contrast to common understandings of motherhood in modern Western culture, in which motherhood is often viewed as synonymous with domestic confinement. Far from restricting her physical mobility, Elene's status as the biological mother of Constantine is precisely what makes possible and indeed necessitates her travels, as well as her new role as a political emissary for Rome.

Politicizing motherhood

Although Elene's motherhood entails her assumption of a political role that takes her far beyond the boundaries of her own home, Cynewulf's overt politicization of motherhood reminds us that even Anglo-Saxon mothers who did not travel were deeply imbricated in public political life. Unlike modern Western culture, which tends to assume a sharp separation between domestic life and national politics, Anglo-Saxon England was a culture in which diplomacy and public politics were conducted within the home, and in which domestic 'confinement' located one squarely within the centres of public political power. Because Anglo-Saxon mothers presided over the home— distributing gifts, bearing mead, mediating between men, and hosting foreign emissaries—motherhood in Anglo-Saxon England, particularly as experienced by royal and noble women, was always a public political role. And as Elene fulfils political duties that fall under the rubric of biological mothering, Cynewulf expands the concept of motherhood itself: he neither reduces it to the act of birthgiving, nor even to the care of biological children, but depicts it as a social role bound up in the preservation of spiritual life and creative expression.

Throughout the poem, Cynewulf invites readers to envision Elene's motherhood figuratively, that is, to view her as a symbol of Church, which was commonly identified in both patristic and early medieval writings through the metaphor of *mater ecclesia*—a metaphor rooted in the belief that one was reborn in the church through baptism. As Wulfstan puts it in his third homily on the Christian life:

Ealle we habbað ænne heofonlicne fæder and ane gastlice modor, seo is ecclesia genamod, þæt is Godes cyrice.[6]

We all have a heavenly father and a spiritual mother, who is called *Ecclesia*, that is, God's church.

The spiritual children whom Elene seeks to convert are the lost Jews; not surprisingly, her spiritual mothering relies heavily on a rhetoric of disappointed parenthood. Citing Isaiah 1: 2–3, Elene assumes the voice of the heartbroken father who has given his children everything and been repaid by their utmost hatred and disdain:

> Ic up ahof   eaforan gingne
> & bearn cende   þam ic blæd forgeaf,
> halige higefrofre;   ac hie hyrwdon [m]e,
> feodon þurh feondscipe   (lines 353–6a)

I have raised up young ones and brought forth children to whom I have given prosperity, holy solace of the mind, but they have scorned me, hated me with enmity.

Elene's progression over the course of the poem from biological to spiritual mother parallels the lives of many Anglo-Saxon queens and noble women, who, after raising their children, often entered monasteries and assumed the role of abbess or *modor*, 'mother', of their communities. Moreover, by the later tenth century, the period in which the Vercelli Book was received, the queen was charged with the duty of overseeing female monasteries, thus making her a kind of spiritual mother of all women religious.

Spiritual motherhood

Elene's movement from biological to spiritual mother also enacts a hermeneutic shift consistent with Christian conversion: the acceptance of Christianity entails a necessary movement from literal to more symbolic orders of representation. One of the most pervasive themes in patristic and early medieval anti-Jewish polemics was that the Jews were unable to read figurally; that is, unlike Christians, who understood the Old Testament as a prefiguration of the New Testament, Jews were bound to the literal letter of the Old Testament and unable to penetrate its deeper spiritual significance. When Elene accuses the Jews of having *herwdon, | fædera lare* ('scorned the teaching of the fathers', lines 387b–388a), what she is referring to is their refusal to read the Old Testament figurally, which they cannot do until they recognize Elene as not only a queen mother from a powerful family but also as a figure for Holy Church. Conversion and rightful understanding of the laws of the fathers are shown to be contingent on recognition of the multiple meanings that accrue to motherhood as well as acceptance of the mother's reinterpretation of patriarchal law—and Cynewulf figures both of these goals as highly desirable.

If Elene ever truly served as a spiritual mother of Jews, she did so during the early fourth century. Yet the rather hazy and anachronistic sense of temporality that informs *Elene*—the poem is set two hundred and thirty-three winters after Christ's birth (AD 233), but also in the sixth year of Constantine's reign (AD 312); and it features such ana-chronistically placed figures as the second-century protomartyr Stephen as Judas's brother—reminds us that Elene was a figure who operated not only within the limited duration of historical time but also the grander and more expansive range of typological history. For Cynewulf, as for so many other medieval writers, Elene was not sim-ply a legendary queen mother from the past, but a figure who bore important meanings for their own cultures. Indeed, throughout late antiquity and the early Middle Ages, writers frequently drew on Helena as an exemplar for royal women, invoking the well-known empress as a model of Christian evangelicism in the hopes of ins-piring their own queens to soften the hearts of their male kin and draw them closer to God. (See Pl. 4 for an Anglo-Saxon queen.)

For some medieval writers, particularly those who heeded biblical injunctions against women as teachers, the idea that royal women might serve as agents of Christian conversion was highly problematic. This sensibility informs Bede's *Historia Ecclesiastica* (AD 731), which takes pains to depict conversion as the rightful work of bishops, missionaries, and monks. Yet unlike Bede, Cynewulf seems wholly at ease with the idea of queen mothers as agents of conversion— figuring Elene as the inspiration not only for the spiritual awakening of the Jews but also for his own conversion.

At the end of the poem, Cynewulf undergoes a spiritual transform-ation analogous to that experienced by Judas. Just as Judas suffers seven nights in a literal *nearu* 'prison' (line 711a) intended to symbo-lize his own spiritual imprisonment and alienation from Christ, so too does Cynewulf endure a metaphorical *nearosorg* 'imprisonment' (line 1260b) *nihtes nearwe* 'in the torment of night' (line 1239a) on account of his inability to receive the true meaning of the Holy Cross. And just as Elene inspires Judas to open his heart to Christ and to find the Cross in a very literal sense, so too does she prove the neces-sary catalyst for unlocking Cynewulf's own frozen breasthoard and enabling him to accept the Cross's true meaning and subsequently reveal it in his poetry. As the critic Joyce Tally Lionarons points out, by the end of the poem, Elene has become the poetic mother-muse who releases Cynewulf from his writer's block and allows him to compose ('Cultural Syncretism', pp. 66–8).

The association between motherhood and artistic inspiration can be traced back to the ancient idea of the three muses, and it is suggested in Anglo-Saxon literature on several occasions. An explicit link between motherhood and artistic inspiration appears in the anonymous eleventh-century *Vita Ædwardi* written in honour of Queen Edith. Although Edith never produced any biological children—a situation rumoured to be the result of Edward's desire to die a virgin and subsequent refusal to consummate their marriage—the author nevertheless casts her as a kind of mother to everyone: to the king, and to the royal boys at court, and ultimately to himself as a poet. In the author's eyes, Edith's solicitude for her husband's royal dress made her seem 'not so much a spouse as a good mother', while her care for the education and rearing of boys with royal blood was illustrative of how she 'showered [them] with motherly love' (p. 25).[7] Similarly, the author casts Edith as the mother-muse of his own poetry—opening the text with an appeal to his female Muse, but happily abandoning her when Edith appears as an intercessor for her mythical sister. Describing himself as having been vowed specially by his Muse to Edith, the poet claims that it was she who 'fixed my feet, restored me as from death, | Put back the pens that I had thrown away; | And these as slaves I dedicate to her' (p. 5). Much as Edith restores the author's powers of creative expression, so too does Elene restore Cynewulf's. In both the *Vita Ædwardi* and in *Elene*, motherhood is allied with the power of creative thought and expression. And in both texts, motherhood is depicted as a cultural phenomenon that encompasses a range of activities beyond biological reproduction. But in the case of *Elene*, maternal inspiration is particularly exciting in that it produces a profound recasting of motherhood as depicted in heroic poetry.

The new heroic mother

Cynewulf's vision of motherhood as a flexible social role that might be enacted in a variety of different forms—biological reproduction, spiritual mothering, and artistic inspiration—significantly expands the fairly narrow range of meanings that are typically assigned to motherhood in Old English heroic poetry. The mothers who are celebrated in heroic poetry tend to derive much of their identity from their sons' successes in battle, a point that is nicely encapsulated in the *Beowulf*-poet's treatment of Beowulf's mother, who is never named but imagined simply as a proud mother basking in the glory of her son's heroic conquests:

> Hwæt, þæt secgan mæg
> efne swa hwylc mægþa   swa ðone magan cende
> æfter gumcynnum,   gyf heo gyt lyfað,
> þæt hyre Ealdmetod   este wære
> bearngebyrdo.[8]

Lo, whatever woman brought forth this son among mankind, she may say, if she still lives, that the God of Old was kind to her in her childbearing.

For those sons whose military exploits are less successful than Beowulf's, their mothers weep. Maternal laments give voice to the sorrow that is so difficult for men to express according to the implicit rules of Germanic stoicism, and also lend dignity and meaning to the deaths of male kin, reminding others that these men have not died in vain but in the interest of protecting their women. As the modern feminist writer Dorothy Dinnerstein puts it: '[Woman's] tears serve not to deter man but to help him go on, for she is doing his weeping for him and he is doing what she weeps about for her.'[9]

One of the stock roles of mothers and wives in heroic poetry is to serve as the 'whetting woman', whose duty it is to wield words that might inspire men to battle. The whetting woman's voice can be heard clearly in *Waldere* (lines 8–11), in which Hildegyth encourages her lover Waldere to engage in a battle in which he ultimately loses his right hand:

> . . . [nu] is se dæg cumen
> þæt ðu scealt aninga   oðer twega,
> lif forleosan   oððe l[..]gne dom
> agan mid eldum,   Ælfheres sunu.[10]

Now the day has come when you, son of Ælfhere, must do one of two things: lose your life or achieve lasting glory among men.

Hildegyth's subsequent statement that she will never have need to blame Waldere for seeing him flee at the sword-play in disgrace or escape to the wall to save his life (lines 12–16a) reveals that the clear win-or-die binary she presents him with is a false one. The whetting woman's role is premised on the need to prevent men from taking the third option of avoiding warfare altogether through flight, and Hildegyth's taunting of Waldere reminds us that adherence to the fight-or-die binary was never the result of any sort of natural male aggression, but a masculinity that was painfully constructed by, among other things, the voices of women.

As Elene assumes the role of a militant *mater ecclesia* urging her lost spiritual sons to accept her maternal love, she interrupts this seemingly endless and inevitable cycle that positions the maternal voice as ever in the service of Anglo-Saxon heroic warfare. Adopting the language of the Germanic whetting woman, Elene translates the imperative to fight into the need to convert. Immediately before Elene has Judas cast into a pit, where he will suffer for seven nights and ultimately emerge as a new Christian convert, she presents him with a choice:

> 'Þe synt tu gearu,
> swa lif swa deað   swa þe leofre bið
> to geceosanne;   cyð ricene nu
> hwæt ðu þæs to þinge   þafian wille.'   (lines 605b–608)

'Two fates are prepared for you, either life or death, whichever is preferable to you to choose. Say now, quickly, what you will assent to in this matter.'

For readers like Cynewulf, steeped in the Latin texts of Christian monasticism, this choice would have recalled the Two Ways—the wide way of spiritual death versus the narrow way of spiritual life—a theme that appears in both the Old and New Testaments, as well as in numerous patristic writings.[11] For readers more familiar with the heroic poetry of the meadhall, these choices would, however, have evoked the live-or-die motif that informs the rhetoric of the Germanic whetting woman. Yet Cynewulf has significantly recast her voice: Elene's words are designed to convince the Jews to fight for spiritual rather than earthly life, and to send them on a quest for eternal glory through spiritual struggle rather than a quest for worldly fame through literal battle.

Indeed glory accrues to Elene not through the reproduction of successful warriors but through the production of believing children. Although Elene does keep in close contact with her biological son back in Rome, those interactions take a back seat to her more pressing work of teaching the Jews to accept Christ as their Saviour. Elene is not concerned at the prospect of watching her battle-fallen sons cremated on a funeral pyre, but at the prospect of watching her lost spiritual sons consumed in the flames of eternal hellfire. The rhetorical energies of the maternal voice are thus directed not towards inspiring war but towards effecting conversion. It is perhaps not surprising that Elene's greatest moment of glory occurs immediately after her spiritual son Judas has proven his internalization of her teachings by bringing her the nails with which Christ was crucified. As he lays them upon Elene's knees, she bursts into tears of joy, and her subsequent visitation by the spirit of the Lord marks her conversion of Judas as the act that ensures her own glory. The identity of the mother is redefined: it is no longer contingent on her warrior son's ability to kill but on her spiritual son's willingness to change.

Revising history

For the Anglo-Saxons the name 'Elene' would have invoked not only the Christian heroine of the *Inventio* legend, but also Helen of Troy, whose matchless beauty and abduction by Paris gave rise to the Greeks' invasion and destruction of Troy. As the prize granted by Aphrodite in exchange for the apple of discord, Helen of Troy was associated with a kind of general female unruliness that would lead to political strife—ideas that are forcefully expressed in the Old English *Orosius*, an anonymous late ninth-century translation that King Alfred the Great deemed one of the texts most necessary for all men to know. Immediately after discussing the Amazon women's penchant for killing men, the *Orosius*-translators embark on a new section of the text that relates how *Priamises sunu þæs cyninges . . . genom þæs cyninges wif Monelaus, of Læcedemonia, Creca byrig, Elena* ('the son of king Priam . . . took Menelaus's wife Helen from the Greek city Lacedaemon' p. 31, lines 23–5) and then discusses the *mære gewinn 7 þa miclan gefeoht Creca and Troiana* ('famous battle and extensive fighting between Greeks and Trojans', p. 31, line 26) that ensued.[12] Although Helen is granted very little agency in this account, she is nevertheless depicted as an exemplar of the female disobedience allegedly found within the pagan past. Contrasting the great *sibb and frið* ('peace and concord', p. 31, line 17) to be found in Christ with the unruliness exemplified by the Amazon women's killing of men the *Orosius*-translators demand to know *Hu wene ge hwelce sibbe þa weras hæfden ær þæm cristendome, þonne heora wif swa monigfeald yfel donde wæron on þiosan middangearde?* ('How do you expect that men had any peace before Christendom when their women were engaged in so much evil throughout the earth?', p. 31, lines 19–21).

Given the very negative light in which women are depicted within Trojan history, it is perhaps not surprising that when Elene berates the Jews for their selective amnesia, that is, their ability to remember all of the minute details of secular warfare but nothing at all about Christ's death, her anger centres on their fascination with the Trojan wars:

> 'Hu is þæt geworden   on þysse werþeode
> þæt ge swa monigfeald   on gemynd witon
> alra tacna gehwylc   swa Troian[ae]
> þurh gefeoht fremedon?'   (lines 643–6)

'How has it come about among this people that you remember such manifold things, all of the deeds that the Trojans wrought in battle?'

When Elene demands that history should centre on Christ's sufferings rather than on Trojan warfare, and when Cynewulf echoes her request by urging all people to remember the story of the Cross, together, they voice an implicit demand that Woman be remembered differently within the historical record—not as the beautiful lover who would instigate familial and political strife but as the Christian mother who would make it possible to know the giver of all peace. As readers meditate on Cynewulf's account of the Invention, Helen of Troy is re-envisioned as Elene: woman is remembered not as the beautiful face that launched a thousand ships but as the wise voice that saved a thousand souls.

A few thoughts

Centralizing feminism in Anglo-Saxon literary culture is not about importing a modern grid through which to read medieval texts; rather it is about situating those texts in their literary and historical contexts. Doing so often reveals astonishingly flexible attitudes toward gender and toward women's assumption of political power, reminding us that women's oppression is not a direct and unchanging trajectory between the Middle Ages and modernity, and that we cannot explain women's oppression as a simple legacy of 'medieval' or 'pre-modern' social structures. Reading Old English texts through a feminist perspective is beneficial to both modern feminists and to Anglo-Saxonists: for modern feminists, feminist Anglo-Saxon studies offer a fresh perspective on contemporary feminist problems; for Anglo-Saxonists, feminist criticism offers a way to keep Old English texts fresh and relevant and also to gain a more complete picture of Anglo-Saxon society.

To be sure, Cynewulf's vision of motherhood in *Elene* cannot be read as a mirror of motherhood as practised in Anglo-Saxon culture. Both hagiographic narratives and heroic poems are comprised of characters who do not encode the complexities of Anglo-Saxon people or their lives but rather the most entrenched stereotypes and social values. These texts were designed to convey spiritual rather than literal truths, heroic ideals rather than realistic experiences, and they were probably meant to foster fervent inspiration rather than strict emulation. Yet upon close examination of the gender stereotypes in these poems, what emerges is the sense that even those texts and traditions which encode the most aggressively colonizing and intolerably misogynist mindsets simultaneously encode revisionist treatments of gender. We need not identify Cynewulf as an early proto-feminist or Elene as a 'mother to think back through' to realize that *Elene* offers an expansive account of motherhood that revises both Anglo-Saxon and modern stereotypes of maternity. Although the rich and varied array of feminist criticism that *Elene* has provoked allows us to chart modern responses to *Elene*, the absence of marginal comments or any other record of the poem's reception renders contemporary responses extremely difficult, if not impossible, to trace. We may never know if *Elene* guided the actions of an Anglo-Saxon mother. However, one cannot help but wonder if Cynewulf's version of the legend, or one like it, may not have inspired Æthelflæd, the widowed queen mother and ruler of Mercia from 911 to 918, who allegedly took the holy eve of the Invention of the Cross, Elene's feast-day, as the auspicious occasion on which to begin her own travels to Scergeat in preparation for battle.[13]

Notes

1. Drucilla Cornell, *At the Heart of Freedom: Feminism, Sex, and Equality* (Princeton: Princeton University Press, 1998), p. 24.

2. Hélène Cixous, 'The Laugh of the Medusa', trans. Keith Cohen and Paula Cohen, *Signs*, 1 (1976), 875–93, at 881; this is a revised version of 'Le rire de la Méduse', which appeared in *L'Arc* (1975), 39–54.

3. All citations from *Elene* are by line number and refer to P. O. E. Gradon, ed., *Cynewulf's 'Elene'*, rev. edn. (Exeter: University of Exeter Press, 1977).

4. Sister Mary Dolorosa Mannix, *Sancti Ambrosii oratio de obitu Theodosii: Text, Translation, Introduction and Commentary*, Patristic Studies 9 (Washington DC: Catholic University of America, 1925), p. 80.

5. *The Anglo-Saxon Minor Poems*, ed. Elliott Van Kirk Dobbie, ASPR 6 (New York: Columbia University Press, 1942), pp. 44 and 45, lines 372–5a, 385–87.

6. *The Homilies of Wulfstan*, ed. Dorothy Bethurum (Oxford: Clarendon Press, 1957), p. 202, lines 41–3.

7. Citations from the *Vita Ædwardi* are by page number and refer to *The Life of King Edward who Rests at Westminster/Attributed to a Monk of Saint Bertin*, ed. and trans. Frank Barlow, 2nd edn. (Oxford: Clarendon Press, 1992).

8. *Beowulf and the Fight at Finnsburg*, ed. Fr. Klaeber, 3rd edn., with the First and Second Supplements (Boston: D. C. Heath, 1950), lines 942b–946a.

9. Dorothy Dinnerstein, *The Mermaid and the Minotaur: Sexual Arrangements and Human Malaise* (New York: Harper and Row), 1976, p. 226.

10. Citations from *Waldere* are by line number and refer to the text contained in *Anglo-Saxon Minor Poems*, pp. 4–5.

11. Catharine A. Regan, 'Evangelicism as the Informing Principle of Cynewulf's *Elene*'. In Robert E. Bjork, ed., *Cynewulf: Basic Readings* (New York: Garland Publishing), 1996, pp. 251–80, at 261–3; first published in *Traditio*, 20 (1973), 27–52.

12. Citations from the Old English *Orosius* refer to *The Old English Orosius*, ed. Janet Bately, EETS s.s. 6 (London: Oxford University Press, 1980).

13. *English Historical Documents*, i: *c.500–1042*, ed. Dorothy Whitelock, 2nd edn. (London: Eyre Methuen, 1979), p. 211.

References and suggested reading

Clayton, Mary. *The Cult of the Virgin Mary in Anglo-Saxon England.* Cambridge Studies in Anglo-Saxon England 2. Cambridge: Cambridge University Press, 1990. A comprehensive study of the figure of Mary in Anglo-Saxon England.

Damico, Helen, and Alexandra Hennessey Olsen, eds. *New Readings on Women in Old English Literature.* Bloomington: Indiana University Press, 1990. An important collection that offers a rich array of essays on Anglo-Saxon women and gender.

Fell, Christine. *Women in Anglo-Saxon England.* Oxford: Basil Blackwell, 1986. An indispensable study of women in Anglo-Saxon England that examines archaeological, literary, and historical evidence, and offers some discussion of women in Roman Britain, Viking society, and post-Conquest culture.

Hollis, Stephanie. *Anglo-Saxon Women and the Church: Sharing a Common Fate.* Woodbridge and Rochester: Boydell Press, 1992. An immensely detailed and absorbing examination of religious women in Anglo-Saxon England.

Lees, Clare A., and Gillian R. Overing. *Double Agents: Women and Clerical Culture in Anglo-Saxon England.* Philadelphia: University of Pennsylvania Press, 2001. A study of women's ambivalent occupations in the Anglo-Saxon historical record.

Lees, Clare A. 'At a Crossroads: Old English and Feminist Criticism'. In Katherine O'Brien O'Keeffe, ed., *Readings in Old English Texts.* Cambridge: Cambridge University Press, 1997, pp. 146–69. An overview of feminist criticism in Old English literary studies, with a brief close reading of *Elene*.

Lionarons, Joyce Tally. 'Cultural Syncretism and the Construction of Gender in Cynewulf's *Elene*', *Exemplaria*, 10 (1998), 51–68. Lionarons explores the performative nature of gender in *Elene*, and argues that the poem's uneasy gender dynamics obtain from Cynewulf's efforts to blend his Latin source material with Germanic literary tradition.

Olsen, Alexandra Hennessey. 'Gender Roles'. In Robert E. Bjork and John D. Niles, eds., *A Beowulf Handbook.* Lincoln: University of Nebraska Press, 1997, pp. 311–24. Olsen offers a comprehensive survey of gender criticism in *Beowulf*-studies and reviews major social roles assigned to women in heroic poetry.

Overing, Gillian R. *Language, Sign and Gender in 'Beowulf'*. Carbondale: Southern Illinois University Press, 1990. A useful and fascinating study of women in heroic culture, particularly *Beowulf*.

Stafford, Pauline. *Queen Emma and Queen Edith: Queenship and Women's Power in Eleventh-Century England*. Oxford: Basil Blackwell, 1997. A valuable historical study of Anglo-Saxon queenship that focuses explicitly on Edith and Emma, but also provides much useful information regarding cultural attitudes toward royal women throughout the period.

12

Wise words: Old English sapiential poetry

Thomas D. Hill

Defining sapiential

The phrase 'sapiential poetry' is modelled on the term 'sapiential' as it is used in biblical scholarship and criticism to refer to those books of the Old Testament such as Proverbs, Ecclesiastes, or (in the Vulgate) Ecclesiasticus, which consist of wise sayings and reflections about life and wisdom. These texts are also sometimes referred to as 'wisdom literature' but one would not normally refer to proverbs as 'wisdom literature' in modern English usage and so for present purposes I use the Latinate equivalent. Other biblical texts, of course, contain sapiential material and such texts were often excerpted and quoted in other contexts in Christian Latin and vernacular works. But the major biblical sapiential texts are both an important and influential biblical genre and an immediate and authoritative model for Old English sapiential literature. There also existed, we may presume, a native Germanic tradition of sapiential literature, which we make inferences about on the basis of what is preserved in written (mostly poetic) texts and from comparative evidence, but concerning which we are much less well informed.

It must be confessed at the outset that the terminology in this area of literary studies is imprecise. Terms such as 'proverb', 'gnome', 'maxim', or 'sentence' are often used indistinguishably and the distinction between 'sapiential' and more generally 'moralistic' poetry is essentially a judgement call. For example, the maxim 'Drive carefully' is a sapiential text, whereas the statement that the speed limit is 65 m.p.h. is a law (or the summary of a law), while extended discourse about the dangers of careless driving would be the modern equivalent of a moralizing homily. But such distinctions are often harder to make in reading Old English poetry than one would like. For the purposes of this discussion I would suggest that Aristotle's definition of a maxim as 'a statement, not however concerning particulars ... but with the objects of human actions, and with what should be chosen or avoided with reference to them',[1] is a useful point of departure. To this we may add statements concerning the natural order, some of which seem to have immediate moral implications and others seem to be direct natural observation.

The Old English corpus

The corpus of Old English sapiential poetry is substantial. Most immediately there are the three poems in the Exeter Book (Exeter Cathedral Library 3501) which are entitled *Maxims I* or the Exeter *Maxims* and which consist of approximately 200 lines of verse. A poem that has always been immediately associated with the Exeter *Maxims* is *Maxims II* or the *Cotton Maxims* and is approximately 66 lines long. The Old English *Solomon and Saturn I* and *II* is approximately 506 lines long and is generally thought like *Maxims I* and *II* to reflect the tradition of Germanic sapiential poetry. The first poem is concerned with the powers of the letters of the *Pater Noster*, an association often thought to derive from the tradition of Germanic runic magic. The second portion of *Solomon and Saturn* is a wide-ranging dialogue in which a pagan spokesman Saturn seeks wisdom from the 'Christian' Solomon. The topics dealt with range widely from the monstrous bird with four heads named the Vasa Mortis, to Christian judgement, the fall of the rebel angels, and the power of time and fate. There are two more relevant poems in the Exeter Book that deserve mention — *The Gifts of Men* and *The Fortunes of Men*. The former is concerned with various talents with which men are gifted, and the latter with the destinies that can befall a young man. These poems, which seem puzzling to the modern literary critic, are none the less very interesting in what they reveal about Anglo-Saxon attitudes to work and society and are included by Dorothy Whitelock in her *English Historical Documents* collection. These texts are the most secular Germanic sapiential texts in the corpus, but there is a substantial corpus of more or less explicitly Christian sapiential poetry including *Precepts, Vainglory, The Order of the World*, the somewhat awkwardly entitled *Homiletic Fragments I* and *II*, and the recently edited *Instructions for Christians*.

In addition to those poems, which consist largely or entirely of sapiential statements, many of the more famous Old English poems contain such discourse. Poems like *The Wanderer* and *The Seafarer*, for example, could be defined as sapiential as readily as 'elegies' since they contain much sapiential material and there is substantial material of this type in *Beowulf*. The wise old king of the Danes, Hrothgar, is particularly prone to sapiential discourse, but other characters such as Wealhtheow, the Coastguard, and Beowulf himself speak on occasion in a similar mode.

As this enumeration of texts suggests, there is a great deal of sapiential poetry preserved in Old English. While scholars and critics would inevitably disagree about what poems and what passages are or are not strictly speaking 'sapiential', the existence of a very significant body of wisdom poetry is beyond reasonable doubt. These poems and this mode of poetry have, however, not attracted much critical or scholarly attention and this neglect is motivated in part by the very real difficulties which this poetry presents and in part by the fact that much wisdom poetry seems very alien to modern and postmodern readers.

Poetry and discourse of a sapiential nature generally is often characterized as difficult and this characterization is well founded. To begin with, sapiential texts define briefly or allude to cultural norms and ideals that can be difficult for those who are not native speakers, and who have no direct access to the culture to understand. Again such statements are often very concise or metaphorical or simultaneously both. A phrase such as 'business is business' can be construed quite differently by different speakers of American English and would have no meaning to someone who did not have at least some familiarity with American culture. Or to take another often-cited example, the American (and British) proverb, 'A rolling stone gathers no moss' is at the same time widely current and quite cryptic. It is hard even for an informed native speaker to determine whether 'gathering moss' is good or bad.

One modern response to this literature which one encounters in critical texts is that sapiential literature is no longer a living genre for educated speakers of modern English. Proverbs admittedly have some currency, but sophisticated and educated 'modern' or 'postmodern' native speakers would never cite a proverb or a maxim seriously in the course of argument. This is a claim which has some force—if one were to submit a sapiential poem to a 'serious' literary journal, it would be rejected out of hand, unless the editors assumed the poem in question was ironic. But I would argue that it is not so much that sapiential literature is no longer a current living genre, as that current 'modern' literature of this kind exists in certain specific generic forms that are no longer recognized as literary. In political and legal discourse, sapiential literature of a very traditional form remains current and important. The claim, for example, that a person who is arrested is 'innocent until proven guilty' is at the same time a maxim and an important and to some degree problematic rule in Anglo-American law. Some such maxims are even formally proverbial in structure. The claim that 'an Englishman's home is his castle' is not literally true and is a figurative (proverbial) condensation of a number of legal ideas about an individual's right to privacy and his or her freedom from official harassment.

One of the difficulties which Old English sapiential literature presents is that we are rarely in a position to gloss a maxim which has legal or social implications with anything like the assurance which a historian of later periods can have. Even so, scholars who are both informed and imaginative can elucidate texts that initially seem quite opaque. One example would be Christine Fell's very interesting discussion of 'Maxims I' (*Exeter Book Maxims*), lines 81–83a:

> Cyning sceal mid ceape   cwene gebicgan,
> bunum ond beagum;   bu sceolon ærest
> geofum god wesan.

A king must 'buy' a queen with wealth, with cups and bracelets. Both must first be generous with gifts.

On first reading, these lines seem brutally misogynistic, but Fell shows that they refer to a tradition of property settlements in the context of royal marriage in which the property rights and authority of the queen were important and duly respected.[2]

Interpretations

The question which often occurs in reading Old English sapiential poetry is how these apparently self-evident truisms can be 'read' as anything other than manifest evidence of an apparent Anglo-Saxon taste for banalities. Obviously a clear and cogent answer to that question would be, in effect, a persuasive interpretation of all or at least the bulk of the corpus of Old English sapiential poetry; neither I nor any other scholar or critic is able to offer such interpretation. But I can offer some suggestions that might advance our understanding of this issue and at the least offer the possibility of new questions. To begin with, in so far as we can discern a specifically native Anglo-Saxon rhetorical tradition, appeals to and citation of traditional wisdom seems to have been a received rhetorical technique. When the coastguard in *Beowulf* hears Beowulf's account of the rationale for the voyage to Denmark, he does not simply grant Beowulf and his men permission to proceed, he prefaces his permission with a wise saying about the necessity for discernment:

> Weard maþelode,   ðær on wicge sæt,
> ombeht unforht: æghwæþres sceal
> scearp scyldwiga   gescad witan,
> worda ond worca,   se þe wel þenceð.   (lines 286–9)

The guardian spoke where he sat on [his] steed, the fearless court official, 'The keen warrior must know how to distinguish both words and deeds, he who thinks well.'

This sentence about the importance of discernment is not necessary for the sequence of the narrative. It simply serves to invest the coastguard's permission to proceed with a certain kind of *gravitas* that would be lacking in a more straightforward speech. He 'adorns' his consent with a wise saying. It would be easy to multiply instances of this kind of rhetorical usage from *Beowulf* and the limited corpus of

'Germanic' Old English poetry, and such usage was also conventional in the tradition of Christian Latin rhetoric—indeed, the coastguard's speech is an instance of the 'words and works' *topos* which is widely attested in Christian Latin and Old English religious texts. And the prominence of sapiential texts in the Bible, which Old English authors would have known in Latin or the vernacular, can hardly be exaggerated. Thus one immediate reason an Old English reader or listener might have been interested in such poetry might have been as a kind of gathering of *sententiae*, which they could use and adapt if they were called upon to speak formally in public.

But this essentially functionalist view of Old English sapiential poetry simply extends and broadens the problem which these texts present. To say that sapiential statements were used rhetorically does not answer the question of why such statements were thought appropriate as rhetorical adornment. To pursue this question it is necessary to speculate: if we assume (and there are reasons for this assumption) that Anglo-Saxon culture was deeply 'conservative' in its sense of the continuity and importance of tradition, appeals to received wisdom had a kind of rhetorical and cultural force which such appeals might not have in a cultural world more orientated to the future—more 'progressive'.

Beyond these generalities one may also note that sapiential discourse can, in some instances, serve to cloak statements that are charged with political meaning. Thus, when Beowulf intervenes in the charged political situation at Hrothgar's court and invites Hrothgar's son Hrethric to the court of the Geats—a move which would effectively protect him from Hrothulf, Hrothgar's grown nephew—Beowulf concludes his speech with a maxim about foreign travel:

> Gif him þonne Hreþric   to hofum Geata
> geþingeð, þeodnes bearn,   he mæg þær fela
> freonda findan;   feorcyþðe beoð
> selran gesohte   þæm þe him selfa deah.   (lines 1836–9)

If Hrethric, the prince's child, intends to come to the courts of the Geats, he may find many friends there; distant places are better sought for the one who is of worth himself.

The concluding aphorism seems to the modern reader conventional enough, but in the context of the dynastic tensions of Hrothgar's court, if Hrothgar were to travel to the court of the Geats he would be protected from any threat from Hrothulf, a threat which Wealhtheow discerns and which we know from Scandinavian sources was a real one. But Beowulf elides the political implications of his invitation with a maxim about the advantages of travel.

The maxim itself may seem something of a truism to modern readers, but it presents some conceptual issues that have not always been recognized by the commentators. To begin with, the conceptual content of the maxim is closely paralleled in the Old Norse Icelandic sapiential poem *Hávamál*:

> Vits er þörf
> þeim er víða ratar;
> dælt er heima hvat.
> At augabragði verður
> sá er ekki kann
> og með snotrum sitr.[3]

He needs wit who travels widely. Everything is easy at home. Someone who is foolish makes people raise their eyebrows when he sits among wise men.

The modern reader tends to assimilate both the Beowulfian maxim and the passage from *Hávamál* to modern truisms about the benefits of travel, but these maxims, and in particular the passage from *Hávamál*, have an edge to them which similar modern maxims do not. One should seek to travel—the wisdom masters say—because one can learn from the experience, an idea with which moderns would agree, and because the foreign court where one no longer has the support of 'kith and kin' is the place where one's intelligence and manly qualities are truly tested. *Dælt er heima hvat* ('Everything is easy at home'), says the *Hávamál* poet and Beowulf insists that distant lands are for those who *selfa dugon* ('are *by themselves* of worth').

The rhetorical function of Beowulf's maxim in this speech is generally recognized; it is indeed obvious enough to require no special comment, but it is not always recognized that one rhetorical strategy in sapiential discourse is to embed a controversial maxim in a context of rhetorically similar material so that the reader or listener may be inclined to accept the authority of the problematical maxim as well. In other words, a series of maxims may be as empty and banal as they seem, but they can serve the purpose of validating one or more problematical maxims that occur in the series. For the modern reader who is not sensitive to the implications and the nuances of Old English sapiential discourse, the problem of 'reading' and interpreting such a text can be formidable.

One example of an ideologically sensitive maxim embedded in what seems to be a neutral context occurs in *Precepts*, a sapiential poem in the Exeter Book, which most critics agree is one of the less interesting poems of this type in the collection. The poem consists of a series of instructions uttered by a 'father' to a 'son' and the moral teaching of the poem is characteristically on a rather high level of generality.[4] Part of the first 'teaching' which the father imparts to his son is a paraphrase of the commandment to honour your mother and father:

> Fæder ond modor   freo þu mid heortan,
> maga gehwylcne,   gif him sy meotud on lufan.   (lines 9–10)

Cherish [your] mother and father in [your] heart and each of [your] kinsmen, if they love God.

These lines are based on the biblical injunction to honour your mother and father. The Anglo-Saxon poet extends the command to include the kinship group generally, an extension which conforms to what we know about the importance of kinship in Anglo-Saxon society; but then the poet goes on to make a crucial exception. The 'son' should honour his mother, father, and kinsmen '*if* they love the Lord'. The 'if' clause imagines a potential conflict between a 'son' who is religious and a kinship group which is much less so, and it is clear in context that the claims of religion transcend the claims of kinship. Since a vocation to the priesthood or the monastic life implies or could imply a celibate life forswearing armed violence, one can easily imagine why an Anglo-Saxon family might be reluctant to see one of their sons make such a commitment and there are a variety of other situations in which the claims of family and religion might conflict. The *Precepts*-poet, however, has in effect pre-empted the family's appeal to the literal text of the Bible. The command to honour your mother and father only applies 'if they love the Lord'. *Precepts* is, in the opinion of virtually all critics, one of the less successful and less sophisticated Old English wisdom poems, and I would not question that judgement. But what might be perceived as the deficiencies of the poet allow us to read and perceive an ideological rupture at this point, which a more skilful poet might have successfully obscured. Poems such as *Precepts*, which few would defend from an aesthetic perspective, can be very revealing from the perspective of the scholar interested in Anglo-Saxon intellectual history and culture.

Reading *Solomon and Saturn II*, lines 364–87

This discussion of Old English sapiential poetry has been relatively general and, to the degree that I have focused on specific passages, I have for the most part summarized received opinion. I shall conclude by looking in some detail at a particular passage in the Old English *Solomon and Saturn II* which has not received much attention, but which is none the less interesting. The analysis I shall offer will attempt to demonstrate that the study of Old English sapiential poetry is of great interest and that there are a number of topics for research and study in this scholarly field.

One of the major concerns of the Old English *Solomon and Saturn II* is *wyrd*, a term often translated as 'fate', and the poet's concern might loosely be paraphrased as how man is situated in history. At one point in the poem the pagan spokesman Saturn and the Christian spokesman Solomon have the following exchange:

Saturnus cwæð:
'Ac hu gegangeð ðæt? Gode oððe yfle,
ðonne hie beoð ðurh ane idese acende,
twegen getwinnas, ne bið hira tir gelic.
Oðer bið unlæde on eorðan, oðer bið eadig,
swiðe leoftæle mid leoda duguðum;
oðer leofað lytle hwile,
swiceð on ðisse sidan gesceafte, and ðonne eft mid sorgum gewiteð.
Fricge ic ðec, hlaford Salomon, hwæðres bið hira folgoð betra?'
Salomon cuæð:
'Modor ne rædeð, ðonne heo magan cenneð,
hu him weorðe geond worold widsið sceapen.
Oft heo to bealwe bearn afedeð,
seolfre to sorge, siððan dreogeð
his earfoðu orlegstunde.
Heo ðæs afran sceall oft and gelome

grimme greotan,   ðonne he geong færeð,
hafað wilde mod,   werige heortan,
sefan sorgfullne,   slideð geneahhe,
werig, wilna leas,   wuldres bedæled,
hwilum higegeomor   healle weardað,
leofað leodum feor;   locað geneahhe
fram ðam unlædan agen   hlaford.
Forðan nah seo modor geweald,   ðonne heo magan cenneð,
bearnes blædes,   ac sceall on gebyrd
faran an æfter anum;   ðæt is eald gesceaft.'

(lines 364–87)

Saturn said:

'How does that come to pass? For good or evil when they are born from one woman, two twins their destiny is not alike, one is wretched upon the earth the other is blessed, very well thought of among the hosts of the peoples. The other lives for a little while weakens in this broad creation and then departs again with sorrows. For which one is their destiny better?'

Solomon said:

'The mother does not determine when she bears a son how his far journey will be shaped throughout the world. Often she raises a son up to grief to her own sorrow—afterwards [he] endures hardships, a time of grief. She must often grimly weep for the child when he goes forth. He has a wild mind, a grieving heart, a sorrowful mind. He errs enough, weary, deprived of joys, parted from radiance; sometimes grieving he lives in the hall, he lives far from the peoples. His lord looks away from that wretch. Therefore the mother has no power when she bears her kin/child, the fruit of a child; but he must go as destined from birth: one after the other—that is the ancient way.'

This exchange raises a number of problems, but scholars (Robert Menner, for example) have elucidated some aspects of it at least. Saturn's initial question reflects a line of argument known in the ancient world directed against astrology and astrological prophecy. If the position of the stars determines human destiny and allows astrologers to predict the future with some accuracy, then how is it that twins, who are born virtually at the same time, often have very different fates? An astrologer could argue, of course, that a few moments of time can make a profound astrological difference, but if parents or other observers cannot distinguish the exact point in time, the objection to astrology remains valid. This line of argument appears to underlie Saturn's question and since Christians agree for the most part that astrology is not a valid or legitimate science, Solomon does not respond directly to Saturn's question. Instead, he gives an extended poetic reflection on the theme that when a mother bears a child, she has no power to protect her child from experiencing the vicissitudes of history. Even a beloved child may suffer the harsh fate of alienation from his lord and the joys of the hall—the fate which is a concern in *The Wanderer*.

The initial response of the modern reader to this passage can only be puzzlement. When a mother bears a child, of course she has no way of knowing what might happen to him or her. Children are born into history and only God knows what is going to happen to them. One could rephrase the last clause from a modern secular perspective—'God only knows' what will happen to them—but both the modern secularist and the medieval Christian would agree that no human, not even the mother, knows what will become of the child. From our perspective, the extended verse paragraph in which Solomon speaks of the helplessness of the mother in the face of historical events seems quite pointless.

In addition to the curious pointlessness of Solomon's claim that the ultimate fate of a young child cannot be known, there is also the question of why Solomon's emphasis on the powerlessness of the mother to determine the fate of her child—*modor ne rædeð, nah seo modor geweald*—is so marked. He says nothing about the role of the father or about the role of the mother and father as a couple. In considering this problem we may begin by observing that a sapiential text which argues against a given practice or belief implies that the belief was in fact current. I would suggest that in this exchange between Solomon and Saturn the poet is condemning two forms of *nascentia*, the pagan magical belief that fate or fortune is determined at birth (for which, see Flint, p. 89). Saturn offers a standard argument against astrology—the problem of the different fates that can befall twins. Since Saturn's speech is essentially consonant with Christian faith, Solomon does not directly reply to Saturn's comment but discusses a somewhat different form of *nascentia*. If the pagan or at least un-Christian belief to which Saturn is alluding is relatively clear, the 'pagan' belief to which Solomon is alluding is more problematical. If Solomon insists repeatedly that the mother has no power to determine the earthly fate of her son, to what belief or related beliefs is he referring? While there is no clear-cut Anglo-Saxon vernacular statement of the belief that mothers have the power to bless (or curse) their children, and that their blessing or curse can significantly affect the fate of the child, this belief was current in medieval and early modern Europe and would explain this otherwise wholly cryptic sapiential passage.

One absolutely clear (if late) instance of this motif occurs in *Harry Potter and the Order of the Phoenix*, in which it is explained that Harry Potter's extraordinary power which enables him to resist Voldemort derives from his mother's blessing, and the blood kinship which bound her to her sister, the otherwise loathsome Aunt Petunia, makes that blessing particularly potent in Petunia's presence.[5] Part of the power and success of this series is based upon its dependence on motifs current in medieval and early modern romance, so this parallel is not as fanciful as it might seem.

The motif of the mother's blessing (or curse) being important for the fate of the child is not, as I have remarked, explicitly expressed in the rather limited corpus of Old English secular literature, but there is no explicit discussion of astrology in Old English either and the astrological interpretation of Saturn's portion of the dialogue has never been questioned. In the narrative of the *fata/fées* who bestow gifts and destiny on the child, a motif current in Germania in the early Middle Ages, the wise women who bestow the gifts can be seen as surrogates for the power of the mother and they certainly come at the behest of the mother. And there is one striking instance of the motif of the power of the blessing, or in this instance the curse, of the mother in a text which was composed in Britain and which is at least roughly contemporaneous with *Solomon and Saturn II*.

The first four stories of the Welsh *Mabinogion*, the 'Four Branches' the *Pedeir keinc y mabinogi* are preserved in later manuscripts, but are thought to have been composed in the mid-twelfth century, and all scholars are agreed that the author of the narratives which we have was drawing on material that was quite archaic. Given the date of composition of the *Pedeir keinc* and the fact that *Solomon and Saturn II* is usually thought to be a relatively late Old English poem, narratives which are preserved in the *Pedeir keinc* can legitimately be thought to be contemporaneous with the Old English poem. The fourth branch of the *Pedeir keinc* concerns, among other matters, the relationship of Aranrhod with her (illegitimate?/incestuously conceived?) son, Llew Llaw Gyffes, and the efforts of Gwydion to persuade or to trick her into fulfilling her role as a mother.

She 'swears a destiny' on her son that only she can name him,[6] and it is explicit in the text that only she has this power. When she is tricked into naming him, she 'swears a destiny' on him that he will never be equipped with arms until she arms him, and when she is again tricked into arming him, she swears a further destiny on him that he can never marry a human wife. The efforts of Gwydion and Math to frustrate Aranrhod's curse by creating the beautiful but unfaithful Blodeuedd out of flowers set the scene for the romantic tragedy of the last part of the narrative.

It is not wholly clear why Aranrhod is so hostile to her son Llew Llaw Gyffes. She was compelled to prove her virginity and when she failed the magical test to prove her virginity, she was delivered of the undeveloped foetus, which grew into the boy. She was thus compelled to give birth and deeply shamed in the process, and her shame and anger motivate her at least in part. But if elucidating the narrative logic of *Math vab Mathonwy* is difficult, it is clear that, as the mother of Lleu Llaw Gyffes, Aranrhod has a crucial role to play in his life which neither he nor Gwydion can ignore. At three crucial moments in the destiny of a warrior (to use Dumézil's phrase), Aranrhod can give or deny him a name, can give or deny him arms, and can permit or deny him the possibility of marriage. An Old English poet could indeed say of a woman like Aranrhod that *ah seo modor geweald* ('the mother has power') over the earthly fate of her son.

But the Old English poet who composed *Solomon and Saturn II* was a Christian poet for whom the power of the mother to speak the destiny of her son was problematical, and just as his pagan brother in wisdom denied the ability of astrologers to read the stars, the Christian speaker Solomon denied the power of a mother to bless or curse her son. For him, as for Martin of Braga in his *De correctione rusticorum*, 12, 'God does not order a man to know future events, but living in the fear of [God] that he should seek governance and help for his life. God alone possesses foreknowledge of events.' Mothers have no power over the course of history.

Conclusion

This interpretation of these lines in *Solomon and Saturn II* is speculative, but it perhaps has the merit of suggesting something of the fascination as well as the difficulty of Old English sapiential poetry. Students who are approaching Old English literature for the first time sometimes have the impression that these texts have been studied so extensively that there is nothing new to be said or done. Even for the canonical texts there is still much to be done, but in the field of sapiential literature the corpus has barely begun to be studied. The only major sapiential poetic text which has ever been provided with a full-scale scholarly edition is the Old English *Solomon and Saturn I* and *II* which was edited by R. J. Menner in 1941. Menner's edition is an excellent one, but it is now over sixty years old and a good deal of work has been done on the poem in the years since his edition first appeared. The remainder of the corpus of Old English sapiential poetry has never even been edited in a modern annotated scholarly edition (though see Shippey).

There is no question that Old English wisdom poetry is less immediately attractive to most modern readers than heroic poetry such as *Beowulf* or *The Battle of Maldon* or the elegies, or the best of Old English religious poetry. And critics have universally agreed that it is very difficult. But the poetic value of the best of the Old English wisdom poems is widely accepted, and if one of the goals of the study of Old English literature is to enable us to better understand this portion of the human past, those texts which directly address the problems of moral values and human choice are of obvious importance. Careful and sympathetic study of these texts can enable us to understand the values and the thought-world of the Anglo-Saxons more immediately and directly than the study of other literary texts. It is also possible that scholars and students who live in a post-modern world of irony and doubt, in which even the possibility of wisdom is questioned, might even learn something from, as well as about, the profoundly different world view of the Old English wisdom poets.

Notes

1. Aristotle, *The Art of Rhetoric*, ed. and trans. John Henry Freese. Loeb Classical Library (London: Heinemann, 1926), ii, 21, pp. 278–9.
2. Christine Fell, *Women in Anglo-Saxon England* (Oxford: Basil Blackwell, 1984), p. 36.
3. *Hávamál*, ed. David A. H. Evans (Kendal: Viking Society for Northern Research, 1986), stanza 5, p. 40. Translation mine.
4. For discussion see Sandra McEntire, 'The Monastic Context of Old English "Precepts" ', *Neuphilologische Mitteilungen*, 91 (1990), 243–9.
5. J. K. Rowling, *Harry Potter and the Order of the Phoenix* (London: Bloomsbury, 2003), pp. 736–7. Rowling's immediate 'source' (assuming that she has one) is likely to be the protective and magical power of Ash Girl's dead mother in 'Aschenputtel' (Grimm no. 21).
6. ' "Ie," heb hi, "mi a dynghaf dyghet idaw, no chaffo enw yny caffo y genhyf i," ' quoted from *Pedeir Keinc y Mabinogi*, ed. Ifor Williams (Caerdydd: Gwasg Prifysgol Cymru, 1961), p. 79. The phrasing of Aranrhod's curses the next two occasions she has to curse her son is similar. See also Rachel Bromwich and D. Simon Evans, eds., *Culhuch and Olwen* (Cardiff: University of Wales Press, 1992), p. 2, line 50, for an instance of a stepmother swearing a hostile destiny on her stepson.

References and suggested reading

Cross, James E., and Thomas D. Hill, eds. *The Prose Solomon and Saturn and Adrian and Ritheus.* McMaster Old English Studies and Texts I. Toronto: University of Toronto Press, 1982. This edition can be used as a guide to the larger European context of wisdom, riddle, and exegetical literature which one must consult in studying Old English wisdom literature.

Deskis, Susan E. *Beowulf and the Medieval Proverbial Tradition.* Medieval and Renaissance Texts and Studies 155. Tempe, Arizona: Medieval and Renaissance Texts and Studies, 1996. A model of what sophisticated modern study of sapiential material can be and one of the few recent books on *Beowulf* which offers new sources and parallels for the poem.

Flint, Valerie I. J. *The Rise of Magic in Early Medieval Europe.* Princeton: Princeton University Press, 1991. Particularly useful within the context of this essay for defining *nascentia*.

Jackson, Elizabeth. 'From the Seat of the þyle? A Reading of Maxims I, Lines 138–40', *Journal of English and Germanic Philology*, 39 (2000), 170–92.

Jackson, Elizabeth. ' "Not Simply Lists": An Eddic Perspective on Short-Item Lists in Old English Poems', *Speculum*, 73 (1998), 338–71. Of the copious amount of periodical literature which discusses Old English sapiential literature either directly or indirectly, both of Jackson's papers deserve special mention, not least because they reflect a well-informed understanding of Old Norse–Icelandic sapiential literature as well as the Old English.

Menner, Robert J., ed. *The Poetical Dialogues of Solomon and Saturn*. New York: Modern Language Association of America, 1941; repr. Millwood, NY: Kraus, 1973, pp. 135–6.

Mieder, Wolfgang. *International Proverb Scholarship: An Annotated Bibliography*. New York: Garland Publishing, 1982; and *International Proverb Scholarship: An Annotated Bibliography, Supplement*. New York: Garland Publishing, 1990. Proverb scholarship as it is conventionally understood is concerned with a somewhat narrower field than 'Sapiential Literature' as I have defined it here, but the field of Proverb scholarship is obviously related, and the student will find these volumes useful for orientation.

Poole, Russel E. *Old English Wisdom Poetry, Annotated Bibliographies of Old and Middle English Literature V*. Cambridge: D. S. Brewer, 1998. An annotated bibliographical guide to Old English wisdom poetry, which is both judicious and comprehensive.

Thesaurus proverbiorum medii aevi | Lexikon der Sprichwörter des romanisch-germanischen Mittelalters | begründet von Samuel Singer, herausgegeben vom Kuratorium Singer der Schweizerischen Akademie der Geistes- und Sozialwissenschaften. 14 vols. Berlin and New York: W. de Gruyter, 1995–. The new Samuel Singer collection. The fullest collection of medieval proverbs and sentences ever attempted. While the base language of the collection is German, the collection is so arranged that the gathering can be used by persons who know little or no German. The entries are organized around base words in German but these terms are glossed in French and English, and the proverbs are drawn from a wide variety of medieval vernacular languages and medieval Latin. There is a great deal of Middle English proverbial material and some Old English material as well. Indispensable.

Shippey, T. A. *Poems of Wisdom and Learning in Old English*. Cambridge: D. S. Brewer, 1976. Perhaps the closest approximation to a modern edition of at least some wisdom poems. Shippey's introduction and notes are very brief, though his translations are quite useful.

Walther, Hans. *Proverbia sententiaeque Latinitatis Medii Aevi; Lateinische Sprichwörter und Sentenzen des Mittelalters in alphabetischer Anordnung.* Vols. 1–6. Göttingen: Vandenhoeck & Ruprecht, 1963–. A very substantial collection of medieval Latin metrical proverbs and sentences. To use this collection one must be able to read Latin, but it is such a full gathering of material that those with at least some knowledge of the language should make the effort to consult it.

Whiting, Bartlett Jere, with Helen W. Whiting. *Proverbs, Sentences, and Proverbial Phrases from English Writings Mainly Before 1500.* Cambridge, Mass.: Harvard University Press, 1968. A gathering of proverbial material that focuses more on Middle than Old English, but is an immensely useful volume and is probably the place to begin in studying Old English sapiential literature.

13

Middle English didactic literature

James H. Morey

Introduction

Didactic verse is the largest single body of Middle English poetry, and there is an even greater amount of didactic prose. Depending on how broadly one defines 'didacticism', one could level the field at a single stroke and claim that nearly all Middle English literature was written with instruction as its primary aim. More modestly, one could claim that didactic literature is the substrate, the body of common knowledge and received wisdom, that underlies more belletristic writing and that would have been familiar even to illiterate commoners. Just as Chaucer offers 'sentence and solas' in his poetry, so didactic verse offers wisdom and comfort: the wisdom to lead a Christian life, and the comfort of knowing that salvation accrues from so living. Popular conceptions of the medieval church, largely based on how Chaucer is taught, are shaped by the assumption that the church was hopelessly corrupt, and that pious promulgations of dogma were the fatigued legacy of a faith system soon to be superseded by the Reformation. But Chaucer was critical of religious practice only in so far as it deviated from the ideal, and in the achievement and expression of that ideal Chaucer's faith was as strong as that of the *Pearl*-poet, William Langland, and any country parson or ploughman. One of the greatest testimonies to the influence of didactic literature is the amount written in, or translated into, English. Chaucer would not have been the only Englishman to be paying very close attention.

Autodidacts: wiser than we know

> God says himself, as written we find,
> That when the blind lead the blind,
> Into the ditch they fall boo   *both*
> For they see not whereby to go,
> So fare priests now by dawe   *by day*
> They be so blind in God's law
> That when they should the people rede   *advise*
> Into sin they do them lead,
> Thus they have done now fulle yore,   *for many years*
> And all is for default of lore.   *learning*

So begins John Mirk's *Instructions for Parish Priests*, a late fourteenth-century manual of religious teaching. The biblical proverb (Matthew 15: 14) leads into an indictment of priests who are ignorant of the fundamentals of the Christian faith, and of how to teach their flock the 'lore'—the learning and wisdom—necessary for salvation. Even as Mirk champions book-learning and launches an extensive review of Christian doctrine, he quotes a proverb with an unmistakable appeal to common sense. The unlearned can acknowledge the truth of the Gospel, and of Mirk's project, just as Piers Plowman acknowledges his guides 'Conscience' and 'Kind Wit' (common sense) at his first appearance in the poem (B.5.539). We are all wiser than we know, if only we are receptive to our innate wisdom. Paradoxically, the faithful are being taught what they already know, or at least what they knew, just as the attainment of paradise is not an arrival but a homecoming. Eden has been lost, but there are ways to return. The purpose of didactic literature is to enable that return. Laments in England over the ignorance of the clergy date at least from King Alfred's Preface to his translation of Pope Gregory's *Pastoral Care* (late ninth century), another guide for priests on how to take care of their flocks. If the clergy themselves are incompetent, what hope can there be for the lay folk? As Chaucer says of his Parson, 'If gold rust, what shall iron do?' (*General Prologue*, line 500). As in any time or place, books are written to meet perceived needs, and if the amount of extant material is any guide, scribes and early printers in fourteenth- and fifteenth-century England saw a profound need for books which served two purposes. First, to resist the tide of light entertainment sweeping the land, stories often based on some trifling French romance, even as authors like Mirk, fighting fire with fire, adopted the French model of octosyllabic couplets. Second, to teach both the 'learned and the lewed', those who know (or should know) and those who do not, the essentials of Christian doctrine.

In a medieval context, where book production was largely in the hands of the clergy, 'religious didacticism' is almost a redundant phrase. Even professional scribes, stationers, and printers of the fifteenth century were acutely aware of the moral dimensions of their work. From homilies and sermons, to drama cycles, to paraphrases of biblical texts and apocrypha, to the massive body of proverbs, wisdom literature, and pastoralia (literature written for the instruction and use of clerics), nearly everything that was written derived its meaning and its claim to authority from the sanction of the church and from the expectation that this literature mediates between the divine and human worlds, between what God says (as Mirk deliberately notes in line 1) and how humans should act. When read in the right way (an essential caveat which puts as much responsibility on the reader as on the writer), all writing offers knowledge about creation, it defines proper human conduct, and it sets the terms for what the Vernon manuscript calls *sowlehele*, literally the healing of the soul. Implicit in the metaphor is the combination of the spiritual and the physical; through proper belief and behaviour the soul can be saved just as a body can be healed. The Vernon manuscript (*c.*1390) is the single largest anthology of Middle English literature, and anyone who takes the time to consult the facsimile by A. I. Doyle cannot fail to be impressed by its size, capaciousness, and that a single scribe was responsible for most of the copying. This library of didactic literature contains, among many other items, the *South English Legendary* (saints' lives), an A-text of *Piers Plowman*, the *Northern Homily Cycle* (liturgically based biblical readings, followed by moralizations and exempla), Robert Grosseteste's *Chasteau d'Amour* (an English translation of an allegory based on a debate among the four 'Daughters of God', Mercy, Truth, Justice and Peace; cf. Psalm 84: 11), the apocryphal *Legend of Adam and Eve* (what the Bible does not tell us concerning what happened to Adam and Eve immediately after the Fall), several translations of Psalms, and the *Estoire del Evangelie* (a synthesis in English of the Gospels from all four Evangelists; such a work is called a 'harmony').

As a *summa* of learning, the Vernon manuscript reflects a sentiment shared by a wide range of medieval authors who cited the words of the Apostle Paul to license the practice of wide reading: 'whatever is written is written for our doctrine, so that through patience, and consolation of the scriptures, we shall have hope' (Romans 15: 4). Paul appears to restrict his injunction to sacred scripture, but medieval writers and translators, including Chaucer in his 'Retraction' and *Nun's Priest's Tale* and William Caxton in his preface to his edition of Malory, often quoted only the first half of the verse in order to extend the claim to literature as a whole. Even classical and pagan literature (notably Virgil) can be read for moral purposes because the authors spoke more wisely than they knew. The divine mind permeates and directs all of creation such that the ox and the ass in the manger and the trees in Egypt on the Flight from Herod bow down to worship the infant Jesus.

Readers encountering didactic literature for the first time will certainly be impressed, and perhaps overwhelmed, by the length of many of the works and their sheer number. Paging through Robert Raymo's entry in the *Manual* is instructive, but daunting. Those who peruse the literature, however, soon learn that these texts derive from sources and traditions that were widespread and almost always well known. A great deal of material is repeated, excerpted, and variously adapted in any number of contexts and formats. There are, in general, two alternatives: material can be spliced into the body of some other text (the *Cursor Mundi* derives some of its prodigious length from this kind of accretion), or material can appear *in toto* or in part in a manuscript composed of other independent texts (such a manuscript is called an anthology or a *florilegium*). The tendency has been to edit and study works in isolation, but one of the most welcome innovations in criticism of the past twenty years has been the placement of Old and Middle English works in their manuscript contexts. Only here can we begin to recover an authentic sense of how the medieval audience itself would have encountered the work.

Official didacts: the church

Beginning with the descent of the Holy Spirit at Pentecost, the church has always had an interest both in spreading the message of the Gospel and assuring its proper understanding. The parables of Jesus teach that it is one thing to hear a story, and quite another to understand it (cf. Mark 8: 18). In order to increase understanding among lay people, the fourth Lateran Council in 1215 required that everyone be confessed and receive communion at least once a year. This major council of the church took place at Rome, during the papacy of Innocent III, one of the most powerful medieval popes. The greater interest in lay spirituality coincided with the rise of the fraternal orders, the Dominicans and Franciscans, who emphasized preaching, confession, and repentance. What can only be called a scribal industry began to produce works dedicated to the instruction of the clergy in pastoral care and preaching. Whereas the much older monastic model of religious life was cloistered, Platonic, and centred on a life of individual reading and contemplation, the fraternal model was de-centred, Aristotelian, and based on a life of freelance preaching. The main difference resides in where the individual chooses to look for the Good, either in the transcendent world of forms (Plato) or the material world itself (Aristotle).

In England in 1281, Archbishop of Canterbury John Pecham (a Franciscan) repeated the charge of Lateran IV in his Lambeth Constitutions, and they entered the vernacular mainstream when Archbishop of York John Thoresby requested that the monk John Gaytryge compose a rhythmical prose version—known as the *Lay Folks Catechism*—in 1357. The word 'catechism', which Gaytryge does not use, derives from a Greek word meaning 'to make hear'. What was an oral form of instruction came to be applied to the book containing such instruction. The operative word for Gaytryge, however, is 'shrift', a Germanic word related to the verb 'to write' and apparently connected to the penance that a priest would prescribe for some sin, in much the same way as we take a prescription from our physician. The term survives today in the expression 'to give someone short shrift', that is, a hasty confession, and in the archaic name

'Shrove Tuesday', the day before Ash Wednesday, when by custom a Christian would confess and prepare for Lent.

Gaytryge conceives of his project as an act of preaching, a 'sermon' (modernized from Perry's edition in EETS o.s. 26):

Here begins a sermon that Dan John Gaytryge made, which teaches how shrift is to be made, and whereof, and in shrift how many things should be considered . . . As a great Doctor shows in his book, of all the creatures that God made in Heaven and in earth, in water and in air, or in anything else, the Sovereign cause and the reason why He made them was his own good will and his goodness. Through this goodness, as He is all good, He would that some creatures of those that He made were communers of that bliss that lasts for evermore. And because no creature might come to that bliss without knowing God, as that clerk teaches, He made the rational creatures Angel and man, of wit and wisdom to know God Almighty, and, through their knowing, love him and serve him and so come to that bliss that they were made to. This manner of knowing had our forefathers in the state of innocence that they were made in, and so should we have had, if they had not sinned. Not so much as holy souls have now in heaven, but much more than man has now in earth. For our forefathers sinned, says the prophet, and we bear the wickedness of their misdeeds. For the knowledge that they had of God Almighty they had it of God beginning, without travail, or affliction, or passing of time. And all the knowing that we have in this world of him, is of hearing, and of learning, and of teaching both of the law and of the learning that belongs to Holy Church, which all creatures that love God Almighty ought to know and to study, and lead their life afterwards, and so come to that bliss that never ends.

In conventional fashion, Gaytryge begins by citing a 'Great Doctor', the learned authority who legitimates what follows. Here the authority is Peter Lombard, the twelfth-century 'Master of Sentences', who compiled (in Latin) his own synthesis of Christian learning consisting mostly of quotations from earlier Doctors of the Church. His *Book of Sentences* (and by 'sentence' we should think, as Chaucer would, of a wise saying, or the moral import of that saying) was itself the subject of commentaries and versifications, and is just one example of the transmission of learning—the *translatio studii*—so characteristic of the Middle Ages. The etymological force of 'translate' is pertinent, since it means 'to carry across' in an effort that is as much physical as intellectual. Copying a manuscript is hard work. A more picturesque image is the 'Golden Chain', whereby teachers instruct pupils who become teachers, and so on.

The commentary, in which materials from the Bible, a church father, or a classical authority are quoted and then expanded upon, was a dominant medieval genre, and commentaries served as vehicles for the transmission of a text. The Bible, for example, would have been most familiar to a medieval scholar in the form of a verse-by-verse commentary, usually of single books, or just part of a book. The commentary could hedge, surround, and often overwhelm the main text in ways similar to how footnotes and glosses can crowd out the primary source in a scholarly edition. (See Pl. 5, for example.) In some cases, we do not have the original texts, but only the commentaries upon them. Macrobius's commentary on Cicero's *Dream of Scipio*, which figures so prominently in Chaucer's dream poetry, is just one example. We can only infer what Cicero wrote in his otherwise lost *Republic*, of which the *Dream of Scipio* was a part, by what Macrobius chose to quote, and comment upon. Whereas Chaucer would sometimes consciously submerge his authority (e.g. Boccaccio, the unnamed but obvious source for *The Knight's Tale*), or invent ones (e.g. Lollius, the named but otherwise unknown source for *Troilus and Criseyde*), authors of didactic literature systematically appropriate, and usually acknowledge, not just the source but also the avowed purpose of the texts.

For Gaytryge, the original sin is the defining moment for humanity. Because of the disobedience of Adam and Eve in the Garden of Eden, we are mortal, broken, and in exile. Through sin mankind has lost the angelic life, with its pure 'knowing' of God. Even in the context of shrift and repentance, Gaytryge offers a positive model of recovery through self-improvement rather than a negative model of guilt and flagellation. Intellectual endeavour enables a homecoming, as the word choices in the climactic last sentence indicate: 'knowing', 'hearing', 'learning', 'teaching', 'learning' (again), 'know', 'study', 'bliss'. Shrift, however, is a more complicated process than at first appears. Even before the confession, which must be done personally, out loud, to a priest, one must feel contrition—that is, one must feel genuinely sorry for the sin. Three more stages follow: a penance must be assigned, restitution must be made (if possible), and absolution must be given. Although the initial impulse—contrition—is personal and interior, the rest of the process necessarily requires an external structure and agent. The point is to bridge the inner and outer life such that the bridge dissolves and the human becomes reconciled with the divine.

Four examples

The following passages supply four instances in which a sinner attempts to connect outer and inner life, the human and the divine, the body and the mind. Healing the soul is the goal, but note that, paradoxically, penance always requires suffering. As C. S. Lewis demonstrates repeatedly in his fiction (e.g. *The Pilgrim's Regress*), the way back is the way forward. In other words, by painfully retracing our wandering, sinful steps, we reach the Edenic zero point. Only then is any real progress possible. The passages concentrate on how types of bodies enact and represent the suffering that the embodied God— that is Christ—suffered in order to make salvation possible. Just as humans were made in God's image (Genesis 1: 27), Christ reverses the process and himself becomes incarnate (Luke 1: 31).

The Book of Margery Kempe: the female body

Margery Kempe, a fourteenth-century wife, mother, and brewer who became a pilgrim and a mystic, recounts these stages in her life in a remarkable autobiographical work known as her *Book*. In chapter 1 the failure to make the connection from contrition to oral confession instigates the crisis which leads to her visions (from Staley's edition, pages 6 and 7):

When this creature was twenty year of age or somewhat more, she was married to a worshipful burgess and was with child within a short time, as nature would. And, after she had conceived, she was labored with great attacks of illness until the child was born, and then, what for the labor she had in childing and for the sickness going before, she despaired of her life, thinking she may not live. And then she sent for her ghostly father, for she had a thing in conscience which she had never shown before that time in all her life. For she was ever hindered by her enemy, the devil, evermore saying to her that, while she was in good health, she needed no confession but could do penance by herself alone, and all should be forgiven, for God is merciful enough. And therefore this creature oftentimes did great penance in fasting on bread and water and other deeds of alms with devout prayers, except that she would not show this sin in confession. And, when she was at any time sick or troubled, the devil said in her mind that she should be damned, for she was not shriven of that sin. Wherefore, after her child was born, she, not trusting her life, sent for her ghostly father, as was said before, in full will to be shriven of all her lifetime as nearly as she could. And, when she came to the point to say that thing which she had so long concealed, her confessor was a little too hasty and began sharply to reprove her before she had fully said her intent, and so she would no more say for aught he might do.

Margery is given short shrift. The passage is clear in its outline of what conventional practice would require, but remarkably ambiguous in its failure to specify what the sin actually was, and whether the fault lies with the priest for reproaching her so harshly or with Margery for concealing the sin for so long. The passage admits an *in bono* (positive) or an *in malo* (negative) reading of confession as it was conventionally practised. A conservative endorsement of confession would fault Margery for failing to confess in a timely fashion. An alternative view could hold that by exposing the priest's insensitivity Margery foregrounds the struggle against patriarchy that defined her life as an unconventional, self-made, female mystic. Without the crisis inspired by her post-partum distress and the harshness of the priest, presumably Margery would not have received the intensely affective and physical visions that defined her new life. Hardship enables recovery. The way up is always through the way down. Regardless of whether or not Margery should have acted as her own confessor, the act of confession is the authorizing narrative for the account of her life and experiences that follows.

Sir Gawain and the Green Knight: the male body

The psychology of sin and its forgiveness undergirds a mythic romance such as *Sir Gawain and the Green Knight*, as one would expect from the anonymous author of *Pearl*, *Patience*, and *Purity*. Gawain faces entwined physical and spiritual challenges that are foreshadowed in an explicitly didactic moment in the story, when the narrator stops the plot and describes Gawain's pentangle (lines 625 ff.). Whereas the Cross, a rudimentary stick figure, is the simplest representation of the human body one can imagine, the pentangle also simulates a human body. The five fives move (starting at the top, moving in either direction) from the five senses and five fingers (head and hand), down to the five Wounds of Christ (foot), to the Joys of

Mary (the other foot), and back up to the knightly virtues (the other hand) which synthesize and embody the knight in action. The significances progress from the purely physical to the more spiritual and abstract, with the wounds serving as the transition point. The pentangle stands on the spiritually charged and explicitly Christian Wounds and Joys. The act of swearing or expressing emotion by the wounds of Christ survived at least through Elizabethan times in the expostulation 'Zounds' (i.e. 'God's wounds'). Secular and religious experience cannot be separated in the pentangle any more than they can be separated in a poem, or in life. Later in the poem Gawain undergoes a series of confessions, and a critique of the validity of the confessions generates much of the drama that exists in the poem. Gawain's own wound, the nick on the neck, becomes yet another challenge: is the wound a reproach or a release?

The Pricke of Conscience: the corrupt body

For every one person who read *Sir Gawain and the Green Knight*, hundreds if not thousands must have read works like the *Lay Folks Catechism* or *The Pricke of Conscience*. Manuscript survival from the medieval period is always random and unpredictable, but surely it is significant that the *Pricke of Conscience* exists in more manuscripts than any other Middle English poem, followed by *Piers Plowman* and *The Canterbury Tales*—from which the *Clerk's Tale*, with its heavy moralization and abject subjection to the will of God, is the one tale copied independently most often. It is worth noting that manuscripts of the Wycliffite Bible and of prose chronicles like the *Brut* are the most numerous of all. *The Pricke of Conscience* is an apocalyptic poem of almost 10,000 lines dwelling upon man's corrupt state, the necessity of the pains of purgatory, and finally a description of the joys of paradise. The early portions of the poem rely heavily on the *contemptus mundi* theme, as the following complaint on the depravity of the times attests (lines 1524–31):

> For swilk degises and suilk manners,
> Als yhong men now hauntes and lers
> And ilk day es comonly sen,
> Byfor this tyme ne has noght ben;
> For that somtyme men held velany
> Now yhung men haldes curtasy;

And that som tyme was courtasy cald
Now wille yhong men velany hald.

For such guises and such manners
Now pursued and learned by young men,
And commonly seen every day,
Before this time have not been,
For what men at one time considered villainy
Now young men consider courtesy,
And what was at one time called courtesy
Now young men consider villainy.

Like Mirk, the author invokes an anterior golden age and defines the present through opposites. The preoccupation with sin and corruption may seem to us morbid and unenlightened, but a compelling logic drives the preoccupation. In the medieval world view, which is also the view of the Evangelists and of Paul, the world is in its seventh and last age, near the end of time. The supreme necessity is to put away the things of this world, and to think on the next, to cleanse the soul and to become reconciled with God. It is no coincidence that the Pope who convened the fourth Lateran Council—Pope Innocent III— also wrote a Latin treatise *De miseria condicionis humane* ('On the Miserable Human Condition'), a famous work adapted by Chaucer in his prologue to the *Man of Law's Tale*.

The ages of the world are the organizing principle of works like the *Cursor Mundi*, the *Polychronicon*, the *Stanzaic Life of Christ*, and even part of the *Ormulum*. The first two works are encyclopaedic world histories, and the last two centre on the life and work of Christ, but they share not only a means of organization but also a commitment to the idea that all of cosmic and human history is providentially entwined. The scholar's duty is to recover and transmit as much of that information as possible (sometimes in massive and tedious hierarchies) before it is too late.

Handlyng Synne: the redeemed body

Robert Mannyng of Brunne's *Handlyng Synne* was one of the best-known penitential manuals of fourteenth-century England. A version appears in the Vernon manuscript, and it is also spliced into texts of the *South English Legendary* and the *Northern Homily Cycle*. As is the custom in most medieval genres, Mannyng draws upon various sources, such as chronicles (William of Malmesbury) and church histories (Bede's *Historia Ecclesiastica*), but his principal source, the French *Manuel des Pechiez*, provides the standard building blocks that one would find in any number of such penitential manuals: the ten commandments, the creed, the *pater noster*, the seven deadly sins counterpointed with the seven sacraments, and so on. Whenever one encounters a collection of texts such as these, one should think of a primer. As the name implies, here one can find the elementary and essential components of the Christian faith.

In Mannyng's case, the text is distinguished by its penchant for narrative in addition to the simple exposition of the sin or virtue, and how best it may be avoided or emulated. Good preaching, like good storytelling, relies on the insertion of exactly the right example in order to render a concrete lesson and to show faith or justice in action. Such a story is what a homilist would call an *exemplum* (the story of the three thieves from the *Pardoner's Tale* is just one example of the genre). These stories could be drawn from the Bible, from history, or from the common fund of folklore and picturesque incident. Mannyng retells, for example, 'The Tale of a Minstrel Killed for Disturbing a Bishop', and 'Why Bishop Grosseteste Loved Music'. The stories appear in succession (the first bishop is anonymous, and is presumably not Grosseteste), and are classic examples of how a quality or activity can be construed *in bono* and *in malo*. Everything can be put to a good or bad purpose, depending on context and the disposition of the reader. Along with the strong penchant for order and counterpoint comes the necessity for some kind of interpretation. Likewise, the parabolic language used by Christ himself throughout the Gospels requires a gloss, a reader, and an interpreting mind, lest the bare letter of the story 'slay' the obtuse reader (2 Cor. 3: 6).

In *Handlyng Synne*, after the prologue and the ten commandments, the bulk of the narrative is taken up by over 5,000 lines on the seven deadly sins. A reader may reasonably ask why what could be subsumed within a brief list should take up so much space, but the point is not just to name the sins, but to amplify, analyse, and apply their natures and consequences. Mannyng's purpose goes beyond providing a rote exposition, or even a 'how-to manual', as the work's title might suggest. Far from being a 'handbook', the metaphor is closer to what we would call 'sin-handling' in the sense of 'manhandling':

Manuel ys handlyng with honde,
Pecchees ys synne to understonde.
These twey words that ben otwynne,
Do hem to gedyr ys handlyng synne.
And weyl is cleped for this skyle,
And, as y wote, yow show I wyle.
We handyl synne euery day
Yn worde and dede al that we may.
Lytyl or mochel synne we do:
The fende and oure flesshe tysyn us thar to.
For this skyl hyt may be seyde,
Handlyng synne for oure mysbreyde,
For euery day and euery oure
We synne, that shal we bye ful soure,
A nouther handlyng there shulde be
With shrift of mouth to clense the.
Handyl thy synne yn thy thought,
Lytyl and mochel what thou hast wroght.
Handyl thy synne to haue drede,
Nothing but peyne is ther for mede,
Handyl thy synnys and weyl hem gesse,
How they fordoun al þy goodness,
Handyl thy synnes all well and even,
Elles forbid they you the bliss of heaven.

'Manual' means handling with hands,
'Pechees' means sin.
These two words that are apart,
Put them together means 'handling sin'.
And it is named well for this reason,
And, as I am able, I will show you.
We handle sin every day,
In word and deed, as far as we are able.
Little or much sin we do:
The fiend and our flesh entice us thereto.
For this reason it may be called
'Handling sin' for our misbehaviour.
For every day and every hour
We sin, that shall we pay for very sorely.
There should be another handling,
With shrift of mouth to cleanse you,
Handle your sin in your thought,
However little or much you have done,

> Handle your sin to have fear,
> Nothing but pain is there for a reward,
> Handle your sins and consider them well
> How they destroy all your goodness.
> Handle your sins well and evenly
> Or else they will forbid you the bliss of heaven.

Once again 'bliss' is the endpoint. Whether the fiend plants the evil thought in one's mind, or whether the flesh entices us, the physical act of *confessio oris*—the confession by mouth—leads one to an intellectual grappling with the sins themselves, through repentance (itself a physical act, such as wearing a hair shirt) and absolution, and eventually heaven. The seven deadly sins are indeed abstractions, but in literary treatments such as those in *Handlyng Synne* and *Piers Plowman* (see passus 5), among many others, the psychosomatic connections between physical and spiritual life are enacted in vivid form. For the same reasons, Bishop Grosseteste adopts the poetic and architectural conceit of a castle in his *Chasteau d'Amour*. The abstract is the literary answer to the philosophical mind–body problem, and it is always best modelled by something we can see, if only in our mind's eye (cf. the allegorical garden in the *Romance of the Rose*, where abstractions are mapped onto structures and landscapes). The theology of this physical and spiritual union rests upon the central mysteries of Christianity: the Incarnation, the Crucifixion, and the Resurrection. The intersection of the divine with the human in the body of Christ makes possible the recovery of the heavenly life humankind would have enjoyed without interruption, were it not for the original sin.

Conclusion

In redeeming sinners Christ is not giving them what an economist would call 'added value'; instead Christ is claiming what was his all along. Likewise, because of Christ's sacrifice the sinner reclaims a lost legacy. Didactic literature is founded on this idea of symmetry and reciprocity, and on the Boethian ideal that everything, even suffering, makes necessary sense from a supernal perspective. Patience and humility are required to read didactic literature, and travellers must exercise the same patience and humility after going in the completely wrong direction. The only alternative is to swallow one's pride, admit the mistake, and go back to the starting-point.

References and suggested reading

Boyle, Leonard E. 'The Fourth Lateran Council and Manuals of Popular Theology'. In Thomas J. Heffernan, ed., *The Popular Literature of Medieval England*. Tennessee Studies in Literature 28. Knoxville: University of Tennessee Press, 1985, pp. 30–43. A concise guide to the subject, with a helpful diagram.

Doyle, A. I., ed. *The Vernon Manuscript: A Facsimile of Bodleian Library, Oxford, MS. Eng. Poet. a.1*. Cambridge: D. S. Brewer, 1987. Likely to be lodged in special collections, but always worth the trip.

Horstmann, Carl, ed. *Yorkshire Writers*, new edn. Cambridge: D. S. Brewer, 1999. Originally published in two volumes (1895–6). Major collection of a peripheral canon of Middle English literature. Manuscript and authorship information is out of date.

Mannyng, Robert of Brunne. *Handlyng Synne*. Ed. Idelle Sullens. Binghamton, NY: Medieval and Renaissance Texts and Studies 153, 1983. A penitential manual based primarily on French sources.

Mirk, John. *Instructions for Parish Priests*. Ed. Gillis Kristensson. Lund Studies in English 49. Lund: Gleerup, 1974. A prime example of pastoralia.

Morey, James H. *Book and Verse: A Guide to Middle English Biblical Literature*. Urbana: University of Illinois Press, 2000. Review of biblically based didactic materials, with indexes.

Morris, Richard, ed. *The Pricke of Conscience*. Berlin: A. Asher & Co., 1863; rpr. New York: AMS, 1973. Still the only edition of a poem existing in more copies than any other Middle English poem.

Perry, George G., ed. *Religious Pieces in Prose and Verse*. EETS o.s. 26. London, 1914. An edition of the *Lay Folks Catechism* from the London Thornton manuscript.

Raymo, Robert R. 'Works of Religious and Philosophical Instruction'. In A. Hartung, ed., *A Manual of the Writings in Middle English*, vol. vii New Haven: Connecticut Academy of Arts and Sciences, 1986, pp. 2255–378 and 2467–582. Exceedingly careful and complete review of the field, with descriptions and summaries followed by manuscript information and bibliography.

Staley, Lynn, ed. *The Book of Margery Kempe*. New York: W. W. Norton & Co., 2001. A convenient starting-point for the study of an increasingly important female mystic.

14

Middle English writings for women: *Ancrene Wisse*

Denis Renevey

Introduction

The *Ancrene Wisse* group consists of a series of texts written in the early thirteenth century in the south-west Midlands area. Not only was this group aimed at a primary audience of women, but it also addressed anchoresses, that is, women who had chosen to lead a solitary life in a private cell, often attached to a parish church, or as part of a group of cells which made an anchorhold. Apart from *Ancrene Wisse*, to which we shall give most of our attention in this chapter, the *Ancrene Wisse* group can be subdivided into the Katherine group and the Wooing group. The Katherine group consists of three virgin martyrs' lives, those of *Seinte Katerine, Seinte Margarete*, and *Seinte Juliene*, a treatise on virginity called *Hali Meiðhad*, and a work on the guardianship of the soul called *Sawles Warde*. The Wooing group consists of four prayers and meditations in rhythmical prose.

While all texts of the *Ancrene Wisse* group demonstrate a concern for the anchoritic life, *Ancrene Wisse* allows best entry into this peculiar mode of life. Probably of Dominican origin, *Ancrene Wisse* provides informal advice to three ladies leading the life of recluses. It is a text written in very elegant style by an author who had a good knowledge of Latin literature and who was also intimate with oral traditions. Although a large number of sources were used for its making, the anchoritic rule *De institutione inclusarum*, by the Cistercian monk Aelred of Rievaulx (1109–66), had a large impact on the structure and thematic scope of *Ancrene Wisse*.

The latter is divided into a preface and eight distinct parts. The tone is sometimes familiar, at other times much more official, and the crisp imagery used by the author throughout the text has contributed to its lasting impact, not to mention its importance as a witness to early Middle English prose. It survives, complete or only in parts, in seventeen medieval manuscripts, some of which attest to its adaptability to new audiences.

Since the anchoritic life was largely a female vocation, the role given to male ecclesiastical supervision of anchoresses accounts for one of the reasons why cells were set, no longer in the wilderness, but rather in the vicinity of parish churches. This essay investigates the question of the role played by communities and social networks in the most distinguished anchoritic work written on English soil in the early thirteenth century, in Middle English, and translated a little later into Anglo-Norman and Latin.

My aim is to see how the treatise constructs a nexus of representations of ideas about communities and social networks throughout its eight parts, which the potential, largely undefined, reading subject can appropriate in order to reform, convert, or construct her (new) subjectivity. Some of these imagined communities refer to either the religious or secular sphere, and are connoted either negatively or positively, while other passages in the treatise make reference to real communities in equally ambivalent ways. Those representations serve an important function by forcing the reading subject to assess her own roles within those communities and to decide whether they are compatible with her function. I contend that the representation of these communities plays a momentous role in shaping the subjectivity, not only of the anchoritic readers of the treatise, but of any reader, medieval or modern, approaching the text with a religious intention in mind and able to create the anchoritic paradigm imaginatively for herself.

Imagining the self and secular communities

Representations of the possible ways by which the reading subject could imaginatively interact with secular communities are found throughout the treatise. The world of the nobility, their manners, and the space they inhabit help in tuning the inner feelings of the reader. The authorial intention to take a cataphatic approach (that is, representing the relationship with God by means of images from everyday life for the construction of an intimate relationship with God) is quite evident in the use made of this specific secular imagery. The besieged lady in her fortress capably resisting the assault of the enemy, the further reference to the female readers as firm-standing towers of a besieged city, and the parable of a king loving a noble poor lady, all combine to create empathy on the part of the readers for a sophisticated textual community. *Ancrene Wisse* assumes knowledge of these literary *topoi* and asks for a transliteration of their use in the religious context, as part of an effort to interiorize religious precepts, such as mastering the sense of sight—which may otherwise lead to lecherous behaviour—fighting against temptations in general, and increasing one's love for the lover-knight who is God in his humanity.

References to a noble and sophisticated textual community apart, the reader also finds invitations to work with representations of other secular communities. Part I, 'Devotion' (p. 19, fo. 7b/10–12; p. 58),[1] asks the anchoress to pray for the community of the sick and sorrowful, as well as prisoners, especially for Christian ones kept in heathen countries. It seems that the main point here is to show the reader how, by means of a sustained imagination triggered by prayer and meditation, she can participate in the betterment of those communities. While she is being asked here to stretch her thoughts beyond the immediate confines of her inhabited space towards the outside world, images of sickness and imprisonment are also called back at other junctures in the guide in order to help the anchoress define her own, largely enclosed, inhabited space, and her inner world.

If the enclosed space of the *reclusorium* plays a momentous role in shaping the subjectivity of the readers, other spaces and other communities are recalled in the treatise. For instance, part V, 'Confession', considered controversial for the ways in which it assumes a much wider readership than an anchoritic one, makes reference to the public spaces of the medieval village or market town. Such a passage assumes a reader who is not at all linked in any practical way to the anchoritic mode of life. Instead, it seems that the assumed speaker here is a lay Christian:

Alswa of þe *stude*: Sire, þus ich pleide oðer spec ichirche, eede o ring, i chirchȝard, biheold hit, oþer wreastlunge, ant oðre fol gomenes; spec þus oðer pleide biuoren wortliche men, biuoren recluse in ancre hus, ed oþer þurl þen ich schulde, neh hali þing. Ich custe him þer, hondlede him i swuch stude, oðer me seoluen. I chirche ich þohte þus, biheold him ed te weouede. (p. 163, fo. 86a/18–24)

The same for *place*: 'Sir, thus I played or spoke in church, joined in the ring-dancing, in the churchyard, watched dancing, wrestling and other silly games; spoke thus or played in front of worldly men, in front of a recluse in an anchorhouse, or at a window where I ought not to have been, or near a holy thing; I kissed him there, handled him, or myself, in such a place; in church I thought this way, watched him at the altar.' (part V, p. 165)

Ancrene Wisse describes a vibrant secular community whose spaces are filled with communal, playful activities, gossip, dancing, wrestling and other games, some of them clearly sexual in intent. Even more interesting for our understanding of the role played by recluses in medieval society, the space of the anchorhold, perceived from the outside, stands in this passage as a landmark of this small but active community. Part V, 'Confession', even more convincingly than other parts of the rule, has an immediate appeal to Christians in general.

Joining the community of the saints

If snapshots of secular life force the self to imagine interactions with the world, other moments in the text situate the self with reference to an idealized holy community, made up of saints, martyrs, and other biblical characters. Such representation takes place appropriately in part III, 'The Inner Feelings', where idealization of the anchoritic life, solidly grounded on spiritual benefits still to come after physical death, relies on a select community of models. The Old Testament

Judith is venerated in *Ancrene Wisse* less for her military and physical prowess at slaying the almighty Assyrian general Holofernes, than for her life of enclosure, shut up in the upper room of her house with only one handmaid. This life of seclusion followed the death of her husband and preceded her military coup. John the Baptist, the Virgin Mary, and even God in his humanity, who fasted for forty days in solitariness, act as models of a spiritual community to which the reading anchoress aspires to belong. Other figures, like Job and some virgin martyrs, are praised not so much for a life of seclusion, but rather for their determination when facing adversity, often experienced in a very solitary way. The virgin martyr narratives are marked by their politics of heroism, thus inviting their readers and those of *Ancrene Wisse* (and other associated texts) to view the solitary as being heroic too. The privilege of belonging to such an élite community can easily be abused by sinful activity, resulting in immediate loss:

Godd wat, he mei beon muche deale sorhfulre þat haueð wið deadlich sunne gasteliche islein godd inwið his sawle—nawt ane forloren þe swete feader of heouene ant seinte Marie his deorewurðe moder, oþer hali chirche (hwen he of hire naueð ne leasse ne mare), ant te engles of heouene ant alle hali halhen þe weren him ear for freond, for breðren ant for sustren. (p. 159, fos. 84a/23–84b/1)

God knows, a man who has spiritually slain God with deadly sin in his own soul can be a great deal more sorrowful—having lost not only the sweet Father of heaven and St. Mary his precious mother, or Holy Church (when he will have neither less nor more from her), but also the angels of heaven and all the holy saints who had been like his friends, his brothers and his sisters. (part V, p. 162)

The loss of the spiritual community through sinful behaviour is described as a murderous act, killing not only father and mother, but also the anchoress's children who are her good works. Representations of imagined communities, be they religious or secular, importantly shape the ways by which the solitary reader addresses her own position with regard to the development of her inner feelings and her growing desire for God.

Social networks: secular communities

Although at times *Ancrene Wisse* loses its close focus on the anchoritic recipients by offering material for the use of a multiple audience, some passages on the other hand construct a precise representation of real social exchanges, which might have been necessary for, or a threat to, the conduct of an anchoritic mode of life. Part II, 'The Outer Senses', admonishes its primary readership against the dangers that inevitable social contacts within the confines of the anchorhold make possible: *Ouer al þat ʒe habbeð iwriten in ower riwle of þinges wið uten, þis point þis article of wel to beo bitunde, ich wulle beo best ihalden* (p. 34, fo. 15a/8–10): 'Above everything that you have written in your rule about outward things, I would have this point, this article about being well-enclosed, best kept' (part II, p. 71). The space of the *reclusorium*, whatever its size and the number of its inhabitants, enables the performance of activities inappropriate to their religious standing. Inevitable interaction with the outside world, often taking place in the parlour, through its carefully described windows, is fraught with dangers, which are closely addressed in *Ancrene Wisse*. One becomes aware that the preservation of solitariness is hard to come by in an environment where social contacts are inevitable. A codification of what is or is not permissible is listed in detail, with reference to the spaces in which those activities can take place. The parlour and church windows play distinct functions, with different levels of permissibility with regard to social interaction. From the parlour window the anchoress should let her maidservant do the talking with her guests, only waving occasionally to them. The church window, on the other hand, fills a sacred function by allowing the sight of the Eucharist: but by performing that function, it also makes visible the parish community attending the Eucharistic consecration at specific times. Indirectly, the anchoress might feel a sense of belonging while witnessing those communal performances. At other times, it was possible for some of the members of this community to come dangerously close to the *reclusorium* by means of its other windows. For those who were well intentioned and useful to the livelihood of the anchoress, like a spiritual guide or confessor, a proper mode of behaviour is stipulated, while emphasis is placed on what the anchoress should or should not do to avoid unnecessary and dangerous social interactions. While the ultimate aim is to flee the world community, possibilities such as kissing a man or making the anchorhouse a space where intensive gossip develops are real enough:

Me seið up on ancren þat euch meast haueð an ald cwene to feden hire earen, a meaðelilt þe meaðeleð hire alle þe talen of þe lond, a rikelot þe cakeleð al þat ha sið ant hereð, swa þat me seið i bisahe: 'From mulne ant from chepinge, from smiððe ant from ancre hus me tidinge bringeð.' (p. 48, fo. 23a/14–19)

It is said of anchoresses that almost everyone of them has some old woman to feed her ears, a gossip who tells her all the local tid-bits, a magpie who cackles about all that she sees and hears, so that the saying now runs, 'You can hear the news from a mill or market, from a smithy or an anchorhouse.' (part II, p. 81)

Representations of social networks and the spaces they create play a part in the process of constructing the solitary self. As a result, it is important to take into consideration the particular conditions in which that self is fashioned. The social visibility and the more general politics which mark thirteenth-century solitary life charge it with images representing exchanges, communication, gossip, and trans-actions. Leading a solitary life in the thirteenth century is not a lonely enterprise, but one carried out for the sake of several communities, physical and spiritual: the immediate community of the parish and the diocese, for which special permission and physical support (cell, food, wood) are necessary, and the larger community of Christians, for whom a life devoted to meditation and prayer infers important spiritual benefits. *Ancrene Wisse* projects a model in which this sense of interaction with the outside world is clearly explicated. It does not occlude the possible dangers of such interactions or of an excess of them, but it is well aware of the necessity of some interactions with those communities for the survival of the model.

Whether social interactions are fought against or connoted posi-tively in *Ancrene Wisse*, their imprint is forcefully encoded in the psyche of its readers. It is significant also that in some parts of the treatise the past of its readers is assumed to be that of former noble ladies, or individuals belonging to the landed gentry, who had had responsibilities within the household, and had entertained guests and given feasts in the not so distant past. The prescriptions against the conduct of secular transactions in part VIII echo those necessary to run the community of a noble household.

Na chaffere ne driue ӡe. Ancre þat is chepilt, þat is, buð forte sullen efter biӡete ha chepeð hire sawle þe chapmon of helle. Þing þah þat ha wurcheð ha mei, þurh hire meistres read, for hire neode sullen. Hali men sumhwile liueden bi hare honden.

Nawt deore dehtren ne wite ӡe in ower hus of oðer monne þinges: ne ahte, ne claðes, ne boistes, ne chartres, scoren ne cyrograffes, ne þe chirch uestemenz, ne þe calices, bute neode oðer strengðe hit makie, oðer muchel eie. Of swuch witunge is muchel vuel ilumpen ofte siðen. (pp. 213–14, fo. 113*a*/8–18)

Do not conduct business. An anchoress fond of bargaining, that is, one who buys to sell for gain, sells her soul to the merchant of hell. Things that she makes, with her director's advice, she may sell for her needs. Holy people often used to live by their hands.

Dear daughters, do not look after other people's things in your house: possessions, clothes, boxes, charters, accounts, indentures, church vestments or chalices—unless need or violence makes it necessary, or great fear. From such guarding much evil has often come about. (part VIII, p. 201)

One ought to note how the comments made here imply that, even though the primary audience *Ancrene Wisse* addresses does not suffer from the deficiencies listed, it is nevertheless assumed that anchoresses elsewhere do participate in business ventures, and interact actively with medieval mercantile society.

Anchoresses, religious communities, and the household

Business interactions of this nature are not recommended. However, their imprint on the psyche of the female reader is significant and seems to suggest an anchoritic model shaped by a market economy. The model anchoress participates in a business transaction with her community, offering in exchange for her permanent and stable place of abode—and the means to sustain her physical life—a spiritual counterpart in the form of prayers and meditations. The good anchoress therefore needs to use discernment in order to check whether the ventures she participates in will make her a better spiritual commodity in her community. There is a price attached to the position of the anchoress, and the regulations offered in *Ancrene Wisse* enable the anchoress to measure her own position in terms of her spiritual marketability.

Recently, serious attention has been drawn towards the succinct, but nevertheless very significant, references to both the English and Anglo-Norman language communities to which the readers of *Ancrene Wisse* belong. In part I, 'Devotion', anchoresses are invited to read from English or French texts, while further on, in part IV, prayers can be made, according to the treatise, in one's own language, thus implying a multilingual anchoritic audience at the time of composition or revision. Such a comment rings with a new tone in light of the work by Jocelyn Wogan-Browne on women's literary culture in Anglo-Norman. The shifts from a single recipient, to the three anchoresses, and finally, in the Corpus version, to the community of English anchoresses are symptomatic. In fact, much of part IV, 'Temptations', is community-orientated and the most significant addition in the Corpus manuscript comes as a natural development to this communal concern:

ȝe beoð, þe ancren of englond, swa feole togederes—twenti nuðe oðer ma. Godd i god ow mutli, þat meast grið is among, meast annesse ant anrednesse, ant sometreadnesse of anred lif efter a riwle, swa þat alle teoð an alle iturnt anesweis, ant nan frommard oðer—efter þat word is. For þi ȝe gað wel forð ant spedeð in ower wei, for euch is wiþward oþer in an manere of liflade, as þah ȝe weren an cuuent of lundene ant of oxnefort, of schreobsburi, oðer of chester. þear as alle beoð an wið an imeane manere. ant wið uten singularite—þat isanful frommardschipe, lah þing i religiun, for hit to warpeð annesse ant manere imeane, þat ah to beon in ordre. Þis nu þenne þat ȝe beoð alle as an cuuent is ower hehe fame, þis is godd icweme, þis is nunan wide cuð, swa þet ower cuuent biginneð to spreaden toward englondes ende. ȝe beoð as þe moderhus þat heo beoð of istreonet, ȝe beoð ase wealle. (p. 130, fos. 69a/13–69b/1)

You are, you anchoresses of England, very many together—twenty, now, or more. May God increase you in goodness—you who live in the greatest peace, the greatest oneness and constancy, and in the concord of a steadfast life: following a single rule, so that all pull one way, and all are turned in the same direction, not away from one another—so it is said. And so you are journeying well and making good speed along your way; for you are all turned toward one another in a single manner of living, as though you were a single convent, in London, Oxford, Shrewsbury or Chester. Since all are one, with a common way of life and without singularity—which is a foul turning away, a low thing in religion, for it breaks apart oneness and a common way of life, which there ought to be in an order—the fact you are like a single convent now makes you greatly honored; it pleases God and is now widely known, so that your convent is beginning to spread toward the end of England. You are like the mother-house from which they have sprung; you are like the spring. (part IV, p. 141)

The Corpus manuscript develops the sense of community that is part of the construction of thirteenth-century solitariness to the greatest extent. The anchoresses find stability in their solitary enterprise by being offered a paradigm for common identification, so that a sense of belonging to community strengthens their identities as solitaries. Not only do they together constitute a convent, but they are also described as forming an order. Although the entire passage should be read metaphorically, as it is clearly indicated when Jesus is described as the prior of that convent, and further reference is made to the cloister as the cloister of heaven, it nevertheless presents the reader with a strong sense of community, and, in view of this passage and other pieces of evidence, it is surely valid to argue for the importance of how community shapes the self in *Ancrene Wisse* in particular, and in thirteenth-century anchoritic culture more generally.

However, at a literal level too, a sense of community, and of the preservation of healthy relationships between its members are frequently expressed by the circulation of written or oral information about its members. Messengers play a significant role in conveying oral or written messages between sisters. The *Ancrene Wisse*-author seems well aware of the means by which information circulates between anchoresses when talking about the content of those messages. A sister should never speak evil about another sister, but she should nevertheless *warni oþer þurh ful siker sondesmon, sweteliche ant luueliche as hire leoue suster, of þing þat ha misnimeð ȝef ha hit wat to soðe* (p. 131, fo. 69b/24–7): 'admonish the other through a very trustworthy messenger, sweetly and lovingly as her dear sister, about anything that she does wrongly if she knows it to be truth' (part IV, p. 141). Despite the absence of conventual space, some of the points raised in the text about friction between sisters reveal many of the practical difficulties that all communities face in their daily routine. There would appear to be a sufficient circulation of information between the *Ancrene Wisse* sisters to allow the development of a set of networks that make possible an exchange of personal, intimate, feelings. Despite not living together within the physical space of a convent, *Ancrene Wisse* offers plenty of evidence that, for the anchoritic readers of the text, the sense of community is a significant signpost for the delineation of their spiritual life, as well as impacting on the way they configure their daily life. The address to *leoue sustren* ('dear sisters') in several passages of the text (especially from part IV onwards) reinforces this sense of belonging.

Secular communities, the community of English anchoresses, language, and religious communities all play a part in shaping the anchoritic model that is offered in this rule. One additional community, that of the household, receives sustained and detailed attention in part VIII, 'The Outer Rule'. This part contextualizes the anchoress in her daily activities, as she surveys and controls the activities of her servants. *Ancrene Wisse* provides information about the practical aspects of her life in her new household, whose architectural space, the anchorhouse, is markedly more spacious than the small cubicles described in liturgical ceremonies of enclosures or represented in manuscript illuminations, such as, for instance, Cambridge, Corpus Christi College, MS 79 (fo. 96a). With unflagging energy, the text covers many aspects of the roles each should play in this particular community. Prescriptions on food and drink, on gifts and possessions, on clothing and occupations, on haircutting and bloodletting, on the rules of conduct for the maidservants, as well as on the teaching by the lady anchoresses of the maidservants, serve to make this final part of the treatise very similar to books of conduct designed for noble households. Despite the idiosyncrasies which mark the anchoritic mode of life, it is easy to find similarities between some of the activities predicated in the treatise and secular activities which a noble lady would undertake in her own household:

Eauer me is leouere se ȝe doð greattre werkes. Ne makie ȝe nane purses forte freondin, ow wið bute to þeo þat ower meistre ȝeueð ow his leaue, ne huue, ne blodbinde of seole ne laz buten leaue . . . As of oðre þinges, kun oðer cuððe hu ofte ȝe underuengen, hu longe ȝe edheolden: tendre of cun ne limpeð nawt ancre beonne . . . Amites ant parures, wordliche leafdis mahen inoh wurchen. Ant ȝef ȝe ham makieð, ne makie ȝe þrof na mustreisun. (pp. 215–16, fos. 114a/16–114b/2)

I would always rather you do the more coarse kinds of handiwork. Do not make purses to win friends, but only for those for whom your director gives you leave, nor caps, silk bandages or lace without leave . . . As for other

things, how often you should receive friends or family, and how long keep
them with you: family feeling is not proper for an anchoress . . . Ladies in the
world can make enough keepsakes and collarbands; but if you make them, do
not make them to show off. (part VIII, p. 203)

Analogies to ladies in the world are recurrent, and not innocent, in
this part of the treatise. The anchoress's role in controlling discipline
within the household bears significantly upon the way she imposes
proper codes of conduct upon her maidservants. In fact, the role of
maidservants in enabling the solitary mode of life in the middle of a
community cannot be stressed enough, since they are the gateway for
information to come in and out of the anchorhouse. The circulation
of information, which they have the power to transmit in and out of
the anchoritic space, may well determine the spiritual quality of the
life experienced by their ladies within. Hence the care with which the
lady anchoress needs to control the moods of her maidservants, bring
them to peace with one another, asking them to kneel in front of her
and to acknowledge their faults. Concern for their education in general, and their literacy, is well documented elsewhere in part VIII. In
fact, as the author suggests, this final 'stucche' or branch, which
should be read each week to the maids, serves as a mini-rule for them,
within the larger rule. The good running of the household relies
heavily on the ways by which the anchoress controls the code of
conduct of her inferiors in the household. The healthy development
of the microscopic community that inhabits the anchorhold necessitates a set of prescriptive rules which the anchoress, as undisputed
hierarchical superior, needs to implement forcefully. The final part of
Ancrene Wisse makes a strong case for a rule written for a religious,
hierarchically organized, household.

Conclusion

The theme of community, which is the concern of this essay,
foregrounds an aspect of anchoritism which is not immediately
visible when approaching this text for the first time. The aim is not
to deny the solitary aspects of the anchoritic life as described in
Ancrene Wisse. On the contrary, the focus on communities in this
text serves to demonstrate what the concept of solitariness in the

thirteenth century entails, how it has to be negotiated, and how solitaries themselves need to configure strategies for preserving their solitary status, within a bustling, mercantile medieval society, whose diverse activities took place not very far from the windows of the anchorhold.

In fact, some of the other early Middle English texts written for women also participate in defining this solitary status. The virgin martyrs' lives offer models of women on their own heroically facing religious and political adversity. *Hali Meiðhad*'s and *Sawles Warde*'s dominant discourses are about sealed bodies and moral intactness. The Wooing group in addition shows what potential for performance solitary life in the thirteenth century offered. Those early Middle English writings for women, like *Ancrene Wisse*, speak in favour of a spirituality of enclosure. However, in doing that, they also point to the tensions which such a life entailed, with the impossible aim of preserving spiritual, moral, and bodily enclosure in a world marked by the interactions of anchoresses with the literal and spiritual communities which constituted medieval society.

Note

1. All references to the Middle English version of *Ancrene Wisse*, by page, folio, and line number, are to the following edition: *Ancrene Wisse, Edited from MS. Corpus Christi College Cambridge 402*, ed. J. R. R. Tolkien, EETS 249 (Oxford: Oxford University Press, 1962). I have provided modern punctuation and expanded all abbreviations silently. Translations, with reference to part and page, are from *Anchoritic Spirituality: Ancrene Wisse and Associated Works*, ed. Anne Savage and Nicholas Watson, The Classics of Western Spirituality (New York: Paulist Press, 1991).

References and suggested reading

Barratt, Alexandra. 'Anchoritic Aspects of *Ancrene Wisse*', *Medium Aevum*, n.s. 49 (1980), 32–56. This essay examines the issue of what it meant to be an anchoress and whether *Ancrene Wisse* is really an anchoritic treatise.

Cannon, Christopher. 'The Form of the Self: *Ancrene Wisse* and Romance', *Medium Aevum*, n.s. 70 (2001), 47–65. This essay offers a convincing exploration of the form of *Ancrene Wisse* and the way it serves for the representation of the bodily self of the anchoress.

Dobson, Eric J. *The Origins of Ancrene Wisse*. Oxford: Oxford University Press, 1976. Even if Dobson's answers have been superseded, his study ploughs the field that all subsequent studies on authorship, recipients, and institutional and cultural contexts have to investigate.

Georgianna, Linda. *The Solitary Self: Individuality in the Ancrene Wisse*. Cambridge, Mass.: Harvard University Press, 1981. This book examines notions of the self in the anchoritic context in general, and in *Ancrene Wisse* in particular.

Millett, Bella, with the assistance of George B. Jack and Yoko Wada. *Ancrene Wisse, the Katherine Group, and the Wooing Group*. Annotated Bibliographies of Old and Middle English Literature 1353–8675 vol. 2. Woodbridge: D. S. Brewer, 1996. The starting-point for any serious research on the *Ancrene Wisse* group.

Millett, Bella. 'The Origins of *Ancrene Wisse*: New Answers, New Questions', *Medium Aevum*, n.s. 61 (1992), 206–28. This piece should be read as a follow-up to Dobson's. It challenges Augustinian authorship, as well as the addressee of the three sisters living in the Deerfold near Wigmore. It suggests Dominican authorship, with a date of composition after 1221.

Renevey, Denis. 'Enclosed Desires: A Study of the Wooing Group'. In William F. Pollard and Robert Boenig, eds., *Mysticism and Spirituality in Medieval England*. Cambridge: D. S. Brewer, 1997, pp. 39–62. This article touches upon the notion of enclosure and the psychological paradigm that it sets for the performance of meditative prayers.

Renevey, Denis. 'Figuring Household Space in *Ancrene Wisse* and *The Doctrine of the Hert*'. In David Spurr and Cornelia Tschichold, eds., *The Space of English*. Swiss Papers in English Language and Literature 17. Tübingen: Günter Narr, forthcoming. This is a companion piece to the one offered as part of this volume. It explores further communities by putting attention on the role of space, more particularly household space, in *Ancrene Wisse* and *The Doctrine of the Hert*.

Wada, Yoko, ed. *A Companion to Ancrene Wisse*. Cambridge: D. S. Brewer, 2003. This book offers some of the most up-to-date research by leading scholars on several aspects of *Ancrene Wisse*. In the context of this volume, the articles by Watson on the use of *Ancrene Wisse* by later medieval authors and by Millett on 'The Genre of *Ancrene Wisse*' deserve particular attention.

Wogan-Browne, Jocelyn. *Saints' Lives and Women's Literary Culture: Virginity and its Authorizations*. Oxford: Oxford University Press, 2001. A ground-breaking book on women's literary culture, with special emphasis on the Anglo-Norman material.

1. Centres of literary and historical significance in medieval England. Map by Niall Brady and Michael Potterton, courtesy of the Discovery Programme, Dublin.

2. Manuscript A of the *Anglo-Saxon Chronicle*: Cambridge, Corpus Christi College, MS 173, folio 26r (*c.*955).

be ꝼæꞅtman ꞅpylce hi him þaꞅ ʒe aðle eoaꝼꝼ ꞅpiðoꞃ onðꞃæ
ðon þon þaꞅe ꞅꞃuman · þe læʒ ꞃe lyꞇʒi ꞃeond æꝼꞇeꞃ ꝼyꞃ
ꞅꞇe ꞅpiðoꞃ ꝼæʒne þ he himið hiꞅ loꞇ pꞃieneū be ꞅpice
þꞃah he hi æꞃ on openū ʒe ꝼeohꞇe oꝼeꞃ eome · ꞇ him þone
ꞅeiðan ꞃꝼyꞃian ꝼoꞃ qæðe · þon oðꞃe pꞃan ꞃync ꞇo mani
ꞇɴne þa pel pyllenðan · on oðꞃe þa æꞅꞅꞇiʒan ·

O�ɴ oðꞃe pꞃan ꞅync ꞇo maniꞇɴne þa pel pyllenðan · on
oðꞃe þa æꞅꞅꞇiʒan · þa pel pyllenðan ꞃync ꞇo maniꞇɴ
ne þ hi ꞅꞃa ꝼæʒnion oðꞃa manna ʒoðꞃa poꞃica · þ him eac
þæꞃ ylean lyꞅꞇe · ꞇ ꞅꞃa ʒylpon hiꞃa nehꞇꞇena ðæða · þ hi
him eac on hyꞇꞇen · ɴimon him byꞃne on hiꞃa ʒoðū poꞃ
cum · ꞇ ʒe þeneen hi ꞃylꝼe miðhiꞃa aʒenū · þe læʒ hi ꞃyn ꞇo
oðꞃa manna ʒe ꝼeohꞇe holðe heapeꞃiaꞃ · ꞇ ne ðon him ꞃyl
ꝼum nan þinʒ · ꞇ þon æꝼꞇeꞃ þam ʒe ꝼeohꞇe eꝼꞇ ꞃy buꞇan
æʒhpyleū eolꞇeane on þiꞃū anðꞃeaꞃðan liꝼe · ꞅe þe on þa
ʒe ꝼeohꞇe þyꞃeꞃ anðꞃeaꞃðan liꝼeꞃ nele ꞃꞃincan ne hiꞅ ꞃyl
ꝼeꞃ ꞇilian he onʒꞇꞇ eꝼꞇ hine ꞃylꝼne · oꝼeꞃ aꞃmen he bið
ꞇ eac ʒe ꞃꞃynð þon he ʒe ꞃꞃiðꞀ · ꞇ ʒe hꞃið þa þe aꞃ pell aʒun
non · þa þa he ioel pæꞅ · Spiðe ꞃꞃiðe þe ʒe ꞃꞃynʒiað ʒꝼ þe
ðꞃa manna ðæða þe pel ʒe ðone bꞃoð ne luꝼiʒað ꞇ ne
heꞃuað · Ac þe nabbað þꞃah nane meðe þaꞃe heꞃunʒe · ʒꝼ
þe be ꞅumum ðæle nellað onʒinnan þ þe ʒe eꞃenlæeeon
þam þeapum þe uꞃ on oðꞃū mannū licyað be þam ðæle
þe þe maʒon · ꝼoꞃ þam iꞅ ꞇo ꞃeʒanne þam pel pyllenðan

4. The dedication page to Queen Emma and King Cnut from an eleventh-century manuscript: Stowe 944 folio 6*r*.

5. Page of commentary: Oxford, Keble College, MS 26, folio 17*v*. (second half of the thirteenth century).

6. *The Book of Margery Kempe,* from the mid-fifteenth-century manuscript: London, British Library, Additional 61823, folio 1r.

7. Rogier van der Weyden, *Annunciation Triptych*, central panel (*c.*1440): Louvre, Paris.

8. Stephan Lochner, *Madonna of the Rose Bush* (*c.*1440): Wallraf-Richarz Museum, Cologne.

9. Paul, Herman, and Jean de Limbourg, April calendar page from *Les Très Riches Heures du Duc de Berry* (1415–16): Musée Condé, Chantilly, MS 65, folio 4*v*.

15

The Middle English *Brut* chronicles

David F. Johnson

Introduction: the Middle English *Brut*

As a genre, the Middle English *Brut* chronicles are defined by their original subject matter: they all deal with the legendary foundation of Britain, beginning with the arrival in and subsequent conquest of the island following the fall of Troy by Aeneas' great-grandson, Brutus (hence the term *Brut*). The prologue to *Castleford's Chronicle* illustrates this myth of origins well:

> Her endys þe Prolog Olbyon, *Albion*
> þat was an yll all wulsome. *island/beautiful*
> Nowe her begynnys þe Boke of Brut,
> And howe he hys awne land fors[o]ke,
> And howe Albyon conqueryd,
> And aftyr hym Brutayne it named,
> þat nowe is callyd Yngland, certanly,
> Aftyr þe name of Engyst of Saxony.

Enduring beyond the Middle Ages as a legitimate and popular form of historiographical writing, the *Brut* in Middle English evolved in two forms, prose and verse. The earliest English prose chronicles were ultimately based on translations of existing Latin and Anglo-Norman texts, and gained momentum as native productions in the late fourteenth century. The Middle English *Prose Brut*, for example, was one of the most popular secular works written in the English Middle

Ages, extant in several versions contained in over 170 manuscripts (Hartung, *Manual*, 2629).

Unlike the *Anglo-Saxon Chronicle* (discussed by Bredehoft in Chapter 8), which emerged initially from the monastic tradition of annotating Easter tables, the Middle English *Bruts* in verse owe a large debt to the creative talents of one man: Geoffrey of Monmouth. His *Historia regum Britanniae* (*History of the Kings of Britain, c*.1185) was the first *Brut*, and it seems, for the most part, to have been the product of his own imagination. The earliest verse chronicles were based on French adaptations of Geoffrey's work;[1] while less widespread than the later prose *Brut*, they are well represented throughout the period. Robert of Gloucester's *Metrical Chronicle* (in two versions, A and B), an anonymous *Short Metrical Chronicle*, Thomas Bek of Castleford's *Chronicle of England*, and Robert Mannyng of Brunne's *The Story of England* were all written between *c*.1300 and 1340, and all recount the history of England from the advent of Brutus in Britain to a point somewhere in the first half of the fourteenth century.

Laȝamon's *Brut*: the poem and its context

The earliest and best-known version of the *Brut* in English is also incidentally the first treatment of Arthurian material in the language: the verse chronicle written by Laȝamon (or Layamon, or Lawman) sometime between 1199 and 1225. Relatively neglected for a number of decades since the appearance of its first modern edition in 1847, the poem has been the subject of a recent surge in interest and the publication of a number of important studies (see References and suggested reading), a development that appears to bear out C. S. Lewis's claim that it 'reveals, in a flash, imaginative power beyond the reach of any Middle English poet whatever' (cited in Bzdyl, p. 1). It is extant in two manuscripts: London, British Library, Cotton Caligula A. ix and Cotton Otho C. xiii. Both versions are probably based on a common exemplar that cannot have been the author's autograph copy, the earlier of the two dating to the middle of the thirteenth century. Cotton Otho C. xiii contains an abridged and altered version of the poem, its idiom changed in significant ways, seemingly to bring it in line with its reviser's linguistic norms.

At over 16,000 lines, the Caligula version is the second longest poem in Middle English. What little we know about the author is derived from his prologue, and current scholarly consensus holds that his main source was in fact the Jerseyman Wace's *Roman de Brut*, a translation into Anglo-Norman rhymed couplets of Geoffrey of Monmouth's massive Latin opus, though scholars have found indications that Laȝamon was familiar with Welsh literature and legend, and especially with the late Anglo-Saxon poetic tradition. Thus far no exact parallels have been identified that would prove Laȝamon knew any of the Old English poetry that has survived to this day, though similarities in form, vocabulary, and tone between his verses and the poetry of his ancestors have been frequently remarked upon. In his use of archaic diction and formulas, Laȝamon seems to look to an earlier age for inspiration, and in stripping away most of what Wace's poem shares with chivalric romance, he has produced a work that has much in common with the earlier heroic epics.

Laȝamon and his sources

It is a well-known fact that medieval authors did not prize originality above all else in the composition of their works. Few texts that include a prologue or preface do not also explicitly note the sources drawn upon in their composition. In most cases such allusions serve to lend authority to the work and establish a literary pedigree for text and author. The case can and should be made that all medieval poetry (and prose, for that matter) should be read and enjoyed for its own inherent qualities, but reading a poem through its identifiable sources can both add a further level of enjoyment and provide insight into the author's own intentions and agenda. Because we know Laȝamon's primary source, his poem is an ideal candidate for such a reading.

Laȝamon claims in his prologue that he combined three books into one to produce his poem:

> Laȝamon gon liðen; wide ȝond þas leode.
> & bi-won þa æðela boc; þa he to bisne nom.
> He nom þa Englisca boc; þa makede Seint Beda.
> Anoþer he nom on Latin; þe makede Seinte Albin.
> & þe feire Austin; þe fulluht broute hider in.
> Boc he nom þe þridde; leide þer amidden.
> þa makede a Frenchis clerc;
> Wace wes ihoten; þe wel couþe writen.   (lines 14–21)[2]

Laȝamon went travelling the length of this whole land, and secured the splendid book which he took as source-text: he took up the 'English Book' which Saint Bede had created, a second he took in Latin created by Saint Albin, and our dear Augustine who brought baptism (the Christian faith) in; a book he took as third source, and set by this his whole course: a French cleric composed it, Wace was what they called him, and very well he wrote it.

The English book by Bede is presumably an Old English translation of the *Ecclesiastical History*, and the Latin book by St Albin has never been satisfactorily identified. Critics have argued that Laȝamon must have included mention of these two sources as a kind of 'pedigree', to lend his endeavour authority. While Laȝamon indeed appears to have taken material from a variety of other sources, it is generally agreed that he follows Wace closely in terms of the structure and contents of his *Brut*, rendering a fairly close translation of the Old French work. This is not to say, however, that Laȝamon's work is slavishly derivative—far from it. Laȝamon clearly had his own agenda, and more often than not it is precisely his additions and omissions *vis à vis* Wace, no matter how subtle or minor they may seem to be, that reveal his attitude toward his subject matter. One key expansion of Laȝamon's text will be examined here to see what it reveals about his stance on two prominent aspects of his poem: violence and kingship.

'Ich am Wulf': violence and wisdom in Laȝamon's *Brut*

One of the chief thematic concerns of Laȝamon's *Brut* (and indeed all of the *Bruts*, based as they are on Geoffrey of Monmouth's *History of the Kings of Britain*) is kingship. In a sense the entire poem consists of a series of narratives about kings and their reigns, each episode describing the ruler's ascension to power, a varying number of details concerning his reign, and his subsequent decline. Some of these narratives are quite brief, with hardly more than a mention of the length of their rule and one or two notable facts about it, as, for instance, concerning King Bladud, about whom Laȝamon tells us that he was a devil-worshipper and an imitator of Icarus. In his case, however, instead of flying too close to the sun, Bladud flies so high that the winds snap the strings on his 'feather-coat', sending him crashing to his death upon the temple of Apollo in London. Bladud's only son and heir is King Leir (more famous as Shakespeare's King Lear), and his story is told here for the first time in English. Other expanded treatments of Britain's most famous kings include the foundation narrative of Brutus himself, and the rather less well-known tale of Brennes and Belinus, two brothers who come perilously close to tearing their realm apart in civil war, yet go on to become the only British kings to conquer Rome. But the undisputed centre-piece of Laȝamon's poem is the story of King Arthur: his conception, birth, rise to power, reign, and fall, an expansive narrative, which, in Laȝamon's version, takes the reader almost to the end of the chronicle.

By means of the individual touches of emphasis he adds to the narratives of his sources, it is clear that one of Laȝamon's main concerns is the question of what makes a good king. In our poet's view, a king must be both a man of formidable prowess and a leader in battle, able to attract to his side powerful 'champions'. Locrin, Brutus's eldest son, embodies the definition:

> þe wes þe wiseste; þe wes þe warreste.
> þe wes þe strengeste; stif he wes on þonke.   (lines 1055–6)

He was the wisest, he was the wariest, he was the strongest, and sturdy of intellect.

Courage, wisdom, the ability to keep the peace and establish law are what Laȝamon values most in a king. Wace tells us that when Brutus established his city of 'New Troy' he gave his people *preceps e leis | Ke pais e concorde tenissent | Ne pur rien ne se mesfeissent* ('mandates and laws so that they would maintain peace and harmony and not on any account hurt each other', lines 1254–6). Laȝamon expands these few lines significantly:

> He heom bi-tahte þa burh; 7 iȝearwod mid þan beste.
> 7 he heom onleide; þat weoren lawen gode.

He hehte þat luue scolde; liðen heom bi-tweonen.
Ælc halden oðren riht. ba bi daie 7 bi nith.
7 wea-saw nolde; he sculde beon iwite.
7 swa vfele he mihte don; þat he sculde beon ihon.   (lines 1039–46)

He entrusted the town to them and equipped it with the best, and gave them legislation in the form of good laws. He instructed that it should be love which linked them together, each upholding the others' rights, both by day and by night, and if any refused, he was to be punished, and for great crimes committed, a man must be hanged. From such good edicts they developed great respect, and became upright men, and loved reasonable words.

Wisdom and courage, *sapientia et fortitudo*, go hand in hand, and to Laȝamon one of the main pillars of *sapientia* is the ability to maintain law and order. Wisdom is to be applied to the benefit of the people, and rash behaviour and anger can destroy the intellect, as we shall see.

The pattern of kings good and bad in the *Brut* is of course already present in Laȝamon's sources, but his expansions and omissions are designed to highlight these traits. Laȝamon's usual practice is to tell us that this king was good and wise and courageous, or that one evil and stingy and cowardly, and he does so by means of epithets of his own addition, sometimes changing the character of a ruler altogether. King Morpidus, for example, is simply 'very fierce and bold and a strong knight' in Wace, whereas Laȝamon expands on this description to good effect:

þes biȝet þesne kinedom; þurh kenschipe muchele.
Cniht he wes swiðe strong; kene and custi muchel and long.
Of alle þingen heo weore god; ȝif heo neore to-wamed.
A-nan se he wes wrað wið eni mon; i þon stude he hine sloh.

.   .   .   .

Ah hit wes muchel hærme. of ane mon swa hende;
þat þurh his wraððe. his wit wes awemmed;

(lines 3172–80)

This man acquired this kingdom because of his great courage; he was a knight most strong, courageous, generous, huge and tall; he would in all things have been good, had he not been highly moody: the moment he got annoyed with anyone, in that spot he would slay him . . . But this was a great fault in such a fine man, that through his anger his intellect was impaired.

Morpidus's eldest son, Gorbonian, succeeds him and is characterized by Wace as a gentle and law-abiding ruler, but most emphatically a righteous one. Laȝamon, on the other hand, stresses quite different traits; his ability to keep the peace and, just as importantly, to keep himself under control:

> He wes swiðe soð-fest; and swiðe wel iðæwed.
> Rad-ful and rihtwis; and a mete run-hende.
> He heold þis lond stille; al æfter his iwille.
> Mid treouscipe gode; þe while his tir læste.   (lines 3258–61)

He was very honest and well-behaved, ingenious and just and most generous with food. In peace he held this land, and by his own demand, with great fidelity, as long as his fame lasted, and kept himself under control until he came to his life's end.

Laȝamon adds a similar emphasis to Gorbonian's younger brother Argal, who in Wace is the opposite of all things good: *Mais maleme se descorda | E malement lui resembla* ('but he was very different and hardly resembled him', lines 3482–4) becomes in Laȝamon:

> Þis we þe for-cuððeste mon; þe æfre hedde kinedom.
> Vnriht him wes leof; and riht-wis-nesse him wes lað.   (lines 3266–7)

This was the most depraved man who ever ruled the kingdom: injustice was dear to him and justice was distasteful.

Many similarly stark contrasts frequently emerge from Laȝamon's adaptation of his sources.

Such alterations can tell us a great deal about Laȝamon's attitude towards his subject, and his own social and political concerns. As the historian Richard Kaeuper notes, 'he waxes enthusiastic for the right kind of violence, at the right time, by the right people' (p. 120 n. 45). Indeed, Laȝamon's apparent taste for violence is often remarked upon. The critic Loomis terms it 'his ferocious streak', and likewise the scholar Tatlock notes his 'huge relish in harsh cruelty where thought fitting' (see Bzdyl, p. 13). An important and relevant counterpoint to the rather superficial impression that Laȝamon relished violent description for its own sake is the observation by critic Françoise Le Saux that Laȝamon's 'lack of interest in technical aspects of warfare is accompanied by a tendency towards compressing battle scenes in general, and toning down of slaughter scenes in particular'. Time and again Laȝamon may be seen to reduce the length and detail of such scenes, and as a result when he does include them they are all the more emphatic. Laȝamon appears to have thought the depiction of violence fitting especially when it pertained to the most important sovereign in the poem, King Arthur. Some of Laȝamon's best-known rhetorical amplifications are applied to Arthur, among them the implicitly violent animal similes (yet another way in which his poem departs from his sources). This is evinced in lines 10624–36, for example:

> Þa isæh Arður; aðelest kingen.
> Whar Colgrim at-stod; 7 æc stal wrohte.
> Þa clupede þe king; kenliche lude.
> Balde mine þeines; buhȝeð to þan hulles.
> For ȝerstendæi wes Colgrim; monnen alre kennest.
> Nu him is al swa þere gat; þer he þene hul wat.
> Hæh uppen hulle; fehteð mid hornen.
> Þenne comeð þe wlf wilde; touward hire winden.
> Þeh þe wulf beon ane; buten ælc imane.
> 7 þer weoren in ane loken. fif hundred gaten.
> Þe wulf heom to iwiteð and alle heom abiteð.
> Swa ich wulle nu to-dæi; Colgrim. al fordemen.
> Ich am wulf 7 he is gat. þe gume scal beon fæie.

Then Arthur noted, that most admired king, where Colgrim offered resistance and made his stand too; then the king called out, loudly and with courage: 'My bold-hearted warriors, march to the hills! For yesterday Colgrim was of all men most courageous, now he's just like the goat holding guard on its hill: high on the hillside it fights with its horns; then the wild wolf comes, on its way up towards them; even though the wolf's alone, without any pack, if there were in one pen a full five hundred goats, the wolf would get to them and would bite them all. In just that way today I shall quite destroy Colgrim: I'm the wolf and he's the goat: that man is going to be doomed!'

In this quotation, the extended metaphor of the wolf and the goat is Laȝamon's unique means of depicting the conqueror and the vanquished. Underlying this metaphor is the implicitly gory imagery of a wolf rending 500 goats to death, but we note that Laȝamon shies away from any such crudely explicit depiction of savage butchery. A scene that does paint Arthur's 'harsher cruelty', and Laȝamon's apparent relish of it, occurs somewhat later in the poem, just as Arthur has consolidated his control of all Britain and is eager for further conquest. He is holding court with representatives of all his dependencies, when a vicious fight breaks out amongst his proud guests, provoked by their rivalry and concern for precedence:

þa duȝeð wærð iwraððed; duntes þer weoren riue.
Ærest þa laues heo weorpen; þa while þa heo ilæsten.
And þa bolln seoluerne; mid wine iuulled.
7 seoððen þa uustes; uusden to sweoren.

(lines 11367–70)

The company became aroused: blows were freely given; first they started throwing loaves, as long as there were some left, and then the silver goblets which were filled with wine, and after that, clutching palms quickly caught up throats!

In the ensuing mêlée seven men are slain, which leads to 'enormous blood-shed, consternation in the court!' (line 11386). It is at this point that Arthur steps in to put an end to the violence:

Þa com þe king buȝen; ut of his buren.
Mid him an hundred beornen; mid helmen & mid burnen.
Ælc bar an his riht hond; whit stelene bro[n]d.
Þa cleopede Arður; aðelest kingen.
Sitteð sitteð swiðe; elc mon bi his liue.
And wa-swa þat nulle don; he scal for-demed beon.
Nimeð me þene ilke mon; þa þis feht ærst bigon.
7 doð wið ðe an his sweore; 7 draȝeð hine to ane more.
7 doð hine in an <ley>uen; þer he scal liggen.
And nimeð al his nexte cun; þa ȝe maȝen iuinden.
And swengeð of þa hafden; mid breoden eouwer sweorden.
Þa wifmen þa ȝe maȝen ifinden; of his nexten cunden.
kerueð of hire neose; 7 heore wlite ga to lose.
And swa ich wulle al for-don; þat cun þat he of com.
And ȝif ich auere-mare; seoððen ihere.
Þat æi of mine hirede; of heȝe na of loȝe.
Of þissen ilke slehte; æft sake are[re].
Ne sculde him neoððer gon fore; gold ne na gærsume.
Hæh hors no hære scrud; þat he ne sculde beon ded.
Oðer mid horsen to-draȝen; þat is elches swiken laȝen.
Bringeð þene halidom; and ich wulle swerien þer-on.
Swa ȝe scullen cnihtes; þe weoren at þissen fihte.
Eorles 7 beornes; þat ȝe hit breken nulleð.

(lines 11387–410)

Then the king emerged from out of his chamber; with him a hundred courtiers, with helmets and with corselets, each carrying in his right hand a broadsword of bright steel. Then shouted Arthur, most admired of kings: 'Sit down, sit down at once, all of you, or you will lose your lives! Anyone who refuses to will be condemned to death. Seize and bring me the actual man who first started this fight, clap a noose around his neck and drag him to the marshes, and fling him in a deep bog and there let him lie, and seize all his closest relatives whom you can discover, and strike off their heads with your broadswords; from the women you can discover among his closest relations carve off the noses and let their beauty be destroyed; in that way I'll quite obliterate the tribe from which he came, and if ever any more I subsequently hear that any of my courtiers, whether great or humble, from this same slaughter should seek revenge after, then no compensation from gold or treasure will atone, neither strong steed nor war gear, to buy him off from death or from being drawn apart by horses, which is the punishment for traitors. Bring here the sacred relics and I shall swear upon them, as shall all you knights who were present at this fight, you earls and barons, that you will never break it.'

Here, the violence serves to underpin Arthur's authority and determination to maintain order. This is, of course, the event that leads to the immediate introduction of the Round Table, where Arthur's men may sit without rancour as equals. Laȝamon's table is crafted by a skilled artisan from Cornwall, seats 1,600 knights and is amazingly portable: Arthur can take it with him wherever he goes (line 11438). Again, it is instructive to compare Laȝamon's account with his main source, Wace (who, incidentally, is the very first to mention the Round Table in writing). In the corresponding moment in Wace's narrative we encounter simply the following:

> Pur les nobles baruns qu'il out,
> Dunt chescuns mieldre estre quidout,
> Chescuns se teneit al meillur,
> Ne nuls n'en saveit le peiur,
> Fist Artur la Runde Table
> Dunt Bretun dient mainte fable.   (lines 9747–52)

On account of his noble barons—each of whom felt he was superior, each considered himself the best, and no one could say who was the worst— Arthur had the Round Table made, about which the British tell many a tale.

Wace makes no mention of a food-fight turned bloody, or the stern yet grimly wise measures Arthur takes to restore order. Laȝamon's expansion illustrates well his pragmatic attitude toward violence in the service of order.

Laȝamon's Arthur evolves quickly into the epitome of the ideal king: a successful leader in battle, a wise judge in peacetime whose chief concern is for justice and the welfare of his people. But Laȝamon realized that Arthur was not simply born to prowess and wisdom, he had to acquire them. An analysis of a final set of passages will show how Laȝamon incorporates a subtle development in the character of his protagonist, one which is, again, entirely lacking in his sources. If one had any doubts as to which qualities our poet admired most in a sovereign before Arthur enters the stage, the way Laȝamon describes Arthur's ascension to power should make it abundantly clear.

The rise of the king

Arthur is only 15 years old when his father King Uther Pendragon dies. Laȝamon's description of Arthur's reaction to the news that he is to be crowned king 'and receive the land from God' is touchingly realistic: at lines 9923–5, we read, *þus heo gunnen tellen; 7 Arður sæt ful stille. | ænne stunde he wes blac; and on heuwe swiðe wak. | ane while he wes reod; and reousede on heorte* ('So they finished talking, and Arthur sat without speaking: one moment he was pallid, and in colour very blanched, next moment he was red and his emotions much aroused'). At his coronation Arthur vows to drive the Saxons out of Britain, and a series of wars against the invaders ensues. After many hundreds of lines, Arthur gains the upper hand. His opponent, Childric, petitions him to allow him to leave the island with his surviving men and never return. Arthur's reply is exultant, and tinged with hubris. He compares Childric to the cornered fox being dug out of his hole, boasts that he has his life in his hands and may choose between beheading and hanging as his punishment, but makes, in Laȝamon's version alone, a fateful decision:

> Whæðer-swa ich wulle don; oðer slæn oðer a-hon.
> Nu ich wulle ȝifen him grið; 7 leten hine me specken wið.
> Nulle ich hine slæ no ahon; ah his bode ich wulle fon.
> Ȝisles ich wulle habben; of hæxten his monnen.
> Hors 7 heore wepnen. ær heo heonne wenden.
> And swa heo scullen wræcchen; to heoren scipen liðen.
> Sæilien ouer sæ; to sele heore londe.

7 þer wirð-liche; wunien on riche.
And tellen tidende; of Arðure kinge.
Hu ich heom habbe i-freoied; for mines fader saule
7 for mine freo-dome; ifrouered þa wræcchen.
Her wes Arður þe king; aðelen bidæled.
Nes þer nan swa reh3 mon; þe him durste ræden.
Þet him of-þuhte sære; sone þer-after.
                              (lines 10419–30)

'I shall neither behead nor hang him but will accede to his request: I wish to take hostages from his highest-ranking men, horses and their weapons, before they go from here, and so they are to travel like wretches to their ships, to sail across the sea to their splendid land, and dwell there dutifully within their realm, and announce the tidings of Arthur the king, of how I have set them free for my father's soul's sake, and from my own generosity have dealt gently with the wretches.' In this affair King Arthur was short of all good judgement, there was no man who was quite so rash as to dare to put him right; this he regretted bitterly a short time after.

Here Arthur strips Childric and his men of their weapons and other gear, as well as their honour, whereas in Wace it is the Saxon leader Childric who offers these terms himself. And Wace makes no mention of Arthur's blunder. Childric and his men set sail, but soon decide upon revenge and make landfall at Dartmouth, where they engage in an orgy of slaughter and brutality (lines 10455–79). The nature of Arthur's error is not entirely clear from this passage, though La3amon's comment upon it leaves no doubt that it was a serious one. Either La3amon felt that Arthur should have killed Childric while he had the chance, or he faulted Arthur's handling of the situation for another reason. Le Saux apparently has the former in mind when she writes that 'Arthur is thus defined as a hunter from the outset, and the predatory nature of the king marks the treatment of his character throughout the poem, while suggesting an underlying irony that the hunter should have let his prey get away, in this case.'[3] It is possible, however, to read Arthur's mishandling of the situation in another light, one that recognizes its relevance for our understanding of La3amon's views on kingship and violence. La3amon never criticizes his protagonists gratuitously, so we must ask ourselves why he inserted this instance of Arthur's failure unless he meant it to serve a purpose. A later passage, in which Arthur finds himself in much the same situation, provides the key.

Having defeated the Saxons and further pacified his own realm, Arthur turns to international conquest, setting his sights on Ireland. His army utterly defeats the poorly equipped Irish, whose king, Gillomaur, flees and is captured. Like Childric before him, he offers Arthur hostages and further promises of peace and tribute. This time, faced again with an enemy in abject defeat, Arthur behaves differently:

> Þis iherde Arður; aðelest king;
> 7 he gan lih3en; luddere steftne.
> 7 he gon andswerie; mid ædmode worden.
> Beo nu glad Gillomar; ne beo þin heorte noht sær.
> For þv ært a wis mon; þa bet þe scal iwurðen.
> For æuere me æhte wisne mon; wurðliche igreten.
> For þine wis-dome; no scal þe noht þa wurse.
> Muchel þu me beodest; þe scal beon þa betere.
> Her forð-rihtes; bi-foren al mine cnihtes.
> For3iuen þe amare; al þæ haluen-dæle.
> Of golde 7 of gærsume; ah þu scalt mi mon bicumen.
> And half þat gauel sende; ælche 3ere to mi[n]e londe.
> Halfe þa steden; 7 halfe þa iweden.
> Halue þa hauekes; 7 halue þa hundes.
> Þæ þu me beodest. ich wulle þe bi-lefen;
> Ah ich wulle habben. þire hæhre monne children;
> Þeo heom beoð alre leofuest. ich heom mai þe bet ileouen;
> 7 swa þu scalt wunien; in wurðscipe þire.
> A þine kine-dome i þine rihte icunden.
> 7 ic þe wulle 3euen to; þat ne scal þe king woh don.
> Buten he hit abugge; mid his bare rugge.
> Þeo hit sæide Arður; aðelest kingen.

(lines 11178–93)

Arthur was listening, most admired king, and he began laughing with a loud bellow, and gave him an answer with most gracious words: 'Cheer up, now, Gillomaur, don't let your feelings be so sore. Since you have been sensible, things will turn out well for you, for people who are intelligent merit sympathetic treatment; you shall not suffer any more, because of your common sense: you have offered me a lot; for that you shall be better off! On this spot, outright, in the presence of all my knights, let there be restored to you the largest part of that half measure of gold and treasury; but you must become my vassal, and send half that tribute each year into my country. Half of the horses, and half of the trappings, half of the hawks and half of the hounds which you were offering me, I will leave to you, but the children I will take

with me who come from your nobility, those whom they love best of all—
then I can trust them the better! And so you will remain in your self-respect,
in your own kingdom, in your rightful inheritance: to you I shall give this so
that no king shall do wrong to you without atoning for it on his bare back!'
So spoke Arthur, most admired of kings.

Laȝamon would have us believe that Gillomaur is not the only one
exhibiting wisdom, for Arthur has learned a thing or two about gaining the co-operation of his defeated enemies. Where his laughter and
exultation had been scornful toward Childric, here it is jovial and
reassuring; where he had previously stripped the defeated Saxons of
all their possessions and sent them packing as wretches (Arthur's
generosity in that case amounting to certain humiliation before the
eyes of their own people), here he grants Gillomaur half of his possessions and his kingdom and, in so doing, his 'self-respect'. Laȝamon
makes it clear in no uncertain terms that Arthur came to regret his
treatment of Childric; here he comments just as emphatically by
means of the repeated epithet, 'most admired of kings', that Arthur
had learned a valuable lesson.

Conclusion

What sets Arthur apart from almost all the rest of the monarchs who
pass before our eyes in the *Brut* is his ability to learn to temper justice
with mercy and wisdom. The description of his treatment of the Irish
king makes this explicit, where it is only implicit, at best, in Geoffrey
and Wace. Where Arthur is concerned at least, Laȝamon exhibits not
so much a 'huge relish' for violence, as a concern with the role of
violence in society and its necessity for maintaining peace and order.
He may at times seem to embrace it, revel in it, celebrate it, though
perhaps not for its own sake. It serves also as a measure of a monarch:
a good king is a strong king, and it is an integral and positive element
in his portrayal of all the leaders in his poem, but especially Arthur.
Laȝamon would have read, as we may, in both Geoffrey's and Wace's
narratives countless instances of power gone awry, with the con-
sequent violence visited upon the heads of the innocent. But as his
changes and additions suggest, perhaps more so than his sources, he
appreciated that power without wisdom was of little use to society.

The application of this lesson to early thirteenth-century England would not have gone amiss.

Even such a cursory comparison as this of Laȝamon's text and his source reveals that his attitudes toward his subject matter were in some potentially significant ways quite different from his French predecessor, Wace. Such a reading demonstrates that he had subtly different concepts of kingship and the role of violence in the world as he knew it. While the examination of the sources, where known, of a medieval work should never eclipse consideration of the work itself, scrutinizing those sources may yield information about a medieval author's attitudes, tastes, intentions, and methodology that he or she would never share with us directly.

Notes

1. In addition to Wace's *Roman de Brut* (see n. 2), the most significant of these was Geffrei Gaimar's *L'estoire des Engleis*.
2. All quotations of Laȝamon's *Brut* are taken from the edition by Brook and Leslie; the translations are based on Allen's, though I have in places modified it slightly. All quotations and translations of Wace's *Roman de Brut* are from Weiss.
3. Le Saux, *The Poem and its Sources*, p. 54.

References and suggested reading

Allen, Rosamund. *Brut*. New York: St Martin's Press, 1992. A verse translation of the entire *Brut*, with an excellent introduction.

Allen, Rosamund, Lucy Perry, and Jane Annette Roberts, eds. *Laȝamon: Contexts, Language, and Interpretation*. King's College London Medieval Studies 19. London: King's College London Centre for Late Antique and Medieval Studies, 2002.

Brook, G. L., and R. F. Leslie, eds. *Layamon: Brut*. Early English Text Society 250 and 270. London, New York: Oxford University Press, 1963 and 1978. The standard edition of *Laȝamon's Brut*, presenting both Caligula and Otho texts on facing pages.

Bzdyl, Donald G. *Layamon's Brut : A History of the Britons*. Binghamton, NY:

Medieval and Renaissance Texts and Studies, 1989. A prose translation of
Laȝamon's Brut.

Eckhardt, Caroline E., ed., *Castleford's Chronicle or The Boke of Brut*. Early
English Text Society 305. London: Oxford University Press, 1963 and 1978.

Hartung, Albert E., ed. *A Manual of Writings in Middle English, 1050–1500*,
xxi: Edward Donald Kennedy. *Chronicles and Other Historical Writing*.
Hamden: Archon Books, 1990.

Kaeuper, Richard W. *Chivalry and Violence in Medieval Europe*. Oxford:
Oxford University Press, 1999. An in-depth treatment of medieval views on
violence as reflected in contemporary literature and historiography.

Le Saux, Françoise H. M. *Layamon's Brut : The Poem and its Sources*.
Arthurian Studies 19. Cambridge: D. S. Brewer, 1989. A ground-breaking
study of Laȝamon's use of his sources.

Le Saux, Françoise H. M. *The Text and Tradition of Layamon's Brut*.
Arthurian Studies 33. Cambridge, Rochester, NY: D. S. Brewer, 1994. This is
an excellent collection of articles on all aspects of Laȝamon's work and the
social and political contexts of his poem.

Tatlock, John S. P. *The Legendary History of Britain: Geoffrey of Monmouth's
Historia Regum Britanniae and its Early Vernacular Versions*. Berkeley:
University of California Press, 1950. A monumental study of Geoffrey's
Historia which sheds light on, among a great deal of other things, the
relation between that text and Laȝamon's poem.

Weiss, Judith. *Wace's Roman de Brut: A History of the British: Text and
Translation*, rev. edn. Exeter Medieval English Texts and Studies. Exeter:
University of Exeter Press, 2002. Text and translation of Laȝamon's chief
Anglo-Norman source.

16

Earlier verse romance

Peter J. Lucas

Introduction: romance and the Breton lay

Love, we are told, was not a theme much favoured by the ancients. Old English poetry, being primarily concerned with the Germanic heroic ethic and with religious themes, paid relatively little attention to the role of women in society. The literature of the period between 1050 and 1200 showed a much greater interest in the relations between people, including emotional relationships between the sexes. Romance is a new genre of narrative verse growing out of this cultural context, elevating the theme of love, and stimulated in England by French models. Romance is not just about deeds of derring-do to deliver boxes of chocolates. Nor are medieval romances just love stories. They are much more celebrations of the power of love and loyalty, not just between a man and woman, but also between members of society. Some early Middle English romances focus on the themes of loyalty and fair play. Romances such as *Havelok* and *Gamelyn* show their heroes fighting off injustice and winning through by a combination of toughness and moral rectitude; their success is marked by their receiving just reward for the display of popular qualities in the form of (re)gaining their true social position. Usually the main characters are super-people in some sense, either through their social position or through some special skill or power, or both.

Soon the predominant theme is romantic love, not just for itself, but also for its potential relationship to social cohesion. We are presented with a social setting that is exclusive to members of the courtly chivalric class, a community of the elect, aristocrats and knights, and we enter an illusory world of ideals and tests where the socio-political conditions that provide the setting are never explained. This courtly society is portrayed so as to evoke an idealized representation of contemporary society; it is a refining influence.[1]

Breton lays were a popular variety of romance that included an element of contact with fairy magic and an enchanted world where time stands still, and where no ethical justification is provided for fairy behaviour. The fashion for them took off in the wake of a series of successful lays by the poet Marie de France in the second half of the twelfth century (c.1160–90). Although the lays were written in French, Marie probably lived in England—they are dedicated to a certain *nobles reis* 'noble king', probably Henry II (1154–89). The genre became quite popular in England and was imitated in the Middle English period up to the fifteenth century, including poems such as *Emaré, The Erle of Toulous, Sir Gowther*, and Thomas Chestre's *Sir Launfal.* The later interest in Breton lays may have been stimulated by Chaucer's attribution of his *Franklin's Tale* to the genre (Lucas, 'Keeping up Appearances').

Among earlier Middle English lays *Sir Orfeo* (c.1330) is a text of outstanding interest and merit. It is all the more interesting because, unlike so many lays, the story itself did not originate in Brittany (although the story was almost certainly filtered through Brittany); on the contrary it is adapted from the original (Greek) version of the classical story of Orpheus and Eurydice, the one that lacked the second loss (or death) of Eurydice (Dronke). This original version survived in at least four eleventh-century Latin poems: the *Liber quid suum virtutis* by Thierry of Saint-Trond; the poem taken to begin *Carmine leniti tenet Orpheus antra Cocyti*, 'With a sweet song Orpheus charms the caves of Cocytus' by a certain Gautier; the *Dialogue with Calliope* by Godefroy of Reims (in the interlude beginning *Non renuenda peto, mihi, Calliopea, faveto*, 'I do not ask for things being refused; favour thou me Calliope'); and the anonymous lyric *Parce continuis, deprecor, lamentis*, 'Cease your endless laments, I beseech you'. The first three of these are from France, indicating that the underlying story at least would have been known in Brittany.[2] In view of the probability that '*Sir Orfeo* was translated from an O[ld]

F[rench] or A[nglo-]N[orman] narrative *lai'* (Bliss, p. xli), the existence of the original version of the story in eleventh-century France
shows beyond reasonable doubt that this original version, which the
Sir Orfeo poet must have used, was indeed available to him, probably
in the form of a narrative lay. So the *matière de Bretagne* supplied the
medium for the transposition of the story into the romance genre. It
was a story that differed from the characteristic Breton lay pattern in
having the couple married from the outset and the hero entering the
Other World before (rather than after) the resolution of the crisis
caused by the lovers' separation. Since the story is one that was
adapted to Breton lay form, it reveals much about what themes
(as opposed to story elements) were considered essential to the
genre. Social and ethical values appear to have been central to the
Middle English Breton lay. Before considering how these values are
celebrated in *Sir Orfeo* we must examine the characteristics of the
Breton lay.

The Breton lay

Usually the stories told in Breton lays follow a common pattern
(Smithers). Often the hero becomes involved in a liaison with a fairy
lady. When he fails to heed her command he loses her, but the rest of
the story tells how he is eventually reconciled with her in a permanent
relationship, and they live happily ever after, usually in the Fairy
World. If the heroine is mortal she usually has a son by her lover, but
is then separated from her lover, and the rest of the story tells how
they are brought back together through the medium of the son. A
common motif in Breton lays is the occurrence of a Rash Promise.
The eliciting of a Rash Promise usually plays an important part in
bringing about the denouement. For example, in *Sir Tristrem* King
Mark promises the minstrel Tristrem to give him whatever he wishes,
whereupon he promptly asks for Mark's wife, Ysonde. By this means
the lovers Tristrem and Ysonde are reunited.

The Prologue to *Sir Orfeo* (which also occurs at the beginning of
Lay le Freine) indicates the main features of Breton lays.

> Layes þat ben in harping
> Ben yfounde of ferli þing: *noble subject matter*

> Sum beþe of wer and sum of wo,   *war*
> And sum of joie and mirþe also,
> And sum of trecherie and of gile,
> Of old auentours þat fel while,   *events*
> And sum of bourdes and ribaudy,   *jokes*
> And mani þer beþ of fairy;
> Of al þinges þat men seþ
> Mest o loue, forsoþe, þai beþ.   (lines 3–12)[3]   *of*

The association with harping goes back to the oral performance of *lais* by Breton *jongleurs*, 'minstrels' who went along with the Crusades, where the verbal element (which Marie de France called a *cunte*, 'story') was accompanied, possibly in the form of interludes, by music played on the harp. The association is of particular resonance in relation to *Sir Orfeo* because Orfeo is a harp-playing genius, and because the harp plays a crucial role in the story. The importance of the harp and the music made with it is suggested by the hospitality extended to harp-players,

> Siker was eueri gode harpour   *Sure*
> Of him to haue miche honour,   (lines 27–8)   *much*

reiterated by the Steward (lines 517–18), and by the care with which Orfeo protects his harp from the elements to which he himself is exposed.

> His harp, whereon was al his gle,   *revelry*
> He hidde in an holwe tre.   (lines 267–8)

It is by playing the harp that Orfeo consoles himself in the wilderness, and the spell-binding quality of the music he makes with it is illustrated by his capacity to attract and bemuse the animals. Though the power of the harp is inherited from the Orpheus legend, in Orfeo's hands it is more wide-ranging and thoroughgoing in its influence, and the greater power given to it emphasizes its importance. For it is through the exceptional skill with which Orfeo plays the harp that the rash promise is elicited from the fairy king and that the Steward recognizes Orfeo on his return. Thus the harp is instrumental in Orfeo's recovery of both his wife and his kingdom; it succeeds where a thousand armed men failed and is in fact the key to his success.

Many of the subject-matter elements indicated in the Prologue occur in the course of the story of *Sir Orfeo*. When Orfeo visits the fairy Other World he sees the victims of war and *trecherie*, but the main theme of the poem is the love between Orfeo and his wife Heurodis (the classical Eurydice), which is tested by fairy intervention. Such a threat often comes from outside courtly society, and is also supplied by the king of the Other World in *Sir Degaré*. *Sir Orfeo* therefore makes particularly productive use of the fairy dimension to threaten blissful human existence, a threat that is encapsulated not only in the seizure of Heurodis, but also in the chamber of horrors seen by Orfeo *wiþin þe wal* when he enters the fairy king's castle to find Heurodis (lines 387–404). The threat also has repercussions, as the abduction of Heurodis leads to Orfeo's abdication of his heirless kingdom; similarly in *Emaré* the heroine's refusal to comply with her father's demands leads to her exile. However, the lack of sexual threat to Heurodis in her abduction is somewhat untypical of Middle English romance. There is no violence inflicted on Heurodis except that which is self-inflicted (and does not last), and even in the Other World she is apparently unmolested, indeed *wiþouten lac* (line 460).

The fairy element in *Sir Orfeo* is suffused with ideas from Celtic thought, now most easily paralleled from Ireland, although no doubt inherited from Celtic Brittany (Allen, 'Orpheus'); these ideas were also generally understood in England at the time.[4] The Other World to which Heurodis is *ynome* 'taken' (lines 193, 403) to *liue wiþ ous euermo*, as the fairy king would have it (line 168), is a living world where the inhabitants are generally kept in statuesque mode in a state of arrested mobility. It is full

> Of folk þat were þider ybrou3t,
> And þou3t dede, and nare nou3t.   *seemed/were not at all*
> (lines 389–90)

Although apparently dead because that is the state they were in when snatched from the human world, they have the potential for motion, and can move about on occasion subject to fairy control, but only something very special (in this poem Orfeo's harp-playing) can bring about the restoration of total mobility and freedom of action, with the exceptional result here that someone *taken* can return to the human world.

The bond of love

In *Sir Orfeo* the bonds of human society are tested, principally by a mysterious, external, supernatural agent, the fairy king. Broadly, the bonds involved are the basic ones. That between a man and a woman is illustrated within a marriage by the mutual love of Orfeo and Heurodis. That between man and man is illustrated in the society of the poem by the loyalty owed to Orfeo as king by his people, especially the Steward.

The emphasis on, and even idealization of, the mutual love between Orfeo and Heurodis is one of the most striking features of *Sir Orfeo*. Just how strong this love is is conveyed first by what they communicate to each other, and secondly what they do. There are two passages in which Orfeo and Heurodis communicate their love.

In the first (lines 102–30) their relationship is thrown into sharp relief because they are under threat of separation. Here they communicate through speech, Orfeo saying to Heurodis:

'O lef liif, what is te,	*dear*
Þat euer ȝete hast ben so stille,	
And now gredest wonder schille?	*cry out, loudly*
Þi bodi, þat was so white ycore,	*exquisite*
Wiþ þine nailes is al totore.	*torn to pieces*
Allas! þi rode, þat was so red,	*face*
Is al wan, as þou were ded;	
And also þine fingres smale	
Beþ al blodi and al pale.	
Allas! þi louesom eyȝen to	*beautiful*
Lokeþ so man doþ on his fo!	*as*
A! dame, ich biseche merci,	
Lete ben al þis reweful cri,	*pitiful*
And tel me what þe is, and hou,	*is wrong/how it happened*
And what þing may þe help now.'	
Þo lay sche stille atte last,	
And gan to wepe swiþe fast,	*very*
And seyd þus þe king to:	
'Allas, mi lord Sir Orfeo,	
Seþþen we first togider were	*Since*
Ones wroþ neuer we nere,	*angry/were not*

> Bot euer ich haue yloued þe
> As my liif, and so þou me;
> Ac now we mot delen ato   *separate*
> —Do þi best, for y mot go.'
> 'Allas!' quaþ he, 'Forlorn ich am!
> Whider wiltow go, and to wham?   *will you*
> Whider þou gost ichil wiþ þe,
> And whider y go þou schalt wiþ me.'   (lines 102–30)

Orfeo's distress is conveyed by his contrasting Heurodis's normal blithe demeanour with her present disfigurement, and Heurodis's by her weeping and inability through shock to indicate what precisely the problem is. Nevertheless, she indicates the harmony that is being disrupted (*Ones wroþ neuer we nere*) and in the last two lines Orfeo indicates his undying devotion to being with her. The couple's speeches suggest a close mimicry of speaking tones, which serves to focus attention on the directness of the assertions. Each assertion is an absolute one. There has never been a single cross word between them at any time during their marriage. Each has loved the other as his or her own life. They will never be separated: togetherness is all. This concentration on their absolute devotion to each other is one of the ways in which the relationship is idealized.

In the second passage (lines 319–30), where they are now separated, they communicate through looks. Orfeo has abdicated his kingdom, leaving the Steward in charge (a somewhat unusual arrangement; more usual was for continuation of the blood-line), and gone to live in the wilderness, where he sees a company of ladies on a fairy hunt, one of whom is:

> His owhen quen, Dam Heurodis.
> Ʒern he biheld hir, and sche him eke,   *Eagerly/also*
> Ac noiþer to oþer a word no speke.
>   (lines 322–4)

Lines 323–4 are perhaps the most moving in the poem and illustrate the frustration of natural human emotion resulting from the separation of the married couple caused by Heurodis's removal to the Other World. One of the reasons why these lines stand out in the poem as being so moving is probably that the word *ʒern*, when construed with *and sche him eke*, contains the only description (as opposed to expression) of emotion on Heurodis's part in the poem. It is notable that there is no recognition scene between Orfeo and Heurodis (such a scene does occur between Orfeo and the Steward), so that the immediacy of their apparent feelings for each other is conveyed more directly. Otherwise emotion is conveyed mainly by implication from what Orfeo and Heurodis do. Heurodis's distracted mutilation of her body following her dream,

> Ac as sone as sche gan awake,
> Sche crid, and loþli bere gan make: *loathsome uproar*
> Sche froted hir honden and hir fet,   *chafed*
> And crached hir visage—it bled wete;   *scratched/face*
> Hir riche robe hye al torett,   *tore to pieces*
> And was reueyd out of hir witt   *driven*
>
>   (lines 77–82)

because it arises from dreaming about her abduction from Orfeo, implies her love for him. When we are told that

> For messais þat sche on him seiȝe,   *discomfort/saw*
> Þat had ben so riche and so heiȝe,
> Þe teres fel out of her eiȝe:
> Þe oþer leuedis þis yseiȝe
> And maked hir oway to ride
> —Sche most wiþ him no lenger abide   *could*
>
>   (lines 325–30)

it is evident (though not overtly stated) that Heurodis, frustrated by not being able to speak to her husband, cried because she saw her husband distraught, and that her distress was seen by her fairy minders to be such that she was removed from him a second time. Similarly Orfeo's love for Heurodis is implied by his reaction, first to the news that she is to be taken from him (lines 175 ff.), and secondly to her actual removal (lines 195 ff.). Because he is deprived of her company he decides to become a 'drop-out': he gives up his kingdom and goes into the wilderness, where he tries to console himself by playing the harp (lines 201–18); he does not set out in search of Heurodis. Later, when he recognizes Heurodis in the company of the sixty ladies hawking, he abandons passive endurance and resolves to follow her *Tide wat bitide*. Not caring whether he lives or dies (line 342), he determines to pursue what seems to him to be the overriding positive value—love.

Corresponding to the private love of Orfeo and Heurodis is the public loyalty of the king's subjects, especially, of course, the Steward. All the king's men are prepared to die in order to prevent the queen's abduction:

> Þai . . . sayd þai wold þere abide,
> And dye þer euerichon,
> Er þe quen schuld fram hem gon   (lines 187–90)

and they beg Orfeo not to abdicate his kingdom:

> Þai kneled adoun al yfere   *together*
> And praid him ȝif his wille were,
> Þat he no schuld nouȝt fram hem go.   (lines 219–25)

In the final episode the beggar answers Orfeo's questions truthfully, the Steward is loyal to Orfeo even though he does not recognize him at first, and all are overjoyed at the king's return:

> Þo al þo þat þerin sete   *Then/those*
> Þat it was King Orfeo vnderȝete,   *realized*
> And þe steward him wele knewe:
> Ouer and ouer þe bord he þrewe,   *table*
> And fel adoun to his fet;
> So dede euerich lord þat þer sete,
> And al þai seyd at o criing: *one*
> 'Ȝe beþ our lord, Sir and our king!'
> Glad þai were of his liue.   (lines 575–83)

Love and social cohesion

It is these human relationships, private love and the public loyalty that is its corollary, which are tested in *Sir Orfeo*, the first by the unmotivated intervention of the fairy king, the second also by Orfeo's return to Winchester in disguise. The Fairy World is *a fair cuntray* described in terms of dazzling artificial beauty (lines 351–76), but behind the façade of this enchanting landscape it is in fact menacing and cruel. This unmotivated hostility is revealed principally in the two main speeches of the fairy king (lines 165–74 and 421–8), as well as in the action of carrying Heurodis off against her wishes. Because of its menace the Fairy World provides a foil for the Human World, which, as we have seen, is marked by the strong emotional bonds of private reciprocated love and public loyalty.

Understanding the poem is to a large extent dependent on the

perception of the role of the fairy visitant as a tester of human relationships. In *Sir Orfeo*, far from being an escapist refuge to which hero
and heroine can retire at the end to live happily ever after, the Fairy
World is a place from which Heurodis must be rescued (although
Orfeo does not set out to do that in the first place). Through the
power of the harp (and maybe by the implied support for harping/
minstrelsy the author was indulging in a little advocacy, even self-
advertisement, as well as carrying on one aspect of the Orpheus tradition),[5] the fairy king is forced to adopt the human virtue of keeping
his word and to be polite (lines 463–71). Whereas often in Breton lays
the fairy outwits the human, in *Sir Orfeo* the reverse is nearer the truth
because fairy power is a foil for testing the bonds of human society.

Conclusion

Since *Sir Orfeo* is a poem involving tests it may be instructive to
compare it (briefly) with a later and more sophisticated romance, *Sir
Gawain and the Green Knight*.[6] In *Sir Gawain* the nature of Camelot
society (with Gawain as its acting representative) is tested. Attention
is focused not so much on whether Gawain is virtuous as on the
degree of his virtue and, through him, on the relative perfection or
degeneracy of Camelot society. *Sir Orfeo* is not like that: no questions
are asked about the degree of moral virtue of Winchester society
(though the very existence of one such virtue is questioned—and
confirmed—in the testing of the Steward's loyalty). Gawain's knight-
hood is subjected to a series of tests: the Beheading Game, the
Exchange of Winnings, the Temptation of the Lady. In *Sir Orfeo* there
are two tests, that of the relationship between Orfeo and Heurodis,
and that of the relationship between Orfeo and his subjects. But these
relationships are seen as pivots of society. Without the personal marital love of the couple at the head of society public stability is threatened, because the king cannot rule without the help and support of
the woman he loves; public responsibility is dependent on personal
happiness and fulfilment. And without the loyalty of the king's subjects society would be undermined. What is at stake, ultimately, is
society's capacity to survive, something it can do only by preserving
the values that hold it together. Whereas *Sir Gawain* is concerned

with relative questions, *Sir Orfeo* is concerned with absolute questions. Hence the differences of outcome. Gawain's success or failure is a matter of ambiguity: Bertilak, alias the Green Knight, considers him *On þe fautlest freke þat euer on fote ȝede* 'the most faultless man that ever went on foot' (line 2363), whereas Gawain views himself as *fawty and falce* 'lacking integrity and dishonest' (line 2382). But Orfeo's success is necessarily absolute, since the breakdown of his relationships with his wife and his people would have dealt a scarcely bearable blow to his society as then constituted.

Sir Orfeo is a poem in which situations are contrived for testing the bonds of society. The two essential elements of society in the poem are private, reciprocal marital love and its corollary, public loyalty. Since these bonds survive against the severest tests, their strength and importance is stressed: human society is vindicated triumphantly and its stability established. Fragile as this stability may be, it is secured by human talent, skill, will-power, and courage when Orfeo finally gets the best of both worlds.

Notes

1. Cf. Erich Auerbach, *Mimesis: The Representation of Reality in Western Literature*, trans. Willard Trask (Princeton: Princeton University Press, 1953), ch. 6; and for a richly allusive and discursive treatment of medieval romance see Pamela O. E. Gradon, *Form and Style in Early English Literature* (London: Methuen, 1971), ch. 4.

2. The reason for the survival of this original version of the story was probably that the story underwent a Christian metamorphosis whereby Orpheus was seen as a Christ-figure. Orpheus was depicted as playing his lyre to sheep (Christ the Good Shepherd) and his descent to the underworld to rescue Eurydice was likened to Christ's harrowing of hell to save sinners.

3. The text is that of Bliss, but with *j* for *i* where it means *j*, the expansion of ampersands, the omission of unnecessary hyphens, and with minor adjustments of punctuation.

4. Alan J. Fletcher, '*Sir Orfeo* and the Flight from the Enchanters', *Studies in the Age of Chaucer*, 22 (2000), 141–77, at pp. 158–62.

5. Ibid. 169–70 for the importance of harpers in the reign of Edward I (1272–1307) in relation to *Sir Orfeo*.

6. J. R. R. Tolkien, and E. V. Gordon, rev. Norman Davis, *Sir Gawain and the Green Knight* (Oxford: Oxford University Press, 1967).

References and suggested reading

Allen, Dorena. 'Orpheus and Orfeo: The Dead and the Taken', *Medium Aevum*, 33 (1964), 102–11. The best analysis of the fairy Other World presented in the poem.

Bliss, Alan J., ed. *Sir Orfeo*. London: Oxford University Press, 1954; 2nd edn., 1966; repr. 1971. The most authoritative edition.

Brewer, Derek, ed. *Studies in Medieval English Romances: Some New Approaches*. Cambridge: D. S. Brewer, 1988. A collection of essays on various aspects, including Derek Pearsall on 'The Development of Middle English Romance'.

Dronke, Peter. 'The Return of Eurydice', *Classica et Mediaevalia*, 23 (1962), 198–215. Essential treatment of the survival of the original Orpheus story, including the modifications to the story by the classical author Virgil, who was followed by Ovid and Boethius.

French, Walter Hoyt, and Charles Brockway Hale, eds. *Middle English Metrical Romances*, 2 vols. New York: Russell and Russell, 1930; repr. 1964. A full collection of texts.

Hardman, Phillipa, ed. *The Matter of Identity in Medieval Romance*. Cambridge: Cambridge University Press, 2002. Essays on the theme of identity, including a suggestive treatment of female vulnerability by Amanda Hopkins, pp. 43–58.

Lucas, Angela M. 'Keeping up Appearances: Chaucer's Franklin and the Magic of the Breton Lay Genre'. In Brian Cosgrove, ed., *Literature and the Supernatural*. Dublin: Blackrock, 1995. Good account of Breton lays with a discussion of the degree to which Chaucer's *Franklin's Tale* conforms to the genre.

Mehl, Dieter. *The Middle English Romances of the Thirteenth and Fourteenth Centuries*. London: Routledge, 1969. A useful survey which attempts to classify the material.

Smithers, Geoffrey V. 'Story-Patterns in some Breton Lays', *Medium Aevum*, 40 (1971), 61–92. The best attempt to analyse the story patterns that characterize Breton lays.

Stevens, John. *Medieval Romance: Themes and Approaches*. London: Hutchinson, 1973. A classic survey.

17

Middle English debate literature

Alan J. Fletcher

Introduction

Debate literature was a pan-European medieval genre. In England, alongside examples in the other two literary languages, French and Latin, debates are well represented in Middle English in poems like *The Cuckoo and the Nightingale* or *The Parliament of the Three Ages* (Conlee). While significant differences distinguish many debate poems, all dramatize an argument and contest of verbal skill between emotionally heated opponents. The most sophisticated example to survive in Middle English is *The Owl and the Nightingale*, chosen for study here even though, by virtue of that very sophistication, it is not entirely typical.

Socially productive binaries

Late-medieval culture dimensioned debating practically as well as textually, and each dimension found reciprocal support in the other. Thus debates were real-time events, played out in a host of institutional settings—in schoolrooms, for example, or courts of law, manorial households, theology faculties, or parlours of bishops—as well as things encountered on parchment in more readerly, literary ways. Whatever the debate's modality, it is no exaggeration to say that the dynamic of debate powered influential circles of late-medieval English society, making that society extremely 'debate conscious'.

From the social point of view, a debate's importance may locate less in its disputed issues and possible outcome than in the communal bonding it fosters. Once the disputants settle into the binary positions in which both agree to differ, they begin to shape identities for themselves out of their opposition. At a deeper level, then, contestation actually binds the disputants together in identities mutually affirmed precisely because they are contrary. Of course, binary thinking, which is a procedure dramatized in and driving *The Owl and the Nightingale*, is a perennial mode of thought. Binaries now, as in medieval times, bond those who subscribe to them in a shared social moment, irrespective of how antithetical the experiences of this shared moment may be. The antithesis simply orientates how we view the content of the shared moment, establishing alternative terms in which that content is available to be perceived. Sometimes, the alternatives may even seem to melt back into each other—there are passages in the poem when exactly this, too, appears to happen. When such coalescence occurs, it seems clearer than ever that what finally matters is the cohesion that the binary has generated. Each apparent polar term becomes a twin partner in one communal, if variously figurable, event. On these occasions, differences start appearing more superficial than significant, as the centre of interest shifts to unity through opposition.

Here, of course, is a tension. The debate normally aims to get somewhere, to resolve issues and close upon a truth. As such, it was a valued heuristic tool in the late-medieval period. Yet our poem, supremely aware of the constructed nature of the debate medium in which truth was traditionally thought to be accessible, comes close to presenting truth equally as a construct rather than an absolute. Further, it seems to ask, 'Who's worried about getting at truth when there's rhetoric?' It could therefore be said to stage a carnival celebration of a key cultural practice dethroned, however temporarily, by a parodic rhetorical counterfeit. The inversion releases potent social force, one consequence of which is the highlighting of the *constructed* nature of personal and social experience. The poem seems to release a sense of a community busily and joyously exploring positions less for the positions' sake than for the sake of forging interchangeable, flexible identities for itself in which it can survive and thrive. We may reasonably suppose that the poem similarly raised the consciousness of its first audiences in this respect.

Exactly how each bird stood for a polar endpoint of a socially, as well as textually, productive binary remains, then, to be seen; likewise, how each sparked off the other to create a potent social force field which, by playing a polyphony of genres in the ears of its audience, caused them to hear the boundaries and dimensions of their cultural awareness.

The debate(d) poem

The intellectual and literary feat that *The Owl and the Nightingale* achieves makes it fully deserve the reputation it has come to enjoy. In it, two birds, an Owl and a Nightingale, battle over the question of who sings the best, while also pulling in all sorts of other topical issues as their debate develops. The plan is that Nicholas of Guild-ford, whom both birds agree is so brilliant and impartial that he makes an ideal judge, will be appealed to for a verdict when the debate is over. No verdict, though, is ever returned; after over 1,700 lines of heated argument, another bird, the Wren, intervenes and advises the disputants to fly off as agreed to Portesham in Dorset, where Master Nicholas lives, to put their case before him and receive his definitive judgement. At this point the text ends as briskly as it began.

Although as it unfolds the poem strikes up all sorts of local genre resonances—I spoke of a genre polyphony—its overarching generic category is dialectic or debate. In one of the two manuscripts in which the poem survives, a Latin heading pre-empts expectation of what may lie ahead: *Incipit* altercacio *inter filomenam et bubonem* ('Here begins the *debate* between the Nightingale and the Owl'). Whether this heading was editorial or authorial is unimportant. It flags the genre to which the poem was perceived to belong, and provides an initial orientation: it was an *altercacio*, a common term designating 'debate' whether as textual or actual practice.

Whichever bird early audiences favoured when the debate was over, it is ironically appropriate that the avian dispute has also set present-day critics at odds, and not only about the issues debated and about whether any judgement between the birds is even possible. Today, it has also generated argument about its original historical circumstances. Questions about who wrote it, for whom, where, and when remain unsettled. Yet current critical discussion, losing confidence that these questions are answerable, has retreated from them, preferring instead to focus on interpretative questions that have been thought to need less historical information to resolve.

But, by that same measure, this criticism is of limited value. The historical questions matter. And even many of the interpretative questions that critics have taken refuge in cannot be properly deliberated unless the poem's historical ones are reckoned with. In order, therefore, to understand the cultural work and positioning of this text, historical questions like author, audience, time, and place persist. Of course, often the required information is simply unavailable for texts from remote periods, having been lost or forgotten. Yet treating our text to the most ambitious retrospective affordable requires that these questions be faced.

The approach to *The Owl and the Nightingale* adopted here, then, maintains that its optimal textual understanding accompanies an understanding of it socially, that both its textual and social enterprises are in some way mutually implicated. The procedure of the approach could be pictured archaeologically. We have various shards of a broken pot. That it was a culturally significant pot is clear because one of the shards, the poem itself, is so sophisticated. But how are all the pieces to be reassembled so that the proportion and shape of the whole can be seen aright? Restoring this totality will help recuperate an understanding of exactly how it served its society. Did it dispense wine, ale, milk, or water? The social situations of drinking each of these liquids, after all, are likely to be very different. Theoretically, there should be some fit between the literary shard and the various historical ones. Yet our sense of the patterns we think we see on the literary shard must not coerce our sense of those we think we see on the historical ones, or vice versa. Nevertheless, somehow the patterns must all join together. With due care, they ought to be cross-referenceable. The emergent pot will necessarily be a hypothesis for debate in itself, but it should at least have hypothetical integrity. So the following discussion will avoid sheltering in narrow, literary considerations that risk occluding the poem from its cultural work and the social mechanisms with which its debate genre affiliates it.

The task, then, will be to try to read the dialectical dynamic of the poem associationally within a particular cultural formation whose temporal and geographical situation we can now try to delimit. Although the information deficit cannot be fully repaired, we can go further than critics traditionally have.

When, where, and who?

First, when was *The Owl and the Nightingale* written? Strictly speaking, the best that can be said for this is some time up to the date limit suggested by the palaeography of its two surviving manuscripts, London, British Library, Cotton Caligula A. ix (hereafter C) and Oxford, Jesus College, MS 29 (part II) (hereafter J). The handwriting of J had long been considered to date to late in the thirteenth century, and that of C to the first half, perhaps to *c.*1250, and therefore sometime in the first part of the reign of King Henry III (1216–72). But recent palaeographical opinion has estimated that C equally belongs to the late thirteenth century (Ker, p. ix); it is perhaps more closely to be compared with a manuscript datable *c.*1284 (Laing, p. 70).

In declaring both C and J to be near contemporaries, these reappraisals have paved the way for a reconsideration of the composition date of the poem. The traditional thinking was that it had been written between the death in 1189 of King Henry II and the accession in 1216 of his grandson King Henry III, a reference within the poem to the soul of a King Henry being interpreted as Henry II's soul (Stanley, p. 19).

But the palaeographical redating of C opens the possibility that the reference is to King Henry III, who died in 1272 (Cartlidge[1] and Cartlidge[4], p. xv). For two further reasons I believe Henry III may indeed have been the king in question. The textual condition of the poem is such that the history of its manuscript transmission must have been relatively brief. It was probably composed shortly before C and J were copied (Wells, p. 519). Also, the poem contains a batch of words that the historical dictionaries tell us appear here for the first time (for example, *afoled, alegge, bataile, carter, dahet, faucun, huing, ipeint, kukeweld, plait, plaiding, stable*). After *The Owl and the Nightingale*, the next dictionary attestations start clustering from *c.*1290 onwards. Were the poem to be dated between 1189 and 1216, we would need to believe that no attestations of the words in question—and none seems particularly abstruse or exotic—were recorded for two, maybe three, generations; that is, that eighty or ninety years lay between their (supposedly early) appearance in the poem and the end of the thirteenth century when their attestations come thicker and faster. Believing this seems to require a greater act of faith than simply believing that the attestations in the poem are in fact near contemporaries with the next earliest ones that the dictionaries cite and that start clustering from *c.*1290. In short, it seems more likely that the lexis thought to be first on record in the poem is more nearly contemporary than previously imagined with that found in texts composed late in the thirteenth century.

Important interpretative consequences, excluded if we believe the earlier dating, automatically follow once we accept the poem as a post-1272, pre-*c.*1284 product; quite simply, times have changed and a different cultural formation than existed *c.*1200 now conditioned the text and its author, contouring differently the horizons of response in the audiences receiving his poem. But let us ask other questions useful to consider before trying to estimate the possible interpretative consequences of a re-dating.

Where in England was the poem written, and of what local histories might it have been conscious? Critics used to think the poem written by someone trained to write either in Dorset, Hampshire, or Surrey (Cartlidge[1], p. 234). Perhaps the author was from Guildford, one of the two place names mentioned in the text (Stanley, p. 18). But the latest work in Middle English dialectology has determined that, while this traditional view could indeed be correct, not enough is known to fix the poem's language to these counties quite so firmly, let alone to Guildford. In fact, it could hail from 'almost anywhere in Wessex, the Home Counties or the south-west Midlands' (Cartlidge[3]).

However, there are good reasons why the traditional association of the poem with Guildford should be respected. Let us look afresh at an old piece of evidence.

If the poem's first audience were familiar with Master Nicholas of Guildford, where were they? The Wren near the end of the debate says that he now lives in Portesham, a relatively out-of-the-way village on the Dorset coast. But the Wren is describing a distant geography, and probably so was the author. Formerly in the J manuscript was a parchment leaf on which appeared a quatrain of doggerel verse. The leaf later got lost, but the quatrain was recorded, courtesy of a seventeenth-century antiquary. Judging by its style and linguistic complexion, the quatrain may have been contemporary with the poem, and it mentioned someone called John of Guildford. The point is, we now have to reckon with *two* Guildford people: Master Nicholas inside the poem, and a certain Master John outside it and inside a text of his own on the leaf now missing. Furthermore, the lost quatrain has the throw-away appearance of one of those scribal whimsies that sometimes turn up in medieval manuscripts and that can help determine the provenance of the manuscript or of texts copied in it. So there is more reason than usually believed for associating some of the contents of the manuscript from which J was either immediately (or ultimately) copied with Guildford by virtue of the two independent Guildford people associated with it. Yet critics have sooner recruited Master John of the missing leaf into the uncertain service of trying to establish who the poem's author was than in helping strengthen any real-time link between his poem and Guildford, even though this seems the best way Master John can be employed.

So the traditional suggestion of some actual Guildford association for the poem is more plausible than has been thought. If a case for taking Guildford or its environs, between 1272 and c.1284, as the poem's geographical epicentre remains intact, the grounds for a hoped-for historicization start to look more promising. But more can be said.

What sort of early readership had *The Owl and the Nightingale?* Amongst whom were its socially productive binaries active? This question too correlates with some of the literary issues that will later be considered. Earlier belief held that no information on this survived. This may no longer be true. C and J—both manuscripts are poetic anthologies—have been said to show no sign of customization for any definable original interest group; their contents appeal to tastes ranging widely from the clerical to the secular. Moreover, not all clerical and secular tastes were necessarily mutually exclusive. Thus C and J may have suited 'a friary, a convent, a cathedral chapter, a magnate's court or the household of a country gentleman' (Cartlidge[2], p. 262). In principle, the poem may indeed have found a wide readership like this, especially once it had left its author's desk and begun travelling in anthologies, which of their nature often cater to a wide range of tastes. The point about the permeability of reading interests across professional divides is an efficient one. This notwithstanding, the facts about the poem's early readership come down to two whose broad consistency is worth recalling: the first is that certainly one copy, and maybe two copies, of the poem turned up in anthologies whose contents were strikingly similar to those of C and J and that had been kept in the library of a religious house of canons in Titchfield, Hampshire; and the second is that the only actual medieval reader of the poem for whom a plausible case can be made was a Dominican friar, and a famous one: the philosopher, preacher, and theologian Robert Holcot, who appears somehow to have encountered it in the early part of the fourteenth century and not far from where it originated, maybe indeed in the very place of its origin (Fletcher, pp. 2–4). In sum, whatever about a possible secular readership of this poem, the one known about for certain was clerical. So, no doubt, was the poem's author, his professional circle, and also the circle in which Nicholas of Guildford was chiefly known and in which the poem imagines him as deserving promotion.

Furthermore, the author not only bonded vocationally with his professional circle in a clerical ideal of community, but he, they, and all his early readers also bonded conceptually in a wider ideal of community that the binding power of his dialectic fostered and projected. This wider, virtual community of the like-minded was one in which all consumers of the poem were invited to participate, whose values they would come intellectually to recognize, and through that recognition, quietly ingest. So, while we do not know who the author of the poem was—though believing him to have been someone who knew Nicholas of Guildford, not Nicholas himself, remains creditworthy (Stanley, pp. 19–22, contested by Cartlidge[4], pp. xiv–xv)— more interesting is the sense of identity that he registers as he fashioned and was fashioned by his poem, and the nature of the circle of the like-minded that he invited his audience to inhabit. This circle's space could never be neutral, as earlier suggested. It was electrically charged, having provided for a simultaneous dimensioning of two socially potent forces: it offered freedom to contemplate with detached clarity the constructed nature of a socially shaping genre and its cultural underpinnings; and it offered room for recognition and acceptance of the *negotiable* nature of the conventions upon which that constructedness depended. In short, the poet wrote a dialectic that raised consciousness not simply about the various issues in dispute—that happens self-evidently—but also about the dialectical process itself and then, by association, about the social stakes of dialectical thinking.

Is there life after dialectic?

Nevertheless, although the poem has forced dialectic to break cover as a genre, it does not follow that dialectic, once seen for what it is—a negotiable system of rhetorical constructs—can be abandoned. The poem's dispassionate take on dialectic may, paradoxically, pave the nearest way towards endorsing and naturalizing it.

Support for an argument that the poem renders dialectic self-reflexive, and does so with socially shaping force, is strong. Further, the self-reflexiveness takes various forms. Having begun by flagging its genre affiliation with dialectic, the poem then proceeds to expose certain assumptions that dialectic routinely otherwise takes for granted. One of these is dialectic's inclination to take itself seriously. Many subscribed to the serious belief that the truth was 'out there' and could be accessed dialectically. Thus dialectic played for serious truth stakes. But it is as if the poem pulls faces at the genre to which it professes affiliation. Consequently, it collapses any ready assumption that dialectic be taken seriously as a heuristic tool. The poem similarly gestures towards its affiliated genre's inclination towards seriousness in another way. Many of the human issues that the birds debate are inherently serious: the plight of battered wives, for instance, or the trap of loveless marriages. Especially shocking is the Owl's unflinching description of a brutalized wife having her husband's fist smashed into her teeth (Cartlidge[4], p. 37, lines 1531–8). But a light-hearted counterbalance to such matter is always at hand in how the poem's serious issues are *staged*; constant reminders never let us forget that the debaters are simply birds, however human-sounding their voices. And so yet another binary in a poem already crammed with them crystallizes here in an opposition between light-hearted and serious, insinuated into the heart of the genre that the poet manipulates and that again contributes towards the genre's exposé as a synthetic construction in its own right. This particular debate poem seems to be on holiday from serious debating as a means for seriously resolving anything. This does not mean that it seeks to deny that debating can ever achieve such resolution; it is just that this particular instance will not achieve it. In a sense, then, the poem enters a dialectic with some of its espoused genre's standard assumptions. Laughter at the genre's expense nevertheless brings the genre up close.

Some other medieval debate poems superficially resemble *The Owl and the Nightingale* in the way they too seem to stage a wry stand-off from their genre in not finalizing a judgement, instead devolving the responsibility for any resolution upon the audience. But the poem seems to work far more single-mindedly at cultivating a dialectical stance towards its own genre than do these related texts. Alongside the unsettling, latent in the deferral of judgement, of regular dialectic's faith that a determination is reachable, several passages in the poem show the narrator reflecting less upon *what* his birds say than upon *how* they choose to say it and upon what the practical consequences of their choice are likely to be. These passages risk being drowned by the din of the birds' sensational slanging match, yet the interest they betray in the inner mechanics and psychology of debate, in debate purely as a set of strategic moves, seems a little unusual in the run of medieval debate literature. It is tempting to see this interest as indicating the poet's acquaintance with sophistic, a branch of rhetoric that the late thirteenth century was finding increasingly fascinating. Sophistic, with its emphasis on the tricks and dodges of debate, and on audience psychology, was transmitted to the later Middle Ages via Aristotle's *Rhetoric*, translated into Latin *c*.1269 by William of Moerbeke, and then further promoted a few years later in the commentary on it by Giles of Rome (Copeland, pp. 121–4). Giles was much interested in the very thing that interested our poet: debate as tactic rather than as content. The net effect of the passages in the poem that betray a similar interest is again to denaturalize and foreground the debate medium by shifting attention away from the message and towards the medium. The social result of this denaturalizing might be a subsequent renaturalizing of the debate genre precisely by forcing a jocular consciousness of its materiality.

Once a genre acquires differentiated social realizations—recall how

real-time medieval debates served a variety of institutional contexts—so through differentiation the genre is potentially liable to
emerge for inspection as a phenomenon in its own right, no longer to
be taken for granted. Being made aware of a genre's different inflections also raises awareness of its very existence and of the ways in
which we agree to recognize its parameters. The method of *The Owl
and the Nightingale* seems to abet this potentiality for self-
consciousness. It argues an author alive to at least some of the guises
that debate assumed in his society. The poem could have been composed only by someone with a relatively high degree of cultural fluency and literate in the discourses of 'debate culture'. This can also be
proved collaterally from the sheer range of other sorts of genres that
the author was able to ventriloquize. His poem is full of voices, and
not just of the two most vocal. Compare the following passage,
part of the Nightingale's attack on the Owl's purported dirty habits,
which also incidentally displays many of the literary qualities
that endeared the poem to an earlier generation of critics (Cartlidge[4],
p. 4, lines 101–26):

> Þat oþer ʒer a faukun bredde—
> His nest noʒt wel he ne bihedde:
> Þarto þu stele in o dai,
> & leidest þaron þi fole ey.
> Þo hit bicom þat he haʒte,
> & of his eyre briddes wraʒte,
> Ho broʒte his briddes mete,
> Bihold his nest, iseʒ hi ete.
> He iseʒ bi one halue
> His nest ifuled uthalue.
> Þe faucun was wroþ wit his bridde,
> & lude ʒal and sterne chidde:
> 'Segget me wo hauet þis ido!
> Ov nas neuer icunde þarto:
> Hit was idon ov a loþ viste.
> Segget me ʒif ʒe hit wiste!'
> Þo quaþ þat on & quad þat oþer:
> 'Iwis, hit was ure oʒe broþer–
> Þe ʒond þat haued þat grete heued.
> Wai þat he nis þarof bireued.
> Worp hit ut mid þe alre wurste
> Þat his necke him toberste!'

> Þe faucun ilefde his bridde,
> & nom þat fule brid amidde,
> & warp hit of þan wilde bowe,
> Þar pie & crowe hit todrawe.

The other year a falcon was breeding. He didn't protect his nest very well. One day you crept up to it and laid your filthy egg in it. When eventually the falcon hatched his eggs and chicks appeared from them, he brought his chicks food, looked at his nest, and saw them eating. He saw that the outside of his nest had been fouled on one side. The falcon was furious with his chicks and yelled out loud and gave them a stern ticking off: 'Tell me, who's done this? This was never your habit. A vile wet fart has been landed on you! Tell me if you know about it.' Then one after the other said, 'Sure, it was our own brother, the one over there with the big head. A pity he's not detached from it. Chuck him out with everything that's nasty so that he breaks his neck.' The falcon believed his chicks and seized that foul bird around the middle and flung it from the wild bough to where magpies and crows ripped it to bits.

Not only have we here a showcase of the author's brilliance in evoking a spoken idiom, we also catch him ventriloquizing a Nightingale ventriloquizing a falcon and then the falcon's chicks. (Multiple voices are also a stylistic asset to a poem that, in terms of plot, is extremely static; since very little actually happens, the dynamism of the verbal action makes a good substitute, and local vistas like this prevent a fixed location, the corner of a field where the debate unfolds, becoming monotonous.) But genres are voices too, and this little tale of daddy falcon and the nest-crashing owlet itself introduces a new genre voice—beast fable—and adds it to the poem's overarching genre of debate. There are many other local examples of the author's genre ventriloquism: lyric, sermon, satire, and others are all grist to his poetic mill. Thus his cultural fluency similarly shows in the way he achieved a genre polyphony, as well as mimicked voices, within the compass of his poem. Since the auditorium of his debate is accommodating, it is not surprising to find that it also welcomes such a densely binary style, because binaries similarly aim at accommodating a totality between their polar endpoints. Furthermore, on reflection, it is clear that binaries themselves are microdialectics; they are mini-debates (war vs. peace, hawks vs. doves, owls vs. nightingales). Consequently, in the encircling debate genre of the poem, binary style might be expected to find a natural habitat. But the more interesting point is that the poet has cultivated this style so emphatically; the poem is strewn with evidence of it. Indeed, it seems iconized in Master Nicholas, who derived his star quality precisely from his ability to discriminate between opposites.

Conclusion

Holding that in mind, we can fold back our inferences about the author and his cultural formation into the geohistorical moment reconstructed earlier. What sort of 'pot' have we?

Hypothetically, it might look as follows. The hostility of the birds dialogically convenes an amiable, community spirit among the readers/audience who witness it. (Most people enjoy a good spat, and spats spectated are consoling reminders of our easeful distance as spectators.) Note, too, that it is a communal ease; at the end of his poem, the author conceived his comfortably positioned audience as a plural like-minded community, curious about how the debate might turn out. Indeed, at the very end he effaces himself as omniscient author, suddenly relocating himself amongst that community, saying that he cannot reveal the outcome because the narrative he has been relating has suddenly expired. He is one with them in being no wiser than they. Not only does he cause his poem to convene him and his plural audience into one emotionally bonded community, but also into a community of shared intellectual interests. The author, on a safe assumption, was clerical. So were the earliest audiences for which there is reliable evidence. Yet he was not so sternly clerical that he quarantined sacred discourse from secular narrative. Nor would the community imagined in his poem have found their mixture offensive; here again they were like-minded. For both author and audience, sacred and secular had dialectical integrity and could prove mutually enhancing.

If late thirteenth-century Guildford really was the poem's geohistorical epicentre, then a cultural formation answering that of the poem was available in only one place. It did not exist in Guildford until 1276, when a royal foundation of Dominican friars was established. Skill in canon and civil law, precisely the sort of legal familiarity evinced in the poem, was something friars were famous for. Perhaps a more specialized aspect of that skill is glimpsed in the poem's preoccupation with marriage issues. To be sure, these were explored in a variety of medieval texts, but their judicial arbitration, in the real world, was almost invariably the prerogative of the ecclesiastical courts. May contact with them have helped stimulate our clerical author's interest? But especially beguiling is the fact that the mendicant Orders, at around the time mooted for the poem's composition, were great mediators to the laity in their English sermons of the scholastic doctrine of contraries, that 'opposites set next to each other are mutually enhancing' (as one Aristotelean epitome in circulation at the time put it). This is the principle, after all, around which the poem also turns.

The first known likely reader of the poem, Robert Holcot, was a Dominican friar. Was it written by a member of his Order in the latter part of the previous century? And like the poem's author, neither was Holcot a stern man. Contrary to modern stereotypes, eminent churchmen are not invariably solemn. In his learned discourse *On Wisdom*, Holcot found time to tell the one about an artist who painted superbly, but whose children were startlingly ugly. When the discrepancy was pointed out, he replied, 'Ah yes, you see, when I'm producing my paintings I work during the day when I can see what I'm doing'. A cleric tolerating such robust humour might be expected to have enjoyed a poem where sacred similarly mingled with secular.

As the superlative example of Middle English debate literature, then, and as part of the social consequence of its superlative achievement, *The Owl and the Nightingale* denaturalized and renaturalized debate as a constitutive cultural force, and connected its author and his community with the exhilarating and dangerous truth that the Truth lay in their hands.

References and suggested reading

Cartlidge, Neil. 'The Date of *The Owl and the Nightingale*', *Medium Aevum*, 65 (1996), 230–47. [Cartlidge[1]]. Taking its central idea from N. R. Ker's work (see below), this argues that a date for the poem after 1272 is possible.

Cartlidge, Neil. 'The Composition and Social Context of Oxford, Jesus College, MS 29(II) and London, British Library, MS Cotton Caligula A.ix', *Medium Aevum*, 66 (1997), 250–69. [Cartlidge²]. This attempts to understand the readership and interests reflected in the C and J manuscripts.

Cartlidge, Neil. 'The Linguistic Evidence for the Provenance of *The Owl and the Nightingale*', *Neuphilologische Mitteilungen*, 99 (1998), 249–68. [Cartlidge³]. Drawing on research currently under way in Edinburgh on early Middle English scribal dialects, this charts the regional affiliations of the C and J manuscripts and of the possible original dialect of the author.

Cartlidge, Neil, ed. *The Owl and the Nightingale* (Exeter: Exeter University Press, 2001). [Cartlidge⁴]. This is the most recent critical edition of the poem.

Conlee, John W., ed. *Middle English Debate Poetry: A Critical Anthology* (East Lansing: Colleagues Press, 1991). This useful anthology contains many of the extant Middle English debate poems other than *The Owl and the Nightingale*.

Copeland, Rita. 'Sophistic, Spectrality, Iconoclasm'. In Jeremy Dimmick, James Simpson, and Nicolette Zeeman, eds., *Images, Idolatry, and Iconoclasm in Late Medieval England*. Oxford: Oxford University Press, 2002, pp. 112–30. This includes a valuable account of the rise in the interest in sophistic in medieval England.

Fletcher, Alan J. 'The Genesis of *The Owl and the Nightingale*: A New Hypothesis', *Chaucer Review*, 34 (1999), 1–17. This adduces possible evidence of the Dominican friar Robert Holcot having been the first known reader of *The Owl and the Nightingale*, and also upholds the centrality of Guildford to the poem's historical consciousness.

Hill, Betty. 'Oxford, Jesus College MS. 29: Addenda on Donation, Acquisition, Dating and Relevance of the "Broaken Leafe" Note to "The Owl and the Nightingale" ', *Notes & Queries*, 220 (1975), 98–105. This discusses some of the issues raised by the leaf lost from the J manuscript.

Ker, N. R. *The Owl and the Nightingale: Facsimile of the Jesus and Cotton Manuscripts*. Early English Text Society o.s. 251. Oxford: Oxford University Press, 1963. The introduction to this facsimile paved the way to re-dating the poem when it arbitrated that the C manuscript was not copied early in the thirteenth century, as had hitherto been believed.

Laing, Margaret. *Catalogue of Sources for a Linguistic Atlas of Early Medieval English*. Cambridge: D. S. Brewer, 1993. This cites an opinion on the palaeographical dating of the C manuscript privately communicated from Malcolm B. Parkes to the author.

Stanley, E. G., ed. *The Owl and the Nightingale*, 2nd edn. Manchester: Manchester University Press, 1972; repr. 1981. Though in general terms now superseded, the introduction to this edition remains of value for some of its arguments and appraisals.

Wells, J. E. '*The Owl and the Nightingale* and MS Cotton', *Modern Language Notes*, 48 (1933), 516–19. This argues that only a relatively short period intervened between the authorship of *The Owl and the Nightingale* and its extant manuscripts.

18

Religious writing by women

Mary Swan

Introduction

The texts which will form the focus of this chapter are usually known today as *Revelations of Divine Love*, by Julian of Norwich, and *The Book of Margery Kempe*, by Margery Kempe. Julian of Norwich lived from around 1342 to some time after 1416. Little is known about her, but it is generally accepted that in her adulthood she became a religious recluse, or anchoress, at St Julian's Church in Norwich, Norfolk. *Revelations of Divine Love* exists in two versions: a shorter and a longer one. Both recount a series of religious visions experienced by Julian when she was 30, and her reflections upon their meaning. The current scholarly consensus is that the shorter version of the text was composed soon after the visions happened, or at least within a few years of this date, and the longer version some twenty years later. The details of Margery Kempe's life are better known, partly because she gives a much fuller account of them in her book than does Julian, and also because this account tallies with, and can be amplified by, independent evidence of the lives of Margery and of her family. She lived from around 1373 until some time after 1439, in King's Lynn in Norfolk, and was the daughter and the wife of prosperous middle-class merchants. Margery's *Book* tells that she had fourteen children with her husband, and that she embarked on a life of spiritual devotion and pilgrimage in middle age; some time after experiencing the first of a series of religious visions. *The Book of Margery Kempe* was probably written down in the mid- to late 1430s.

Writing by women in the late Middle Ages

Women's relationship to literature in the later Middle Ages has been the subject of increasing scholarly interest over the last few decades. This had led to a broad definition of that relationship, which extends from the physical inscription of texts by women, through the dictation by women to male scribes, and women commissioning men to compose texts, to women playing a more indirect supporting role as the intended audience for some literary texts. Some medieval women writers have been known to scholars for a long time, and more are identified from time to time. The authors of the very large number of anonymous surviving medieval texts, and the scribes of anonymous medieval manuscripts, were routinely assumed to be men, but more recently these assumptions have been subjected to more critical scrutiny, and as a result evidence for women authors and scribes is being uncovered. Recent work on particular genres, especially the popular devotional literature of the later Middle Ages, which includes Saints' Lives and meditatory and regulatory texts, identifies women as one of their key intended audiences (see Chapter 14). As a result of all of these trends in scholarship, a more nuanced picture is being built up of the ways in which women shape and are shaped by literature in the later Middle Ages.

The writings by women which have interested scholars for some time are those which fit into the modern category of 'literary' works, such as the romance-influenced *Lais* composed in Anglo-Norman by Marie de France in twelfth-century England, and the works of Christine de Pizan, written in French and in France in the late fourteenth and early fifteenth centuries. Many texts composed by women, however, have received less critical attention because they are not 'literary' in the modern sense of the category, but are rather practical or theological in style. Amongst these are the texts composed by, and on behalf of, women which describe their religious experiences, often including supernatural visions and prophecies. These writings started to attract substantial scholarly attention in the 1980s, and since then have grown into a major focus for research, in the form of editing, translating, and analysis.

Of the writings attributed to medieval women mystics, two texts which have prompted a particularly large amount of critical study, and which are also often included in undergraduate and graduate courses, are *Revelations of Divine Love* by Julian of Norwich, and *The Book of Margery Kempe*. These two texts will form the central examples of this chapter.

Mystics and their writings

Mysticism is a term used to describe spiritual communion with the divine, and it characterizes very large-scale trends in Christian thinking and practice in later medieval Europe. These trends are a reflection of changes in social structure and ideology, and they are manifested in the often passionate and emotional participation of lay people in a new and popular spirituality, which stresses the humanity of Christ, and espouses a style of devotion centred on individual meditation and connection with the divine. These new styles of devotion are now known as 'affective piety', and are often characterized by modern scholars as feminized, in that they stress the bodily and experiential, and are rooted in everyday life.

Women seem to have been particularly drawn to the resulting new modes of Christian living, and they form the core of some interesting religious movements, which emerge throughout Europe from the thirteenth century onwards. These movements are a combination of the para-monastic and the worldly, and they usually involve women who are not professed nuns choosing to live a life of chastity, poverty, and religious devotion without joining a formal nunnery, but instead by living in isolation, or in communities of like-minded women.

These new directions in religious conduct promoted new forms of religious experience, and the ultimate form of this is the vision: the experience by the visionary of direct contact with the divine. This is usually facilitated by deep meditation and asceticism (which can include sensory deprivation of various kinds, such as isolation, lack of sleep, starvation, and self-harm) on the part of the visionary, and results in an increased depth of knowledge of the divine, and an increased personal authority as mediator of this knowledge.

This increased personal authority was often accompanied by a sense of responsibility, or in some cases compulsion, to communicate the visionary experience and to use it to deepen the spiritual understanding of others. For this reason, a surprisingly large number of women visionaries produced written accounts of their experiences; either by writing or dictating them themselves, or by allowing men to write about them on their behalf. Almost all of the surviving written accounts of personally experienced divine vision are by or about women. The texts draw on other kinds of writing, most notably Saints' Lives, romances, and devotional works. They often became very popular with women and men throughout Europe, and circulated widely, so that in some cases we can trace the transmission of ideas and narrative structures from one text to another, and can thus see this body of writings as constituting a new genre.

Current scholarly debates on women mystics

The vibrant field of studies of women mystics covers a range of approaches and disciplines, and is engaged in the discussion of a number of important issues. Some single-discipline work is produced: literary studies analyse the texts in terms of their relationship to each other and to other genres, and examine the style and language of individual texts; historical work seeks to identify the context for the production of the texts, and the details of the lives of their producers; theological studies show how the texts respond to other religious texts and debates of the time. Much more common, however, are interdisciplinary studies of women mystics, which analyse the women and their writings as cultural actors and products, and which show how different aspects of their context—the spiritual, the material, the autobiographical, the emotional—are interwoven and influence each other.

Perhaps the most popular issues in current scholarship are the following:

1. Authority. The debate on this topic stems from the essential tension in the works of all women mystics between their authors' lowly social and spiritual status as women and the spiritual and sometimes social authority bestowed on them by their visionary experiences. This debate draws on wider work on gender and patriarchal social structures in the Middle Ages.

2. Agency. This debate centres on the question of who wrote a given text. In some cases we know that a text about a woman mystic has been written by a man—often a man, such as her priest or confessor or spiritual adviser, who has an authoritative and influential position relative to the woman. In many cases, however, it is not clear whether the narrative voice in a text is really that of the woman mystic, who is writing down (or having written) her own words, or whether it is that of her scribe, who is adopting her voice but inventing it too. This debate involves questions of gender and writing style, and concepts of identity and individuality which increasingly draw on work from feminist studies and queer theory.

3. Psychology. This debate is long-standing, but has shifted its terms away from a desire to pathologize and thereby explain away women's visions, towards a more socially rooted reading which seeks to trace the psychology of internalized oppression and of female empowerment in the context of late medieval religious experience.

4. Everyday life. This debate foregrounds the domestic as the context for women's visionary experiences, and also for their accounts of them. It aims to counteract the downgrading of the domestic, familial, and everyday in traditional scholarship, and to revalidate these particularly female spheres of experience as a way of reading women mystics in something approaching their own terms.

Scholarship specifically on Julian of Norwich and Margery Kempe has followed the general trends of scholarship on women mystics, but has often treated these two writers very differently from one another. Margery and her *Book* have attracted considerably more scholarly attention than Julian and her writings, but until recent years the critical reception of Margery has been much more negative than that of Julian. Even Julian has not been taken seriously as a theologian and an author until relatively recently.

Earlier scholarship on Julian exhibited a tendency to scrutinize her texts for autobiographical details which might allow the construction of a personality-based context in which to read her work. The scholarly focus is now changing to an interest in her theology, and how it relates to other theological traditions of the later Middle Ages, and in her negotiation of her gender and her authority.

Recent scholarship on Margery is attempting to take her seriously as a mystic and an author, and is thus moving away from earlier, and influential, deeply negative and judgemental assessments of her as 'out of control' or disordered, artless, and unselfconscious as a writer, and towards an appreciation of the productive tension between her worldliness and her spirituality, and between Margery and her scribes. Another strand of current work on Margery is the investigation of the influence on Margery's *Book* of popular contemporary female visionary religious role models, in particular St Bridget of Sweden.

Current scholarship on both Julian and Margery centres on the question of authority. A major subject of current critical interest is the agency of these two women as writers. The debate on this topic focuses on irresolvable but important questions about exactly what input they had into the texts as we have them today: did they both dictate them to a scribe, who wrote down verbatim what they said, and did not add anything; or did their scribes substantially reshape the women's words, and thus produce texts whose real authors, in stylistic terms, are not Julian or Margery; or are parts of each text directly composed by Julian and Margery, and other parts interpolated or revoiced by the scribes? Margery tells us repeatedly that she could not write, while Julian is less clear on this point, but a central theme in both their texts is the tension between their status as women (and, as their texts put it, 'creatures'), as spiritual authorities, and creators of books.

Excerpts from the texts, with critical analysis

The issues outlined above provide a context for the composition of *Revelations of Divine Love* and *The Book of Margery Kempe*, and also a context for our interpretations of these works. In this section, the act of interpretation will be rooted in very close attention to the texts, and in particular to their structure, language, and style. The method of analysis which is described below is particularly suited to under-graduate students, but can also be used by students and scholars at any point in their career. In order to make the steps in this method of analysis completely clear to students encountering medieval mystical writing for the first time, the description which follows is directly aimed at such readers, and addresses them as 'you'; this mode of address is intended to stress the importance of individual responses to the texts as a first step in building a rooted critical analysis.

The two excerpts which will provide the data for this analysis form part of the descriptions of the crucifixion visions in *Revelations of Divine Love* and *The Book of Margery Kempe* (See Pl. 6).

Julian of Norwich, *Revelations of Divine Love*, Long Text, chapter 4, crucifixion vision (Glasscoe edn., pp. 5–6)

In this sodenly I saw the rede blode trekelyn [trickling] downe fro [from] under the garlande, hote and freisly [freshly] and ryth plenteously, as it were in the time of his passion that the garlande of thornys was pressid [pressed] on his blissid [blessed] hede, ryte [right] so both God and man, the same that sufferd thus for me. I conceived [understood] treuly and mightily that it was himselfe shewed it me without ony [any] mene [intermediary]. And in the same sheweing [showing] sodenly the Trinite fullfilled the herte [heart] most of ioy [joy]. And so I understood it shall be in hevyn withoute end to all that shall come there. For the Trinite is God, God is the Trinite; the Trinite is our maker and keeper, the Trinite is our everlasting lover, everlasting ioy and blisse, be our lord Iesus Christ. And this was shewed in the first and in all; for where Iesus appereith [appears] the blissid Trinite is understond [under-stood], as to my sight. And I said 'Benedicte domine!' ['Blessed be you, God!'] This I said, for reverence in my meneing, with a mighty voice; and full gretly was astonyed [astonished] for wonder and mervel [marvel] that I had that he that is so reverend and dredfull will be so homely with a synfull creture liveing in wretched flesh.

The Book of Margery Kempe, chapter 80, crucifixion vision (Windeatt edn., pp. 345–6)

Another tyme sche saw in hyr contemplacyon owr Lord Jhesu Crist bowndyn [bound] to a peler [pillar], and hys handys wer bowndyn abovyn hys hevyd [head]. And than sche sey sextene [sixteen] men wyth sextene scorgys [scourges], and eche scorge had viii babelys [8 spiked lumps] of leed [lead] on the ende, and every babyl was ful of scharp prekelys [prickles], as it had ben the rowelys [spiked wheels] of a spor [spur]. And tho men wyth the scorgys madyn comenawnt [made a covenant] that ich [each] of hem schulde yevyn [give] owr Lord xl strokys [40 strokes].

Whan sche saw this petows [piteous] syght, sche wept and cryid ryth [right] lowde as yyf [as if] sche schulde a brostyn [should have burst] for sorwe [sorrow] and peyne. And whan owr Lord was al-to-betyn [all beaten up] and scorgyd [scourged], the Jewys losyd [loosened] hym fro the peler and tokyn hym hys crosse for to beryn [bear] on hys schuldyr [shoulder]. And than hir thowt [it seemed to her] that owr Lady and sche went be another wey for to metyn [meet] wyth hym, and whan thei mettyn wyth hym, thei sey [saw] hym beryn the hevy crosse wyth gret peyne; it was so hevy and so boystows [large] that unethe [hardly] he myth bere it.

And than owr Lady seyd unto hym: 'A, my swete sone, late me help to ber that hevy crosse.'

And sche was so weyke that sche myth not [could not help] byt fel [falling] down and swownyd and lay stille as [as if] it had ben [she were] a ded woman.

In first encountering a text in Middle English, the easiest way to recognize the equivalents of words in present-day English, and also to understand the rhythm and flow of the writing, is to read it out aloud, trying to pronounce every letter. Medieval manuscript texts do not use punctuation in the way that it is used in present-day English, and therefore most edited texts, including the excerpts given above, impose modern punctuation. This usually marks the sense units of the text (clauses, sentences, paragraphs), and so it is useful as an aid to following the text, and need not skew our analysis of it.

On first reading any text, it is worth keeping informal running notes of your impressions, however uninformed or naïve or judgemental these might seem. Your first impressions of a text, which might include some very impressionistic or obvious-seeming statements—'this is a bit lengthy'; 'this is moving very quickly'; 'I didn't expect this to come next'; 'this is very predictable'; 'this is boring'; 'I don't understand this part'; 'a theme seems to be being set up here'; 'this reminds me of an earlier part of the text'—are often the best key to identifying the effect it has on you as a reader. Once you have begun to identify its effect on you, you can go back to the specific points of the text in question, and make a detailed stylistic analysis of them to work out how they achieve that effect.

Of course some of a modern reader's impressions of a text may be very far from those of a medieval reader or hearer, and result from the modern reader's cultural distance from the context in which the text was produced. This is not a problem, since you will be able to identify which of your impressions fall into that category, and they will include those which are generated by your lack of familiarity with particular aspects of medieval culture—details of medieval Christian practice, for example—or with medieval literature—perhaps the conventions of a certain genre. Your identification of those aspects will give you a list of topics to find out about if you want to deepen your reading of medieval literature.

What will be left is a list of impressions which are likely to include some which are common to present-day and medieval readers, and some which are the result of reading the text through the lens of post-medieval concepts, such as particular psychological or political ideologies. All of these impressions are useful ones to work with, since they will enable the production of analyses of the text which either approach it on its own terms (inasmuch as we can tell what these are), or which shed new light on it in modern terms.

To undertake a thorough and consistent stylistic analysis of a passage of medieval literature, it is necessary to have a good edition of the text, and to be confident about how it would translate into present-day English. Using the edition (which should be photocopied or written out, with plenty of space in between and around the lines), the main sense units—sentences, clauses, and sub-clauses, most of which will be signalled in some way by the editorial punctuation—should be marked up so that they stand out. Any notable features should now be marked up, preferably using a different colour. These might include repeated words, phrases, or structures; notable breaks or disjunctures; climaxes of narrative or structure; or other things which strike you. You will now have your own mapped-out copy of the text, and you can use it to produce data for a detailed stylistic analysis.

A good set of criteria for undertaking a stylistic analysis is:[1]

1. Voice
2. Vocabulary
3. Syntax
4. Imagery and patterning
5. Rhythm
6. Tone, attitude, point of view

It will be possible to find examples of everything on the above list in almost any textual excerpt. So, with the excerpt in front of you, you should make notes on each point, describing what you find with detailed reference to the text, and defining each of the topics on the list. Then you can refer back to your list of initial impressions, and see if any of the stylistic features you have identified can explain your reactions.

If this sequence of analysis is applied to the first textual example, from chapter 4 of *Revelations of Divine Love*, the resulting notes might look like this:

Voice

First-person narrator is also the character experiencing the events described, and the speaker reported. Dramatic direct speech (*Benedicte domine!*), in *a mighty voice*, emphasizes the narrator's direct part in the vision and her access to Christ. Astonished (*sodenly, Benedicte domini* exclamation in direct speech) but also didactic.

Vocabulary

Dramatic (*sodenly, hote and freishly*); fairly colloquial language of popular devotion (*his blissid hede, ioy, it shall be in hevyn withoute end, the Trinite is our maker and keeper, wonder and mervel*). Some focus in the vocabulary on terms for seeing and understanding, and the differences between them (*saw, conceived, understood, was shewed, as to my sight*).

Syntax

Mostly sentences of medium length. Some parataxis, mostly in the first half of the extract (*And in the same shewing, And so I understood, And I said*). Some hypotaxis in the latter part of the extract (*for the Trinite is God . . .*).

Imagery and patterning

Vivid and focused on minute detail of physical scene (colour of blood, heat, movement) at the start, and then moves away from that to discuss relationship of speaker with Christ. Refers to Bible narrative of the Passion (*as it were in the time of his passion*), but is very selective in what it includes from the Bible version: relies on the reader's knowledge of the context and explication of the scene.

Rhythm

Sentences and sense units of fairly regular length and rhythm, which makes for smooth reading and steady momentum. Patterning of vocabulary and structure within sentences (*the Trinite is God, God is the Trinite; the Trinite is our maker and keeper, the Trinite is . . .*) draws attention to key words and concepts.

Tone, attitude, point of view

Earnest, eager to communicate. First-person narration from an informed but also humble (*a synfull creture living in wretched flesh*) perspective. Narrative voice does not criticize or question what is described, but imparts it to the reader.

From this set of fairly preliminary notes, it is already clear that the excerpt has a shape which changes from the dramatic and immediate and relatively simply structured to the more complex and doctrinal. If the analysis were extended to the remainder of this chapter of *Revelations of Divine Love*, it would show that this trend is carried through, and that the rest of the chapter is used to expound and exemplify some complex aspects of Christian doctrine on the virgin birth.

Analysis of this excerpt also shows Julian to be creating a narrator's voice which juggles authority and humility. She writes in the language of popular religious devotion, rather than high theology, but she treats complex theological issues clearly and assertively, without expressing uncertainty or inadequacy.

Going through the same sequence of analysis for the second textual example, from chapter 80 of *The Book of Margery Kempe*, might result in the following notes:

Voice

Two layers of voice in this excerpt: the third-person narrator and the directly reported voice of the Virgin Mary. Margery's voice in the vision is reported indirectly, in the description of her crying.

Vocabulary

Some vocabulary of perception and levels of perception (*sche saw in hyr contemplacyon, sche sey, sche saw, hir thowt*), which could be compared with that in the excerpt from *Revelations of Divine Love*.

Syntax

Parataxis (*And . . . and . . .*) is the dominant mode of linking clauses and sentences in this excerpt. Sense units are fairly regular in length and structure. The dramatic narrative of the excerpt is propelled by this regularity and pattern, and also by the striking images depicted.

Imagery and patterning

There are echoes in the details of this excerpt of two other surviving late medieval English interpretations of the Crucifixion which may well have been familiar to Margery and some of her readers: in a painting in Norwich Cathedral, Christ has his hands tied behind his head and his torturers hold scourges, and in the Wakefield Play of the Scourging, the Virgin Mary offers to help carry Christ's cross.

Sensory images are built up in this excerpt through descriptions of the texture and weight of the torture implements (*scharp prekelys, hevy, hevy and boystows*), and of the noise of Margery's distress (*sche wept and cryid ryth lowde*).

Rhythm

Regular rhythm is established both by the even syntax, and by the repetition of selected vocabulary items (*and, bowndyn, babyl, scorgys, peler, crosse, metyn, hevy*). This extensive repetition also reinforces the sense of cumulative torture—both of Christ and of Margery as viewer.

Tone, attitude, point of view

Engaged and emotional and involved. Third-person narration from a very involved perspective, which switches in and out of reporting Margery's experiences and neutrally describing what is happening without positioning Margery as the person experiencing it. The narrative voice does not criticize or question what is described, but the third-person narrator does express Margery's distress and incomprehension at what she experiences; partly by describing her crying, and partly by reinforcing the horror of the scene through descriptions of the instruments of torture and through describing the Virgin Mary's collapse.

This excerpt, in comparison to that from *Revelations of Divine Love*, is full of action as well as description of scenes, and this difference between the two works is a consistent one. Typical of *The Book of Margery Kempe*, too, is the overlay of personal voice and emotional reaction. This often muffles debates on theological issues, or filters them through the metaphor of Margery's strikingly described experience, which often includes her participation in biblical scenes.

Echoes of mystery pageants, and narrative details which are paralleled in late medieval art, have also been identified elsewhere in the *Book of Margery Kempe*, and these show some of the store of resources used to build up the *Book*'s version of Christian history and theology. Recent scholarly work has added to this list of Margery's influences a range of popular and more high-status religious writings, and this is helping shift the older perception of her as unlearned and naïve, and is showing that her narrative voice is a very careful mediation of complex ideas and texts through a resolutely worldly and colloquial register.

As you continue to study the text in question, you will read critical studies of it (for recommended critical studies of the texts, see the list at the end of this chapter). These will cause you to rethink, question, and often modify your understanding of the text, and therefore it is useful and interesting to return periodically to your notes on initial impressions, to see whether they all still hold. It is also vital to return to the text itself after spending time noting your impressions and analysis and reading those of others. If the primary text is re-read at this point, your own work and secondary reading will fall into perspective, and you will re-connect with the text, and be able to write about it with more authority and accuracy.

Conclusion

Analysing excerpts of the texts in this way makes it possible to identify the sorts of voice constructed in each of them—both the voices of the narrators, and those of the characters whose words they ventriloquize—and also to show how this construction is achieved, and its effect on the individual reader. It will also be possible to propose some of the effects the texts may have had on their medieval readers, and to hypothesize about what cultural work the text's authors may have intended them to perform.

What can be seen from the excerpts analysed above is that Julian of Norwich and Margery Kempe construct subtly different voices in their texts, but that both of them are obliged to operate as visionaries and as authors in a cultural context which devalues them because they are women. They respond to this in different ways: Julian's writing shows her acquaintance with male theologians, and her ability to adopt their register, but this is counterbalanced by her creation of an ideology of the everyday, which makes her writings accessible to laywomen as well as to highly educated male members of religious orders. Margery, by contrast, produces a text whose register seems much more colloquial, and whose style seems much less conscious and dignified than Julian's. On more detailed examination, however, it becomes clear that she has internalized, and understands, the discourse of élite Christian intellectual life, and that this informs her work without dictating its style.

Working with these two texts in the ways outlined in this chapter allows us to avoid trying to measure them directly against twenty-first-century concepts which might seem applicable, but which in fact reduce or marginalize the texts because they do not fit their culture. One of the most problematic of these modern concepts is the modern idea of popular autobiography, with its expectations of transparency, objectivity, truth, verifiable experience, and access to an individual personality. Instead, the close analysis of these two works allows us to deal with them as texts: deliberate, conscious pieces of writing. They are shown to be carefully constructed, dealing in big theological and social questions, and positioned very precisely at different points of the stylistic and ideological continuum between the formal, élite, theological explication and the popular, enabling devotion of later medieval Europe.

Note

1. I would like to express my gratitude to Professor Barbara Raw, who taught me how to analyse texts in this way.

References and suggested reading

Editions and translations

Blamires, Alcuin, ed. *Woman Defamed and Woman Defended*. Oxford: Oxford University Press, 1992. A collection of translated excerpts from medieval writings on women, and a good source of examples of the textual tradition of misogyny.

Julian of Norwich. *A Revelation of Love*. Ed. Marion Glasscoe. Exeter: Exeter University Press, 1993: revised edition. An edition of the longer version of the text, with introduction and glossary.

Julian of Norwich. *Revelations of Divine Love*. Trans. Elizabeth Spearing. London: Penguin, 1998. A translation of the shorter and longer versions of the text, with introduction and notes by A. C. Spearing.

Petroff, Elizabeth Alvilda, ed. *Medieval Women's Visionary Literature*. New York and Oxford: Oxford University Press, 1986. An anthology of translated excerpts from writings by or about a wide range of women mystics, with excellent introductory sections.

Windeatt, B. A. trans. *The Book of Margery Kempe*. London: Penguin, 1985. A translation of the text with introduction and notes.

Windeatt, Barry, ed. *English Mystics of the Middle Ages*. Cambridge: Cambridge University Press, 1994, pp. 181–213. An edition of the shorter text of Julian of Norwich, *Revelations of Divine Love*.

Windeatt, Barry, ed. *The Book of Margery Kempe*. Harlow: Longman, 2000. Edition of the text with very useful introduction, glossary and footnoted translations of hard words and phrases.

Studies

Beckwith, Sarah. *Christ's Body: Identity, Culture and Society in Late Medieval Writings*. London: Routledge, 1993. A good discussion of many relevant themes.

Bynum, Caroline Walker. *Holy Feast and Holy Fast*. Berkeley: University of California Press, 1987. A ground-breaking study of women, food, and devotional practice in the later Middle Ages, which generated an ongoing debate on these subjects. Its introductory chapter, 'Religious Women in the Later Middle Ages', is an excellent survey of the field.

Staley Johnson, Lynn. 'The Trope of the Scribe and the Question of Literary Authority in the Works of Julian of Norwich and Margery Kempe', *Speculum*, 66 (1991), 820–38. A useful introduction to the interrelationship of authority and authorship in the later Middle Ages.

Websites

Femina: Medieval Women and Gender website
www.haverford.edu/library/reference/mschaus/mfi/mfi.html
Labyrinth: Medieval Resources website
www.labyrinth.georgetown.edu

19

The *Gawain*-poet

Michael W. Twomey

Introduction: authorship, manuscript, and language

We presume that one person wrote *Pearl, Cleanness* (or *Purity*), *Patience*, and *Sir Gawain and the Green Knight*, the four poems in London, British Library, Cotton Nero A. x, which is also the sole manuscript in which the poems survive. This presumption is based on similarities in vocabulary, syntax, style, versification, imagery, and themes. We can be fairly certain that the manuscript's scribe was not the author, because metrical irregularities in *Pearl* and *Sir Gawain* indicate that the author's pronunciation always included final -*e*, but the scribe's pronunciation included it only when it was grammatically necessary; for example, in adverbs.

All attempts at identifying an author are frustrated by uncertainty about the dates of the poems—not only the decade, but also the order in which they were written. The manuscript is dated by its handwriting and its twelve illustrations (four for *Pearl*, two for *Cleanness*, two for *Patience*, and four for *Sir Gawain*) to about the year 1400. Failing any public record of the author's identity, scholars have attempted to make a case from evidence in the manuscript itself. The problem with this evidence—the scribal hand, the illustrations, the marginal notes added by medieval readers—is that it is later than the poems. A reader's marginal note tells us more about the readership than the authorship of a text in a manuscript.

The closest we have come to a profile of the author is the 'Cheshire hypothesis', which proposes that the poet was a clerical member of Richard II's Cheshire retinue. This hypothesis accounts for the poet's combination of religious and secular learning, his familiarity with court life, and his intimate knowledge of the general area around Cheshire, which is probably the setting for Gawain's journey to Hautdesert and his encounter with the Green Knight at the Green Chapel. The itinerary mentioned in lines 697–701—North Wales, Anglesey, the Holy Head and the Wilderness of the Wirral—brings Gawain to the threshold of that area.[1] The toponymic *Hautdesert* and many of the words used for landscape features in the third fitt (or section) seem to point to the territory around Swythamley Grange in Staffordshire, which in the fourteenth century was on the property of the Cistercian abbey at Dieulacres, just to the south, near modern Leek. The *Linguistic Atlas of Late Middle English* in fact places the dialect of the poems in Cotton Nero A. x in this very corner of Staffordshire near the Cheshire border. Most attempts at identifying the author derive him from families who lived in this general area.

If the poet were a member of Richard II's Cheshire retinue, he would have been culturally and linguistically at home in French, like his king. The world that he animates in *Sir Gawain* is essentially French. Aristocratic characters in the poem show their courtesy with French phrases (*graunt mercy*, etc.). *Sir Gawain* employs about 750 Anglo-Norman French words (compared to 1,650 English and 250 Scandinavian words), some of which are nativized via English morphology. Many of the French terms that describe material culture are architectural, such as *barbican*; others describe armour and weapons, such as *giserne* (battle-axe). A good many words describe social activities, such as *daunsying*. The poet is so comfortable in French that his syntax is sometimes French, as in the phrase *cros Kryst*, which renders the prayer formula *crois Christ*. Of the 2,650 different words used in *Sir Gawain*, few of the French words have disappeared from the English language, whereas a good many of the native English words and virtually all of the Scandinavian imports, both of which are so vital for creating the atmosphere of an ancient poetic tradition, have long since passed from use. It is even possible that the alliterative long line is itself partly French in origin, inspired by the Old French *laisse* used in *chansons de geste*, and not entirely the product of an 'alliterative revival' of ancient English poetic forms once believed to be part of a cultural protest against the Frenchified London court of the Plantagenets.

Sir Gawain and the Green Knight in the context of medieval literature

So much of our sense of the poet comes from *Sir Gawain* that the present chapter will focus only on it. The one secular poem among the four in the Cotton Nero manuscript, *Sir Gawain* is regarded as the supreme achievement of English medieval Arthurian literature before Malory's *Morte Darthur*. *Sir Gawain* inhabits the world of aristocratic patrons and audiences whose values, manners, and material culture animated medieval romance. The poet presents himself as a minstrel reading a *laye*, which places *Sir Gawain* in the same category as the French *lais* of Marie de France and their English counterparts (*Launfal, Orfeo*), thus hinting that this will be a tale of fairy magic and love. In beginning and in closing, the poet also labels his tale an adventure (lines 27, 29, 2522), another French term, implying that *Sir Gawain* will involve a quest, marvellous adversaries, and demonstrations of chivalric prowess. The word 'romance' gathers up the lay and the adventure into the embrace of a vast literary mode. However, the modern reader of *Sir Gawain* must abandon the assumption that 'romance' is synonymous with 'fiction'. Romance-writers routinely set Arthur's adventures in periods of peace between the wars of Arthur that were narrated in the so-called *Brut* chronicles. *Sir Gawain* opens with the medieval belief that Arthur was descended from Brutus (hence 'Brut'), great-grandson of Aeneas, who, according to the English foundational myth, had colonized the island that was later believed to be named after him. It closes by affirming the historicity of Gawain's adventure, claiming the *Brutus bokez* as witnesses.

The pleasure of reading *Sir Gawain* is heightened by the poet's deft use of an English, Scandinavian, and French vocabulary that changes to suit the circumstance. Thus, when Gawain arrives at Bertilak's castle, Hautdesert, the poet describes the protocols of hospitality in terms that evoke similar scenes in other romances. Then when Gawain is tempted on three successive mornings by Bertilak's wife, his conversations with the Lady exploit the vocabulary of the courtly love lyric. It is chiefly the poet's use of the long alliterative line that obscures comparison of Gawain's *luf-talkyng* with Middle English love lyrics—the roundels, *virelays*, and *balades*, including those of Chaucer, that used an Anglicized French diction, metre, and form.

Ethics and culture

It is tempting to think of *Sir Gawain* as a direct reflection of the secular and religious value-systems of fourteenth-century England, but sociologizing the text without regard for its literary conventions is risky business. Indeed, *Sir Gawain*'s secular culture is chivalry and its religious culture is Christianity. The geography, material culture, and lifestyles depicted in the poem are contemporary, but *Sir Gawain* otherwise inhabits the past. Unlike his contemporaries Chaucer and Langland, the *Gawain*-poet is uninvolved in current events. Nevertheless, Gawain's situation is never treated as quaint or anachronistic; indeed, one reason why *Sir Gawain* appeals to modern readers is that more than other medieval romances it manages to invite serious consideration of its main character's plight, despite its lack of realism.

The Green Knight's challenge is aimed at the reputation of the king and the court, who, he says, are known for chivalry and courtesy.[2] Gawain accepts the challenge in order to protect the honour of his king and the rest of the court. This is the ancient ethos of the *Männerbund* (German for 'male cohort'), in which honour is held collectively as well as individually. The Green Knight reiterates the honour motive towards the end when he explains to Gawain, at lines 2456–8, that he was sent by Morgan le Fay. In the end, neither the Green Knight nor Camelot seem to consider Gawain a failure, so why does Gawain?

Like Malory's knights, Gawain believes that, once lost, his good name cannot be restored. Although unwitnessed except by the Green Knight, Gawain's failure at the Green Chapel has in his mind been a public failure that requires a public accounting at Camelot:

'Þis is þe bende of þis blame I bere on my nek,	*band*
Þis is þe laȝe and þe losse þat I laȝt haue	*injury/latched, i.e. received*
Of couardise and couetyse þat I haf caȝt þare;	
Þis is þe token of vntrawþe þat I am tan inne,	*taken*

And I mot nedez hit were wyle I may last.   *wear*
For mon may hyden his harme, bot vnhap ne may hit,   *it may not be undone*
For þer hit onez is tachched twynne wil hit neuer.'   *part*
                              (lines 2506–12)

The public dimension of Gawain's identity is best illustrated by the
pentangle that he wears on his shield. The poet calls it a *syngne þat
Salamon set sumquyle | In bytoknyng of trawþe* that *acordez to þis
knyȝt and to his cler* [fair] *armez, | For ay faythful in fyue and sere fyue
syþez* [in five ways and five times in each] | *Gawain watz for gode
knawen* (lines 625–6, 631–3). The pentangle represents Gawain's
trawþe, but it is an abstract symbol of the knight himself. Its five sets
of five virtues detail physical abilities, social virtues, and religious
faith. All of these are elements of the active life of a knight, a secular
person. Gawain's religious faith is focused on the wounds of Christ
and the joys of Mary—nothing requiring any great theological
sophistication, only the hard experience of a man who bleeds for his
lord while trying to win his lady's grace.

Although he does not suspect it at first, Gawain's reputation as a
lady's man (which carries over from French romances) is also at
stake. At Hautdesert his host's wife (correctly called 'the Lady', not
'Lady Bertilak') attempts to seduce him on three successive mornings
while the host himself goes hunting for the evening meal. Gawain's
arrival at Hautdesert has occasioned a good deal of buzz about his
manerez and *luf-talkyng*, and it is on this basis that the Lady demands
that he perform, at lines 1228–37. It is only by denying that he is the
person she has heard of (lines 1242 ff.) that Gawain is able courte-
ously to avoid having sex with her. For three days he fends off the
Lady's attempts to trap him into living up to his reputation as a lover,
but when she offers him a magical green girdle that is supposed to
protect the wearer from harm, he takes it as a token of their 'love'.

As a romance, the plot of *Sir Gawain* draws every aspect of
Gawain's adventure together into a search for meaning, and it does so
symmetrically. If Gawain's pentangle is a symbol of the man in his
identity as knight, the green girdle, as Gawain himself tells Bertilak
and later Arthur's court, is a symbol of his failure in this adventure.
Gawain has made his agreement with the Green Knight by his *seker
traweþ*, as he says ('assured faith', line 403). The pentangle represents
that *trawþe* (line 626) and the girdle the *vntrawþe* (line 2509) by
which he failed. Knowing that, once off, his head cannot be restored,

he chooses life with disgrace over death with honour. Gawain has no magic sword, no ring of invisibility, no impenetrable armour. Although magic is conventionally part of the natural universe of romances, often it aids the hero; in *Sir Gawain*, it is unavailable to him. Even the green girdle does not work. The magic in *Sir Gawain* is not 'pagan' magic, since it does not correlate with a 'real-world' pagan culture. It is purely literary convention—the magic of the fairy lay and the romance, where magic and Christianity exist side by side.

Gawain inhabits a Christian culture that offers the possibility of forgiveness for sin, but he lives in it as a resident alien. Back in Camelot, he speaks his shame not as a Christian for whom sin and guilt are spiritual stains on the immortal soul, but as a knight for whom dishonour and shame are physical scars, like the one on his neck. In lines 2506–10, he 'latched' his injury and loss, 'caught' his cowardice and covetousness, was 'taken' in *vntrawþe*. If Arthur's blood endowed Gawain's body with honour (line 357), his own blood has now endowed it with shame. Gawain's religion is skin-deep. The mechanisms and talismans of the church are ever-present: Gawain hears Mass, goes to confession, prays when he is in trouble, venerates an image of the Virgin on the inside of his shield. But when the Green Knight's axe comes down on his neck, Gawain pulls away his head. It is the Green Knight's chiding, '*þou art not Gawayn . . . þat is so goud halden*' ('considered so good', line 2270), not his confidence that his soul will fly off to God along with his head, that makes Gawain go through with his bargain. By saving his body, Gawain believes he has lost both his honour and his identity as a man of *trawþe*, the very qualities for which his body has served, up to now, as a vehicle.

Overview of critical approaches

How editions of the text influence interpretation

Critical reading of *Sir Gawain* begins with the text of the poem, which most modern readers encounter in the edition of Tolkien and Gordon and more recent editions based on it, in the edition of Andrew and Waldron, or in a translation such as Borroff's. There is no substitute for reading the poem in Middle English, but readers must be aware that editors have already interpreted *Sir Gawain* for them via the very aids that make the poem intelligible: the punctuation in the text and the annotation and glossary at the back (or margins).

The manuscript is written in a small, workmanlike hand on vellum pages measuring only 170 × 125 mm. Not only does it lack punctuation, but it also uses capital letters irregularly except to divide sections, it employs the abbreviations commonly found in medieval manuscripts, and it does not separate stanzas. The punctuation in printed editions is editorial, and as a result there are places where editorial decisions about connecting or separating phrases and clauses may actually misrepresent the poem's syntax. When there is only one base manuscript, as in the case of *Sir Gawain*, editors lack the checks and balances that may be provided by other surviving copies of the text. However much editors may strive for objectivity, they inevitably must depend on their judgement, and thus they may misunderstand what the scribe has written. Consider lines 2445–6, where Bertilak identifies himself to Gawain, here transcribed as they appear in the manuscript, with italics used to indicate scribal abbreviations:

> Bertilak de hautdesert I hat i*n* þis londe
> Þurʒ myʒt of morgue lafaye þat i*n* my ho*us* lenges

One kind of problem here is lexical. Despite the lack of precedents in other English Arthurian texts, editors have always transcribed the first part of the name of Morgan le Fay as *Morgne* because they have regarded the name as a form of *Morgan*. However, it was not until Malory's *Morte Darthur* (1469–70) that *Morgan* was established for speakers of English. Before Malory, when both French and English versions of Arthurian narratives circulated, two French forms of Morgan's name were known in England: *Morgue* and *Morgain*, the latter being the form that gave Malory his spelling, *Morgan*. Given this fact, and since the *Gawain*-scribe makes the letters *n* and *u* exactly the same way (as is common in fourteenth-century English manuscripts), *Morgne* must be an editorial misreading.

Another kind of problem is syntactical. The phrase *þurʒ myʒt of morgue lafaye* refers either forward or back. If it refers back, it works as an adverbial phrase to modify *I hat in þis londe*. The lines would thus be translated, 'Bertilak de Hautdesert I am called in this land through the power of Morgan le Fay, who lives in my house.' If, on the other hand, *þurʒ miʒt of morgue lafaye* refers forward, the resulting clause must sprawl awkwardly over the next several lines, and lines 2445–6 must be considered either a scribal error or a false start in Bertilak's speech. In their note to line 2446, Tolkien and Gordon suggest that a line is missing between *I hat in þis londe* and *þurʒ miʒt of morgue lafaye*, and for this reason they insert a full point after *I hat in þis londe*. Other editions adopt their punctuation. However, there is no reason to separate line 2445 from line 2446 other than denial of Bertilak's subordination to Morgan le Fay. Thus we may read: '*Bertilak de Hautdesert I hat in þis londe | þurʒ miʒt of Morgue la Faye, þat in my hous lenges.*'

The legacy of the 'Celtic school' of interpretation

Like many readers in the twentieth century, Tolkien and Gordon suppressed Morgan's relationship to Bertilak because they thought of the poem as a narrative about two male principals, Sir Gawain and a Green Knight, apparently ignoring that the title, imposed by the poem's first editor in 1839, is not authorial. The text in the manuscript is untitled. Most early twentieth-century scholars persisted in the view that the characters in *Sir Gawain* are fourteenth-century versions of (ultimately unconnected) Celtic antecedents, even though they also believed that *Sir Gawain* was drawn primarily from French sources.

For about 100 years, critics read *Sir Gawain* by keeping its intertextual relationship to contemporary Arthurian literature somewhat at arm's length. In view of evidence that the legend of Arthur developed and was transmitted orally by Celtic (Welsh, Breton) story-tellers for many years before Arthurian narratives were written by Chrétien de Troyes and others, scholars in the early to mid-twentieth century under the general influence of Jessie Weston, Robert Graves, and Carl Jung tried to tease out traces of Celtic pagan, mythic originals in Arthurian literature. Although the existence of Celtic oral tradition cannot be doubted, reconstructing it with any certainty is blocked by the lack of textual witnesses. Nevertheless, scholars in the 'Celtic school' believed that all Arthurian figures and plots pointed back to recoverable originals, as if over the centuries each subsequent generation of Arthurian writers had reverently preserved traces of these originals for later generations to find.

Thus Bertilak's name was supposed to be a corruption of Irish *bachlach* (churl) and Gawain was an etiolated sun-god. The narrative was composed of three separate 'motifs' from earlier Celtic 'tradition', labelled 'beheading game', 'exchange of winnings', and 'temptation'. On the other hand, the Celtic school successfully identified a number of French analogues for various plot elements in *Sir Gawain*, in effect pointing to the contemporary literary culture that the poem more likely inhabits.

Contemporary interpretation

Over the past fifty years, since *Sir Gawain* has become a favourite in medieval literature courses taught in the expanding universities of English-speaking countries, academic readers have interpreted *Sir Gawain* by means of virtually every critical approach, but chiefly via close reading, historicism, 'exegesis', and feminism, sometimes combining methodologies. This situation is to be celebrated rather than deplored. Newer readings do not displace older ones so much as build on them. The ability of *Sir Gawain* to 'speak' to succeeding generations of modern readers puts it in that vexed category of canonical, must-read texts which re-invite investigation. Every new reading only confirms that canonical status. What then do modern readers see in it?

As Bertilak tells Gawain in lines 2445–62, *Sir Gawain* is a tale about Morgan le Fay's attempt simultaneously to test the reputation of Arthur's court and frighten Guenivere to death. Although Morgan fails in her second motive, she succeeds in her first. All readings of *Sir Gawain* recognize the Green Knight's *Crystemas gomen* as an occasion for testing the chivalry of the court via its surrogate Sir Gawain. The beheading game, exchange of winnings, and temptation still define the plot. The poet's particular genius is getting readers to experience the adventure without dramatic irony, so that all along we know no more than Gawain. We are just as surprised as he is to learn that the beheading game has been subsumed into the exchange of winnings, which in turn includes the bedroom temptations. We cease to see the narrative through Gawain's eyes only after Bertilak explains that Gawain's failure was the trivial offence of concealing the green girdle (lines 2338–68), at which point Gawain looks for someone to blame, lashing out first at women, and then at himself.

To the extent that all reading involves finding patterns in language and imagery, determining structure and theme, analysing character and plot, all criticism of *Sir Gawain* depends on close reading. The poem demands it, for despite the constraints of its form—three alliterating syllables per long line, a 'bob' and 'wheel' (a rhyming quatrain) at the end of every stanza—the language of *Sir Gawain* is rich and purposeful, even in seemingly minor passages. For example, at the beginning of fitt 2 the narrative fast-forwards in time to Gawain's departure, meditating on transience and mortality via a description of the changing seasons. Fitt 1 has closed with an admonishment to Gawain not to shirk this *auenture*, and fitt 2 opens with a reminder that it was Arthur's desire for adventure that started it all. In light of the poet's earlier remark that Arthur is *sumquat childgered* ('somewhat boyish') with a *brayn wild*, it is not difficult to see the irony of calling the Green Knight's visit a *hanselle* ('New Year's gift'), exactly the sort of *ȝelping* ('boasting', but also 'yelping') that satisfies Arthur's custom of not eating until he has heard of an adventure. In lines 495–6, Gawain's present optimism contrasts with the death he faces in one year: *Gawan watz glad to begynne þose gomnez in halle, | Bot þaȝ þe ende be heuy haf ȝe no wonder.* Gawain's mind finally turns to that 'heavy end'—a reference to the cutting edge of the Green Knight's axe as well as to death?—in the very last lines of the second stanza, when the Michaelmas moon (29 September) now hangs in the sky as a reminder of the coming of winter: *þen þenkkez Gawan ful sone | Of his anious vyage* ('anxious journey', lines 534–5). In between, the cycle of the seasons has run its course in some of the English language's most beautiful nature poetry.

The circularity of natural time contrasts with the linearity of human time. Nature returns to life every spring, but humans move only towards death. The Green Knight, whose very colour suggests nature, can survive decapitation, but Gawain cannot. Despite the liturgical feast of St Michael the Archangel as a reminder that Christianity provides an escape from death and the devil, Gawain does not seem particularly confident of eternal life. For him, Michaelmas is only a day on the calendar. In the end, even though he confesses his sins on the night before his appointment at the Green Chapel, Gawain pulls his head away from the Green Knight's axe.

If close reading is common to all criticism, what distinguishes interpretations is the textual evidence they emphasize and the contexts within which they place it. For example, 'exegesis'—interpretation based on Christian theology—has persistently supplied a context for reading *Sir Gawain*, even though Gawain himself is not exceedingly devout. Gawain's adventure is associated with important feasts on the liturgical calendar. Besides Michaelmas, three other feasts mark off the action: All Souls (2 November, the day of Gawain's departure from Camelot), Christmas, and, the most important of these, New Year's. Gawain makes his contract with the Green Knight on New Year's Day, and then meets him on the same day a year later. Gawain's nick on the neck is at least a reminder that New Year's is the Feast of the Circumcision—sign of man's covenant with God. One argument about the significance of this allusion would be that Gawain is renewed—baptized in blood, as it were—by the Green Knight's axe. And yet it is also possible to see in the nick on the neck a confirmation of the *vulnus naturae* (Latin for 'wound of nature') incurred by Adam in the fall—the tendency towards sin which theologically speaking is the inheritance of all mankind as the result of Adam's disobedience in Eden.

Feminist readings have led in two different directions. Marxist feminist readings, for example, see the beheading game and exchange of winnings as illustrations of aristocratic male power and privilege, while insisting that the women, running the now-familiar gamut from 'goddess' (in one sense, the Virgin Mary on Gawain's shield; in another, Morgan) to 'whore' (the Lady), are marginalized. In the poem's conclusion, the male bond is affirmed by a final exchange in which Gawain claims the Lady's girdle as a personal token and returns to his originary male cohort, who make the girdle into an item of livery. Deconstructionist feminist readings upset the commonsense understanding of the plot as a set of agreements between males, instead enlarging the roles of the women, especially Morgan. In the conclusion, Gawain's adoption of the girdle as a *luf-lace* shows that the temptation scenes, not the beheading game or the exchange of winnings, define Gawain, and his discovery that the entire adventure was orchestrated by his aunt Morgan le Fay upsets his understanding of himself as the nephew of Arthur, whose blood in his veins he had earlier (line 357) cited as the only source of his worth.

Conclusion: *Sir Gawain* as an Arthurian romance

Joined with historicism, feminism has led to profound changes in the interpretation of *Sir Gawain*, for by allowing Morgan le Fay to return from the banishment to which the Celtic school had sentenced her, feminism has ultimately led to reading *Sir Gawain* as a fourteenth-century Arthurian romance indebted to the Vulgate (or Lancelot-Grail) Cycle of prose romances written in France in the early thirteenth century, particularly the Prose *Lancelot* and *Queste del Saint Graal*. Except for Arthur's and Gawain's, names in *Sir Gawain* are in the French of the Vulgate Cycle. In his editorial notes, the poem's first editor Frederic Madden (1839) connected Morgan's hatred for Guenivere to the Prose *Lancelot*, and since then a number of scholars have extended that observation. The temptation scenes in *Sir Gawain*'s third fitt have parallels in the Prose *Lancelot*. The scene at the Green Chapel may be meant to evoke similar scenes at hermitages in the *Queste del Saint Graal*. The names of the Round Table knights are given in their Vulgate Cycle forms. Even elements that are not in the Vulgate Cycle have correlatives elsewhere in French Arthurian literature. The 'beheading game' resembles that of the Old French *Caradoc*, part of the First Continuation of Chrétien's *Perceval*. Social interaction is depicted in terms that may be adopted from the romances of Chrétien de Troyes.

Sir Gawain may be read as an episode out of the Vulgate Cycle, where Morgan's attempts to abduct Arthurian knights such as Lancelot anticipate her removal of Arthur to Avalon after the final battle. Morgan's motive is explained in the Prose *Lancelot*, where Guenivere expels Morgan from court when she learns that Morgan has been having an affair with Guiomar, Guenivere's cousin. In the wilderness, Morgan learns Merlin's magic, and then she proceeds to establish a realm of her own along the margins of Arthurian society. Knights who wander into her sphere are imprisoned, and occasionally Morgan attempts to kill someone at court directly via subterfuge. This is the Vulgate identity of Morgan, and it is revealed in Bertilak's speech to Gawain, lines 2445–55. This scene—which adapts the conventions of the 'recognition scene' in medieval romances—invites

Gawain (and the reader) to look back over the events of the past few days, and to recognize that the old hag Gawain saw with the Lady (lines 947–69) and at the high table (lines 1001–2) is Morgan herself. Her placement at table betrays her status as the castle's feudal power, a thought which has not occurred to Gawain until now.

Traces of Morgan's presence have been in the text all along. The Green Knight's colour and the red eyes that he rolls *runischly* may be considered 'fairy symptoms'. Some in Camelot recognize this with their first glimpse of the Green Knight, *for fantoum and fayry3e þe folk þere hit demed* (line 240), and later when Gawain departs, some tongues cluck about the folly of letting him go off to be *Hadet wyth an aluish mon for angardez pryde* (line 681). Gawain's approach to the castle Hautdesert takes him into the realm of one of Morgan's fairy accomplices in the Vulgate Cycle, the Queen of North Wales. On Christmas Eve, Gawain looks up from his prayer to see a castle where he had seen only thickets just a moment before (lines 740 ff.). Although Gawain thanks Jesus and St Julian for providing him with lodging, an Arthurian analogue for this scene exists in the Vulgate Cycle's *Mort Artu* which suggests that another power is at work. There, Arthur stumbles across the castle of Morgan le Fay in an uncharted wilderness, is lodged for the night, and does not recognize his sister until she identifies herself to him the following morning. As in *Sir Gawain*, the episode culminates in a recognition scene. In the *Mort Artu*, however, Arthur is confronted with evidence of Lancelot's adultery with Guenivere. *Sir Gawain* takes place earlier in Arthurian history, before the Round Table is threatened by adultery and treason. The Green Knight's challenge and Gawain's failure of *trawþe* are perhaps meant to provide the first hints of the tragedy to come.

Notes

1. All citations to the text of *Sir Gawain* are to the edition of Malcolm Andrew and Ronald Waldron in *The Poems of the Pearl Manuscript*, 3rd edn., Exeter Medieval English Texts and Studies (Exeter: University of Exeter Press, 1996), which in places I have silently re-punctuated.

2. '*þy bur3* [city] *and þy burnes* [men] *best ar holden,* | *Stifest vnder stel-gere on stedes to ryde . . .* | *And here is kydde* [displayed] *courtesy, as I*

haf herd carp [tell] | . . . *if þou be so bold as alle burnez tellen,* | *þou wyl grant me godly þe gomen* [game] *þat I ask'* (lines 259–60, 263, 272–3).

References and suggested reading

Borroff, Marie. '*Sir Gawain and the Green Knight*: A Stylistic and Metrical Study'. Yale Studies in English 152. New Haven: Yale University Press, 1962. Still the most comprehensive discussion of the poetics of *Sir Gawain*.

Brewer, Derek, and Jonathan Gibson, eds. *A Companion to the Gawain-Poet*. Arthurian Studies 38. Cambridge: D. S. Brewer, 1997. An excellent orientation to most aspects of *Sir Gawain* and the other poems of the Cotton Nero manuscript, including theories of authorship, historical and cultural context, the manuscript, language, magic and the supernatural, religious and secular values; includes a bibliography of critical studies.

Brewer, Elisabeth. *Sir Gawain and the Green Knight: Sources and Analogues.* Arthurian Studies 27. 2nd edn. Cambridge: D. S. Brewer, 1992.

Burrow, J. A. *A Reading of Sir Gawain and the Green Knight.* London: Routledge, 1965. A fitt-by-fitt close reading of the narrative within its historical and Arthurian setting.

Clough, Andrea. 'The French Element in *Sir Gawain and the Green Knight*, with Special Reference to the Description of Bertilak's Castle in ll. 785–810', *Neuphilologische Mitteilungen*, 96 (1985), 197–208. The Anglo-Norman French vocabulary of *Sir Gawain*.

Fisher, Sheila. 'Leaving Morgan Aside: Women, History, and Revisionism in *Sir Gawain and the Green Knight'*. In Christopher Baswell and William Sharpe, eds., *The Passing of Arthur: New Essays in Arthurian Tradition.* New York: Garland, 1988, pp. 129–51. Reprinted in Stephanie Trigg, ed., *Medieval English Poetry*. Longman Critical Readers. London: Longman, 1993, pp. 138–55. Feminist approach to *Sir Gawain*.

Lindley, Arthur. 'Pinning Gawain Down: The Misediting of *Sir Gawain and the Green Knight'*, *Journal of English and Germanic Philology*, 96 (1997), 26–42. How the edition of Tolkien and Gordon preserves scholarly views of the early twentieth century.

Putter, Ad. *An Introduction to the Gawain-Poet.* Longman Medieval and Renaissance Library. London and New York: Longman, 1996. A cultural profile of the author, plus close readings of the four poems in the Cotton Nero manuscript.

Shoaf, R. A. *The Poem as Green Girdle: Commercium in Sir Gawain and the Green Knight.* University of Florida Humanities Monograph 55. Gainesville, FL: University of Florida, 1984. A historical approach to the exchanges between Gawain and the Green Knight in their economic, legal, political, and theological dimensions; *Sir Gawain* as a reflection of the late medieval conflict between chivalric and commercial values.

Twomey, Michael W. 'Morgan le Fay, Empress of the Desert'. In Bonnie Wheeler and Fiona Tolhurst, eds., *On Arthurian Women: Essays in Memory of Maureen Fries.* Dallas, TX: Scriptorium, 2001, pp. 103–19. The 'fairy symptoms' in *Sir Gawain*, location of Hautdesert, editorial problems in Bertilak's speech, and the feudal relationship of Bertilak to Morgan le Fay.

20

Middle English prologues

Andrew Galloway

Introduction: the importance of the prologue

> Whan that Aprill with his shoures soote . . .

Although students (and teachers) no longer routinely memorize poetry, most can finish this sentence.[1] Deep-rooted school-room conventions, and the sentence's compact brevity but euphony and lexical variety, have made this the most famous sentence in all English. Its charms are both more obvious and more elusive because of its unparalleled familiarity. Its lines have, for example, ingrained in generations of reciters' minds Chaucer's suavely innovative, Continentally derived iambic decasyllabic line; yet its initial headless iamb, 'Whan', opens the poem with a stressed first syllable, as clearly as *Beowulf* and other Old English poetry begin with the clarion 'Hwæt!' That initial stress pushes the metre of the line's first half forward, from iambic into trochaic metre, as if the poem were not '× –' but '– ×'. This impression is corrected by the stutter of weak syllables at the caesura ('*with his* **shour***es* **soot***e*'), and more by the regular iambs of the following line; together, the opening rhythms display the urgent but quickly harnessed energies of spring. In eighteen lines the reader's and listener's perspective falls like a raindrop down through the cosmos of spring from the heavens to the earth, funnelled rapidly by the sentence to the seemingly casual story-gathering and literary labours of the narrator in the tavern. But some will have already noted the display of a powerful poetic creator at work, stirring wry ambiguity everywhere, as in the initial mixing of the urges of spring from growing pains to mating pains to praying pains. The sentence is full of poetic *tours de force* and signs of careful crafting, from the eager 'running' of the *yonge sonne* after the Ram of Aries—as if the spring sun were itself a lamb following an older parent—to the goading sense of a 'pricking' anticipation of love that drives the *smale foweles* to sleep *with open ye*, to the instant transfer of these impulses to people longing for a seasonable pilgrimage. Such human pilgrims of life emerge filled with 'ful devout' gratitude both to saints and April, both of which have freed them from the long winter that has kept them as frozen, dry, and moribund as the roots and birds were before spring and the poem began. Such ambiguous *ful* hearted urges of life push insistently forward in the first eighteen lines, until the sentence makes a double stop at a reflective and penitential moment, with the *rime riche* of *for to seke* and *whan that they were seke*. Even here it is not clear if the sickness remembered is of the soul or the winter-tormented body. In either case, the commemorative and penitential pause is brief, quickly followed by a continuation of the urges already unleashed *to make a start*, in a hundred different directions, including, as soon emerges, a literary one.

Even if the obligation to memorize it, or, later, the familiarity of having memorized it, may dull appreciation, such an opening sentence deserves the fame it has received, and deserves it in its own right, even though it is what might be called 'the prologue to Chaucer's *General Prologue*'. The rest of the *General Prologue* is properly read as a work in its own right too, since, like the *Wife of Bath's Prologue* and the Prologue to the *Legend of Good Women*, it constitutes a rich, complicated and self-sufficient satire. Chaucer did not fulfil the *General Prologue*'s promise of fifty-eight further stories—just as he did not finish the Legends even though he carefully revised the Prologue to the *Legend of Good Women*. The *House of Fame* (*HF*) remains similarly unfinished, lacking its final 'point' or 'denouement', but not its three elaborate prologues—the first including a long preliminary further prologue now titled the 'proem', before moving through the 'invocation' and then the first 'story', which in turn ends up being a framework or preliminary setting for another story, that of Virgil's

Aeneid—whose opening words we hear and see most fully, framed in an ideally monumental form:

> But as I romed up and doun,
> I fond that on a wall ther was
> Thus writen on a table of bras:
> 'I wol now singe, yif I kan,
> The armes and also the man . . .'   (*HF* 140–4)[1]

Beginnings for Chaucer are objects of poetic attention for their own sakes. In spite of the awkward, non-Virgilian line-filler, *yif I kan*, the narrator's discovery of Virgil's bronzed opening words shows how productive the idea of a prologue was to him, especially one displaying a monumentality Chaucer's narrator never openly aspires to (even if, by a historical irony, the opening of the *General Prologue* has become precisely that). Pondering Virgil's opening does not lead the writer of *The House of Fame* to become an 'English Virgil', but instead to advance a series of perspectives on the idea of literary fame, and on the sense of history that makes it hard for later poets to speak in turn, to start to tell their 'tidings'—which, notoriously, *The House of Fame* never does. Instead, it expends attention endlessly on the doubts and worries of any post-Virgilian Christian writer, minstrel, court poet, scientific treatise writer, or even gossip news reporter trying to get down to his task: understandably, since those doubts concern essential matters for establishing a literary profession in such terms and circumstances, such as the value of classical materials—and 'fame' itself—in a Christian world; the trustworthiness of a writer who depends heavily on the past, yet cannot help remaking that past; the need for history and tradition and sources, but the equal necessity of altering and rehandling history and tradition; above all, the unnerving sense that all literary history has involved just such a progression of rehandlings and distortions, based on 'tidings' that ultimately are no more reliable than those of a crowd of gossipy pilgrims, *With scrippes bret-ful of lesinges* (*HF* 2123).

That this attention to beginnings is inordinately protracted is not simply our judgement. The *Wife of Bath's Prologue* includes a comment on just this tendency: 'This is a long preamble of a tale!' (III.831), the Friar declares—before the Summoner makes that preamble even longer by picking a fight with him, thus establishing the grounds for their own stories. If some preambles become ends in themselves, others emerge from chance quarrels (and indeed the Wife's initial feisty posture shows this applies to hers too). No tablet of brass frames the Friar's and Summoner's inception of stories against each other's professions, but rather a simile of a fly falling into food and other *mateere: a flye and eek a frere | Wol falle in every dyssh and eek mateere*, the Summoner proclaims. *In medias res* indeed: the pun seems deliberately to degrade Horace's famous dictum on how to start a story by stumbling 'into the midst of things' (*Ars poetica*, line 148). Probably less learned a pun about the technical terms for starting a story is the word used for ten of the fifteen introductions to tales in the unique Middle English version of the *Seven Sages of Rome* found in an early fifteenth-century manuscript (London, British Library, Cotton Galba E. ix): these introductions are, in this work only, called 'prolongs'—fittingly enough, since in this *Thousand and One Nights* kind of story, the tales that these 'prolongs' introduce alternately defer and re-impose the death penalty on the king's innocent son.

Middle English prologues are never overtly monumental, in the sense of standing removed, in brassy frames or icy heights, from more 'common' and communal aspects of life. Instead, they show efforts to weave themselves into living communities and ongoing histories, even while offering vehicles for their writers to define various degrees of vocational and intellectual authority and some proprietary claim on the works, in a culture and literary context that offered few other means to make such claims. These functions, variously defined, could be in tense conflict. There is abundant evidence that in Chaucer's period and London context they were. But throughout Middle English literature, a writer's claims to vocational and intellectual authority were delicately balanced against the writer's subservience to a living community of readers, and beyond those to a vast range of human and divine history.

The evidence of this tension in Chaucer's time and place is, foremost, the size and complexity, and often the ambiguous moral or vocational claims, of prologues. Chaucer's London contemporary William Langland appears equally obsessed with the problem of making a start in his lifelong literary labour we know as *Piers Plowman*; indeed, it has been noted repeatedly that that poem, with its series of dreams and awakenings and self-doubting reflections, is continually starting over. Langland's narrator's posture at the opening as he *lay and lenede and loked on the watres* and *slombred into a slepyng, it swayed so murye*, looks idyllic at first, another luscious early spring moment of beginning; later, after we hear his incessant debates with Christian and learned authority, and his struggles to reconcile appearance and substance in all social roles, social labour, and spiritual authority, we are likely to worry at just how idyllic or clear his own vocational self-presentation is, with his garbing of himself in sheep's clothing (like the proverbial and biblical wolf: Matthew 7: 14–15), and his ambiguous initial claim to a religious vocation: *In habite as an heremite unholy of werkes* (line 3; emphases added). What sort of authority and vocation this might be frames the broader question of what sorts of authority, social or moral, any of the professions in Langland's sweeping prologue possess. Another major late fourteenth-century London poet, John Gower, wraps his longest English work, the *Confessio amantis* ('confession of a lover'), in a system of Latin verses and Latin glosses that mark his work with heavily clerical framing, and his prologue dwells on the 'division' between and among the clergy and the laity in relation to an ideal original clarity of vocation (whose precise historical 'moment' shifts continually in his prologue). Yet this claim for a reverence to the past is irreconcilable with his narrator's opening assertion that it is 'good' for him to *wryte of new som matiere*, that is, to alter radically the past he claims to worship. And as a layman involved in the historical and moral knowledge traditionally deployed by the clergy—he even invents for himself the oxymoronic intellectual role of a *burel clerk* (a simple, unlearned, or lay clerk; Prol. 52)—his posture exemplifies precisely the collapse of such traditional distinctions between laity and clergy he deplores. Hence his own suggestion in the Latin margins of an equally oxymoron title, a 'lover's confession' (book 1, iv, line 295 marg.). The traditional and novel vocational claims of medieval vernacular poets seem here at the point of flying apart; instead, they result in particularly distinguished and complicated narratives where an author makes a start.

Material history and the modes of beginning

Book history intertwines with literary history. The printed title page and author's name were still to come, but the bulging prologues of late Middle English poetry indicate that although this moment had not yet arrived, the reasons for it were gathering. In print culture, we look to titles for how a book identifies itself; this sort of 'opening' is, from the early sixteenth century on, part of the author's creative language.[2] In manuscript culture, titles have a place, but they are not often the work of authors, and they offer only skeletal information, functioning as stark reminders about the genre and subject. The Gospel of Matthew opens 'The book of the generation of Jesus Christ', where the first word in the original Greek, *biblos*, became the name for the entire Bible. This importance of first words can be found in earlier Greek histories; Herodotus, for example, defines himself and his history in the first three words, a convenient strategy of 'prologue' for an author in the age of scrolls. Christian writings tend to stress from the outset their works as *books*, and this coheres with evidence that the codex, the form of the book as we know it, was created along with Christianity, replacing the scroll, and offering easier citation of Jesus' words, and easier comparison between what were now called the 'Old' and 'New' Testaments. A book's substantial first page offered a frame for an engagement with the reader longer than the first few words. Henceforth, initial stretches of writing appear addressing a reader to declare the writer's intention, and the utility and authority of the subsequent written book: 'Forasmuch as many have taken in hand to set forth in order a narration of the things that have been accomplished among us, according as they have delivered them unto us, who from the beginning were eyewitnesses and ministers of the word; it seemed good to me also, having diligently attained to all things from the beginning, to write to thee in order, most excellent Theophilus, that thou mayest know the verity of those words in which thou hast been instructed', as the Gospel of Luke opens.

Important books gained universally accepted titles, but few medieval vernacular writers proceed as if they had a set title as such. Instead, the prologue bears the burden of defining a work, usually in terms other than those we consider standard. Most vernacular writers open by declaring they are a story 'about' something; even Chrétien de Troyes's mid-twelfth-century French romance *Cligés*, which makes lofty claims for his and the book's authority, opens by recalling only that 'that man who made a story about Erec and Enide' and other subjects now will tell a new one 'about a vassal who was in Greece from the lineage of King Arthur'. This discursive style signals the importance of oral address and community, even while retaining the importance of bookishness. Even an epistolary prologue—a common way of opening medieval Latin writings—suggests an exchange with a living person. Vernacular works are still more likely to open by speaking, praying, singing, even staging long debates about the circumstances and value of writing the work that follows, as well as defining its subject and identity. Thus John Trevisa opens his 1387 translation of Ranulph Higden's Latin world history by showing a 'knight' (a flatteringly learned and clever portrait of Trevisa's patron, Sir Thomas Berkeley) out-arguing a 'clerk' (a parodically reluctant version of Trevisa himself) on the moral and social grounds for translating such works 'out of Latyn into Englysch'.[3] About the same time Chaucer used a similar structure of debate and of patrons' compulsion to introduce his *Legend of Good Women*.

By these oral postures, Middle English authors commence by defining some intimate connection to a living world, stressing continuities with history (however understood) and with an immediate community of listeners (however defined), who may also but not necessarily have been readers, and in any case would not be silent ones (Joyce Coleman, author of the best recent study of the evidence for literary performance, has persuasively argued that the norm of reading literature aloud, even when one is alone, persists well into the Renaissance[4]). But these oral modes are less simply reflections on the dominance of oral storytelling as such, than signs of the general tendency of medieval works to define literature's continuities with history and community. Sidney in the late sixteenth century, following Horace, condemned medieval and contemporary works that opened 'from the beginning'—'do they not know that a tragedy is tied to the laws of Poesy, and not of History?'[5] But the tendency of medieval literary works to open by defining themselves as mere episodes in some larger historical trajectory—the nationalist *Brut* history, for example, commencing *Sir Gawain and the Green Knight*—is not a sign of their being 'primitive' (as the scholar A. D. Nuttall declares in his splendid consideration of the classical tradition of works opening 'in the midst of things'[6]), but rather of how medieval literature often deftly locates its own modest existence within a large community or context, and then proceeds to use its intervention to transform our understanding of that larger context. *Sir Gawain* returns at the end to its opening rehearsal of the *Brut* history, but we now see that as filled with disruptions of personal identity, and with continuous remakings of community. In evoking and inserting themselves into such communities and continuities, medieval works open with phrases elegantly long to capture attention (and hold it until a main verb appears), or especially euphonious, or bluntly interruptive and commanding. Middle English drama may open with *I command silyns!*— and with speeches of actors playing kings, whose socially powerful speech within the play is thus doubly defined as socially powerful speech within the playing area. Such characters' introductory words may be flattering or wryly satiric ways to overlap the internal and external audiences, so that the townsfolk audiences these stage-emperors address are being called (as in the panoramic fifteenth-century play of 'Mary Magdelene') *kingges, and conquerors kene | Erlys, and barons, and knytes that byn bold, | Berdes* [maidens] *in my bower, so seemly to sene*. Both imagined and actual communities are transformed by such overlapping identities.

When medieval vernacular authors offer titles for their works, they do so in the course of an introductory discussion with the reader, even when the work also presents itself as an intricate text suited to further textual explication and commentary. Thus the thirteenth-century *Roman de la rose* opens by declaring the authority of the deep meanings lurking 'couvertement' in dreams, defending that with mention of the ancient commentator Macrobius, and then concludes this prologue with the authority of the dream that the *Rose* presents in particular, of a young man setting forth in May into an allegorical garden of courtly life and love. That prologue claims for this vision an encyclopedic capaciousness, in the course of which the narrator offers the work's title as if this named the enclosed, visionary, and (as it soon turns out) quite socially exclusive garden of love that readers were being invited into, as well as naming the 'romance' (i.e. the French poem) itself:

> Et se nus ne nulle demande
> Comment je veil que cis romans
> Soit appellés, que je commans,
> Que c'est li *Romans de la rose*,
> Ou l'art d'Amors est toute enclose.   (lines 34–8)

And if anyone should want to ask how I want this poem to be called that I am now beginning, it's the *Romance of the Rose*, in which the art of love is wholly enclosed.

Given its influence, and its demonstrations of the potential depth and complexity of a work based on a love allegory, the *Rose*'s importance in defining the possibilities of vernacular European literature is inestimable. Its ambitious and self-authorizing opening owes much to the clever use of Latin prologues to ancient works known as *accessus ad auctores*, commonly produced in academic culture from this period on, where commentators introducing ancient texts present title, author, intention, subject material, and a range of other information. These introductions often included such information as the work's 'quality' or stylistic and rhetorical mode (much like our notion of 'genre'), its structure, its moral or other utility, and its position in the branches of learning; in a scheme increasingly popular from the mid-thirteenth century, such commentaries framed this material in terms of Aristotelian 'causes': the author (efficient cause), subject (material cause), structure and genre (formal cause), and didactic purpose (final cause).[7] Yet that form is only one of several structures of prologues influential on later medieval vernacular literature, all of which find various ways of balancing claims to literary vocation and authority against claims of participation in living communities and common traditions.

Four types of prologue

We may identify four general kinds of literary labour in prologues as particularly important for Middle English literature in particular. As general categories, these are merely preliminary tools, since actual prologues frequently present several or many of these forms in combination or succession.

The redactor's prologue

First is what might be called the 'redactor's prologue', in which the writer's role as collector, editor, or translator is the basis for the prologue. The most significant, well-represented, and carefully developed strand of this are historians' prologues, whose influence on this aspect of Middle English poetry needs further exploration.[8] From Eusebius (Greek, fourth century; translated into Latin almost at once) to Bede (the famous Latin historian of eighth-century Anglo-Saxon England), to all later medieval chroniclers and encyclopaedists, the action of collecting materials 'that have been scattered by our predecessors and culled, as from some intellectual meadows, the appropriate extracts from ancient authors' (Eusebius, *Ecclesiastical History*, 1.4) is a primary basis for the profession of the writer producing histories and other compilations or cumulative works (whence the term *florilegium*, 'collection of flowers'). The fashion of assembling books out of carefully arranged and often identified and situated portions of earlier, more authoritative texts became especially pronounced in the twelfth and thirteenth centuries, when academic styles began to pervade all manner of writings, from history to literature. One of the earliest major Middle English poems, Laȝamon's *Brut*, an early thirteenth-century translation of Wace's French version of the history of King Arthur, opens with an account of the journeying of the author *wide ȝond þas leode* ('far throughout this land') to gather three key texts: Bede (in *Englisca*); a mysterious book in Latin made by *Austin* (Augustine of Canterbury, who introduced Christianity) and *Seinte Albin* (Albinus or, more likely, Alban, the first English saint); and the *Frenchis* history made by Wace, which in fact is almost his sole written source of the elaborately expanded historical epic that follows. After claiming to collect these three books, Laȝamon lovingly gazes upon these monuments of successive English civilizations and languages (*he heom leofliche biheold*), all instances of cultures that often violently replaced previous cultures on the island; and, taking a quill pen in his fingers, presses it into the parchment, *and þa þre boc þrumde to are* ('and pressed the three books into one', lines 1–35). The act of compilation is here like a priestly consecration of the Eucharist, the Trinity of God; Laȝamon's prologue thus sanctifies the English history before the coming of the Anglo-Saxons, and piously implies the preciousness of prior monuments of that history, and thus of his own.

From the mid-thirteenth century, the redactor's prologue often exploited the authorizing features found in academic prologues. Chaucer, who commonly emphasizes in prologues his role as a florilegist, whether culling bits from *olde bokes* or from the tales told by a *compaignye* assembled *In Southwerk* (*CT* I.717–18), always manages to convey a set of 'causes' in the academic tradition. This is reflected in his attention to the diversity of the circumstances and purposes behind the sources he presents. Thus where Laȝamon delights in the unity he imposes on the diverse materials he claims as his sources, Chaucer uses a display of his sources in prologues to denounce such unifying purposes in compilation. The *Legend of Good Women* initially emphasizes Chaucer as a carefree reader and compiler of a vast array of very different materials, whose truth he cannot swear to, then shows his encounter with the God of Love and Alceste who impose on him the 'penance' of gathering diverse stories for a particularly monolithic end: the *makyng of a glorious legende | Of goode wymmen . . . And telle of false men that hem bytraien* (*F* 483–6). So too, Chaucer's *Wife of Bath's Prologue* features a set of stories *bounden in o volume* (III.681) by virtue of a particularly narrow purpose: to portray *wikked wyves* (a sort of compilation that actually circulated in late-medieval culture); but when these are retold by their resistant listener, the Wife, the stories regain diversity of meaning, character, and pathos. The skill of a compiler in gathering *variae* into a conceptual and material unity, the focus of almost every compiler's prologue, is thus recast as a demonstration of how separate materials resist such narrowing of their meanings. So too the putatively unified intentions of misogyny are displayed as in fact involving a complex set of erotic, violent, professional, and personal relationships between compiler, reader, and further hearer, who is also the stories' repeater, to the pilgrims and to us.

Testimonial prologues

In Middle English prologues from Laȝamon through Gower through Lydgate, compilation becomes an account of personal experience. The second type of prologue is thus closely tied to the previous one; it might be called the 'testimonial prologue', by which a direct experience, visionary or historical, is introduced and framed. A common testimonial prologue involves the initial gesture, prolifically found in

French literature, where a wandering narrator, often in spring, stumbles into a scene, debate, lament, or other 'happening'. Although modern scholars have defined this as the 'genre' of *chanson d'aventure*, such a stratagem offered a flexible means of entering any number of kinds of material, especially those known as the *reverdie*, the name given to descriptions of the return of spring, found in many French poems. The sense of 'dropping in' on something at a pleasant time of year allows a seductive suspension of judgement as well as a verification of the immediate 'truth' of what is presented. Thus *The Owl and the Nightingale* offers a minimal version of this French form by identifying the narrator as happening to be in a very out of the way place (*In one sufle diȝele hale*, line 2), in the warmth of summer, and hearing the loud voices of the debate: the remoteness of the setting suggests a place for free speculation and judgement. Many lyrics elaborate this gesture further, and, along with the *reverdie*, it plays a key role in *Piers Plowman* and Chaucer's *General Prologue*.

A more remotely situated genre, but with equal claim to testimonial authority, is the dream vision; as with *Piers* this may be linked to the *chanson d'aventure* opening. Falling asleep is a vehicle for defining both the casualness, the uncalculated nature of a vision to the memory of which the narrator now bears witness, and the vision's profound sublimity. The western medieval tradition of such visionary testimonial prologues begins with Boethius' *Consolation of Philosophy* (sixth century), whose dramatic debate between the narrator and Lady Philosophy over the meaning of his misfortunes resonates throughout medieval literature as a model of 'testimonial allegory', from Alan of Lille in the twelfth century, through the *Rose* in the thirteenth, to *Piers* in the late fourteenth—and a host of other Middle English works such as Gower's *Confessio* and the prose *Testament of Love* by another London contemporary, Thomas Usk (who, like Boethius, was actually incarcerated and executed for political reasons amidst political turmoil, Usk in 1388).

The immediacy of such 'testimonial' gestures obviously loses out to the sense of literary tradition: Boethius was already more or less overtly revisiting Aristotle, Plato, Cicero, and other writers, as well as offering a compendium of literary verse forms. Alan of Lille and the *Roman de la rose* also revisit their precedents. But literary tradition may add to, not lessen, the feeling of depth and mystery in the 'testimonial' form: when *Piers* opens its prologue with its narrator wandering *on a May morwenynge on Malverne Hilles* to a *brood bank by a bournes syde* and falling asleep *as I lay and lenede and loked on the watres* (line 9), only to dream *a merveillous swevene* (line 11), early readers might have slid into a reverie of literary association. The May opening and dream vision recall the *Roman de la rose* where the dreamer wanders toward *une riviere* (line 104); the openings of various Breton lays like those influencing *Sir Orfeo*, with their supernatural materials, are briefly evoked by *Piers*'s *Me bifel a ferly, of Fairye me thoghte* (just as *Sir Orfeo* notes that *mani lais ther beth of fairy*). Some might have recalled other western, alliterative Middle English poems that in fact seem to lie directly behind *Piers*, especially *Wynnere and Wastoure*, a likely source although extant in a single copy. Here, the prologue (actually the second prologue, after an introduction condemning upstart poets and the dangers of going to London, *southewarde*, line 8) presents the narrator's slide into socially visionary sleep:

Þe bourne full bremly rane þe bankes bytwene.	*river very fiercely ran*
So ruyde were þe roughe stremys and raughten so heghe	
That it was neghande nyghte or I nappe myghte	*nearly night before*
For dyn of the depe water and dadillyng of fewllys	*chirping of birds*
Bot as I laye at the laste þan lowked myn eghne	*lowered my eyelids*
And I was swythe in a sweuen sweped belyue . . .	*swept quickly into a dream*

(lines 41–6)

In one way this more originally elaborates the *Roman de la rose* than does Langland's opening: the river that in the *Rose* leads into the garden, and in *Piers* leads into sleep, here makes so much noise that it keeps the dreamer awake. The apparatus of the literary dream-vision tradition briefly threatens to prevent the vision from starting.

Given the sense of literary depth yet claims to direct experience, and the portentous importance of the experience, 'testimonial prologues' readily yield mixtures of social and allegorical materials, as is clear in *Piers*, *Wynnere*, and the vast range of works with some debt to the *Roman de la rose*. (See Pl. 10.) This is so even when apparently stark social realism is the main approach. When Chaucer's *General Prologue* uses the 'testimonial' strategy with detailed social literalism, the sense of a need for further explication remains. Such explication is both allowed and rebuffed by how fully the narrator enters into the points of view of his fellow pilgrims: their motives are portrayed in endlessly deepening wells of irony, whose surface descriptive detail and narrator's approval give way not only to the pervasive satires against their self-promoting notions of their ways of life, but even to the haunting sense that their self-consciousness is potentially keen enough to share that satiric awareness of themselves and others. While not usually seen as allegorical, Chaucer's social types, however presented as witnessed directly, become ciphers requiring some deeper commentary on the meaning of such socially and profession-ally atomized existence. The only path offered for satisfying such a need to understand further is the (unfinished) series of tales that follow.

The commentary prologue

A third type might be called the 'commentary prologue', where an initial or later explication is offered or initiated, or simply promised. The form is particularly suited to visionary works of the sort that also constitute the 'testimonial prologue', although the commentary pro-logue may also be applied to the visions of others. In the latter sense it is most influentially established by Macrobius' massively learned fifth-century *Commentary on the Dream of Scipio*. The form is hand-ily manipulated by the writers from Chaucer's period onwards. Chaucer's *House of Fame*, probably directly indebted to Macrobius as was his *Parliament of Fowles*, and as behind that was the *Roman de la rose* (although the mention of Macrobius in the prologue to the *Roman* may have allowed Chaucer more assertions of this debt than reality would allow), opens with an initial set of explanatory terms for dreams whose differences become less clear the more he defines them. So too, the second passus of *Piers Plowman* begins as if now starting the 'real' poem, proposing to offer full explanation of the vision that the Prologue of that work has offered: *What this moun-taigne bymeneth and the merke dale | And the feld ful of folk, I shal yow faire shewe.* But this claim of starting the 'real' explanation leads instead to more visions, and thus still more interpretive doubt. Holychurch's elaborate 'lesson' so baffles the narrator that he must turn to yet another vision, this time of the 'false' antitype, Lady Meed, to try to satisfy his desire to understand.

Gower's Latin glosses and Latin verses to the skilfully philosophical and quietly ironic English tales of the *Confessio amantis* present the gesture of the commentary prologue in its clearest academic form;

but his glosses do not in fact proclaim more authoritative explication than the English text, and the Latin verses that repeat the gesture of a commentary prologue throughout the poem often present at least as much ambiguity as the English. And Chaucer's *Wife of Bath's Prologue* presents in its initial 162 lines—that is, until the Pardoner interrupts her and changes her style of prologue to a more probingly self-reflective one—a kind of anti-commentary prologue, since she claims that scripture need not be approached with more than everyday 'experience' and commonsense physicality. Most medieval copies of the Wife's *Prologue* frame her words in Latin glosses, identifying her texts and adducing others, sometimes commenting further in opposition to her.[9] A few of these glosses may conceivably go back to Chaucer himself; at a minimum they indicate a destabilizing from shortly after Chaucer's time of what authority a commentary has in relation to a poem, a question that is made more rather than less pressing with the influence on vernacular works of the 'academic' prologue.

The literary autobiographical prologue

The last type, considerably rarer in medieval literature, might be called the 'literary autobiographical prologue': here the present work is introduced as another in a series of works by the present author. The opening of the Book of Acts, referencing the Gospel of Luke, offers a tiny version of the form; it is more elaborately found in the prologue to Chrétien's *Cligés*, noted above. There it probably derives from Virgil's supposed original opening of *The Aeneid*, preserved by early grammarian commentators in their prologues, where the verse opening alludes to Virgil in the first person as the maker of previous noted works: 'that man I who [*Ille ego qui*: compare Chrétien's opening *Cil qui*] once tuned my song on a slender reed, then, leaving the woodland, constrained the neighbouring fields to serve the husbandmen . . . now of Mars' bristling [Arms I sing, and the man . . .]').[10] The literary autobiographical prologue is rare in Middle English, perhaps in part because the apocryphal opening of *The Aeneid* was not widely known. More, the type requires a strong sense of a literary career and, as every scholar of Middle English literature knows, piecing that together struggles against writers who themselves were rarely eager to declare such a career. Chaucer, who almost certainly did not know the apocryphal opening of *The Aeneid* (as his quotation of the standard opening in the *House of Fame* shows), is an exception in Middle English generally: he offers an oblique version of the literary autobiography in the Prologue to the *Man of Law's Tale*, commandeering one speaker's prologue into his own, to mention a series of the works that *Chaucer . . . Hath seyd . . . in swich Englissh as he kan* (II.47–9). Chaucer's indictment before the God of Love and Alceste in the Prologue to the *Legend of Good Women* allows a more extended gesture of this type, with a similar modest disclaimer about the very poetic abilities being extolled (*Al be hit that he kan nat wel endite*, F 414–30).

Chaucer reveals throughout his works a remarkably developed sense of a literary career, the ultimate basis for any claim to the profession of a writer but one rarely displayed by medieval, especially non-Latin, writers. Of other Middle English poets, only Gower approaches the literary autobiographical gesture by listing his three main works, and he relegates this list to a Latin *epistola* found at the very end of many copies of the *Confessio amantis*, where it is attributed to 'a certain philosopher'. The revisions of this list, bringing it successively up to date, suggest it was a record of accomplishments carefully maintained by Gower himself. But Chaucer's and, earlier but probably unknown to him, Chrétien de Troyes's uses of this type of prologue go even further, presenting astonishingly confident assertions of literary professionalism. Even for Chaucer and Chrétien, however, such hints of more 'modern' assumptions of literary identity and contemporary poetic authority are woven into traditional medieval assertions of social, historical, and literary continuities: the cycle of the seasons; the endlessly continuous stories of Arthur; the promise of telling yet more stories than the writer can ever fulfil— above all, the use of that humble genre, the prologue, to make the strongest case for literary authority and originality.

Notes

1. Quotations of Chaucer are from Larry D. Benson, gen. ed., *The Riverside Chaucer*, 3rd edn. (Boston: Houghton Mifflin, 1987). Other Middle English works cited here are from these editions or from works in 'Further

Reading': *The Seven Sages of Rome*, ed. Killis Campbell (Boston: Ginn, 1907); G. C. Macaulay, ed., *The English works of John Gower*, 2 vols., EETS e.s. 81–2 (London: Oxford University Press, 1900); 'Mary Magdalene', in David Bevington, ed., *Medieval Drama* (Boston: Houghton Mifflin, 1975); Laȝamon: *Brut*, ed. G. L. Brook and R. F. Leslie, EETS 250 (London: Oxford University Press, 1963); *The Vision of Piers Plowman*, ed. A. V. C. Schmidt, 2nd edn. (London: J. M. Dent, 1995); *Sir Orfeo*, ed. A. J. Bliss, 2nd edn. (Oxford: Oxford University Press, 1966); *The Owl and the Nightingale: Text and Translation*, ed. and tr. Neil Cartlidge (Exeter: University of Exeter Press, 2001); 'Wynnere and Wastoure', in Thorlac Turville-Petre, ed., *Alliterative Poetry of the Later Middle Ages: An Anthology* (London: Routledge, 1989).

2. See Anne Ferry, *The Title to the Poem* (Stanford: Stanford University Press, 1996).

3. Printed in Burrow and Turville-Petre, *A Book of Middle English*, pp. 215–17.

4. Joyce Coleman, *Public Reading and the Reading Public in Late Medieval England and France* (Cambridge: Cambridge University Press, 1996).

5. Sir Philip Sidney, *An Apology for Poetry, or The Defence of Poesy*, ed. Geoffrey Shepherd (London: Thomas Nelson, 1965), p. 135.

6. Nuttall, *Openings*, pp. 59–60.

7. See Minnis, *Medieval Theory of Authorship*.

8. See A. Galloway, 'Authority', in Brown, *Companion to Chaucer*, pp. 23–39.

9. Susan Schibanoff, 'The New Reader and Female Textuality in Two Early Commentaries on Chaucer', *Studies in the Age of Chaucer*, 10 (1988), 71–108; Hanna and Lawler, *Jankyn's Book of Wikked Wyves*, pp. 84–7.

10. See H. Rushton Fairclough, ed. and tr., *Virgil*, rev. edn., vol. 1, Loeb Classical Library 63 (Cambridge, Mass.: Harvard University Press, 1967), pp. 240–1; also Nuttall, *Openings*, pp. 1–32.

References and suggested reading

Brown, Peter, ed. *A Companion to Chaucer*. Oxford: Blackwell Publishers, 2002. A set of essays introducing a range of topics pertinent to Chaucer's literature and its contexts, social and literary, with further readings.

Burrow, J. A., and Thorlac Turville-Petre, eds. *A Book of Middle English*. 2nd edn. Oxford: Blackwell Publishers, 1996. A clear introduction to Middle English grammar and literary style followed by a set of annotated excerpts spanning Middle English literature, with references to full editions.

Gertz, Sunhee Kim. *Poetic Prologues: Medieval Conversations with the Literary Past*. Analecta romanica 56. Frankfurt am Main: Vittorio Klostermann,

1996. Scrutiny of a range of rhetorical uses of conventional notions of historical progression in a range of medieval writers' prologues (Latin, French, Italian, and Middle English), especially the *topos* of 'transferral of culture and empire', that writers adapt to claim both continuity with tradition and their own importance as offering commentaries on or fulfilments of such traditions.

Hanna, Ralph, and Traugott Lawler, eds. *Jankyn's Book of Wikked Wyves.* Vol. 1. Athens: University of Georgia Press, 1997. A full discussion and edition of the kinds of Latin materials lying behind *The Wife of Bath's Prologue*, including the kinds of real collection resembling Jankyn's book and the misogamist ideologies that informed them.

Middleton, Anne. 'The Audience and Public of *Piers Plowman*'. In David A. Lawton, ed., *Middle English Alliterative Poetry and its Literary Background.* Cambridge: D. S. Brewer, 1982, pp. 101–24. A key discussion of the use of the brief introductory gestures of *chanson d'aventure* throughout *Piers Plowman*, with consideration of the 'internal' and 'external' (real) audiences of the poem and the kinds of claims to 'truth' such fictional postures allow.

Minnis, Alastair. *Medieval Theory of Authorship: Scholastic Literary Attitudes in the Later Middle Ages.* London: Scolar Press, 1984. An examination of academic Latin prologues to ancient authors and the uses to which these were put in Middle English prologues.

Nuttall, A. D. *Openings: Narrative Beginnings from the Epic to the Novel.* Oxford: Clarendon Press, 1992. A series of essays on how a long sequence of major works in Western culture frame their beginnings, with particular attention to the development of the ancient notion of beginning 'in the midst of things'.

Said, Edward. *Beginnings: Intention and Method.* New York: Columbia University Press, 1985. A broad literary, cultural, and philosophical overview of the problems of making literary beginnings, primarily focusing its examples on nineteenth-century English literature.

Smith, Vance. *The Book of the Incipit: Beginnings in the Fourteenth Century.* Minneapolis: University of Minnesota Press, 2001. A discussion of *Piers Plowman* as perpetually starting over, and thus participating in the cultural and philosophical difficulties of defining legitimate origins of all kinds in late fourteenth-century England.

Wogan-Browne, Jocelyn, Nicholas Watson, Andrew Taylor, and Ruth Evans, eds. *The Idea of the Vernacular: An Anthology of Middle English Literary Theory, 1280–1520.* University Park, Penn.: Pennsylvania State University Press, 1999. A collection of Middle English Texts presenting or implying views or theories of vernacular literature, notably including prologues.

21

The Middle English lyrics

Anne Marie D'Arcy

Introduction

At the close of Umberto Eco's novel *The Name of the Rose*, the narrator describes the vestiges of a vast monastic book collection as 'a kind of lesser library, a symbol of the greater vanished one: a library made up of fragments, quotations, unfinished sentences, amputated stumps of books'.[1] Reading these lines calls to mind one of the principal problems concerning the study of Middle English lyrics. Even though many lyrics have been preserved, many more have perished, or survive only as fragments. Most of the surviving poems are religious, including four of the earliest, composed by St Godric of Finchale (*c*.1065–1170) but, as G. L. Brook, editor of the authoritative edition of the Harley lyrics, points out, this is largely due to 'the part played by monasteries in the preservation of manuscripts and does not necessarily reflect contemporary taste'.[2] There are no dance songs extant in Old English literature, but singing and dancing in churchyards on saints' days seems to have gained currency by the last quarter of the twelfth century. We may note the story recorded by Gerald of Wales concerning a parish priest in the diocese of Worcester who endured a sleepless night due to such singing and dancing. In the course of celebrating Mass the next morning, instead of singing the usual *Dominus vobiscum* or 'Peace be with you', he inadvertently blurted out the refrain of one of these songs, *Swete lamman dhin are* or 'Sweetheart have mercy'. This catchy ditty was swiftly anathematized by the scandalized bishop, William de Norhale (1186–90), throughout the diocese.[3]

Indeed, as the critic Rosemary Woolf observes, the word 'lyric' has come to mean something in this vein, a song or poem, 'short, delightful, and melodious, and with a sweetness and light-heartedness that distinguish it from more serious and reflective poems'. While these characteristics may be discernible in some of the secular lyrics, particularly those which draw on French traditions in terms of subject matter and style, they are hardly typical of Middle English religious lyrics: 'Many of these are long, few were set to music, and all of them are devotionally and didactically serious' (Woolf, p. 1).

The religious lyrics

Mariological lyrics

This function of communicating and celebrating the doctrine and tradition of the Christian faith is borne out elegantly by the early fifteenth-century *I sing of a Maiden* (Davies, p. 155), which has been described by several critics as 'the finest of all the English religious lyrics'. In terms of metre and structure, the poem is simple, yet crystalline in its simplicity, possessed of 'perfect proportion and balance' (Gray, pp. 101–2). Its seamless blend of metrical austerity and doctrinal polyvalence combines translucently literal, theologically precise language with a 'fullness of suggestion' (ibid. 102) that is pregnant with meaning in a multiple of allegorical senses:

> I sing of a maiden
> That is makeles: *without equal, mate*
> King of alle kinges
> To here sone she ches.   *she chose for her son*
>
> He cam also stille   *as*
> Ther his moder was,
> As dew in Aprille
> That falleth on the grass.
>
> He cam also stille
> To his moderes bowr,
> As dew in Aprille
> That falleth on the flowr.

> He cam also stille
> Ther his moder lay,
> As dew in Aprille
> The falleth on the spray.
>
> Moder and maiden
> Was never non but she:
> Well may swich a lady   *such*
> Godes moder be.

The first stanza celebrates the dogma of Mary's perpetual virginity; her status as *aeiparthenos* (Ever Virgin), confirmed by the Second Council of Constantinople of 553 and the Lateran Council of 649, is underscored by the use of the present tense. She is lauded as *Makeles*, a doctrinally exact description of her matchless singularity; Mary remains *sola in sexu femina*, or alone of all her sex, as she is described in a fifth-century poem from the *Paschale carmen* of Sedulius (Corpus Scriptorum Ecclesiasticorum Latinorum, hereafter CSEL, 10, 48). There would seem to be further plays on the word in that, as a virgin, she is without a *mak* or 'mate' and she is *sine macula*, 'without stain' (Song of Songs 4: 7; Wisdom 7: 26), which reaffirms her unspotted sinlessness, a concept found in Western theology as early as St Augustine (*De natura et gratia*, 36, 42, CSEL 42, 164), but also may suggest her Immaculate Conception. However, the implicit paradoxes raised by the suggestion that Mary was conceived without sin remained unresolved during the Middle Ages, and the suggestion, which was particularly popular in England, was opposed by several theologians, most notably St Bernard; indeed, it did not become dogma until the apostolic constitution of 1854, *Ineffabilis Deus.*

The poet also emphasizes her free consent and active co-operation in the Incarnation; it is her choice that the king of all kings becomes her son. The three middle stanzas describe the actual process of the Incarnation, which is suffused by an atmosphere of almost unearthly stillness; the action suggested by the verb *cam* is counterbalanced by the adverb *stille*. Here, the pivotal image of the dew falling gently and silently, which no one can observe, is directly related to another metaphor used to explicate the Virgin's conception. Exegetes interpreted the dew that fell upon Gideon's fleece in Judges 6: 36–40, yet allowed the surrounding earth to remain dry, as a type of the Incarnation, or, more particularly, Mary's womb (St Ambrose, *De Spiritu*

Sancto, 1, 8–9, *Patrologia Latina*, hereafter *PL*, 16, 705; St Jerome, *Epistola* 108, *PL* 22, 886). Authority was also derived from Psalm 71: 6 'He shall come down like rain upon the fleece; and as showers falling gently upon the earth', and the *Rorate coeli*, the Latin text of Isaiah 45: 8: 'Drop down dew, ye heavens, from above, and let the clouds rain the just: let the earth be opened, and bud forth a saviour',[4] which was set to music for use during the Advent season. Moreover, there is the evocation of the virgin's womb as a grassy meadow; a popular metaphor, especially in the East, established in the early fifth century by Proclus of Constantinople (*Oratio de laudibus sanctae Mariae*, 1, *Patrologia Graeca*, hereafter *PG*, 65, 681–2). Mary is described not only in terms of a flower, such as the lily which represents her chastity in the iconography of the Annunciation, but also as a sprig or branch, which suggests her role as the *radix sancta*, a title derived from Romans 11: 16 found in the twelfth-century Marian antiphon *Ave regina coelorum*. As the 'holy root' of salvation, Mary made the Incarnation and therefore the Redemption possible; thus, the messianic prophecy of Isaiah 11: 1: 'And there shall come forth a rod out of the root of Jesse, and a flower shall rise up out of his root' was applied to her by generations of exegetes, most notably St Jerome (*Commentariorum in Esaiam*, 4, Corpus Christianorum Series Latina, hereafter CCSL, 73, 147–9). The fertile potentiality of the dew is endorsed by the April locus, traditionally depicted in both secular and religious texts as the month of rejuvenating showers and the dawning of new life. In fact, there is a skilful interpenetration of sacred and profane imagery throughout the poem; the almost imperceptible advent of Christ is not only reminiscent of the covert lover of courtly literature, who steals up on the lady in her *bowr*, or *thalamus*, but also the emergent iconographic motif of the angelic herald 'creeping silently' into the Annunciate's *thalamus*, which is given memorable expression in the thirteenth- or fourteenth-century Latin carol *Angelus ad virginem subintrans in conclave* (Gray, p. 104), and such fifteenth-century Netherlandish artists as Rogier van der Weyden and Petrus Christus.[5] Finally, the use of the word 'lady' in the closing stanza, which centres on the *mater et filia* motif, emphasizes her nobility and divine maternity as *Theotokos*, or 'Godbearer', the lofty title bestowed on her by the Council of Ephesus in 431.

Christological lyrics

According to the influential thirteenth-century liturgist William Durandus, there are three decorous modes of depicting Christ: as an infant on His mother's lap, as the suffering man on the Cross, and as the enthroned *Maiestas Domini* or Lord in Majesty, returning in glory to judge the quick and the dead (*Rationale divinorum officiorum*, 1, 3, 6, Corpus Christianorum Continuatio Mediaevalis, hereafter CCCM, 140, 37). Of these iconographic motifs, 'English devotional lyrics are most fond of the first and the second, those, significantly, of Christ in his humanity' (Gray, p. 76). The Passion is the fulcrum of popular medieval piety, and is the subject of a vast number of lyrics, particularly during the later Middle Ages. The art historian Erwin Panofsky notes the radical shift in emphasis in artistic treatments of the subject at this time from that which typified the preceding centuries: 'the hieratic symbol of the crucified Christ came to be replaced by the heart-rending image of the Broken Body, now ineffably mild and sad, now grim to the point of gruesomeness'.[6] The expressive potentialities of the suffering of Jesus were consistently exploited throughout the later Middle Ages. Jack Bennett has pointed out that *blody* and *blo* or 'livid' are 'the characteristic epithets for the rent body on the Rood. Such emphases grew more marked as painted rood-screens or crucifixes became the focus of vision in every monastery and church, and the Crucifixion became a fixed part of the iconographic programme of psalters, Books of Hours, and missals' (Bennett, p. 39). An early example of this tendency is the fourteenth-century lyric beginning *Whanne ic se on Rode* (Davies, p. 99), which is preserved 'in seven related versions' (Woolf, p. 34):

Whanne ic se on Rode	*I*
Jesu, my lemman,	*lover*
And besiden him stonden	
Marye and Johan,	
And his rig iswongen,	*back/scourged*
And his side istungen,	*pierced*
For the luve of man;	
Well ou ic for to wepen,	*ought*
And sinnces for to leten,	*abandon*
Yif ic of luve can,	*if/know*
Yif ic of luve can,	
Yif ic of luve can.	

Here, we are presented with Christ on the Cross, flanked by the intercessors *Marye and Johan*, recalling 'one of the paintings of the Passion, which by the second half of the thirteenth century were becoming quite common in churches' (Woolf, p. 34). In describing the scene the poet places a strong emphasis on Christ's suffering; we are exhorted to visualize his punctured, bleeding back and his side, pierced by the centurion's lance. This is reminiscent of those images of contemplation that feature the motif of the *imago pietatis* or Man of Sorrows, which shows Christ stripped bare in his Passion, but divorced from the Cross in a timeless, sometimes eucharistic setting. In this context, his suffering is often emphasized by means of the *ostentatio vulnerum* gesture, in which he shows his wounds to the spectator, especially the *vulnus lateris* or spear wound in his side,[7] or points to the rivulets of blood that run from these wounds into a chalice as testament to his ever-living sacrifice.[8] Here, however, the poet not only evokes the Crucifixion but also asks us to see it as though it is happening before us. Like the watchful donors often found in the company of the Virgin and St John the Evangelist in later medieval altarpieces,[9] the narrator is engaged in a spiritual exercise that involves imagining oneself standing at the foot of the *Rode*, capable of entering into the omnitemporal reality of the Passion, but at a respectful distance. This type of affective meditation stems from the Cistercian tradition, exemplified by Aelred of Rievaulx's *Letter to his Sister* in which she is instructed to envision herself standing and watching in empathy with Christ's mother and the Beloved Disciple at Golgotha (*De vita eremitica, ad sororem liber*, 63, PL 32, 1470). A profound sense of intimacy is discernible in the reference to Christ as *my leman*, who suffered and died *For the luve of man*. This personal tone is sustained in the second movement of the poem, where, in a pained examination of conscience, the narrator comes to the realization that the sweet tears of compunction can flow only from personal knowledge of Christ's love: *Well ou ic for to wepen, | And sinnes for to leten, | Yif ic of luve can*. This is a popular theme of Cistercian mysticism, found in the writings of St Bernard, but more particularly in those of his friend William of St Thierry, a Benedictine who became a Cistercian towards the close of his life. For William, 'love of God itself is knowledge of him; unless he is loved, he is not known, and unless he is known, he is not loved. He is known only insofar as he is loved, and he is loved only insofar as he is known.'[10]

Moral lyrics

Finally we turn to a recurrent theme in the Middle English religious lyric also found in pagan antiquity, the moral life as a preparation for the inevitability of death. 'This is hardly surprising,' as Gray points out, 'since it is obvious that death is a subject which is not without interest for the non-Christian poet as well as for the Christian. Indeed, it is remarkable that some medieval "religious" poems on death seem only nominally connected with Christianity' (Gray, p. 176). Certainly, the most familiar of all medieval meditations on mortality, the *ubi sunt* formula, has its origins in the classical period where it is used to memorable satiric effect by the Greek rhetorician Lucian (*c.* AD 120–90). In his *Dialogues of the Dead*, Menippus, the Cynic anti-hero, enquires as to where, among the shadowy ossuary of Hades, are all the once proud beauties such as Hyacinth, Narcissus, Achilles, Helen, and Leda.[11] Indeed, the plaintive cry of *ubi sunt* is distinguished by an almost classical sense of *gravitas* in the Old English poem *The Wanderer*. However, it would seem that the Middle English devotional tradition inherited the *ubi sunt* formula from biblical and patristic sources and it is usually deployed in a moralizing, didactic context. It is also generally linked to the *De contemptu mundi* motif, which holds the things of this world up to contempt, as in these oft-quoted, intensely eidetic lines from the late thirteenth century (Davies, pp. 56–7):

Where beth they, beforen us weren,	
Houndes ladden and havekes beren,	*led/carried hawks*
And hadden feld and wode?	
The riche levedies in hoere bour,	*their chambers*
That wereden gold in hoere tressour,	*wore/head-bands*
With hoere brighte rode?	*shining faces*
Eten and drounken and maden hem glad;	*entertained themselves*
Hoere lif was all with gamen ilad:	*spent wholly in pleasure*
Men keneleden hem beforen.	*kneeled/them*
They beren hem well swithe heye,	*most proudly*
And in a twinkling of an eye,	
Hoere soules weren forloren.	*utterly lost*

The poem is based on a Latin meditation on the salutary aspects of *timor mortis*, or fear of death, formerly ascribed to St Bernard (*Meditationes piissimae de cognitione humanae conditionis*, PL 184,

491). However, the poet has infused his recollection of the transitory joys of the world with a reflective delicacy, rather than a 'marmoreal severity' (Woolf, p. 109), and a miniaturist's attention to detail that is absent from the homiletic prose original. We are presented with a shimmering, albeit evanescent, triptych of the refinements of aristocratic living: the hawks and hounds, the gold fillets of the haughty ladies, the leisurely feasting and gaminess. In the second stanza, this courtly *otium* or leisure, the vellumy frailty of a life spent whiling away the time, stands in rueful contraposition to the equalizing suddenness of death, which comes 'in the twinkling of an eye' (1 Corinthians 15: 52), during which the souls of these merrymakers *weren forloren*.

According to Johan Huizinga: 'No epoch has laid so much stress as the expiring Middle Ages on the thought of death.'[12] However, largely due to the influence of Huizinga, there is a tendency 'to oversimplify medieval attitudes towards death: the men of the Middle Ages did not spend all their waking moments thinking upon their end; nor were they surrounded by shrouds and grinning skeletons' (Gray, p. 176). Indeed, it seems appropriate to end our discussion of the religious lyrics with an early sixteenth-century poem, which, although acknowledging the inexorability of death, also reaffirms the vestigial allure of human creativity and the poet's art in particular. The *ubi sunt* formula is central to William Dunbar's *Lament for the Makaris* (Davies, pp. 250–2). Here, 'trublit now with gret seiknes', the Scottish poet contemplates the ineluctable progress of 'all estatis' of mankind, including his own, towards *That strang, unmerciful tyrand*:

I se that makaris amang the laif	*poets/rest*
Playis heir ther pageant, syne gois to graif:	*then go to the grave*
Sparit is nought ther faculte.	*profession, art*
Timor mortis conturbat me.	*The fear of death confounds me*

The sonorous Latin refrain is proverbial and is taken from the responsary at the third nocturn, seventh lesson of the Office of the Dead, yet Dunbar gives the *ubi sunt* formula an added impact by listing a cavalcade of latter-day poets headed up by 'noble Chaucer', then John Lydgate, who had been a monk of the powerful Benedictine monastery of Bury St Edmunds, then John Gower. This triumvirate is succeeded by the Scottish *makaris*, the word consciously recalling the etymology of 'poet', which is ultimately derived from the early Greek word for 'maker'. In conclusion, it seems significant that even though the razing inevitability of death reasserts itself in the closing stanzas, Dunbar's act of naming is possessed of a certain demiurgic quality. Even though there is a poignant irony in the fact that not all of the dead Scottish brethren listed can be identified today, by making this epitaph he gives them, and himself by implication, a literary afterlife and a modicum of defiant satisfaction against that most prosaic of enemies.

The secular lyrics

Images of nature and love

The themes of nature and love are central to one of the Harley lyrics, *Lenten is come with love to toune*, but the poem is also illustrative of the cross-pollination of these themes and the exegetical iconography of the religious lyrics. Although several other Harleian manuscripts contain lyrics, the term 'the Harley lyrics' is now taken to mean the group of poems collected in a single manuscript (London, British Library, Harley 2253), which dates from the 1340s. In many respects, the poem is typical of this group, with alliteration and an elaborate stanza form (Davies, pp. 84–6):

Lenten is come with love to toune,	*Spring has come*
With blosmen and with briddes roune,	*the song of birds*
That all this bliss bringeth.	
Dayeseyes in this dales,	*these*
Notes swete of nightegales,	
Uch fowl song singeth.	*Each bird*
The threstelcok him threteth oo.	*song thrush wrangles all the time*
Away is huere winter wo	*their*
When woderofe springeth.	*woodruff*
This fowles singeth ferly fele,	*Vast numbers of birds are singing*
And wliteth on huere wynne wele,	*and warbling in their abundant joy*
That all the wode ringeth.	

This is a love song couched in the form of a *reverdie*, a favoured Continental form that focuses on the association between nature and love: a theme which is ultimately derived from medieval Latin poetry. It welcomes *Lenten*, or spring, to town and all the *blisse* that this season brings in its wake. Except for the references to woodruff and daisies *in this dales*, this first stanza focuses on the chorus of birds, and such verbs as *singeth*, *threteth*, *wlyteth*, and *ringeth* describe and create the resonant sense of sound.

In the second stanza, however, there is a more balanced division between the floral imagery and the tonal effects. The first six lines emphasize the beauty of renascent nature by means of the images of the rose, verdant foliage, the lily, fennel, and chervil or wild thyme. As Reiss points out, these images, allied to those of the nightingale and the thrush, 'are traditional in medieval love literature. The red of the rose and the white of the lily (or lily of the valley), combining in the red and white of the English daisy, present colours traditionally seen as those of earthly love; and the birds listed here have similar associations' (Reiss, p. 70). The flowers are also familiar from the religious lyrics; the lily is interpreted as a figure of Mary's virginity and, in a characteristic typological paradox, her fertility. Mary is frequently saluted as *rosa sine spinis*, the rose without thorns, in Latin hymns (cf. Sirach 24: 18). Such patristic exegetes as St Basil the Great (*c.*329–79; *De peccato, Sermones viginti quatuor de moribus*, 7, *PG* 32, 1211) and St Ambrose (*c.*340–97; *Hexaemeron*, 3, 11, *PL* 14, 175) associated it with the idea that in the Earthly Paradise the rose was not only unfading, thus a symbol of eternal life (as opposed to the transient bloom of the postlapsarian rose found in classical poetry; cf. Wisdom 2: 8) and Mary's incorruptibility, but also thornless: an apt symbol of Mary's sinlessness, thorns being part of the wages of sin in Genesis 3: 18. The rose was principally associated with her coronation as *Regina coeli*, the matronly yet virginal Queen of Paradise, who is often surrounded in later medieval art by red and white roses,[13] or actually crowned with garlands of roses.[14] The symbolic combination of red roses with white lilies was also associated by exegetes with Song of Songs 5: 10, 'My beloved is white and ruddy', which was taken to apply to Christ as well as his mother. By the later Middle Ages, the common daisy, which combines the colouring of the rose and lily, was interpreted 'as a symbol of the Christ Child in his innocence' (Reiss, p. 70). Furthermore, the moon was also interpreted as a symbol of Mary, stemming from Song of Songs 6: 9, where the beloved is described as 'fair as the moon, bright as the sun'. This is not to suggest, however, that the poet is specifically alluding to the Virgin and her son, or that these lines should be viewed as a veiled religious allegory. Rather, this evocation of the sacred and profane suggests the fecund purity of the new season; the earthly paradise seems reborn in a secular setting.

This image of unspoiled, prelapsarian bliss is rudely undercut by the last six lines of this stanza, which are concerned with discordant, brutish sounds. We are initially confronted by the vigour of the animal world, *Wowes this wilde drakes*, the male duck being infamous for the prodigious ferocity of its rutting, but the frenzied pace set by the drakes and other *miles*, or animals, is compromised by the fact that the poet is reminded of nothing more cataclysmic than a gently flowing *strem*. This sense of ironic torpor is also discernible in his plaintive cry that he is one of those thwarted in love; thus he is estranged from the reproductive joys of nature. Moreover, his apparent resolve to forsake *toune* and lead a frustrated, fugitive existence *in wode* seems to invite offers from members of the opposite sex, however *proude* they may appear, to rectify the situation. After all, and as the *ubi sunt* formula so often reminds us, their aloof disdain will not avert the unpalatable eventuality of bedding down with the worms that *woweth under cloude*, just as nature intended. Women should seize the day, embracing humility (and by implication the poet) while they can, a virtue which is literally grounded in humus in this instance. As Reiss remarks, 'Whereas so many medieval poems take very seriously man's alienation from nature, this poem would seem to play with it and use the threat of it as a means of seduction' (Reiss, p. 73).

Images of women

Female presumption is also brought low in an early fifteenth-century carol that features the exploits of *joly Jankin*, which is ostensibly written from a woman's perspective, but to bawdy and parodic effect. The opening echoes that of a *chanson d'aventure*, a type of lyric that usually involves a man setting off on his travels with the greening of spring, only to encounter a pretty girl by chance. Here, however, the speaker tells us that it was she that roved out, but as it was Christmas Day, her progress was limited to joining the Mass procession, where-

upon she recognized Jankin the clerk by his *mery ton* or sonorous
voice (Davies, pp. 162–3):

> Kyrie, so kyrie,
> Jankin singeth merye,
> With Aleison.

This represents a witty reversal of the usual gender roles and there is
an added piquancy in the fact that the liturgical invocation, *Kyrie
eleyson* 'Lord, have mercy', not only plays on the girl's name 'Aleison',
but also suggests the conventional lover's cry for mercy in the
fin'amors tradition. There are many poems about clerics' love affairs
in Goliardic verse and the vernacular, and the name was stereotypic,
as the *Wife of Bath's Prologue* suggests. The cleric proceeds to sing the
parts of the Mass, as he intones the Office in the second stanza, the
girl assumes that he is directing the 'Kyrieleyson' towards her. This
thought strikes her again as he reads the Epistle in the third stanza
and, by the time he has launched into the *Sanctus* in the fourth, we
begin to suspect that there is more to their relationship than meets
the eye of the other parishioners. She tells us in an aside that she
payed for his cote; clerics in minor orders being the proverbial
scrounging, penurious students of the Middle Ages, with a reputation
for feckless lechery to boot. Nevertheless, Jankin's ecclesiastical role as
a cleric and a scholar is highlighted in the sixth stanza by the fact that
he carries the *pax-brede*, the disk or tablet kissed by the congregation
during the kiss of peace. Here, immediately after the *Agnus Dei*, he
finally salutes his paramour on the sly: *He twinkled but said nowt,* |
And on my fot he trede. Again, there is an implicit irony in the fact that
he is passing her a wink as well as the *pax*, which hints at a more
carnal embrace than the kiss of peace. Our suspicions are correct,
and while Jankin is left holding the *pax*, signifier of his pre-eminent
standing in the community,[15] by the *Benedicamus Domino*, or Final
Blessing, in the concluding stanza, the girl reveals that she will be left
in *shame*, holding the unwanted *childe*. The fact that we are supposed
to find this 'somehow inherently funny: embarrassing, inconvenient,
but fundamentally well deserved, her own fault' (Boklund-
Lagopoulou, p. 220) does little to convince us that this lyric is in fact
composed by a woman, but perhaps by some clerk who is in no doubt
about what every woman wants, or at least has coming to her if she
listens to a clerk's song. The content of this lyric, with its dissonant

counterpoint between the Mass and the sexual act, may seem surprisingly ribald, if not verging on the blasphemous, but there are several extant carols that deal with this theme. John Skelton, who was himself a parish priest in Norfolk, employs the Office and Mass of the Dead to similar parodic effect in *Phyllyp Sparowe*, a mock elegy for the death of a young girl's pet bird.

That the conventions of the courtly ideal of female beauty increasingly became the object of literary parody in the later Middle Ages can be demonstrated by comparing an early fourteenth-century lyric, *A waile whit as whalles bon* (Davies, pp. 80–2), with Thomas Hoccleve's roundel, which Davies entitles *A Description of his Ugly Lady* (Davies, p. 165). *A waile whit as whalles bon* is characteristic of the Harley lyrics in its elaborate stanza form and alliteration, and it makes full use of the ekphrastic techniques of twelfth- and thirteenth-century Latin poetry, which established the feminine paradigm of *fin'amors*. The *descriptio puellae* formed part of the Latin school curriculum whereby 'every schoolboy learned how to describe a woman's beauty and how to write an invective against women'.[16] Thus, this courtly portrait of a lady would seem to be derived from the rhetorical tradition rather than personal observation, and calls to mind the stylized noblewomen in the calendar pictures of that masterpiece of Franco-Flemish painting, *Les Très Riches Heures du Duc de Berry*.[17] She is ivory-skinned, as *whit ase whalles bon*, her hair is as fair as a *grein in golde*, she has *eyen gray* which have wounded her beholder with the dart of love. Her *bente browen* or arched eyebrows *bringeth blisse*, as does her *comely mouth*, which is, although the poet does not specify in this particular instance, no doubt small and reminiscent of a rosebud. That the lady is everything we might expect her to be as an object of desire suggests that this lyric is more concerned with the refined, poetic sentiments she inspires in the poet than a heartfelt asseveration of love, as his claim in the first stanza demonstrates: *Hire gladshipe nes never gon | Whil I may glew* ('Her joy shall never pass away while I can make songs').

Writing in the early fifteenth century, Hoccleve, on the other hand, mocks the use of rhetorical *descriptio* by abusing it in a riotously sardonic fashion. His lady's *golden foreheed is full narw and smal*, her suntan being indicative of the low breeding of one who toils in the fields, while her low forehead suggests bovine intelligence. Her eyebrows are as red and bushy as a coral plant, while her jet black eyes imply a lascivious disposition. The burden sets the tone for the stanzas; her *bowgy cheekes been as softe as clay* and are distinguished by *large jowes*, a further sign of low breeding in late medieval treatises on physiognomy. Her nose slopes like *a pentice* or overhanging roof, but still fails to overshadow the generous expanse of *hir mouth thogh she uprights lay*. Indeed, the poet's description of the mouth as *nothing scant* is unusually understated, but it is enhanced by a pair of lifeless, rubbery *lippes gray* that hang down over her chin, which can scarcely *be seen at al*. Her portly figure complements her face, being shaped *as a footbal*, while her voice is reminiscent of the dulcet tones of a parrot, rather than the nightingale of the *fin'amors* tradition. Davies finds Hoccleve's description 'crude and shocking' (Davies, p. 337), but it reflects a contemporary tendency in the visual arts, also discernible in the calendar pictures of *Les Très Riches Heures*,[18] to represent 'the quaintness of the lower classes, in short the genre and particularly the *genre rustique*'.[19] This lyric not only detonates the courtly ideal of *fin'amors*, but also caricatures the common woman.

It seems fitting to end with these two poems, which are typical of the sustained formulaic and thematic power of the Middle English lyric over a span of several centuries: a form which was sufficiently elastic and sophisticated to parody its own myriad themes and conventions. Moreover, this brief outline can only attempt to trace some of the textual contours and visual hinterland of an almost inexhaustibly rich field.

Notes

1. Umberto Eco, *The Name of the Rose*, trans. W. Weaver (London: Secker and Warburg, 1983), pp. 514–15.
2. *The Harley Lyrics: The Middle English Lyrics of MS. Harley 2253*, ed. G. L. Brook (Manchester: Manchester University Press, 1956; repr. Manchester, 1968), p. 1.
3. Gerald of Wales, *Gemma Ecclesiastica*, 43, *Giraldi Cambrensis Opera*, ed. J. S. Brewer, J. F. Dimock, and G. F. Warner, Rolls Series 21, 8 vols. (London: Longman, Green, Longman, and Roberts, 1861–91), vol. ii, p. 120.
4. All biblical references and quotations in English are taken from the Douai-Rheims translation of the Vulgate.
5. Rogier van der Weyden, *Annunciation Triptych*, central panel, *c.*1440

(Louvre, Paris. See Pl. 7.); Petrus Christus, *Annunciation and Nativity*, 1452 (Staatliche Museen, Berlin).

6. Erwin Panofsky, *Early Netherlandish Painting: Its Origins and Character*, 2 vols. (Cambridge, Mass.: Harvard University Press, 1953), vol. i, p. 73.

7. Master Francke, *Christ as Man of Sorrows*, *c*.1425–30 (Kunsthalle, Hamburg); Petrus Christus, *The Man of Sorrows*, 1444–6 (Birmingham Museum and Art Gallery, Birmingham).

8. Jacob Cornelisz van Oostsanen, *Eucharistic Man of Sorrows*, *c*.1510 (Mayer van den Bergh Museum, Antwerp).

9. Rogier van der Weyden, *Crucifixion Triptych*, *c*.1445 (Kunsthistorisches Museum, Vienna).

10. William of St Thierry, *Exposition on the Song of Songs*, trans. C. Hart, intr. J. M. Déchanet (Shannon: Irish University Press, 1970), song 1, stanza 7, p. 64.

11. Lucian, *Dialogues of the Dead*, 5, *Lucian*, ed. and trans. A. M. Harmon, K. Kilburn, and M. D. Macleod, Loeb Classical Library, 8 vols. (London and Cambridge, Mass.: William Heinemann and Harvard University Press, 1913–67), vol. vii, pp. 20–5.

12. Johan Huizinga, *The Waning of the Middle Ages: A Study of the Forms of Life, Thought, and Art in France and the Netherlands in the Fourteenth and Fifteenth Centuries*, trans. F. Hopman (London: Edward Arnold, 1924; repr. Harmondsworth: Penguin, 1990), p. 134.

13. Stephano da Zevio, *Madonna in the Rosary*, *c*.1410 (Museo di Castelvecchio, Verona); Stephan Lochner, *Madonna of the Rose Bush*, *c*.1440 (Wallraf-Richartz Museum, Cologne. See Pl. 8.).

14. Stephan Lochner, *Triptych with the Virgin and Child in an Enclosed Garden*, *c*.1445–50 (Wallraf-Richartz Museum, Cologne); Master of St Severin, *Altarpiece of the Rosary Brotherhood*, *c*.1510–1515 (St Andrew's Church, Cologne).

15. See Eamon Duffy, *The Stripping of the Altars: Traditional Religion in England, 1400–1580* (New Haven and London: Yale University Press, 1992), pp. 126–7.

16. F. J. E. Raby, *A History of Secular Latin Poetry in the Middle Ages*, 2 vols. (Oxford: Clarendon Press, 1934), vol. ii, p. 45.

17. Paul, Herman, and Jean de Limbourg, 'April' from *Les Très Riches Heures du Duc de Berry*, *c*.1411–16 (Chantilly, Musée Condé, MS 65, fo. 4*v*. See Pl. 9.).

18. Limbourg brothers and Jean Colombe, 'September', from *Les Très Riches Heures du Duc de Berry*, *c*.1411–16 and 1485–9 (Chantilly, Musée Condé, MS 65, fo. 9*v*).

19. Panofsky, *Early Netherlandish Painting*, vol. i, p. 70. On this point see Jonathan Alexander, '*Labeur* and *Paresse*: Ideological Representations of Medieval Peasant Labor', *Art Bulletin*, 72 (1990), 443–52.

References and suggested reading

Bennett, J. A. W. *Poetry of the Passion: Studies in Twelve Centuries of English Verse*. Oxford: Clarendon Press, 1982. Although this learned study is not specifically medieval, it traces the origin and development of the motif throughout the Middle Ages.

Boklund-Lagopoulou, Karin. *'I Have a Yong Suster': Popular Song and the Middle English Lyric*. Dublin: Four Courts Press, 2002. Although this work is idiosyncratic in some of its conclusions, it also provides some stimulating responses to received critical opinion.

Davies, R. T., ed. *Medieval English Lyrics: A Critical Anthology*. London: Faber and Faber, 1963. All quotations (with some minor emendations to Davies's translations) are from this edition.

Duncan, T. G., ed. *A Companion to the Middle English Lyric*. Cambridge: D. S. Brewer, 2005. A significant collection of essays on different aspects of the subject, including moral and penitential lyrics, social and political lyrics, love lyrics, courtly lyrics, preaching and poetry, prosody, and the manuscript tradition.

Gray, Douglas. *Themes and Images in the Medieval English Religious Lyric*. London: Routledge and Kegan Paul, 1972. Full of insight, this lively and scholarly work gives a rich analysis of the iconography which informs the lyrics.

Manning, Stephen. *Wisdom and Number: Toward a Critical Appraisal of the Middle English Religious Lyric*. Lincoln: University of Nebraska Press, 1962. This study provides a close reading of a range of lyrics, with a strong emphasis on the influence of exegetical method.

Moore, A. K. *The Secular Lyric in Middle English*. Lexington: University of Kentucky Press, 1951. Although dated, this study remains a clear, accessible introduction to the secular lyrics.

Greentree, Rosemary. *The Middle English Lyric and Short Poem*. Annotated Bibliographies of Old and Middle English Literature 7. Cambridge: D. S. Brewer, 2001. This is an annotated bibliography of editions and critical works that goes up to 1995, citing works published up to 1997, with a particularly useful subject index.

Reiss, Edmund. *The Art of the Middle English Lyric: Essays in Criticism*. Athens: University of Georgia Press, 1972. This study provides a close reading of several religious and secular lyrics, with a strong emphasis on prosody.

Woolf, Rosemary. *The English Religious Lyric in the Middle Ages.* Oxford: Clarendon Press, 1968. Although this work may seem initially daunting due to the breadth and depth of its scholarship, it remains the standard, authoritative introduction to the subject.

22

Medieval dream visions: Chaucer's *Book of the Duchess*

William A. Quinn

Defining the dream vision

The term 'dream vision' or 'dream-vision' has no Middle English pedigree; indeed, it did not become a comfortable critical label until 1906. Yet, Chaucer clearly recognized and frequently toyed with an established genre when he composed his four major dream narratives: the *Book of the Duchess*, the *House of Fame*, the *Parliament of Fowls*, and the *Legend of Good Women*. The immediate *raison d'être* for each of Chaucer's dream visions seems straightforward enough. After some ruminative preliminaries, Chaucer eventually reports *in propria persona* that he fell asleep; that he had a *sweven* ('dream'); that he witnessed wonders; and that, now awake (except at the end of the F-Prologue to the *Legend*; cf. G 544), he will report everything as it honestly happened.[1]

Such a dream may be presented as a preternatural visitation or as an excursion into the dreamer's subconscious—or both. At worst, dreaming offers a robotic excuse for didactic exposition. At best, the dream vision provides an entertaining excuse for teaching a true fantasy, or *narratio fabulosa*. In prose or verse, in ancient, medieval, or modern literature, the dream vision can be at once idiosyncratic and archetypal, anecdotal and philosophical, didactic and enigmatic, autobiographical and universal.

The rather free-fall fiction of dreaming often appeals to post-modernist sensibilities, but the thematic intent of a medieval 'maker' was usually quite antithetical to the interpretative assumptions of many post-structuralist readers. Chaucer did not doubt that dreams could convey a *trouthe*. Although their significance too often becomes only *afterward . . . apparunt*, some *swevenes* do come true; the Bible said so; Plato said so; Cicero said so; Virgil said so; so, who could say 'no'—other than sceptics like Pandarus (cf. *T&C*, 5. 362)? Chaucer's contemporaries questioned instead the legitimacy of a largely post-medieval understanding of *fiction* (see *OED* s.v. def 2b). As a true-lie, the dream vision negotiates the imaginary terrain between facts and wisdom on the one hand and 'fables and lesynges' (*Romaunt*, lines 2–5) on the other. In modern literary dictionaries, dream vision is frequently subsumed under relentlessly reductive definitions of allegory. However, the dream premise assured medieval readers that the reported experience really did happen—in a sense.

To interpret such a narrative, Chaucer inherited a precise terminology from *An authour that hight* [was named] *Macrobes*, and it was quite common to refer to the explicator of a dream as its 'reader'. In his *Commentary on Cicero's 'Dream of Scipio'*, Ambrosius Theodosius Macrobius (fl. AD 400) had designated five types of dreams: the *somnium*, or enigmatic dream, which offers an adumbrated truth clearly in need of interpretation; the *visio*, or prophetic vision, which comes true; the *oraculum*, or admonitory appearance of an authority figure; the *insomnium*, or nightmare; and the *visum*, or phantasmic apparition which commonly occurs during the threshold of waking. This authoritative cataloguing of dreams licensed an extraordinary diversity of medieval dream visions. Indeed, Jean de Meun's continuation of the *Roman de la rose*, John Gower's *Confessio Amantis*, the *Gawain*-poet's *Pearl*, and William Langland's *Piers Plowman* have almost nothing in common—except the premise of an individual dreamer reporting his ultimately therapeutic vision(s). Dreaming provides such a strong yet flexible paradigm for interpreting visionary narrative that many include Boethius's *Consolation of Philosophy* and Dante's *Divine Comedy* as exemplars of the genre, although neither author reports actually having fallen asleep. A modern sense of *fiction* can thus be readily imposed upon the *truth* of any dream vision, reading it as a merely ludic exercise. Medieval dream visions normally maintained a more definite contact with reality, however, with much stronger convictions regarding true interpretation. Chaucer's *Book of the Duchess*, for example, once mirrored a specifically anticipated frame of reference—the Lancastrian court.

Standard readings of Chaucer's first dream vision

Most studies of the *Book of the Duchess*—which a later hand in the manuscript, Oxford, Bodleian Library, Tanner 346, labelled *Chaucer's Dream*, and Thynne in 1532 likewise titled *The Dreame of Chaucer*—focus on its literary sources, the historical circumstances that occasioned its composition, and its allegorical significance. All three interpretative approaches illuminate discrete sections of Chaucer's dream vision, but no single reading of the text seems to account for its serial cohesiveness as an actual recitation.

The *Book's* prefatory comments function as a sort of self-diagnosis *cum* reader-response criticism that establishes Chaucer's self-deprecating persona. The first scene also proposes a fellowship of sorrow between the poet and his patron; the action (such as it is) then establishes an analogy between Chaucer as reader of *Ovid* and the readers of *Chaucer*. After falling asleep, Chaucer conjoins *seriatim*: a *descriptio*—in which his bedroom becomes an imaginary cathedral resonant with the harmony of a choir of birds and illuminated by windows glazed with glosses of both the *Histoire de Troie* and the *Roman de la rose*; a transitional interlude that celebrates *venery* (superficially hunting, subliminally sex); a mini-journey to some other world; Chaucer's rehearsal of the knight's mourning; and finally the dreamer's somewhat rope-a-dope *débat* with that knight. On first reading or hearing, the narrative progress of the *Book of the Duchess* seems to be *ydel* or random. However, the dream vision's discrete scenes offer a thematically informed progress of analogous episodes.[2]

Since Chaucer quilted much of this content together from a number of roughly contemporary French sources and from other *clerkes ... in olde tyme*, interpretations based on source studies risk inviting informed readers to conclude that this *Book*, defined as a sequence of discrete parts, remains a rather derivative effort. Chaucer's apparent lack of originality suggests, in turn, his immaturity as a poet. And the dreamer-narrator does occasionally make what seem young mistakes in writing his first significant *Book* (*c*.1368–72). For example, there are some prosody problems. Chaucer apparently confuses Macrobius with Cicero (cf. *PF* 29–84). He calls both Duke Scipio and Pharaoh 'king'—probably by analogy to King Seys (rather than Lancaster). And Chaucer even reduces John of Gaunt's age.[3] There is a certain accidental flattery to this alleged ineptness.

Alceste's reference to *the Deeth of Blaunche the Duchesse* in the Prologue to the *Legend of Good Women* validates reading the *Book*'s *man in blak* specifically—which is not to say exclusively—as John of Gaunt in mourning. It is neither trivial nor wrong-headed to delight in considering the pageantry that may once have informed the original occasion for presenting the *Book of the Duchess*. Such a milieu probably once invested its now elusive enigmas with immediate and easy significance. And many readers still delight as antiquarians in the richness of the *Book*'s lore regarding hunting, chess, rhetoric, and most of all *courtesie*. Detailed footnotes alone do not, however, offer an adequate decoding of the dream vision's entire mystery.

Allegorical readings, on the other hand, would completely despecify the historical reality of the *Book of the Duchess*. Though blind to many of its peculiarly occasional references, such interpretations do insulate the *Book of the Duchess* from critical dismissal as mere ephemera. Gaunt's real identity is masked by puns. The man in black with his back turned to an oak tree more patently represents Melancholy personified; he so names himself: *For y am sorwe, and sorwe ys y*. The rhetorical flourish of this chiasmus only ornaments his solipsism. Likewise, though *Good faire Whit* translates the dead Duchess Blanche's French *name ryght* in a *roman à clef*, her image also readily reads as 'Purity' in an allegory. Allegory allows more universal themes—such as questions of *fortuna* and mutability, pathos and melancholy, rhetoric and *consolatio*, memory and expectation, human perfection and the Fall—to attach themselves to the details of Chaucer's dream vision.[4]

But Chaucer's tonal hiccups are difficult to incorporate simply as 'comic relief' into either an allegorical or a strictly funereal reading of the *Book of the Duchess*. The *Book of the Duchess* must somehow be read in a fashion that harmonizes its immediate referentiality and its universal significance, its funny and sad elements, its recollection of the past and its anticipation of a future. To reconstruct the unifying tension of the *Book*, it is mandatory to reinvest the text with overtones of its original presentation. Though Chaucer recollects his dream as a past vision—'This was my sweven'—his dream vision seems to be presented as a current *show*.

A re-vision of Chaucer's dream

For 290 lines before the dream proper begins—that is, for about a quarter of the entire poem—Chaucer reflects upon the potentially fatal dangers of his insomnia *be this lyght*. Allegoresis interprets this detail as *Illuminatio*; actual performance simply asks for the prop of a candle. Chaucer's prefatory reading of the sad 'romance' of Seys to Alcyone includes what may be designated a foiled *oraculum*. Alcyone prays for a *certeyn sweven*, but the apparition that comes to her seems more a *visum*.[5] Chaucer's own *Defaute of slep* may have been caused by a variety of melancholies. His specific (and perhaps once well-known though unspecified) 'sicknesse' remains more or less a moot interpretative issue, however. Macrobius had considered any *insomnium* resulting from such a condition to be, like the *visum*, unworthy of interpretation. Chaucer thus ironizes the truth of his own dream on an a priori basis.

In the *House of Fame*, Chaucer will despair of ever comprehending the puzzling variety of dreams and their causes—interpretative categories that never quite contain the labyrinthine play of Chaucer's own dream visions. He hopes instead only for the best. It is this same hope that informs, after many melancholic digressions, the end of the *Book of the Duchess*. From its start, however, Chaucer announces that his own dream had been *so ynly swete* and *so wonderful* that it defies interpretation: *Y trowe* [believe] *no man had the wyt | To konne wel my sweven rede*. Neither biblical nor classical authority could decipher this dream. Nor can Arab mathematicians *rekene even | The wondres me mette* [I dreamt] *in my sweven*. These hyperbolic declarations of the dream vision's resistance to any manner of explication are especially vulnerable to comic recitation. The poet's confusion of Macrobius with Cicero is so casually wrong, yet confident; his internal *man/Affrikan* rhyme, so pat; and the end-rhyme *than*, so flat—that Chaucer's initial performance pose may have seemed deliberately clumsy rather than simply amateurish or ignorant. In a performance context, furthermore, Chaucer's patron-audience has in fact commissioned and so expects to appreciate on first hearing the import of what Chaucer can himself now *rede*. In this same situation, Chaucer's transparently wrong-headed claim that his dream vision defies authoritative reading anticipates the knight in black's more sincere, and so more dangerous, assumption that his sorrow resists any remedies prescribed by either poets or physicians.[6]

Before sleeping, Chaucer is himself attended by an unnamed servant. This attendant's only function is to fetch a book. This minimal service proves emblematic, however, of both the dreamer's own minimal ability to cure the knight's grief and of the poet-courtier's service to Gaunt. Chaucer presents himself as bringer of a dream vision, but cannot play Lady Philosophy—an identity more closely approximated by the absent Duchess. The knight in black had been her blank canvas, or *tabula rasa*, in love. But the *Book of the Duchess* assumes a profound scepticism regarding any purely rational acceptance of the providential inevitability of death—the fundamental premise of Boethius's *Consolation of Philosophy*.

The *things smalle* of Ovid's *Metamorphoses* promise 'better play' than any games of chance. Chaucer's highly edited epitome of the tale of Ceyx and Alcyone exemplifies primarily the inability of mere (because merely natural) knowledge to cope with the loss of a loved one. Indeed, Chaucer explicitly notes the restricted insights of this pagan text: *While men loved the lawe of kinde, | this bok ne spak but of such thinges*. Ovid's text offers a diagnosis but does not itself cure the reader's melancholy. Rather, the anguish of the story actually harms Chaucer:

> That trewly I, that made this book
> Had such pittee and such rowthe   *pity*
> To rede hir sorwe that, by my trowthe,
> I ferde the worse al the morwe   *fared*
> Aftir to thenken on hir sorwe.   (lines 96–100)

It is the distraction of reading more than the content of the book that helps (lines 222–5).

To discover the fatal truth, Chaucer has Alcyone promise to become *hooly* Juno's nun *wille, body, herte and al.* Chaucer impersonates Alcyone's grief until she swoons and falls into a *dede slep* (lines 108–27), which Chaucer himself still cannot do. Chaucer then becomes utterly distracted by the dream lore within Ovid's pathetic tale, especially by its promise of a cure for his own insomnia. In the *Metamorphoses,* Juno sends Iris to Sleep; in Chaucer's retelling at lines 133–84, Juno employs a male messenger who is well-acquainted with Morpheus—an occasional variant that may have once mocked a notoriously sleepy servant (i.e., a heretofore healthy Chaucer). Juno's instructions and the messenger's relatively long *katabasis* through a dark valley to the hellish Cave of Sleep creates a somewhat Gothic mood. But this eeriness is then dispelled by some potentially comic details. The heir-apparent is especially idle. Naked, snoring nappers comprise the court. The messenger's need to blow his horn directly into Sleep's ear and the god's minimal reaction thereto sounds almost slapstick. Chaucer's distortion of Ovid's *exemplum* is difficult to accommodate to a strictly funereal interpretation of the *Book of the Duchess,* except as tonal blunders—unless cajolery was as much a part of Chaucer's performance strategy as *consolatio.* In either case, the messenger's emphatic imperative is *Awake* from this pseudo-wake.

Juno's instructions are reported; *Hyt ys no nede reherse hyt more* (line 190). Juno is obeyed. The naked truth is quoted (lines 201–11). Alcyone is informed. And so dies three days and three lines later:

> But what she sayede more in that swow   *anguish*
> I may not telle yow as now;
> Hyt were to longe for to dwelle   *delay*
> (lines 213–17)

Such 'dwelling' during Chaucer's recital would be as unwelcome as Alcyone's news. Returning at last to his *first matere* (line 218), Chaucer concludes his book report with a sort of colophon that gives the *goddess of slepyng* equal billing with King Seys. The handicap of Chaucer's own *sorwful ymagination* at line 14 is promptly illustrated by his inability to extract any real significance from *everydel* of Ovid's tale. He foregrounds only its suggestion that sleep can be conjured.

Chaucer is moved to a confused or playful (lines 233–9) or else apostate attempt at pagan prayer. *To make me sleep*, Chaucer offers Morpheus (or whomever) the votive *Yifte* of a white sale—a prolonged list of bedding (lines 246–61) that does nothing but divert the reader's attention again—which is exactly the point. What looks on the page like irrelevant cataloguing (cf. *CT* 1. 2913–66) plays as a caricature of the rehearser's distracted state of mind. Like Alcyone's prayer, Chaucer's mock petition is granted instantly. The book becomes his pillow (lines 270–4).

At lines 305–57 Chaucer wakes up in his dream to a seemingly idyllic vision, a joyful celebration of both nature and art. The sweet and merry harmony of the birds outside dispels the oppressive isolation of Chaucer's real bedchamber. It is the exterior openness of a cloudless sky during a golden spring that offers some promise of therapeutic escape from the claustrophobic, book-bound interiors of Chaucer's melancholic imagination. The dreamer's own cure begins when he gets up and gets out. Chaucer is dream-awakened by a potentially anagogic horn *T'assay* (*test* and hunting term at line 346; cf. 552, 574).

Chaucer discovers that the beautiful people celebrate the rebirth of spring with ritualized killing, and he is suddenly himself *ryght glad* to mount a dream-convenient horse to give chase. He finds that Octavian's (i.e. King Edward III's) *gret route* (line 360) of servants have maintained all the proprieties of the hunt—and all in vain. The hart still *staal away* |... *a privy way*, and the hunt is called off *wonder faste* (lines 381–5). Chasing the *Book*'s running pun on *hart* (i.e., 'deer', 'heart', and 'hurt') serves as a miniature metaphor for the elusiveness of the text as a whole.

A seemingly sudden transition that transports the dreamer from this futile hunt scene to the apparition of a whelp—after Chaucer has apparently been unhorsed—is usually read (and then dismissed) as a realistically baffling dream feature. The two chase scenes (lines 344–86 and 387–97) are, however, highly resonant of each other, and both foreshadow the dramatic core of the dream—rhetorically chasing a lost love. The hart hunt exemplifies a deliberate, yet frustrated, quest. The inexplicable appearance of a puka-like (if not psychopomp-like) puppy (which also served as a heraldic image of marital fidelity) leads Chaucer to discover an unsought quarry. Yet the escape of the whelp from Chaucer's grasp parallels Octavian's failure to catch the hart.

Whatever else this whelp might signify, its fawning demeanour and its narrative function as a well-intentioned yet rather powerless attendant who *Koude no good* offers a self-deflating image of Chaucer, who serves only as he *best koude* (line 517) while asleep—or as he *kan best* (line 1333) when awake. At lines 398–443 Chaucer intrudes on a *floury grene*, which seems a *locus amoenus*, *As thogh the erthe envye wolde | To be gayer than the heven* where flowers (an emblem of the ladies in court) outnumber the stars. Chaucer portrays himself as an *arriviste* who finds himself on the margin of this dream court's sport, like a squirrel among the *bestes* and big trees.

This natural stage is *litel used*, but it is not a completely private space. To the dreamer it seems, a garden of regenerative forgetting:

> Hyt had forgete the povertee
> That wynter, thorgh hys colde morwes,
> Had mad hyt suffre, and hys sorwes;
> All was forgeten, and that was sene,
> For al the woode was waxen grene;
> Swetnesse of dew had mad hyt waxe.   (lines 410–15)

Though the hunt has already been (prematurely?) abandoned, this shadowy place is crowded with deer.

Again, left behind and alone as the herd moves on *wonder faste*, Chaucer sees—*at the laste | I was war* (lines 444–5)—the likewise forsaken image of his patron—whom the audience recognizes as a *wonder wel-farynge knyght* (line 452) despite the fact that he is now sitting upright on the ground. Chaucer hears the *dedly sorwful soun* (line 462) of a fellow exile from *worldes blysse*. Like Alcyone's incurable despair—and Chaucer's own perhaps still curable sickness—the knight's grief defies natural moderation. Or perhaps Nature is merely indifferent to such individual melancholy *Thogh Pan, that men clepeth god of kynde, | Were for hys sorwes never so wroth* (lines 511–13).

Though, at lines 749–52, the knight in black does temporarily pose as Chaucer's mentor, the rest of Chaucer's dream hardly seems an *oraculum*. The dreamer's unhooding at line 516 and his use of formal second-person pronouns do defer to the higher status of his patron, not his paternal authority. Indeed, in the dream, despite all his talking, the knight's role is unconsciously that of student. Status aside—but never completely aside—Chaucer encounters Gaunt on foot, on common ground, presuming, without being presumptive, a fellowship *by kinde*. The dream reported within the dream vision of the

Book of the Duchess seems, therefore, primarily a pseudo-*somnium* in need of explication.

Chaucer, no Algus himself, quotes eleven lines at 475–85 of the knight's *rym ten vers or twelve | Of a compleynte* (lines 463–4). Since the dreamer himself is explicitly presented as an unseen and unheard witness to the knight's complaint, and since this lyric discloses the literal reason for the knight's melancholy, the rest of Chaucer's rehearsal seems an exercise in *dramatic* irony. The narrator's patent obtuseness is now habitually read as a deliberately therapeutic ploy. Only the knight in black, at line 1305, thinks Chaucer himself a well-meaning dimwit: *Thow wost ful lytel what thow menest.*

Chaucer's first impersonation of his patron's private mourning is a brief song without music (lines 471–85). His direct quotation of the knight's following complaints against fickle Fortuna at lines 598–709 for taking away his perfectly faithful *fers* or 'queen' should be read, all agree, as a sincerely moving re-enactment of grief. But Chaucer's impersonation of the knight's increasingly amplified and contrived and periphrastic rhetoric dispels much of the pathos of his initial, simple sigh. It is specifically the fictional opportunity Chaucer then gives his lord to speak his sorrow aloud to an attendant that hopefully heals.

The sympathetic heart of the *Book of the Duchess* (lines 560–1297) actually needs little further explication because it dramatizes so well what it is: the recollected experiences of extreme love and loss. Gaunt will continue to commemorate Blanche as a translunary light, celestial in beauty and holier than the apostles. But *The Book of the Duchess* begins and ends in an occasional moment. The composition of this dream vision had obviously been completed prior to the start of its recital (line 96); yet the therapeutic activity of its composition is merely anticipated at the end of the *sweven* itself. The intervening occasions—the business of writing, reciting, reading—achieve analogously consoling acceptances of grief by Chaucer as well as by his audience—that is, by John of Gaunt, his courtiers, and the sympathetic reader. But in no sense does the *Book of the Duchess* document the dreamer's *power* to cure Sorrow.

By exhausting melancholic hyperbole in a series of monologues, the knight escapes the suicidal sarcasm of his initial soliloquy: '*Allas, deth, what ayleth the, | That thou noldest taken me*' (lines 481–2). Chaucer's dream pose during this cathartic process is essentially passive. As the *Book*'s real reciter, however, Chaucer's verbatim (and so not at all satiric) re-enactment of the knight's wordy woe exhausts his real audience and thereby dramatizes the mourner's unhealthy obfuscation of a prosaic fact: *She ys ded!* (line 1309). The knight at this moment must confess in public what he has already been quoted at lines 477–9 as having admitted in private: *Now that I see my lady bryght ... Is fro me ded and ys agoon.* At lines 1309–24, any further debate is promptly dismissed: *'Nay!' 'Yis, be my trouthe!'* Chaucer the dreamer's final confession of literal comprehension—*Is that youre los? Be God, hyt ys routhe*—sounds minimal but sincere and all that really can be said—*al was doon.* This critical moment of rhetorical stripping echoes both King Seys' *I am but ded* (line 204) and Chaucer's *but that is don* (line 40); it also anticipates the *Book*'s own conclusion: *now hit ys doon.*

Since it is now generally assumed that the *Book of the Duchess* was originally commissioned for some *solempne service* commemorating an anniversary of Blanche's death, the melancholy tone of such an interpretative context often shrouds Chaucer's concluding meiosis. But the *Book* as a whole seems intended to put the Duke's grief to rest, not just to eulogize the memory of the dead Duchess. Whereas Ovid had offered an admonitory tale, Chaucer's *Book* should be read according to the more 'comic' (in Dante's sense) conventions of medieval dream vision. And it is this less romantic yet more therapeutic reading of Chaucer's dream vision that suggests a happier, transitional occasion for its initial presentation. Such an interpretative context would propose a date several years after Blanche's death, closer to 1374 than 1368—after, that is, John of Gaunt had *by processe of tyme* (line 1331) contracted his marriage to Constanza of Castile and León and/or had fallen in love with his mistress and future wife, Chaucer's sister-in-law, Katherine Swynford.[7]

Like the *Consolation of Philosophy* (the text that immediately precedes Chaucer's *Dreame* in Thynne's 1532 edition), the *Book of the Duchess* confronts undeniable death. Whereas Boethius had considered the inevitability of his own future, Chaucer now addresses the irreversibility of his patron's past. Whereas Boethius had written a universal consolation for himself as a man doomed to die, Chaucer now performs a specific dream vision for a patron who mourned surviving his dead wife. Chaucer's poem does enshrine his patron's lament, but it also offers an implicit *apologia* for getting on with one's life: as the reanimated corpse of King Seys advised his wife, *Awake! Lat be your sorwful lyf* (line 202). Unfortunately, Queen Alcyone refused this therapeutic answer from Juno to her prayer—the imperative to *shewe hir shortly, hit is no nay* (line 147).

The *Book of the Duchess* is, after all, merely such a showing with—one hopes—a happier denouement than Ovid's ancient exemplar. Chaucer awakes himself to the promise of new activity *as I can best, and that anoon* (lines 1324–33). However, this *ex post facto* virtue has informed the voice of his dream vision from its start: *That wil not be mot be left* (line 42). It is not so much the content of Chaucer's dream vision as the very act of dreaming (or reading) that heals. In terms of such a recitative occasion and interpretative context, Chaucer's otherwise curiously digressive description regarding *al that falles | To a chambre . . . of oo sute* (lines 257–61) may have originally served as a playful epithalamion. Once upon a time, to John of Gaunt, and to the general reader still, Chaucer offered an interlude to mourning. The healing to be read in the *Book of the Duchess* remains anticipatory, not memorial.

Notes

1. Chaucer falls asleep: *Book of the Duchess*, BD 275; *House of Fame*, HF 114; *Parliament of Fowls*, PF 94; *Legend of Good Women*, LGW F 209/G 103. Chaucer starts to have a dream: BD 276; HF 119; PF 95; LGW F 210/G 104.
2. The choir of birds: BD 291–320; the illuminations: BD 321–34; venery: BD 344–86; the otherworld: BD 387–442.
3. John of Gaunt: BD 455; Cicero: BD 284; Pharoah and Scipio: BD 282 and 286.
4. Name puns: BD 949–50, 1318–19; Melancholy: BD 445–6, 560.
5. Cf. BD 48, 52.
6. *That the holy roode* [cross] | *Turne us every drem to goode* (HF 57–8); references to BD in this paragraph may be found in lines 276–572.
7. Antithetically, the *Book of the Duchess* was frequently followed by the anti-matrimonial *Lenvoy de Chaucer a Bukton* which John Urry (1721) thought was addressed to John of Gaunt.

References and suggested reading

Brown, Peter, ed. *Reading Dreams: The Interpretation of Dreams from Chaucer to Shakespeare*. Oxford: Oxford University Press, 1999. A collection of six essays (four of which consider Chaucer) by various authors that collectively provide a survey of the literary *topos* of dreaming from medieval and Renaissance perspectives.

Clemen, Wolfgang. *Chaucer's Early Poetry*. Trans. by C. A. M. Sym. London: Methuen, 1963. New York: Barnes and Noble, 1964. [*Der Junge Chaucer*, 1938]. An early but still influential appreciation of Chaucer's 'early' poetry (i.e., the *Book of the Duchess, House of Fame, Parliament of Fowls*, and several lyrics) as significant artistic achievements and not merely curious juvenilia.

Eckhardt, Caroline. 'Genre'. In Peter Brown, ed., *A Companion to Chaucer*. Oxford: Blackwell Publishers, 2000, pp. 180–94. Situates Chaucer's use of the dream vision among his experiments with other medieval classifications of literature.

Edwards, Robert R. *The Dream of Chaucer*. Durham, NC: Duke University Press, 1989. Analyses Chaucer's dream visions as a compendium of the poet's own critical theories regarding language, representation, and the imagination.

Kruger, Stephen F. *Dreaming in the Middle Ages*. Cambridge: Cambridge University Press, 1992. Reviews both positive and negative theories of dream interpretation available to medieval writers of dream vision.

Lynch, Kathryn L. *Chaucer's Philosophical Visions*. Cambridge: D. S. Brewer, 2000. Explores the scholastic expertise and sophistication of philosophical inquiry that informs Chaucer's dream visions.

Minnis, A. J., with V. J. Scattergood and J. J. Smith. *Oxford Guides to Chaucer: The Shorter Poems*. Oxford: Clarendon Press, 1995. A magisterial study of Chaucer's dream visions and minor poems, including an intriguing analysis of the homosocial subtext of *The Book of the Duchess*.

Pearsall, Derek. 'John of Gaunt and *The Book of the Duchess*'. *The Life of Geoffrey Chaucer*. Oxford: Basil Blackwell, 1992, pp. 82–93. Details the historical and biographical background to the performance of the *Book of the Duchess*. Maintains that Chaucer's person and persona played as one and the same in the presence of John of Gaunt. Pearsall acknowledges the possibility that the *Book* contains an implicit (perhaps presumptuous) suggestion that Gaunt get on with a new love. Assuming a date of actual presentation closer to Blanche's death, Pearsall emphasizes the sympathetic, sincere, and commemorative strategy of Chaucer's poem.

Spearing, A. C. *Medieval Dream Poetry*. Cambridge: Cambridge University Press, 1976. An enduring model of lucid formal interpretation and psychological insight. After a survey of the Latin and French precedents for the Middle English type, offers close readings of Chaucer's four 'dream poems', of the major alliterative visions, and finally of the subsequent imitators of Chaucer (from Lydgate through Skelton).

St John, Michael. *Chaucer's Dream Visions: Courtliness and Individual Identity*. Aldershot: Ashgate, 2000. Provides separate chapters for each of Chaucer's four major dream visions. Considers the philosophical subtexts of each. Emphasizes the dream visions' importance in developing a medieval sense of self-reflexive subjectivity and in establishing the role of courtliness as a social bond.

Wimsatt, James. *Chaucer and the French Love Poets: The Literary Background of the Book of the Duchess*. Chapel Hill: University of North Carolina Press, 1968. Details Chaucer's indebtedness to French *dits amoureux* as the love narrative had progressed from the time of Guillaume de Lorris to 1369. Explains the special influence of Guillaume de Machaut and other French contemporaries on Chaucer's form and content.

23

Late romance: Malory and the *Tale of Balin*

Ad Putter

Introduction

This chapter focuses on Sir Thomas Malory's *Tale of Balin*. My aim is to shed light on some of the original qualities (both good and bad) of Malory's writing—his 'newness'—but also on that aspect of his imagination that led him to recapture the essence of romance: his feeling for adventure. Since the enjoyment of medieval romance depends on a sympathetic response to the element of adventure, I shall try to explain why Malory could treat adventure so solemnly when so many of his later readers thought it frivolous. I shall begin by considering some of the features that make Malory's *Morte Darthur* an example of *late* romance, paying particular attention to his choice of the prose form; I then turn to his sense of adventure which, I believe, justifies his status as a classic writer of late *romance*.

The medium of prose

The story of Balin begins as follows:

Than the kynge lette make a cry that all the lordis, knyghtes and jantilmen of armys sholde draw unto the castell called Camelot in tho dayes, and there the kynge wolde lette make a counceile generall and a grete justis. So whan the kynge was com thidir with all his baronage and logged as they semed beste, also ther was com a damoisel the which was sente frome the grete Lady Lyle of Avilion. And whan she com byfore kynge Arthur she tolde fro whens she com, and how sche was sente on message unto hym for thys causis. Than she lette hir mantel falle that was rychely furred, and than was she gurde with a noble swerde, wherof the kynge had mervayle and seyde, 'Damesell for what cause ar ye gurte with that swerde'? (61.17–28)[1]

The first thing to note here is that Malory writes in prose. This is apt to strike modern readers as unremarkable, but medieval English readers had different expectations of romance. In France, the earliest Arthurian romances (c.1170), by Chrétien de Troyes, were in octosyllabic rhyming couplets, but within the space of thirty years Arthurian matter was being amplified into long prose cycles. Although these cycles were widely read in Britain, English romancers stuck resolutely to verse. Thus the prose romances of the French Vulgate Cycle (c.1215–35) were all initially translated into verse. The first translation of Arthurian matter into prose, the *Prose Merlin*, dates from the middle of the fifteenth century, and only then did the shift from verse to prose become widespread in romance. When, in the 1460s, Malory endeavoured to produce a full account of the deeds of Arthur and his Round Table knights, based on all the sources available to him,[2] the choice of prose was a relatively new phenomenon, which set Malory apart from earlier generations of romance writers.

An important factor in the transition from verse to prose is that the traditional forms of versification (tail-rhyme and short couplet), though suitable to oral delivery and aural reception, had come to seem outmoded and lowbrow in the eyes of a growing audience of readers. Fifteenth-century romancers with courtly and artistic aspirations responded to the changing fashions by adopting newly prestigious 'Chaucerian' forms, such as the rhyme-royal stanza or the longer five-beat couplet; but prose offered an obvious alternative. As the language associated with historical truth and moral gravity, prose avoided the stigma of wild improbability with which the genre of romance had increasingly to contend. And to Malory, who conceived of his *Morte Darthur* as a chronicle rather than a romance, prose had the added advantage of allowing him to recount events 'as they had happened', to meet the demands of history without bowing to those of rhyme and metre.

The avoidance of artistic elaboration is also evident from the kind of prose that Malory wrote, the characteristics of which will become clearer if we compare it with its opposite, 'curial prose'.[3] Descended from the administrative prose of court records, curial prose is marked by syntactical complexity, particularly the subordination and correlation of clauses, and the foregrounding of cohesion, typically by means of anaphora (such as 'the aforesaid', 'the which'). Consider, for example, the following sentence from Henry Watson's translation of *Valentine and Orson* (c.1500):

After that the nyght was passed in the whyche Adramayne had betrayed Pacolet and ledde away the fayre Clerymonde, through the cyte of Acquytayne was made great lamentacyons for the losse of the lady, for the gardes of the palays that myssed her made so great lamentacyons and soo great noyse in the mornynge that throughe oute all the cyte was the tydynges. (p. 190)[4]

The main clause (beginning 'through the cyte') is flanked on either side by subclauses. The first subclause ('After . . . Clerymonde') contains another subclause ('in the which . . .') and also a change of tense from past to pluperfect ('*had* betrayed') to indicate a chronological retroversion; the second explanatory subclause ('for the gardes . . .') contains both a relative clause ('that myssed her') and a clause of result, signalled by the correlatives *soo* and *that*.

If this sentence marks out one end of the spectrum of possibilities for Middle English prose, the extract from the beginning of Malory's *Tale of Balin* marks out another extreme. Malory avoids syntactical complexity. All verbs are in the past tense, and no order is imposed on the actions other than the natural one of chronology. If clauses are linked, the co-ordinating conjunction *and* is preferred to a subordinating conjunction, and, where subordination occurs, the clausal relationships are *temporal* rather than *logical* (e.g. *So whan . . . and whan*). Malory's style most closely resembles that of contemporary prose chronicles,[5] which also leave events to speak for themselves. Significantly, Malory only interrupts the story to state that Arthur's castle was 'called Camelot in tho dayes', an intervention that reveals his belief in the historicity of his story. As Malory later notes, 'the cite of Camelot . . . ys in Englysch called Wynchester' (92.1–2); and

Winchester being its current name, Malory cannot responsibly call it Camelot without adding that this is its historical name. By the same token, characters, being historically real, must have names, and Malory makes it his business to give identities to people who are anonymous in the Old French. For example, 'Sir Peryn de Mounte Belyarde' and 'Garnysche of the Mount' from the *Tale of Balin* are both nameless characters in Malory's source, the *Suite du Merlin*;[6] and in the passage above Malory specifies the name of the damsel's lady as 'Lady Lyle of Avilion', where the Old French merely says that the lady is *from* the Isle of Avalon. Malory seemingly wanted the historical realism of a proper name.

Malory's paratactic style is for the most part well suited to his matter, but his limitations are exposed in passages that demand a more complex calibration of events or propositions. The *Tale of Torre and Pellinor* in the *Suite du Merlin* is a fine example of interlace: three story lines, tracing the adventures of three different knights, Gawain, Torre, and Pellinor, are interwoven, the narrative cutting back and forth between them with the aid of elaborate instructions, such as: 'But now the story is silent about them and returns to King Pellinor' (p. 238). Clearly, then, we are asked to imagine the adventures of the three knights as unfolding simultaneously. Although the same must be true for Malory, his expression often suggests otherwise. For example:

AND THUS ENDITH THE ADVENTURE OF SIR GAWAYNE THAT HE DUD AT THE MARIAGE OF ARTHURE.
    Whan sir Torre was redy he mounted uppon horsebacke and rode afftir the knyght with the brachett. (109.4–7)

AND HERE ENDITH THE QUESTE OF SIR TORRE, KYNGE PELLYNORS SON.
    Than Kyng Pellynore armed hym and mownted upon hys horse . . . (114.8–10)

The authorial instructions have been reduced to a minimum, and from what remains it seems that Sir Torre rides out after Gawain has come back, and that Pellinor has been waiting for Torre's return before departing himself. Malory relies, as always, on his favourite adverbs *when* and *then* and on the simple past tense, but what he really needed was a pluperfect combined with a retroverse adverb ('Some time earlier, Torre had got ready . . .'). Malory struggles with complexities of this kind: he gives us one thing after another—

'and another, and another, and still another', as Mark Twain complained.[7]

When it comes to expressing logical relationships, Malory can also be muddled. A symptom of this weakness is his lack of discrimination between analytical connectives (e.g. *for, therefore*) and enumerative ones (e.g. *and*). Take, for example, the following non-sequiturs in *Balin*:

And the name of thys knight was called Balyne, and by good meanys of the barownes he was delyverde oute of preson, *for* he was a good man named of his body, *and* he was borne in Northeumbirlonde. *And so* he wente pryvaly into the courte . . . (62.36–63.3)

'A, fayre damesell', seyde Balyn, 'worthynes and good tacchis and also good dedis is nat only in araymente, but manhode and worship ys hyd within a mannes person; and many a worshipful knyght ys not knowyn unto all peple. *And therefore* worship and hardynesse ys nat in araymente.' (63.22–7)

In the first example, *for* takes us into an explanatory subclause, but, despite the expressed link with the next clause ('*and* he was borne in Northeumbirelonde'), this additional information is obviously *not* causally related to Balin's release. We also discover from this passage, if we have not done so already, that the force of the adverb *so* is typically temporal in Malory. In the second example, the writing is only superficially logical. The position that a man's valour is not dependent on his outward appearance is first developed (hence many an honourable knight is not recognized as such), but then, suddenly, this *entailment* is presented as *proof* of the initial position (*And therefore*), as if it were the major premise in a syllogism. Actually, the strength of the argument is emotional rather than logical: discursive complexity in Malory is always a sign that he strongly feels what he writes.

Fortunately, deductive reasoning is not in great demand in romance, where the meaning of events is often mysterious, and causes and consequences are withheld from the reader until the adventure is over. In epic, by contrast, actions are weighted with advance significance. Whereas the epic hero fights, say, for the fatherland (and carries the burden of knowing it), the romance hero fights to discover why he is fighting. It follows that in romance the 'wherefore' and 'therefore' are not indicated by the author but must be discovered by the knight (and the reader). In this context, Malory's weaknesses are far from debilitating; indeed, they can paradoxically become sources of strength. Two cases will illustrate my point. My first example is from the end of the above-cited extract:

And whan she com byfore kynge Arthur she tolde fro whens she com, and how sche was sente on message unto hym for thys causis. *Than* she lette hir mantel falle that was rychely furred, *and than* was she gurde with a noble swerde, wherof the kynge had mervayle . . .

Strict logicians would call this careless writing. The objection to Malory's *and than*, which implies temporal succession, is that the damsel was already girt with the sword *before* she let her mantle drop. Baines, in his 1962 translation, amended the sentence to 'she drew aside her gown and revealed a handsome sword; and the *Suite* lets the damsel disclose: '*Roi, veschi une espee . . .*' ('King, see here a sword . . .', p. 4). But the reason why few readers would object to Malory's version is that the impact of the revelation, its 'marvellous-ness', depends precisely on the unspecified relationship between the two co-ordinated clauses: first we see a lady in a rich fur coat *and then* we see a lady girt with a sword. By not resolving the relation-ship between these two propositions, Malory comes closer than the French writer (and much closer than Baines) to *showing* the marvel—which would evaporate in the attempt to integrate the two clauses, but survives intact in the illogical succession that Malory has given us.

These illogical successions recur at the level of plot episodes, as my second example illustrates. The damsel sent by the Lady Lisle of Avilion challenges the courtiers to draw the sword from its sheath, but warns that the successful candidate must be strong, virtuous, and nobly born (the last condition is unique to Malory). Although Arthur and his knights fail, Balin feels confident and persuades the damsel to give him a chance. When he succeeds, the damsel pleads with him to return the sword, warning him that 'ye shall sle with that swerde the beste frende that ye have and the man that ye moste love in the worlde, and that swerde shall be youre destruction' (64.9–11). Balin, however, keeps the sword, saying he will 'take the aventure' that God will ordain for him, whereupon the damsel repeats her prophecy and leaves. After a second visitor arrives at court, Merlin tells us what all this means:

'Now shall I sey you', seyde Merlion; 'thys same damesell that here stondith, that broughte the swerde unto youre courte, I shall tell you the cause of hir commynge. She ys the falsist damesell that lyveth—she shall not sey nay!' (67. 21–5)

Merlin explains that the damsel had a lover who was killed by her brother in combat. Plotting revenge, she went to the Lady Lisle of Avilion, whose evil plan is that the damsel should carry a sword to Arthur's court; a knight fulfilled with prowess will draw it and 'with that swerde he scholde sle [her] brothir' (68.4).

It is difficult to see how Balin's adventure of the sword and Merlin's subsequent 'explanation' of it fit together. If the whole point of the damsel's mission is to entrust the sword to a brave knight who can kill her brother, then why does she do her utmost to persuade Balin to hand the sword back? The sword is inscribed in two contradictory narratives: on the one hand, it is an instrument of revenge, foisted on an unsuspecting knight by 'the falsist damesell that lyveth'; on the other hand, the sword is the cause of tragic disaster, which a compassionate damsel naturally tries to prevent. In the *Suite*, it is just about possible to reconcile these two narratives. Here the *damoisele* is indeed keen to rid herself of the sword, offering it as a trophy to any knight who is successful. Admittedly, she then asks Balin to give the sword back but she is content when he refuses: 'then so be it, since it pleases you' (p. 187). Mission accomplished. In Malory, however, the damsel's behaviour is fatally at odds with her role as evil avenger. She never does offer the sword as a prize and appears genuinely distressed by Balin's success: 'I am passynge hevy for youre sake' (64.17). To make matters worse, Malory then has her *leave* in evident despair that her mission has failed: 'So with that departed the damesell and grete sorowe she made' (64.20). Unfortunately, her presence at Arthur's court is required later, when Merlin presides over her unmasking. The upshot of these changes is that the adventure of the damsel remains entirely impervious to Merlin's attempt to 'explain' it; we do not, of course, disbelieve him, but can now only accept his words as another 'marvel'. Taken individually, the damsel's behaviour and Merlin's explanation make sense; in combination, they do not. The virtue of the resulting conflict, however, is that the first 'marvel' is not diminished but deepened by Merlin's revelation, which now constitutes a second 'marvel'; and both marvels are all the greater for not adding up.

The meaning of adventure

The lack of internal coherence should be seen in the context of Malory's general tendency to remove explanations and thereby to increase the 'distance' separating the events from the knight and the reader who confront them.[8] The advantage of a narrative whose incidents are not internally consistent is that it persuades us more powerfully of the influence of external forces of causation (destiny, fate, grace). Malory repeatedly alludes to these forces, and thinks of *aventure* as the means by which the knight can discover the relationship between these external forces of causation and the forces that lie under his own control. To follow Malory's thinking it is necessary to insist on the primary sense of *aventure* as a chance event, which invites the knight to pursue it by virtue of its very remoteness from him. The later senses of adventure as a 'daring feat' or 'an exciting or strange incident' (see *OED* s.v. *adventure*, sb. 5 and 6) lie behind the misleading view that adventures—and by extension romance—must contain prodigious deeds of prowess or fantastical occurrences. This view mistakes the accidental properties of adventure for its essential ones. Romance adventures often demand passive endurance (in Malory's telling words, they must be *abided* as well as *taken*), and they need not take fantastical forms; indeed, Malory worked steadily to reduce the supernatural element in his sources.

To get to the heart of adventure, let us consider an example of it from Malory's *Tale of Balin*. Arthur, who is unwell, pitches his tent in a meadow:

and there he leyde him downe on a paylet to slepe; but he myght have no reste. Ryght so he herde a grete noyse of an horse, and therewith the kynge loked oute at the porche dore of the pavilion and saw a knyght commynge even by hym makynge grete dole.

'Abyde, fayre sir,' seyde Arthure, 'and telle me wherefore thou makyst this sorrow.'

'Ye may litill amende me,' seyde the knight, and so passed forth to the Castell of Meliot.

And anon aftir that com Balyne. And whan he saw kyng Arthur he alyght of hys horse, and com to the kynge on foote and salewed hym.

'Be my hede,' seyde Arthure, 'ye be wellcom. Sir, right now com rydynge thys way a knyght makynge grete mone, and for what cause I can nat telle. Wherfore I wolde desire of you, of your curtesy and of your jantilnesse, to fecche agayne that knight other by force other by his good wylle.' (79.10–28)

Balin follows the knight, whom he finds accompanying a damsel at the edge of a forest. The knight reluctantly agrees to return with Balin, on condition that Balin will guarantee his safety. On the way back, however, the knight is struck dead by an invisible knight named Garlan. Balin, having failed to give the knight safe-conduct, swears to take up his mission. The dying man instructs him to 'ryde to the damesell and folow the queste that I was in as she woll lede you, and revenge my deth when ye may' (80.14–16).

The beginning of this adventure is characterized by an almost dream-like quality. An unknown knight rides past, lamenting, while Arthur lies on his sickbed. In the French source Arthur leaves his bed and rushes out of his tent to see what is up (p. 203); in Malory the scene is focalized, more effectively, from within the pavilion. This dream-like quality is enhanced by the looseness of the link between the passing knight and the immediate context of Arthur's convalescence: what does this knight have to do with Arthur? The human desire for relevance, which prompts Arthur to ask if he can be of any use to the stranger, is only further excited by the knight's frustrating answer: 'you can't help'.

What this shows is that the essence of adventure is not its fantastical nature but rather the fact that it falls outside the normal continuity of life (a visit to Arthur from his physician would *not* be an adventure, even if the latter were a dwarf). At the same time, however, the apparently unmotivated and external accident must make contact with a knight's inner destiny (if a giant passed by without any meaningful impingement, this would not be an adventure either). To quote the philosopher Georg Simmel:

by adventure we always mean a third something, neither the sheer abrupt event whose meaning—a mere given—simply remains outside us, nor the consistent sequence of life in which every element supplements every other toward an inclusively integrated meaning. The adventure is no mere hodge-podge of these two, but rather that incomparable experience which can be interpreted only as a particular encompassing of the accidentally external by the internally necessary.[9]

To provide that incomparable experience, Balin comes in. Being merely a second passer-by, his relationship to the unknown knight is even more tangential than Arthur's, but it is nevertheless *his* adventure, not Arthur's, in the sense that he is to discover the connection between external accident and individual destiny. It has been prophesied that Balin is to strike the 'dolorous stroke', and he will later do so in self-defence when King Pellam tries to kill him for murdering Garlan, the king's brother. And, of course, Garlan *is* the invisible knight, whom Balin has sworn to kill as a result of this present adventure. Pure chance has been reconfigured as destiny: by pursuing adventure the knight has encompassed the 'accidentally external' within the 'internally necessary'.

Chance and destiny

I would like to take a closer look at this interplay between chance and destiny by following it to its chilling conclusion. Having struck the 'dolorous stroke', Balin wanders on only to fulfil the inexorable prophecy that he will kill the man he loves most. The final denouement begins as follows:

And within thre dayes he cam by a crosse; and theron were letters of gold wryten that said: 'it is not for no knight alone to ryde toward this castel'. Thenne sawe he an old hore gentylman coming toward hym that sayd, 'Balyn le Saveage, thow passyst thy bandes to come this waye, therfor torne ageyne and it will availle the,' and he vanysshed awey anone.

And soo he herd an horne blowe as it has ben the dethe of a best. 'That blast,' said Balyn, 'is blowen for me, for I am the pryse [prey], and yet am I not dede.'

Balin is welcomed by the inhabitants of the castle, but, in accordance with the custom of the castle, he must fight a knight on a nearby island. Balin submits:

'I wolde be fayne ther my dethe shold be.'

'Syr,' sayd *a knyght* to Balyn, 'methynketh your sheld is not good; I wille lene yow a byggar, therof I pray yow.'

Wearing a different shield, he crosses to the island and fights an unknown knight. Both are fatally wounded. As he lies dying, Balin speaks:

'What knyghte arte thow? For or [before] now I found never no knight that matched me.' 'My name is,' sayde he, 'Balan, broder unto the good knight Balyn.'

'Alas!' sayd Balyn, 'that ever I sholde see this day,' and therwith he felle backward in a swoune. (88.3–90.4)

Outside fiction, Malory's imaginary universe, where strangers know your name and your destiny, resembles the mental world of the paranoid. Although it is normal to relate what we see and experience to our own concerns, in the case of the paranoid this egoistic striving for unification has gone into overdrive, so that the most irrelevant and extraneous incidents are drawn powerfully into the ego's territory. (The paranoid thinks that words engraved on a tombstone, or uttered by a complete stranger, are crucial messages meant for *him*.) Inside fiction, we first encounter this universe in the romances of Chrétien de Troyes, except of course that this hyper-rational mode of experiencing life is utterly vindicated by the postulates of the genre. The passage from the *Tale of Balin* makes the point perfectly. The sign that Balin meets along the way is indeed a warning directed specifically at him. The French source emphasizes this by specifying that the cross is 'brand new' (p. 217). Malory does not connect the cross to Balin's particular situation; the objects are, in Jill Mann's formulation, 'distanced' from him, just as we are distanced from Balin's reasons for continuing on the quest. True, Malory hints once or twice at Balin's desire to traverse the course of his destiny ('I wolde be fayn ther my deth scholde be') but these are moments when the complicity of character and plot is laid bare, not invitations to psychologize. Balin's death-drive cannot be separated from that of the narrative. In the same way, Balan's operatic self-identification—'My name is,' sayde he, 'Balan, *broder unto the good knight Balyn*' (italics mine)—is powerfully voiced over by the narrative demand that the irony of fate must be exposed for the benefit of the brothers and the reader. If we interpret such utterances in terms of psychological realism, we will be rewarded much more poorly than if we hear in them the duet of character and plot, or, to return to the theme of adventure, of an individual and his fate.

The most ominous hint that Balin's own will and that of destiny are about to join forces is his response to the sounding of the horn: 'That blast', said Balyn, 'is blowen for me, for I am the pryse, and yet am I not dede.' This 'paranoid' realization is much more powerful in Malory than in the French, where the hero shrugs it off with a smile, secure in the knowledge that he is, surely, not captured: 'When he heard it, he began to smile and said to himself, "What is it? Do they who signal the capture think that I have been captured?"' (p. 218). By contrast, Balin's formulation 'and yet am I not dede' does not just fend off the awful thought that the horn-blast signifies his death (yet construed as an adversative adverb), but also embraces it, by intimating that death is only a matter of time (yet construed as a temporal adverb). As Balin's response to the sound of the horn indicates, Malory's distancing of narrative incidents goes hand in hand with the hero's close identification with them; 'adventure' is therefore characterized neither by the knight's distance from an event nor by its bearing on the knight's being, but rather by what Simmel called an 'experiential tension', which seeks relief in the belief that the accidental and the destined are ultimately united in some transcendent design. Malory's handling of the anonymous knight who suggests the change of shields contributes to this tension. From one perspective, this man is central in the unravelling of Balin's destiny, since Balan could not have failed to recognize his brother if he had worn his own shield. The knight's participation in Balin's destiny is highlighted by Balin's exclamation (unique to Malory): 'Allas', saide Balyn, 'all that made an unhappy knyght in the castel, for he caused me to leve myn own shelde to our bothes destruction' (90.15–17). However, the 'unhappy' knight's involvement in Balin's destiny does not alter the fundamental haphazardness of his intervention (Malory's unhappy means 'unlucky'). The combination of necessity and gratuitousness is reminiscent of the stunning moment in the final book when Arthur's and Mordred's armies face each other in a tense stand-off. Both sides have agreed to a truce but both are poised to attack should any knight take up his sword. Then an adder bites:

Ryght so cam oute an addir of a lytyll hethe-buysshe, and hit stange a knyght in the foote. And so whan the knyght felte hym so stonge, he loked downe and saw the adder; and anone he drew hys swerde to sle the addir, and thought none othir harme. And whan the oste on bothe partyes saw that swerde drawyn, than they blewe beamys, trumpettis, and hornys, and shouted grymly, and so bothe ostis dressed hem togedyrs. And kynge Arthur toke hys horse and seyde, '*Alas, this unhappy day!*' and so rode to hys party, and sir Mordred in lyke wyse. (1235.20–9; italics mine)

The caprices of chance, the bite of an adder, the offer of a shield, turn out to be acts of destiny. Similarly, a couple of 'nobodies' (a knight stung in the foot, an 'unhappy' knight whom Balin meets *en passant*) are revealed to be fatal accomplices. Yet, while registering their importance, Malory boldly eliminated all hints of their personality. In the *Suite*, the knight who offers Balin a shield is a central character: he is Balin's host, the seneschal of the castle (p. 218); similarly, the *Stanzaic Morte Arthur* (Malory's source for the adder episode) makes it clear that the knight who reaches for his sword belongs to Mordred's party (line 3346). Since, as we have seen, Malory's usual habit was to identify anonymous characters, his de-specification of them at this point is all the more remarkable. In both cases, they become faceless strangers ('a knyght'), though, also in both cases, their *marginalization* is countered in Arthur's and Balin's exclamations ('Alas! . . .') by a recognition of their *centrality* in the hero's fatal destiny. What Malory does, then, is to make the narrative pull in two opposite directions, and, by sustaining the contradiction, to suggest that 'external accident' and 'internal necessity' are in some mysterious way aspects of one and the same thing.

Conclusion

We must conclude by setting these remarks about Malory's vision of adventure in the context of his self-understanding as the chronicler of Arthur's reign, for if we are persuaded by the argument that Malory's sense of adventure led him to the heart of romance, we might well wonder how he got there when he thought he was writing history. The answer lies in Malory's typically medieval conception of history as a process which, though it has an integrity of its own, also participates in a larger providential design. This conception is inscribed in the very organization of the *Morte*. Individual knights (Balin, Lancelot, Tristram, and so on) are given their own stories, and to some extent these are self-contained units with their own 'beginning' and 'end'. Thus Malory begins the *Tale of Balin* with a historical *incipit*—'After the deth of Uther regned Arthure' (61.1)—just as he concludes it with an *explicit* ('THUS ENDITH THE TALE OF BALYN AND BALAN', 92.16). But it would be most misleading to regard Balin's 'history' as an independent narrative, or to suggest, as Vinaver did, that Malory did all he could to isolate it. First, the historical *incipits* in Malory function partly to insert the histories of individual knights into Arthur's biography. More importantly, Malory carefully inter-linked Balin's fate with that of Arthur. Thus Malory seized on the numerical coincidence that Arthur, in the *Tale of Merlin*, wages wars on *eleven* kings, and that Balin later helps to defeat *twelve* kings: King Rions plus the *eleven* kings said to be allied to him (54.24–5). This coincidence led Malory to identify Arthur's opponents with those defeated by Balin, and to cement the connection with an early prophecy (by Merlin) that two ill-starred brothers will deliver Arthur from his enemies:

'For thes eleven kyngis shall dye all in one day by the grete myght and prouesse of armys of two valyaunte knyghtes,'—as hit telleth aftir. 'Hir names ben Balyne le Saveage and Balan, hys brothir . . .' (40.3–7)

Thus Balin, as well as being a hero, or anti-hero, of his own life, also plays a crucial part in the overarching history of Arthur. Merlin's prophecy is one of many passages that insist on this point and so disprove the hypothesis that Malory conceived of the *Tale of Balin* as an independent work.

The numerous prophecies contained within the *Tale of Balin* likewise open Balin's history out onto later histories, which fulfil challenges earlier faced by Balin. The first such prophecy is made by Merlin after Balin has killed Launceor, and Launceor's lady has committed suicide. Merlin marks the place with a tombstone:

'Here shall be,' seyde Merlion, 'in this same place the grettist bateyle betwyxte two knyghtes that ever was ever or ever shall be, and the trewyst lovers, and yette none of hem shall slee other.' (72.5–8)

The prophecy looks forward to the moment (in the Book of Sir Tristram) when Tristram and Lancelot will fight in circumstances at once different and similar: in the very same place where two true lovers (Launceor and his lady) are slain the two truest lovers will fight but live. Balin's history is thus at once continued and renewed by the later history of Tristram. The last such prophecy, fulfilled during the

Siege of Benwick, is that the sword used by Balin to kill Balan will be used by Lancelot to similar effect: 'And Launcelot with thys swerde shall sle the man in the worlde that he lovith beste: that shall be sir Gawayne' (91.24–5). In this instance, too, the history of Lancelot's fateful wounding of Gawain reproduces the traces of an earlier history.

In Malory's view, then, history has a purpose of its own, but, although events have their own unstoppable momentum, adventures are opportunities when the immanent will of individuals can make contact with the will of history itself. That this is true for Balin and his own history (which definitely has a will of its own) I hope to have shown; it remains for me to note that it is also true for Balin's involvement in the larger history of Arthur's reign. This involvement partakes of the same paradoxical combination of contingency and necessity, extraneousness and centrality that marks the adventure. Balin's defeat of King Rions is necessary because it has been prophesied, and central to Arthur's history because it secures Arthur's initially precarious rule; at the same time, however, Balin's entanglement in Arthurian history is curiously contingent and peripheral, for Balin does not defeat Rions to further Arthur's political interests but in order to regain royal favour after he has beheaded the Lady of the Lake with his cursed sword. Balin's historical importance thus comes about precisely *by adventure*, as Balin's wish to regain Arthur's favour is 'accidentally' subjoined to the historical necessity of King Arthur's rise and fall.

The great turning-points in Arthurian history (Arthur's pulling of the sword from the stone, Balin's capture of Arthur's political enemies, a knight's stabbing of the adder) are governed by the law of unintended consequences. And since providential history executes its will by taking advantage of our immanent will, the 'distance' that separates the knight from his actions should be seen as a measure of Malory's far-reaching historicism. I am led to a similar conclusion concerning Malory's place in literary history. His creation of a 'narrative of distance'—an achievement to which the *Morte Darthur* owes its canonical status as a romance—is perhaps in the final analysis the 'happy' by-product of his will to write history. He produced one of our finest romances by adventure.

Notes

1. *The Works of Sir Thomas Malory*, ed. Eugène Vinaver, rev. Peter Field, 3 vols. (Oxford: Oxford University Press, 1990). All subsequent references to Malory are to this edition.
2. Malory's main sources are the French Vulgate Cycle, the post-Vulgate *Roman du Graal*, the *Prose Tristan*, and the English stanzaic and alliterative versions of the *Morte D'Arthur*.
3. See David Burnley, 'Curial Prose', *Speculum*, 61 (1986), 593–614.
4. *Valentine and Orson*, ed. Arthur Dickson, EETS o.s. 204 (London, 1937).
5. See Field, *Romance and Chronicle*.
6. I cite the *Suite* from the edition by M. D. Legge, *Le Roman de Balain* (Manchester: Manchester University Press, 1942) whenever the original wording matters; where not, I cite the translation by Martha Asher, 'The Post-Vulgate, part I: *The Merlin Continuation*' in *The Old French Arthurian and Post-Vulgate in Translation*, ed. Norris Lacy (New York: Garland Publishing, 1996), vol. iv, pp. 163–277.
7. Mark Twain, *A Connecticut Yankee at King Arthur's Court*, ed. Justin Kaplan (Harmondsworth: Penguin, 1986), p. 140.
8. See Mann, 'Taking the Adventure'.
9. 'The Adventure', in *Georg Simmel, 1858–1918*, ed. Kurt H. Wolff (New York: Free Press, 1950), pp. 243–66.

References and suggested reading

Archibald, Elizabeth, and A. S. G. Edwards, eds. *A Companion to Malory*. Arthurian Studies 37. Cambridge: D. S. Brewer, 1996. A reliable introduction, with essays devoted to the eight books of Malory's *Morte* and to wider issues (Malory's life records, sources, prose style, critical issues, and his literary afterlife).

Bennett, J. A. W., ed. *Essays on Malory*. Oxford: Clarendon Press, 1963. A useful collection of essays on Malory, including one by C. S. Lewis, on Malory's temperament, and by D. S. Brewer, on the links between the individual books and the unifying story of Arthur's life.

Cooper, Helen. 'Romance after 1400'. In David Wallace, ed., *The Cambridge History of Medieval English Literature*. Cambridge: Cambridge University Press, 1999, pp. 241–52. Cooper offers an excellent overview of romance at the end of the medieval period.

Dover, Carol, ed. *A Companion to the Lancelot–Grail Cycle*. Arthurian Studies 54. Cambridge: D. S. Brewer, 2003. A guide through the maze of Arthurian prose cycles, with essays by Fanni Bogdanow on the *Suite du Merlin* and Helen Cooper on Middle English versions, including Malory's.

Edwards, Elizabeth. *The Genesis of Narrative in Malory*. Arthurian Studies 43. Cambridge: D. S. Brewer, 2001. Contains an interesting discussion of episodic inconsistencies in Malory.

Field, Peter. *Romance and Chronicle: A Study of Malory's Prose Style*. Bloomington: Indiana University Press, 1971. The best study of Malory's distinctive prose style. It reveals, amongst other things, the connections between Malory's style and that of contemporary prose chronicles.

Lambert, Mark. *Style and Vision in Le Morte D'Arthur*. New Haven: Yale University Press, 1975. An illuminating stylistic study of the *Morte Darthur*, good both on verbal detail and on Malory's broader emphases.

Mann, Jill. ' "Taking the Adventure": Malory and the *Suite du Merlin*'. In T. Takamiya and D. S. Brewer, eds., *Aspects of Malory*. Cambridge: D. S. Brewer, 1981, pp. 71–92. An exemplary close reading of Malory's *Tale of Balin*, which shows Malory's tendency to distance events from the knight and the reader. Her later book, *The Narrative of Distance: The Distance of Narrative in Malory's Morte Darthur*, William Matthews Lectures (London, 1991), extends this argument to the *Morte* as a whole.

Parins, Marylyn, ed. *Sir Thomas Malory: The Critical Heritage*. London: Routledge, 1995. This edition brings together earlier critical responses to Malory, from the sixteenth century up to the twentieth.

John Stevens. *Medieval Romance: Themes and Approaches*. London: Hutchinson, 1973. An exploration of the nature of romance, and of the essential and non-essential characteristics of the genre.

24

Scottish literature

Nicola Royan

Introduction

In a collection organized primarily by genre, the intrusion of a geo-political topic requires some explanation. It cannot be claimed that medieval Scottish literature is always instantly distinguishable by language, style, or indeed attitude from that written in England, and, while there are some genres that are more Scottish than English, an overall generic distinction cannot be imposed. Given these facts, then, it is legitimate to ask why Scottish literature should be treated separately in a collection of essays such as this. There are perhaps two justifications. First, notwithstanding the absence of infallible and instant markers noted above, it is possible to differentiate a Scottish tradition from the English one. Particular Scottish political, linguistic, and cultural inflections are evident in a broad range of writing; such inflections are not necessarily dependent on English versions of similar material, but draw on a range of European models and texts. Secondly, an examination of medieval Scottish literature can enable a critique of metropolitan assumptions about the development of literature in English. For instance, rhymed verse and alliterative verse exist together later in Scotland than in England; Scots romances appear in verse far more than in prose, even into the sixteenth century. The English pattern of change is not the only one and, at the very least, medieval Scots literature is proof that the path from Chaucer to Shakespeare is not as straight as it sometimes appears from more recent critical perspectives.

Definitions

This chapter is concerned primarily with material written in Older Scots, a variety of English. This excludes material written in the other languages of the medieval Scottish kingdom, such as Latin and French, the prestige languages of court and learning, and Gaelic and Old Norse, the languages of the Western and Northern Isles. Despite the exclusive focus of this essay, the multilingual context of Older Scots material is important: like their English contemporaries, most Scottish poets would be fluent in at least one other language, usually Latin or French, and in consequence, draw their influences from Continental Europe as well as their locality.

Older Scots was distinct from other varieties of Middle English, to the extent that it can be considered as a language, rather than as a dialect. A case can be made for this designation on linguistic grounds, since it is possible to distinguish between Older Scots and Northern Middle English, for instance, in the use of *is, ar* for *es, er*, or the use of *gif* for 'if'.[1] However, the most compelling reasons are sociolinguistic and political. Older Scots was certainly used across all registers and uses, including legal documentation and official correspondence. A letter survives from the Earl of Douglas to Henry IV; the Acts of Parliament appear in Scots from 1424. This range fits with a common model of a language, where it is used for all functions, from the official to the informal; this is certainly true of Older Scots.

Although Older Scots is usually defined as lasting from 1350 to 1700, this essay concentrates on a shorter period, between 1375 and 1513: 1375 is an internal date of John Barbour's romance epic, *The Bruce*; 1513 saw the completion of Gavin Douglas's translation of the Roman epic the *Aeneid* into Scots. During that period some of the greatest poets of medieval Scotland were working, including James I (1396–1437), Robert Henryson (*c.*1460–1505), William Dunbar (?1460–?1513), and of course Barbour (*c.*1320–95) and Douglas (*c.*1474–1522). There are also works by lesser known and anonymous poets, such as Richard Holland's *Buke of the Howlat* (*c.*1450) which contribute to our understanding of the whole. However, like all attempts to put clear dates on cultural phenomena, these boundaries stress discontinuity, whereas literary patterns and influence reach across political and temporal borders. Our understanding of Barbour is limited because we have no extended writing in Scots prior to *The Bruce*; many of the Scots poets of the later sixteenth century foreground their inheritance from previous poets, and there is plenty of evidence to suggest that their medieval predecessors were read widely throughout the sixteenth century.

Nevertheless, while accepting the caveats above, these dates make sense. Politically, between 1375 and 1513, the realm was relatively stable. Despite four minorities and a series of unfortunate kingly ends (including two murders and a cannon-related accident), the Stewart monarchy was unchallenged, with a clear and accepted line of succession. During the later fifteenth century, the Northern Isles and the Western Isles became incorporated into the realm and, although there were various skirmishes between the Scots and the English along the Border, the English monarchs, under pressure from rebellions within, did not attempt the type of invasions practised by Edward I and Edward III. The Scots benefited from English instability, and from their continued political ties with France, but such security did not last. The year 1513 also saw Flodden, a crushing defeat resulting in the death of the Scots king, James IV. James had undertaken the campaign in response to the English invasion of France; his death plunged his realm into another minority.

Among the features that distinguish James V's minority from that of his predecessors are two crucial cultural changes, arriving directly from Europe: first, the arrival of humanism, demonstrated by Douglas's translation of the *Aeneid*, and secondly, the beginnings of the Reformation, first on the Continent, but then gradually making its presence felt in Scotland. Both of these would have dramatic effects on the literature written in Scotland. As a result, despite the continued literary tradition, it makes sense to conclude this discussion at 1513.

Cultural confidence

The comparative political stability of the fifteenth century seems to have contributed to a flowering of Older Scots literature. Compared to what survives of English literature of the same period, it is a small collection. It is, nevertheless, also diverse: there are dream visions, allegories, fabliaux, didactic poetry, both political and spiritual, historiography, and lyrics. Barbour's text becomes a model for Hary's *Wallace*, the other indigenous romance; there are also several Arthurian and Alexander romances, as well as one stemming from the Charlemagne tradition. The poets and writers too seem to have had diverse circumstances. Some are known to be writers of the royal court, such as Barbour, James I, Douglas, and Dunbar: such poets are not as common as might be expected.[2] Others were attached to noble households, or else received patronage from them, such as Hary, whose *Wallace* was patronized by two Border lairds. Still others seem to have had no clear attachment: of these, Henryson is a distinguished example, since his poems deliberately anonymize their authorizing patrons.

In contrast to some of their more recent successors, few Older Scots poets show any sign of 'linguistic or cultural cringe': neither Henryson nor Dunbar, for instance, choose their register or other linguistic variants in order to assert their national identity. Indeed, Dunbar refers to his language as *Inglis* and presents himself as sharing Chaucer's language as well as his literary inheritance. 'Scots' begins to be deployed as the term for the language at the very end of the fifteenth century, codifying a confidence in the language and insisting on its equality with English. The best-known early usage, in Douglas's *Prologue* to the *Eneados*, occurs in a discussion about the difficulties of translating from Latin, and the anxiety that is expressed is directed at least as much towards the pressures of translation as it is towards potential inequalities between English and Scots. If any inferiority regarding language is to be traced, moreover, it is soon replaced by superiority in reading, for Douglas condemns both Chaucer and Caxton for their celebration of Dido, in flat contrast to Virgil's representation. A key characteristic of Older Scots literature, therefore, is self-assurance; how this assurance is expressed is the central theme of the rest of this essay.

The Scots and literary tradition

At least part of that assurance has its roots in a familiarity with the trends of western European culture. Gavin Douglas in particular shows off his knowledge in *The Palice of Honoure*. The list below is illustrative of the range of writers, especially poets, whom Douglas sees as intrinsic to the Court of the Muses:

The suddand sycht of that fyrme Court foresaid	*sight/steadfast*
Recomfort weil my hew tofore wes faid.	*restored my colour that before had faded*
Amyd my brest the joyus heit redoundyt	*heat/flowed back*
Behaldand quhow the lusty Musys raid,	*beholding/how/rode*
And al thair Court, quhilk wes so blyith and glaid,	*which*
Quhois merynes all hevynes confoundyt.	*whose merriness/heaviness*
Thair saw I, weil in poetry ygroundyt,	*well trained*
The gret Homere, quhilk in Grew langage said	*who in Greek*
Maist eloquently, in quham all wyt aboundyt.	*most/intellect*

Thare wes the gret Latyn Virgillyus,	
The famus fathir poet Ovidius,	
Ditis, Daris, and eik the trew Lucane.	*also the true*
Thare wes Plautus, Pogius and Parsius.	*Poggio Bracciolini*
Thare wes Terens, Donat, and Servius,	
Francys Petrark, Flakcus Valeriane.	*Valerius Flaccus*
Thare wes Ysop, Caton and Alane.	*Aesop, Cato and Allan [of Lille]*
Thare wes Galterus and Boetius.	*Walter [of Châtillon]*
Thare wes also the greit Quintilliane.	

Thare was the satyr poete, Juvinale.	*satirical*
Thare was the mixt and subtell Marciale.	*varied and subtle*
Of Thebes bruyt thare wes the poete Stace.	*fame/Statius*
Thare wes Faustus and Laurence of the vale,	*Fausto Andrelini/Lorenzo Valla*
Pomponeus quhais fame of lait, sans fale,	*Guilio Pomponio Leto/late*
Is blawin wyd throw every realme and place.	*blown wide*
Thare wes the morale wyse poete Orace,	
With mony other clerkis of gret avayle.	*weight*
Thare wes Brunell, Claudyus and Bocace.	*Leonardo Bruni*

Sa gret a pres of pepill drew us nere	*press of people*
The hunder part thare namys is not here.	*hundredth*

Yit thare I saw of Brutus Albion	*from Brutus' Albion*
Goffryd Chaucere, as *A per se*, sance pere	*without equal*
In his wulgare, and morell John Gowere.	*in his vernacular*
Lydgat the monk raid musand him allone.	*rode alone thinking*
Of this natioun I knew also anone	*at once*
Gret Kennedy and Dunbar, yit undede,	*alive*
And Quyntyne with ane huttok on his hede.	*a hat*

Howbeit I couth declare and weil endyte	*even if I could declaim and write it well*
The bonteis of that court, dewlye to wryt	*bounties/accurately*
Wer ovir prolyxt, transcendyng myne engyne.	*would be/ingenuity*
Twychand the proces of my panefull syte.	*concerning the course/sorrow*
Belive I saw thir lusty Musys quhyte	*lovely white Muses*
With all thair route towart Venus declyne,	*company/divert*
Quhare Cupyd sat with hir in trone divyne	
I standand bundyn in a sory plyte	*I standing bound*
Byddand thair grace or than the dedly pyne.	*awaiting their grace or otherwise*

(lines 889–933)[3]

Douglas is apparently keen to show *how weill in Poetrie ygroundit* he was, but we should not dismiss his account as mere boasting. While he probably only knew Homer by reputation, the others are part of the common intellectual currency of his time, classical (Virgil, Ovid, Juvenal), medieval (Boethius, Allane, Gautier), and humanist (Petrarch, Boccaccio, Pomponius). Douglas initially organizes his list by genre, rather than by chronology or by country. This suggests that Douglas was familiar with more than simply the names of these writers. For example, the line *Plautus, Poggius, and Parsius* not only alliterates, it also brings together three poets with leanings towards satire: Plautus is the Roman playwright, Persius a Roman satirist, and Poggius is Gian Francesco Poggio Bracciolini, an Italian poet of the fifteenth century with a talent for invective. Douglas is also up with the gossip: Pomponius's fame may well have rested on his spectacular funeral in 1498.

Of the poets listed, we can trace direct influence from only a few. These frame the list: Douglas clearly makes use of Ovid and Virgil, Ovid particularly for *The Palice of Honoure*. It is also obvious that Douglas is influenced by the English triad as well as by his Scots contemporaries. In terms of his expressed admiration, Douglas does not here differentiate between his contemporaries and the English poets, nor indeed between those who write *in his wulgare* and those who write in Latin or other languages. This is an inclusive view of the Court of the Muses, from which any aspiring poet might draw courage and indeed inspiration.

Douglas's response to the poetry of Chaucer and the English poetic tradition of the fifteenth century is clear throughout the poem, at almost every level. For instance, Douglas uses some grammatical forms, such as *ygroundit*, which are not typical of Scots and seem instead to be imitations of the Chaucerian (although not necessarily Chaucer's) style. The nine-line verse forms used in *The Palice of Honoure* are highly ornate, with intricate rhyme schemes. These too might be described as Chaucerian, although it is typical of Douglas that he would take forms usually used for short pieces, such as complaint, and use them for a poem as long and as detailed as *The Palice*. Douglas shares his passion for intricate form with Dunbar; it is arguably a feature of Older Scots verse during the sixteenth century.

Although its subject is more easily paralleled in French poetry, *The Palice of Honoure* can also be considered a Chaucerian poem in genre—dream vision—and also in thematic approach. It seems to respond to *The House of Fame*: Douglas further develops a foolish and comic dreamer, the prosaic and sometimes comic guide (Douglas's dreamer has a nymph), and the quest for an abstraction. However, whereas Chaucer's poem seems to undermine the whole concept of fame, Douglas's vision affirms the value of honour. In so doing, Douglas maintains a difficult equilibrium between the standards of his family and the standards of his church. The Dreamer's guide, a nymph, makes a clear distinction between *wardly honoring* (line 1973), given for state, and true honour, a reward for virtue. Such a position is borne out by Honour's attendants, all personifications of virtues, for instance Gud Werkis and Charitie (lines 1789–1827). However, the representatives of true honour present in Honour's court are all successful military leaders, including Robert Bruce. This mismatch is compounded by a discrepancy in the two earliest witnesses for the poem in line 1921: one describes Honour as *omnipotent*, suggesting a religious reading; the other has *armipotent*, suggesting a military reading. The poem does not explicitly resolve the dilemma, but only insists on Honour's value as a guiding principle for life.

Implicitly, the poem seems to suggest that one should adopt the path to Honour most appropriate to one's circumstances. This is borne out by the Dreamer's own quest, where his path to Honour is through poetry. In the first part of his dream, the Dreamer sees various groups of people go past on their way to the Palace, one following Minerva, one following Diana, and one following Venus. None of these is suitable; in fact, the Dreamer composes a short ditty to satirize Venus as she passes, and consequently finds himself bound in front of her, awaiting judgement. It is at this point that the Muses and their train arrive, to find the Dreamer in chains. It is clear that the Dreamer finds himself most comfortable in the Muses' Court, to which he is attached once Calliope has extricated him from Venus's wrath. It is also the train which brings him closest to Honour, even though he cannot look at Honour directly. While martial honour clearly befits a king, as outlined in the dedication to James IV, for a churchman the text suggests that poetry, particularly of an epic nature, is a better, if no less arduous, route to Honour. Certainly the company kept in the Court of the Muses is distinguished.

Despite its boasting, Douglas's poem is not divorced from his Scottish surroundings. Of the Scots poets whom Douglas mentions, one is unidentifiable today: *Quyntyne with ane huttock on his heid* remains obscure, and reminds the modern audience, as such references always do, of how much Older Scots literature has been lost. *Greit Kennedy* is best known as Dunbar's opponent in their poetic contest, *The Flyting*. This piece of work, in which the poets hurl extravagant insults at one another, is often considered very Scottish, and it is true that it seems to have inspired several further similar contests during the sixteenth century. However, what is more significant is the evidence *The Flyting* provides, especially when taken together with *The Palice of Honoure*, of the huge range of styles and forms used by writers in Older Scots. *The Flyting* strengthens its insults by framing them in words of Germanic and Norse derivation and patterning them by heavy alliteration as well as rhyme (for instance, *Revin, raggit ruke, and full of rebauldrie,* | *Skitterand scorpioun, scauld in scurrilitie* ('Raven, ragged rook, and full of obscenity | defecating scorpion, scold in scurrility').[4] While *The Palice of Honoure*, far more akin to another of Dunbar's poems, *Ryght as the stern of day begouth to schyne*, uses a more consistently French and Latinate vocabulary, it still employs alliteration and rhyme to heighten rhetorical effect. Instead of intensifying insults, these technical features shape the list of poets and reinforce the Dreamer's miserable position, *standand bundin in ane sorie plit,* | *Bydand thair grace or than my deidlie pine.* An acute awareness of poetic form and its potential is characteristic of Older Scots poets; this includes a mixing of styles, bringing together alliteration and rhyme, heavy rhythm with chivalric motifs. This is not to imply that Older Scots poets had richer metrical and technical resources, since nearly all the techniques found in Older Scots can also be found in Middle English verse. Rather, it seems that the Scots were prepared to use a greater range than their English contemporaries, perhaps because they continued to use verse for genres where English and indeed French custom had moved to prose, such as romance. Douglas and Dunbar are the most extreme, but they are not so very unusual.

Scottish concerns

A passion for verse forms, however, may not be enough to underpin a medieval Scottish tradition of poetry. In conclusion, therefore, I want to consider two concerns sometimes highlighted as peculiarly Scottish. The first is the most obvious, namely national identity. Are Scottish medieval writers concerned to assert their Scottishness? Some writers are: for instance, chroniclers and historians are naturally concerned to justify their subject. In particular, in the dominant Latin chronicle, Walter Bower's *Scotichronicon* (1449), national identity is fought out in terms of kinglist and sovereignty. The kinglist, stretching back to Fergus Mac Ferthar, who arrived in the West of Scotland in 330 BC, and beyond that to the origin figures of Gathelos, a Greek prince, and Scota, an Egyptian princess, asserts the antiquity of the Scots and denies any claim to overlordship implicit in the Brutus origin myth common in English material. Among the descendants of these mythical figures were all Scottish kings, and a constant line of kings demonstrates continuous Scottish sovereignty, again in opposition to English claims of subordination. Similar assertions of Scottish independence are to be found in most histories and chronicles written in this period, whether in Latin or in Scots: in this, the Scots are no different from the French or the English chroniclers.

Literary self-assertion

Periodically, of course, history interfered with assertions of independence. For the Scots, this happened most significantly during the first War of Independence (1296–1314), when Edward I invaded to claim his rights as overlord and when the English army, under Edward II, was finally defeated at Bannockburn. This conflict is central to Scottish definitions of identity; the Scottish leaders, Robert Bruce and William Wallace, become national heroes. Their centrality is both created and demonstrated by their eponymous epics, *The Bruce* and *The Wallace*. Written for the court of Robert Bruce's grandson, King Robert II, *The Bruce* is concerned with the Bruce dynasty as much as with the realm. Bannockburn occurs in the very middle of the text; the second half describes Robert's kingship of the Scots, but also his brother Edward's attempted conquest of Ireland. While Barbour is clear that Robert is fighting a noble cause, the identification of the Scottish cause with the Bruce cause may be questioned. For instance, early in his poem, Barbour presents the following well-known lines:

> A, fredome is a noble thing,
> Fredome mays man to haiff liking,   *makes/pleasure*
> Fredome all solace to man giffis,   *gives*
> He levys at es yat frely levys.[5]   *at ease that freely lives*
> (I. 225–8)

These are often given a patriotic reading, yet the interpretation of 'fredome' is not quite so straightforward. For Barbour, freedom is certainly a noble quality, and it seems to be in part Bruce's right to hold what is his by dynastic right, namely the Scottish kingdom, rather than specifically for the Scots themselves to be free of English rule.

What is muddied in *The Bruce* is very clear in *The Wallace*. Its hero has rather more humble origins than Bruce, and scrupulously refuses the kingship. Hary holds Wallace up as a contrast to Bruce, as a man driven by duty and honour rather than self-aggrandisement and ambition, and as a man consistently loyal to his vision of Scottish sovereignty. This contrast is made explicitly in various scenes between Wallace and Bruce in *The Wallace*; it also lies implicitly in the borrowings and references that Hary takes from Barbour's poem. Furthermore, in separating the issue of Scottish sovereignty from the successful presence of an adult king, Hary suggests a more widely shared identity than that presented in *The Bruce*.

Advice to the rulers—William Dunbar

The security of identity implied by Hary's *Wallace* surely lies behind the absence of such discussions from poets such as Henryson, Douglas, and Dunbar. Like Barbour, Douglas and Dunbar write for their king; unlike Barbour, neither poet questions or celebrates the very existence of a sovereign king, although they do address poems to him. Douglas's concluding dedication in *The Palice of Honoure* is addressed to the *maist gracius prince, our soverane James the Ferd* ('most gracious prince, our sovereign James the Fourth', line 2145). His earlier discussion of English and Scottish poets makes clear his understanding of Scotland and England as different and equal; this is reinforced by this conclusion. Dunbar writes more frequently to his king and queen as patrons of his work. One poem in particular, however, is concerned with their rank. *Quhen Merche wes with variand windis past* ('When March was past with changeable winds') is associated with James's marriage to Margaret Tudor. It takes the form of a dream vision, where the dreamer is sent by May out into a garden; there he sees Nature call three meetings, one of beasts, one of birds, and one of flowers, and appoint kings for each realm. As kings, the Lion and the Eagle are exhorted to justice; because of his *busche of speiris* (line 130), the Thistle is considered fit to defend the realm. The Lion and the Thistle are both symbols of the Scottish king; to exercise justice and to defend the realm are the basic duties of a medieval monarch. Crucially, however, these symbolic features receive their kingship from Nature, God's lieutenant: no other authority intervenes. James's sovereignty over his realm is thus assumed without further comment.

Perhaps it is the confidence in their national identity that encourages nearly every Scottish medieval poet to proffer advice to his king. It has been argued that a willingness to engage in advice to princes is a characteristic of medieval Scottish writing. Even *Quhen Merche wes with variand windis past* gives advice as it praises. The Lion is instructed by Nature to *Exerce iustice with mercy and conscience | And lat no small beist suffir skaith na skornis | of greit beistis that bene of moir piscence* ('Exercise justice with mercy and conscience | and let no small beast suffer harm nor insults | from great beasts that have more power', lines 106–8). This is common advice to kings, and appropriate to Nature's appointment. However, the advice given to the Thistle is more pointed. He is instructed:

> And sen thow art a king, thow be discreit.　　　　*since*
> Herb without vertew hald nocht of sic pryce　*the same value*
> As herb of vertew and of odor sueit　　　　　*sweet scent*
>
> .　　　.　　　.　　　.　　　.　　　.
>
> Nor hald non vdir flour in sic denty　　*other/such esteem*
> As the fresche Ros of cullour reid and quhyt,　*red and white*
> For gife thow dois, hurt is thy honesty.　　　*if you do*
> 　　　　　　　　(lines 134–43)

The *Ros of cullour reid and quhyt* is Margaret Tudor, for not only do the colours suggest the model of medieval beauty, but the Tudor symbol brought together the White Rose of York with the Red Rose of Lancaster; the *herbs without vertew* in this context would seem to be James's many mistresses. Although couched in general terms, this celebratory poem nevertheless seems also to deliver a specific rebuke to Dunbar's patron—and to have been accepted in good part.

Robert Henryson

Other advice material is more general in its application. This is particularly true of Robert Henryson's *Moral Fabillis*.[6] Three of the *Fabillis* are provided with overtly political moralities: *The Sheep and the Dog, The Lion and the Mouse, The Wolf and the Lamb*. Each of these tales concerns justice and mercy, one of the essential duties of a good king identified by Dunbar in *Quhen Merche wes with variand windis past*. Henryson draws particular attention to this theme in *The Lion and the Mouse*. The reader's attention is drawn to the significance of this fable by two means: first, its place in the sequence, which is usually seventh in a series of thirteen, and secondly, by its presentation as a dream vision. The placing puts the narrative in the centre of the sequence; the vision allows Aesop, the avowed authority for the collection, to present the fable and the moral directly. The story of the fable is straightforward. The lion is fast asleep after a successful hunt; a group of mice think he is dead and run all over him. When the lion wakes and catches the leader of the mice, only the mouse's fluency persuades the lion not to take his revenge. Later, the lion is trapped by angry hunters—for he does not discriminate between *tayme and wyld* (line 1512). On this occasion, the mice are able to release him, precisely as the chief mouse had promised.

Aesop offers a political reading of the fable: the lion is *ane king with croun* (line 1575), the mice the *commountie* ('the common people', line 1587). The duty of care lies with the prince, since:

Thair lordis and princis quhen that thay [the commounitie] se	*when/common people/see*
Of iustice make nane executioun,	*fail to exercise*
Thay dreid na thing to make rebellioun	*do not fear*
And disobey, for quhy thay stand nane aw,	*because they have no fear*
That garris thame thair soueranis misknaw.	*which causes them to disregard*
(lines 1589–93)	

A failure to provide justice and to *mitigate with mercy crueltie* (line 1597) provokes rebellion and leads to disaster, for the king as much as for the realm. To take responsibility for justice, however, is not merely to enact it, but also to live as an example: the lion's heavy slumber after his hunt is condemned as *lustis, sleuth and sleip* ('lusts, sloth, and sleep'), instead of his duty to be a *walkrife gyde and gouernour* ('wakeful guide and governor', lines 1576–7). Some critics have read this fable, with its focus on the king, as a direct comment on the reign of James III. This reign was a troubled one, eventually ending in a rebellion against the king led by his son, James IV; the mis-enactment of justice, particularly the granting of remissions for money, was a central issue. However, to insist on such a directed reading is unhelpful. The personal duty of the king towards his own moral standing and the stress placed on his essential vulnerability to Fortune are familiar medieval tropes. *The Lion and the Mouse* does not offer specific remedies to specific, contemporary problems; instead it reiterates traditional advice in response to a recurrent problem, namely that of oppression of the powerless by the powerful.[7] It is a problem that concerned many medieval Scottish writers, from the historiographers, such as Walter Bower, to court poets like Dunbar, to writers like Henryson, not at court, not in a monastery or at a university. Despite its endemic presence in medieval Scotland, all these writers suggested ways to address it, apparently in the profound hope that change was possible, and all focused on the king as the essential pivot.

The centrality of the king brings us back to national identity, for as well as being the fount of justice, he was also the guarantor of the existence of the Scottish realm. For most medieval Scots poets, it appears that a good king was a blessing; a poor king might be reformed; and all kings might benefit from advice and good examples. Even *The Palice of Honoure*, not overtly in the advice to princes tradition, in line 2027 points out Scottish models for James IV, namely Robert Bruce, Kenneth McAlpine (who united the Picts and the Scots), and Gregor (who defeated the Danes). All three are valiant warriors, all three go on to be lawgivers: just like his predecessors and successors, James IV has subjects keen to point out standards to maintain.

Conclusion

The geo-political definition outlined at the beginning of this chapter has become much more straightforwardly political. To talk about Older Scots as a language is already to suggest a political situation, one where a different tradition of literature might be traced. This essay argues that it is possible to find one in the detail of style and technique, and in the broad impression of theme and assumption. Of course, such a summary as this necessarily drives a particular view, and it would be wrong to insist that all medieval Scottish literature is concerned with good kingship, or that its technical prowess is always astonishing. For instance, one of the most distinguished poems in Older Scots, *The Testament of Cresseid*, does not fit easily under either of these headings. Nevertheless, more does than does not and so it seems possible to postulate a medieval Scottish tradition. Such a tradition is expressed in a particular variety of language, but stretches that variety to its rhetorical limits. Its writers are not culturally insular, but respond to developments outwith their geographical and linguistic boundaries, and experiment widely in genre and style. As all other traditions, medieval Scottish literature is shaped by its political and geographical circumstances, in this case leading to recurring examinations of familiar problems through many different means. Although applying 'Scottish' to a collection of medieval literature may seem to be a modern imposition, in fact the geo-political title describes an organic tradition.

Notes

1. Alex Agutter, 'Middle Scots as a Literary Language', in *Jack, The History of Scottish Literature*, vol. i, pp. 13–25. See also R. Jordan, *Handbook of Middle English Grammar: Phonology*. Trans. E. J. Crock (Paris; The Hague: Mouton, 1974), pp. 18–19.
2. Mapstone, 'Was there a Court Literature in Fifteenth-Century Scotland?'
3. All quotations are taken from Gavin Douglas, *The Palis of Honoure*, ed. D. Parkinson (Kalamazoo: Medieval Institute Publications/TEAMS, 1992).
4. William Dunbar and Walter Kennedy, 'Schir Johine the Ros, ane thing thair is compild' (*The Flyting of Dumbar and Kennedie*), in *The Poems of William Dunbar*, ed. P. Bawcutt, 2 vols. (Glasgow: Association of Scottish Literary Studies, 1998), vol. i, pp. 200–18, lines 57–8. All quotations from Dunbar are taken from this edition.
5. *Barbour's Bruce*, ed. M. P. McDiarmid and J. A. C. Stevenson, 3 vols. Scottish Text Society 4th series, 12, 13, 15 (Edinburgh, 1980–5), vol. ii: I: 225–8.
6. All references to Henryson's works are to Robert Henryson, *Poems*, ed. D. Fox (Oxford: Oxford University Press, 1981).
7. See R. J. Lyall, 'Politics and Poetry in Fifteenth and Sixteenth Century Scotland', *Scottish Literary Journal*, 3/2 (1976), 5–29.

References and suggested reading

Aitken, Adam J., 'How to Pronounce Older Scots'. In A. J. Aitken,
    M. P. McDiarmid and D. S. Thomson, eds., *Bards and Makars, Scottish Language and Literature: Medieval and Renaissance*. Glasgow: University of

Glasgow Press, 1977, pp. 1–21. This is the essential guide, written by one of the most eminent Scottish philologists. It appears in the first of a series of collections of essays arising from the major international conference in Older Scots literature, another of which appears below.

Bawcutt, Priscilla. *Gavin Douglas: A Critical Study*. Edinburgh: Edinburgh University Press, 1976. An excellent introduction to Douglas and his work.

Bawcutt, Priscilla. *Dunbar the Makar*. Oxford: Oxford University Press, 1992. This is an outstanding and advanced guide to Dunbar and all his poetry, written by one of his most distinguished editors.

Fradenburg, Louise O. *City, Marriage, Tournament: Arts of Rule in Medieval Scotland*. Madison: University of Wisconsin Press, 1991. This is a stimulating and an unusual discussion of the Scottish cultural context, and is particularly interesting on Dunbar.

Goldstein, R. James. *The Matter of Scotland: Historical Narrative in Medieval Scotland*. Lincoln, Nebr., and London: University of Nebraska Press, 1993. One of the few book-length studies of *The Bruce* and *The Wallace*.

Gray, Douglas. *Robert Henryson*. Leiden: E. J. Brill, 1979. A very clear and humane guide to Henryson and his poetry.

Kratzmann, Gregory. *Anglo-Scottish Literary Relations 1430–1550*. Cambridge: Cambridge University Press, 1980. As the title suggests, this explores the relationships and influences between Scottish and English literature during the later Middle Ages. In common with most critics of Scottish literature, Kratzmann sees it as a two-way process.

Jack, R. D. S. ed. *The History of Scottish Literature*. vol i: *Origins to 1660*. Aberdeen: Aberdeen University Press, 1987. This is a good introductory guide to most of the genres and major authors of Older Scots literature; it also has articles on Latin and Gaelic writing.

Lyall, R. J. 'Politics and Poetry in Fifteenth and Sixteenth Century Scotland', *Scottish Literary Journal*, 3 (1976), 5–29. In this context, this piece is particularly useful for its discussion of Henryson's *Fables*.

Mapstone, Sally. 'Was there a Court Literature in Fifteenth-Century Scotland?', in *The Language and Literature of Early Scotland*, special issue, *Studies in Scottish Literature*, 26 (1991), 410–22. This examines the usual circumstances of composition of Older Scots literature, suggesting a different model from that in England. The collection in which this appears is particularly rich, and has many other interesting articles.

25

Medieval drama: the Corpus Christi in York and Croxton

Greg Walker

Introduction

At the centre of late-medieval piety was the Corpus Christi. Represented pictorially, sculpted into images, meditated upon in spiritual
exercises, and embedded at the heart of the liturgy, the material
body of Jesus was the prime focus of Catholic devotion. The Feast
of Corpus Christi itself, established in 1311, fell somewhere between
21 May and 24 June on the first Thursday after Trinity Sunday. It
celebrated the fundamental mystery of Catholic Christianity: the
miracle of the Mass, whereby the eucharistic bread and wine were
transformed as the priest spoke the words of consecration into the
actual body and blood of Jesus through a process known as Transubstantiation. By the later fourteenth century, a more emotionally
engaged, meditative form of popular worship known as affective
piety made that body the focus of newly intense scrutiny. As the
critic David Aers observes: 'The humiliated, tortured, whipped,
nailed down, pierced, dying but life giving body of Christ, the very
body literally present in the eucharist ... became the dominant
icon of the late medieval church and the devotion that the church
cultivated and authorised.'[1] This chapter will examine two very different dramatic texts that reflect the importance of the body of
Christ and the miracle of the Mass to late-medieval culture. The

first, the great cycle of pageants performed in York and known as the York Mystery or Corpus Christi Play, represents the life and death of Christ himself as the central events in universal history. The second, the less well-known but equally vibrant East Anglian Miracle Play known as the Croxton *Play of the Sacrament*, also has the body of Christ as its central figure, but this time in the form of a eucharistic wafer, which is 'tortured' by a group of Jews before it finally provides a spectacular demonstration of its own divine nature.

Any representation of the divine was contentious in the medieval period, but seeking to 'play' God, whether on the streets of York or in the villages of East Anglia, was especially controversial given the traditional associations of play-acting with frivolity and licentiousness. Hence, as one surviving attack, *The Tretise of Miraclis Pleyinge*, put it, drawing a stinging parallel between the actors and Christ's original tormentors,

syþen [since] þes myraclis pleyeris taken in bourde the ernestful werkis of God, [there is] no doubte that thei scornen God as diden þe Jewis þat bobbiden [beat/tormented] Cryst, for þei [the Jews] lowen [laughed] at his Passioun as these [the actors] lowyn [laugh] and japen of þe myraclis of God. þerfore, as þei [the Jews] scorneden Crist, so þeese [the actors] scorne God.[2]

Criticism of religious drama came from both ends of the religious spectrum. It came from strict, orthodox Catholics, like the author of the *Tretise*, concerned that the religious plays were diverting attention from true devotion towards mere representations—audiences were weeping as they watched Crucifixion plays out of a sentimental concern for the actor playing Christ rather than from any realization of their own sinfulness.[3] There was criticism too from those with a more radical agenda, such as the Lollards, who rejected the Miracle of the Mass altogether, and saw plays like the York Cycle as simply adding one form of idolatry to another. But, far from toning down their own histrionic qualities in an attempt to appease such critics, the York and the Croxton plays each exploited their own theatricality to flamboyant effect. Neither is 'pious' in a solemn sense. In each, raucous laughter is heard more frequently than prayer, and broad, impious comedy is often the prevailing mode. Yet these are in no sense irreligious plays. Their humour is an integral part of their spiritual agenda, whether they aimed to deepen their spectators' sense of their own sin and need for grace, or to refute the claims of heretics.

The York Corpus Christi play

Divided into fifty-one pageants, each performed on a wagon by one of the craft guilds that dominated the civic economy, the York play closely reflected the emphases of affective piety. If the body of Christ was the dominant icon of later medieval piety, then on the streets of York that icon was displayed with a new and captivating vitality. The play depicted the whole of universal history from God's creation of the world to the Last Judgement, but its focus was the Incarnation, the making flesh of God in Jesus. A Nativity sequence took the story from the Archangel Gabriel's visit to the Virgin Mary at the Annunciation, through the birth of Jesus in the Bethlehem stable and the visits of the shepherds and Magi to the Holy Family's flight into Egypt to escape the wrath of Herod. Then followed the Passion relating the events of Christ's adult life from his baptism to the Crucifixion and Resurrection.

Whereas the Nativity focuses on the miracle of Christ's birth, the very fact that God was made flesh on earth for the redemption of humankind, in the Passion pageants it is the bodily suffering of that same flesh that provides the central motif. And in each case those qualities so criticized by the author of the *Tretise*, play-acting and laughter, are conspicuously foregrounded. In each of the pageants the largely silent figure of Jesus is surrounded by loud-mouthed, mocking, and often excessively violent interlocutors who are intent upon forcing him to play a role that they have invented for him, whether as a 'warlock', a cheap conjurer, or a false prophet. In the first of the interrogation pageants, *Christ before Annas and Caiaphas*, written like those that follow by an unknown playwright known to scholars as the York Realist, a self-reflexive dimension is added to the theatre of cruelty by turning the violence itself into a game. When the high priests Annas and Caiaphas have finished interrogating Jesus, they tell the guards to teach him a lesson before taking him to Pontius Pilate. In the pageant this ordeal, popularly known as the Buffeting (what the *Tretise* called the *bobbid[ing]*), is inflicted as a game of 'pops', a vicious variant of Blind Man's Buff. Christ is seated on a stool and blindfolded, whereupon the soldiers take it in turns to beat him, jeeringly inviting him to guess which of them struck the blow. The guards evidently take a keen, sadistic pleasure in the game. Tying the blindfold, the Third Soldier (III MILES) jeeringly puns on the *faire flappe*—both a piece of fabric and a slap—with which he will fasten it.

> . . . and þer is one! [*He strikes Jesus*], and þer is ij;   *two*
> And ther is iij; and there is iiij!
> Saye nowe, with an neville happe   *an ill chance*
> Who negheth þe[e] nowe? Not a worde? No?   *approaches*
> (lines 366–9)

Then II MILES strikes him, joking that the blow will stop him from napping (line 370). Finally, when Jesus is beaten unconscious, they rouse him again with festive cries of 'Wassaille! Wassaylle', a call to drink and revel, joking that they will wake him from his slumbers to continue the fun.

On the surface the pageant offers a simple narrative of torment and suffering, but there are levels of irony at work that create considerable dramatic and theological depth. As the soldiers shout at Jesus, joking at his expense and seeking to draw the audience into their 'games', they expand the actions described in Matthew's Gospel into a carnivalesque mockery of both Christ himself and the scholarly, Latinate culture through which Christian belief was mediated. Hence when III MILES, following Matthew's account, scorns Christ's claims to divinity, derisively referring to him as a prophet, he does so by quoting the Latin of the Vulgate Bible itself, thus defamiliarizing it and exposing it to laughter.

Prophete, Y saie, to be out of debate,
Quis Te percussit? Rede yffe þou may.   *Who struck You?* (Matthew 26: 68)
(lines 375–6)   *Prophesy [that] if you can.*

In this way the playwright does indeed seem, as the *Tretise* alleged, to be repeating the offences of Christ's tormentors, both literally (by representing them) and symbolically, by imagining himself or herself in their place, ventriloquizing their words, and giving them all the best lines. Were not the spectators being encouraged to laugh at and scorn Christ too? The author of the *Tretise* may well have thought so. And yet, to allege as much is, of course, to miss the point of the scene. For, despite the soldiers' volubility, their taunts and blows are ultimately fruitless when set against Jesus's dignified, silent, suffering, as IV MILES unconsciously acknowledges.

Those wordes are in waste, what weres þou he wate?
                                 [ironically] *do you think he understands?*
It semys by his wirkyng his wittes were away   *behaviour/lost*
                                 (lines 377–8)

Hence the dramaturgy here is actually complex and subtle. In this short pageant the playwright first aligns drama squarely with the forces of sin, presenting the Buffeting as itself a form of play-acting, and filling the playing area with the boisterous, histrionic activity of the soldiers who abuse Christ under cover of the licensed misrule of a game. But then, having secured the audience's engagement with this ostensibly companionable bloodsport, the pageant slowly allows a different kind of drama quietly to emerge amid the noise. In this movement the very *in*activity of the actor playing Christ, initially so seemingly undramatic, becomes the focus of the audience's attention and sympathy. His silence finally speaks louder than all the soldiers' taunts and jests, as III MILES's words emphasize. In this way the 'playful' histrionics of the soldiers works against itself. The silent body of Christ becomes the still centre of a whirl of words and fruitless human activity,[4] and his willingness to suffer on behalf of humankind, despite humankind's manifest desire to hurt and reject him, is graphically presented.

The same pattern is repeated in later Passion pageants, in each of which Jesus is subjected to acts of highly theatrical humiliation and violence. In *Christ before Herod*, Herod and his 'Dukes' dress him in a fool's white coat and bellow at him in a bizarre mixture of English vernacular and cod-courtly French (*saie beene-venew, in bone fay,* | *Ne plesew et parle remoy?* ('I say, welcome, in good faith, | Does it not please you to talk to me?', lines 146–7)), trying to bully him into displaying his miraculous powers for their amusement. In *Christ before Pilate II* he is brutally scourged before being handed over for crucifixion. In the *Crucifixion* pageant, produced with resonant irony by the York Pinners guild (the makers of nails), all the themes of the earlier pageants are revisited and brought to fruition. The soldiers, focusing on the awkward business of nailing Christ's body to a cross seemingly designed for a much bigger man (a problem they 'solve' by stretching his arms until the tendons snap, allowing them to drive the nails through his hands into the specially prepared holes) amuse themselves during their labours by mocking him (*'Say, sir, howe likes you nowe, | þis werke þat we have wrought?'* (lines 249–50)). Meanwhile, Christ lies silently in their midst, out of sight of the audience, on the top of the pageant wagon. The soldiers exchange heavy-handed puns with each other:

> I MILES: Thoo sawes schall rewe hym sore,
> For all his sauntering sone.
>
> He'll soon sorely regret all those saws [wise sayings]
> he spoke during all his babbling.
>
> (lines 69–70)

And they joke at each other's expense, vying for the audience's sympathies (I MILES promises to come to the aid of his fellows, but then adds in an aside for the spectators' benefit, 'Full snelly [*swiftly*] as a snayle', line 118).

Theatricality and the York *Crucifixion*

With Jesus effectively invisible beneath the rim of the wagon for much of the action, the audience is obliged to focus upon the difficulties facing the soldiers as they struggle with recalcitrant nails, hunt for tools, and try to lift the unexpectedly heavy cross (heavy, symbolically, because its occupant carries the sins of the world on his shoulders). In a bravura display of artistic risk-taking, the York Realist thus makes the suffering of Christ's murderers the centre of the *Crucifixion* pageant ('I MILES: *grete harme have I hente, | My schuldir is in sounder* [dislocated]. II MILES: *And sertis I am nere schent* [ruined], | *So longe have I borne undir* [the weight of the Cross]' (lines 189–92)), making *them* the most immediately sympathetic characters for most of the pageant, and inviting the audience to identify with their labours rather than with the suffering of Christ or the theological significance of his death.

It is only when the Cross is finally dropped into place with one last ligament-shattering jolt, that the brilliance of the playwright's strategy becomes apparent. Having previously been bound up, both intellectually and emotionally, in the actions of the soldiers, the spectators are now able to realize the full significance of what they have witnessed. Only now, having experienced by proxy what it might be like to crucify Jesus, are they able to appreciate, emotionally as well as intellectually, the weight of the Christian dictum that all believers share in the responsibility for Christ's death because they all share in Original Sin. Then, as the image of the crucified Christ, that single most powerful icon in Christian culture, is raised before their eyes, the actor playing Jesus delivers the second of the two short speeches given to him in the pageant. In a brief, lyrical act of forgiveness he offers himself to the spectators and all humankind as a tangible, corporeal symbol of God's love for the world:

> Al men þat walkis by waye or street,
> Takes tente þe schalle no travayle tyne
> > *Be sure you overlook no aspect of my suffering*
> Byholdes myn heede, myn handes, and my feete,
> And fully feele nowe, or þe fine   *before you pass by*
> Yf any mourning may be meete   *appropriate*
> Or myscheve measured unto myne.   *suffering*
> My Fadir, þat alle bales maye bete,   *suffering/relieve*
> Forgiffis þes men þat dois me pyne.   *torment*
> What þei wirke, wotte þai noght;
> Therfore, my Fadir, I crave,
> Latte never þer synnys be sought,
> But see þer saules to save.   (lines 253–64)

The audience, in one of the most powerful moments in the entire Cycle, is placed literally as well as figuratively at the foot of the Cross, and is able to feel the power of the Christian dictum that, just as each of them shares equally in responsibility for Christ's death, so each of them shares also in God's forgiveness, granted freely and unprompted through grace at the Redemption.

But the pageant does not end here. The soldiers continue to mock him, and in doing so mark themselves out as unredeemable sinners by their refusal to respond to Christ's forgiveness:

I MILES: We! Harke, he jangelis like a jay!
II MILES: Methynke he patris like a py!   *chatters like a magpie*

III MILES: He has ben doand all þis day,   *doing*
     And made grete mevyng of mercy.   (lines 265–8)   *spoke much about*

They remain models of sinful worldly men, unable to see beyond
their own immediate concerns to the wider significance of their
actions in the universal drama of the Redemption. Their words have
carried ironic subtexts for the knowing, Christian audience throughout the pageant, effectively underscoring the theological significance
of the greater deed that they are unwittingly performing. II MILES in
particular speaks lines that illuminate the role of the Crucifixion in
the economy of Christian salvation, albeit he has no idea of the
significance of what he says. He talks of his work as '*þis unthrifty*
[unprofitable] *thyng*' (line 90), but at another point observes that
'*This werke is wele, I will warande*' (line 104). The statements seem
contradictory, but from a Christian perspective both are true. The
Crucifixion does not benefit the soldiers, but only because they
choose to ignore Christ's offer of redemption, and it is indeed an
unprofitable, grisly job that they perform. But it is also, paradoxically,
the most profitable work imaginable, as Christ's death will offer
humanity eternal life. Hence when II MILES punningly observes that it
is '*þe foulest dede* [death] *of all*' that Christ will die '*for his dedis*' (lines
26–7), he is both literally accurate and theologically mistaken: the
form of death is indeed foul, but it is for the soldiers' deeds, and those
of all humankind, that Christ is willing to suffer it, not for his own
uniquely sinless life.

Consequently, all the time that the soldiers go about their grim
business, their conversation offers an ironic commentary on the
resolutely worldly perspective from which they view events. As the
actor playing Jesus observes, speaking a paraphrase of the biblical
Christ's words from the Cross: '*What þei wirke, wotte þai noght*'
('They know not what they do'). And the extent of their ignorance is
made graphically clear to the audience, most obviously when I MILES
actually swears, anachronistically, by Christ himself and the
Redemption, telling his companions to '*Strike on þan harde, for hym
þe[e] boght*' ('for he who saved you'). Then the soldiers, having
drawn lots for Christ's garment, leave the place with a final dismis-
sive gesture: '*þis travayle here we tyne*' ('we're wasting our time
here'), which is of course both completely true: they have gained
nothing from their experiences but sore backs, and a misjudgement

of spectacular proportions: for what they have done has changed the universe forever.

The York Passion sequence, then, deploys all those devices objected to in the *Tretise of Miraclis Pleyinge*: overt theatricality, scornful laughter, and the emotional manipulation of the audience, to represent a deadly 'earnest' religious mystery. And it does so in the full knowledge of the effects they will create. The result is a masterful display of controlled stagecraft in which theatricality and theology work symbiotically, emphasizing and reinforcing each other, and contributing to a bravura moment of iconic spectacle in the revelation of the Corpus Christi at the elevation of the Cross.

The Croxton *Play of the Sacrament*

The body of Christ, and the revelation of the Corpus Christi, are also central to the late fifteenth-century Croxton *Play of the Sacrament*, albeit in different ways. As in the York Cycle, Christ's body undergoes physical torments in the course of the play. But, far from suffering in silence like the York Jesus, the Croxton Corpus Christi refuses to take its punishment lying down. Rather it strikes back at its tormentors in acts of violent retaliation, culminating in an altogether different exposure of the wounded body of Jesus.

Unlike the York Cycle, the Croxton play does not represent biblical material. It concerns a reputed miraculous appearance of Christ in Heraclia, in the Spanish kingdom of Aragon, in 1461. It is thus the only surviving English example of a genre, the Miracle or Conversion Play, that was popular in western Europe in the medieval period. Such plays, like the powerful iconographic tradition they drew upon, seem designed to assert Christian doctrine and reinforce belief against the claims of heretics or sceptics. Hence the Croxton play's insistence that it is representing real historical events is part of its strategy. And, given that it asserts the belief that the eucharistic bread and wine do indeed become the body and blood of Christ at the moment of consecration, entirely replacing the substance of the original materials, it is highly likely that it was designed to refute the scepticism of the Lollards, who rejected the doctrine of what is termed the 'Real Presence' of Christ in the eucharistic host (wafer).

The play concerns the attempt by a group of Jewish merchants to test the veracity of the doctrine of Transubstantiation in a very practical way. They bribe a Christian merchant, Aristorius, to obtain for them a consecrated host, which they subject to a series of violent assaults, each one symbolically re-enacting the tortures undergone by Jesus during his Passion, in an attempt to see if it will react. If it does, then the Jews will convert to Christianity. If it does not, they will conclude that Christianity is a fraud. What the play offers is thus a Passion sequence in miniature, in which the Jews *grev[e] Our Lord gretly on grownd,* I *And put hym to a [new] Passyon* (*banns,* lines 37–8). Aristorius's theft of the host and sale of it to the Jews echoes Judas's betrayal of Christ to the Jewish authorities. When the five Jews, led by Jonathas, each stab the host with a knife, they re-enact the Five Wounds Christ received during the Crucifixion. They then nail the host to a post (the Crucifixion itself), before removing it again (the Deposition), wrapping it up and placing it in a cauldron (the Burial), and then throwing it into an oven (Christ's descent into Hell and his liberation of the condemned souls at the Harrowing of Hell), which subsequently explodes to reveal the figure of Christ himself (the Resurrection) to the astonished Jews, who, having been granted so spectacular a demonstration of the power of the sacrament, promptly become Christians.

Pictorial representations of host profanation stories were popular in Continental Europe at the time, the most famous examples being the *predella* (the series of panel paintings below the altarpiece) designed for the church of Corpus Domini in Urbino by Paolo Uccello in 1467–8, and the numerous *Hostienfrevelkirchen* (host-desecration churches) in southern Germany. Dramatic representations of the theme also survive from France and Italy. What links these European examples to the Croxton play is the iconography of the bleeding host and the eventual redemption of the Christian who sells the host to the Jews. Unlike these European examples, however, the Croxton play does not end with the execution or beating of the Jews, but their conversion. This change further suggests that the play was motivated, not by anti-Semitism *per se*, but by a desire to refute the arguments of the Lollards and reconcile them to orthodoxy: hence all the participants are offered the prospect of salvation, not simply the erring orthodox figure.

Although there are strong thematic links between the Croxton play and the Passion sequence, however, the host, as I have suggested, does not behave at all like the passive, suffering Christ of the York pageants. If the latter offered spectators Christ as the Man of Sorrows, the former gives its audiences a taste of Christ Militant in the form of a real, and very pugnacious, presence, unafraid to mete out condign punishments to those who try to desecrate it. The result of the various 'tests' to which Jonathas and his fellows subject the host is a series of grotesque comic episodes in which their expectations are violently confounded at every turn. They describe their own actions (initially simply stabbing the host with their daggers) as if they were heroic blows in a battle:

> Now am I bold with batayl hym to bleyke,
> Þe mydle part of all for to rene,
> A stowte stroke also for to stryke;
> In þe myddys yt shal be sene.   (lines 197–400)

Hence there is something of the swaggering cruelty of the York MILES to their actions. But, since their target is a tiny wafer rather than a suffering human being, the tone of these scenes is very different to the Buffeting or Scourging pageants. Where the York soldiers had been genuinely dangerous as well as laughable in their malice, the Croxton Jews are simply ridiculous, their efforts entirely disproportionate to their visible effects. Their bombast is quickly punctured when the host offers a miraculous demonstration of its divine substance. It bleeds. And the mere sight of the blood sends its tormentors into paroxysms of fear.

> Ah, owt, owt! Harrow! What devyll ys thys?
> Of thys wyrk I am in were!   *amazed*
> It bledyth as yt were woode, iwys!   *mad*
> But yf ye helpe, I shall dyspayre!   *unless*
>   (lines 401–4)

Jonathas then picks up the host and tries to throw it into the cauldron. But it miraculously sticks to his hand, provoking further histrionics:

> Out, out, yt werketh me wrake!
> I may not avoyd yt owt of my hond! (lines 419–20)

And here, as the stage direction states, '*he runneth wood with þe host in hys hond*'. Once he has calmed down, his fellows try to remove the wafer by nailing it to a post and pulling, but rather than the wafer coming loose they sever his arm at the wrist, and all the Jews fall in a heap while, as the stage direction laconically notes, '*þe hand shall hang styll with þe sacrament*' (line 450).

Then, as the action descends into slapstick, the main plot freezes and the quack doctor, Master Brundyche ('Brown-Ditch') of Brabant and his boy, Colle, enter to perform a conventional comic routine. Colle jokes about his master's fraudulent cures and general incompetence ('*He seeth as wele at noone as at nyght,* I ... *And* ... *Can gyff a jud[g]yment aright* [as well]; I *As he þat hathe noon eyn* [no eyes]' (lines 457–9)), while the Doctor boasts of his prowess. Jonathas is, however, unimpressed by the seemingly fortuitous arrival of a doctor, and gives Brundyche short shrift, before, apparently undeterred by the loss of his hand, throwing the host into the cauldron. The result of this renewed assault is, predictably, another demonstration of its miraculous nature, for the cauldron immediately boils over, and the oil runs blood red. Finally, the tormentors hurl the host into the oven, sealing the doors with clay. But this only brings on the last, cataclysmic revelation of the host's transubstantiated state. As the stage direction (line 632) describes it: '*Here the ovyn must ryve asunder, and blede owt at þe cranys* [cracks] *and an image* [of Christ] *appere owt with woundys bledyng.*' This 'image' then reproaches the Jews in uncompromising terms:

> O ye merveylous Jewys,
>
> .   .   .   .   .   .
>
> Why blaspheme yow me? Why do ye thus?
> Why put yow me to a newe tormentry,
> And I dyed for yow on the Crosse?
>> (lines 639, 651–3)

At this the Jews fall to their knees and cry for mercy. Christ forgives them all, restoring Jonathas's hand for good measure. It is left to Episcopus to gather up the host and lead everyone in procession to the Church, where Aristorius confesses his part in the profanation and receives penance. Finally, having '*Crystene[d] the Jewys with gret solempnyte*' (line 871), Episcopus leads both actors and audience in the singing of the *Te Deum Laudamus*.

Croxton's 'gothic' theatricality

The Croxton play is in many ways a remarkable piece of theatre—a graphic demonstration of the 'gothic' capacity of medieval drama to contain different modes and patterns. What might initially appear a naïve and chaotic assemblage of elements—slapstick, grotesque comic violence, gross racial stereotyping, and moments of high cere-monial seriousness—reveals on closer inspection a unified focus in the all-pervading importance of the Corpus Christi. The absurd vio-lence of the Jews' tests, the miraculous properties of the host, and the extended acts of reconciliation and worship: all reinforce the sense of superiority, comfort, and awe inspired in the Christian community through its reaffirmation of faith in the Corpus Christi (both the historical sacrifice of Jesus and the contemporary miracle of Transubstantiation). Even the seemingly irrelevant intrusion of Brundyche and Colle has a bearing upon the transubstantive, redemptive theme. For, as their exchanges reveal, they offer its par-odic counterpoint. Brundyche brings only a travesty of healing, while Christ is the true healer of souls. Thus Jonathas's rejection of the false doctor prefigures his later acceptance of the true healer through bap-tism. In addition, Colle offers a comic inversion of Transubstanti-ation for he seems to summon up the devil in Brundyche's wine bottle:

Here, master, master, ware how ye tugg!	*swig!*
The Devyll, I trowe, within shruggys	*is moving inside*
For yt gooth 'rebyll-rable'	(lines 518–20)

Taken as a whole, the play thus offers a combative assertion that, despite the various divisive elements present in a complex and devel-oping society—incipient international capitalism, materialism, petty crime, inter-religious strife—the Corpus Christi provides a focus for communal unity among believers who themselves form 'the body of Christ' in his church. Hence the final act has cast and audience join together in singing the *Te Deum*, a harmonious action that signals the new wholeness of the Christian community in celebration of its shared faith.[5]

And yet, despite this unity of purpose and the intensity with which it mocks the disbelief of the Jews, the play is none the less problematic. Its dramaturgy—and in particular those features singled out for criticism by the *Tretise of Miraclis Pleyinge*, overt theatricality and impious laughter, raise as many problems as they solve. As the scholar Janette Dillon observes, the play is anxious to assert theological truth, and it denounces tricks and tricksters like Braudyche. Yet its method of validating spiritual truth is a series of stage tricks such as the bleeding host, detachable hand, and exploding oven.[6] If the play was in part a counterblast to Lollard scepticism, then the idea of refuting heretics (some of whom claimed that the Mass itself was a charade designed to keep the ignorant in awe) through the use of a stage-show ran the risk of confirming their worst suspicions.

In the Croxton play there is no sense of that gradual disenchantment with the allure of boisterous theatricality that characterized the York Passion, nor of the scepticism about drama's capacity to produce powerful effects that paradoxically allowed the York Realist to achieve the sublime climax to the *Crucifixion*. Rather than being encouraged first to identify with and then to reject the creative energies of seemingly festive 'play', the Croxton spectators are prompted to align themselves with the forces of theatrical 'boarding' throughout. The grotesque punishments meted out to Jonathas and the Jews enjoy the same degree of authorial validation as the equally feigned 'miracles' of the bleeding host and the appearance of the image of Christ. Does this make the Croxton play less accomplished than its York counterpart, more naïve in its awareness of its own theological implications? Perhaps. Certainly the York pageants seem better able to interrogate their own procedures. But this is as much a reflection of the cultural roles of the two plays as a commentary upon their writers' abilities. The York Cycle was a text—or rather a constantly evolving tradition of performance—that was refined and rendered smooth by over two centuries of use. It was a site in which a sophisticated urban community expressed and reflected upon its own complex beliefs. By contrast, the Croxton play was probably an immediate response to a particular perceived threat, whether from the activities of a particular heretical group or endemic local scepticism. Forged in the heat of controversy as a piece of dramatic propaganda, it was probably better suited to its purpose than a play that relied upon the subtle modulation of an audience's aesthetic and intellectual sensibilities. And, for all its directness, it was not without sophistication.

It adapted a powerful tradition of anti-Semitic iconography to local circumstances. Trying to judge between the qualities of two such different texts would be invidious. But the fact that each focuses upon the physical and theological implications of the body of Christ suggests both the cultural centrality of the Corpus Christi as an icon and an idea, and the ways in which drama could serve political and religious ends in this period.

Notes

1. Aers, p. 1.
2. Walker, pp. 197–8.
3. Ibid. 198.
4. Johnston, pp. 1–2.
5. Scherb, pp. 68–70.
6. Dillon, p. 172.

References and suggested reading

Aers, David, 'Figuring Forth the Body of Christ: Devotion and Politics', *Essays in Medieval Studies*, 11 (1994), 1–11. A stimulating essay on the centrality of the Corpus Christi to medieval culture and a critical overview of recent work on the subject.

Beadle, Richard, ed. *The Cambridge Companion to Medieval English Theatre*. Cambridge: Cambridge University Press, 1994. Probably the best single-volume introduction to early English drama in all its forms.

D'Arcy, Anne Marie. 'Holy Vessell and Blyssed Bloode: Malory's Personal Symbolism of the Grail', in Peter J. Lucas and Angela M. Lucas, eds., *Middle English from Tongue to Text*. Frankfurt: Peter Lang, 2002, pp. 293–318. Contains an excellent account of manifestations of Christ and his blood in medieval texts.

Dillon, Janette. 'What Sacrament?: Excess, Taboo and Truth in the *Croxton Play of the Sacrament* and Twentieth-Century Body Art', *European Medieval Drama*, 4 (2000), 169–80. An insightful essay on the paradoxes of the Croxton play's focus on the body.

Johnston, Alexandra. 'At the Still Point of a Turning World: Augustinian Roots of Medieval Dramaturgy', *European Medieval Drama*, 2 (1998),

1–19. A thought-provoking essay on the theological emphases of the Cycle plays.

Lavin, Marilyn Aronberg. 'The Altar of Corpus Domini in Urbino: Paolo Uccello, Joos van Ghent, Piero della Francesca', *Art Bulletin*, 49 (1967), 1–24. An excellent discussion of the narrative and iconographic traditions behind host profanation stories.

Rubin, Miri. *Gentile Tales: The Narrative Assault on Late-Medieval Jews.* New Haven and London: Yale University Press, 1999. A valuable survey of anti-Semitism in the later medieval period.

Scherb, Victor I. *Staging Faith: East Anglian Drama in the Later Middle Ages.* Madison, Wis.: Fairleigh Dickinson University Press, 2001. Contains a useful section on the Croxton play.

Schrenckenberg, Heinz. *The Jews in Christian Art.* New York: Continuum, 1996. Contains a fascinating section on profanation of the host stories, including numerous illustrations.

Sinanoglou, Leah. 'The Christ Child as Sacrifice: A Medieval Tradition and the Corpus Christi Plays', *Speculum*, 48 (1973), 491–509. A good introduction to the use of motifs of the eucharistic feast in the Cycle plays.

Walker, Greg, ed. *Medieval Drama: An Anthology.* Oxford: Blackwell Publishers, 2000. A comprehensive collection of early dramatic texts. All quotations from the plays and *The Tretise of Miraclis Pleyinge* in this essay are from texts in this anthology.

General Index